Greenhill Books

SOVIET CASUALTIES AND COMBAT LOSSES IN THE TWENTIETH CENTURY

SOVIET CASUALTIES AND COMBAT LOSSES IN THE TWENTIETH CENTURY

General Editor
COLONEL-GENERAL G. F. KRIVOSHEEV
Kandidat of Military Science

Authors
G. F. Krivosheev, V. M. Andronikov, P. D. Burikov, V. V. Gurkin,
A. I. Kruglov, Ye. I. Rodionov, M. V. Filimoshin

Foreword by John Erickson

Greenhill Books, London
Stackpole Books, Pennsylvania

Soviet Casualties and Combat Losses in the Twentieth Century
First published 1997 by Greenhill Books, Lionel Leventhal Limited
Park House, 1 Russell Gardens, London NW11 9NN
and
Stackpole Books, 5067 Ritter Road, Mechanicsburg, PA 17055, USA

British Library Cataloguing in Publication Data
Soviet casualties and combat losses in the twentieth century
1. War – Casualties (Statistics, etc.) – History – 20th century 2. Soldiers – Soviet Union
I. Krivosheev, G. F.
355.4'747'0904

ISBN 1-85367-280-7

Library of Congress Cataloging-in-Publication Data
Grif sekretnosti sniat. English.
Soviet casualties and combat losses in the twentieth century / edited by G. F. Krivosheev;
translated by Christine Barnard; Foreword by John Erickson.
p. cm.
ISBN 1-85367-280-7
1. Soviet Union—History, Military—Statistics. 2. Soviet Union—Armed Forces—History—Statistics.
3. Battle casualties—Soviet Union—Statistics. 4. World War, 1939–1945—Casualties—Statistics.
5. Korean War, 1950–1953—Casualties—Statistics. 6. Hungary—History—Revolution, 1956—
Casualties—Statistics. 7. Czechoslovakia—History—Intervention, 1968—Casualties—Statistics.
8. Afghanistan—History—Soviet occupation, 1979–1989—Casualties—Statistics. I. Krivosheev, G. F.
DK54.G75 1997   97-19004
                                                                                                                        CIP

Publishing History
Soviet Casualties and Combat Losses in the Twentieth Century is the first English edition of
Grif Sekretnosti Sniat (Moscow, 1993), translated from the original Russian by Christine Barnard
and with a new Foreword by John Erickson.

Printed and bound in Great Britain by Creative Print and Design (Wales), Ebbw Vale

Contents

Editor's Note

This book was written by a team of authors from the Russian General Staff, and published in Russian in 1993. Since that time the book has been highly praised by historians, demographers and other specialists.

The authors hope that the English edition of this book will not only increase the number of readers, but will also contribute to an understanding of the problems regarding the combat casualties and losses of the Soviet Union, its allies and enemies in past wars and conflicts.

The authors welcome suggestions and critical remarks from readers, and will try to address them in future studies.

The authors are grateful to Lionel Leventhal of Greenhill Books, to the translator Christine Barnard, and to the Russian General Staff officer Major Dmitri Tcherepanov for his help in reviewing the translation of special military-historical terminology.

Colonel General Professor Grigori Krivosheev
Editor and head of the team of authors
Moscow, 1997

Foreword

In Moscow more than thirty years ago I had the rare opportunity of attending an editorial discussion of the proofs of the sixth and final volume of *The Great Patriotic War of the Soviet Union 1941–1945*. (*Istoriya Velikoi Otechestvennoi voiny Sovetskogo Soyuza 1941–1945, Tom 6, Itogi Velikoi Otechestvennoi*, Moscow, 1965). It was intended to be a summation of the course and costs of the war the Soviet Union waged, and the question of Soviet war losses inevitably intruded itself. Though a considerable body of data was available, much of which has now been declassified, the late Marshal Koniev categorically insisted that as long as he and his wartime commanders still lived no detailed loss figures for specific Red Army operations would ever be published. Not so many months later Marshal Koniev took it upon himself in his Statement to a press conference convened on the 20th anniversary of Victory, 30 April 1965, to announce that 'the total number of Soviet soldiers and officers who had perished in the war', including those who died from wounds or in captivity, was 10 million.

We have not been short of gross numbers and unqualified figures to account for wartime losses in the Soviet Union. Many of these were justifiably denounced and sardonically decried as nothing more than 'simple arithmetic' (*prostaya arifmetika*), their purpose distortion, their effect prolongation of public anguish, their intent defamation. As early as February 1946 Stalin himself produced the figure of 7 million for Soviet losses in the 1941–45 war, aware that this was an ultra-conservative estimate of battlefield loss, if indeed that was what he was referring to. A war-ravaged, battle-damaged Soviet Union could not afford to reveal its weaknesses to the world, nor see Stalin indict himself and his system for vast profligacy with human life.

In the 1960s Nikita Khrushchev advanced the widely quoted figure in East and West of 'an excess of 20 million', to include both military and civilian losses. Two decades later, when the wall of silence was breaking down and the seals of secrecy were gingerly removed, all that the *Encyclopedia of the Great Patriotic War* (*Velikaya Otechestvennaya voina 1941–1945. Entsiklopediya*, Moscow, 1985), edited by Army General M. M. Kozlov, adduced by way of clarification was the re-assertion of a familiar figure, 'upwards of 20 million Soviet citizens, *part of them civilians*, perished in the Hitlerite death camps, from Fascist brutalities, illness, hunger'.

The availability of greater information inevitably sparked off not only a 'numbers game' but also recrimination about the inordinate scale of Soviet losses in the 1941–45 war. What was deemed inordinate was also castigated as unnecessary—worse still, a case of criminal negligence combined with monstrous incompetence on the part of Soviet wartime leaders, Stalin in particular, and field commanders at large. Bizarre arithmetic was employed to support this contention, buttressed by assertions that the Red Army suffered losses wholly disproportionate to those of the Wehrmacht, exaggerated, for example, in the order of 10:1. The overall result was a bitter political controversy in which, for their own political reasons, the several parties strove either to minimise or maximise battlefield loss figures. This bestowed neither dignity nor authenticity on an issue of commanding importance.

Not until the spring of 1990 was some of the long-standing mystery substantially dispelled and the persistent furore momentarily stilled with the publication, in *Military-Historical Journal* (*Voenno-istoricheskii Zhurnal*), March 1990, of an interview with the Chief of the General Staff of the Soviet Armed Forces, Army General M. A. Moiseyev. General Moiseyev acknowledged that the excessive and prolonged secrecy was 'our fault', generating much of the confusion and turmoil over the question of losses.

In 1988–89 two commissions began analysing records available to the General Staff, one concerned with human losses, the other with losses of *matériel*, weapons and equipment. The 'global figure' for battlefield loss in human lives was less than the exaggerations which had appeared in the press but was 'nonetheless large'. 'Irrecoverable losses' were defined as those killed in action, missing in action, non-returned prisoners of war and those dying from wounds, illness or accident—a total of 8,668,400. Medical casualties—the wounded, concussed, frost-bitten and ill—amounted to 18 million.

As for the question of the competence of command and its responsibility for excessive and unnecessary losses, General Moiseyev chose an extraordinary example, the appalling fate of the 2nd Shock Army in 1942, the army commanded by General A. A. Vlasov, who in captivity transferred his allegiance to the Germans. In 36 hours the 2nd Shock Army lost 3,000 men, the final casualty toll rising to more than 66,000. Given space, General Moiseyev might also have mentioned General (later Marshal) G. Zhukov's order of 30 March 1942 castigating the 'criminally negligent attitude' of commanders towards their men, resulting in unacceptable and 'abnormal losses' (*nienormal'nye poteri'*).

General Moiseyev's article and similar studies opened the flood-gates of comment and criticism. The main line of attack concerned the genuineness of the loss figures and the objectivity of the data. There was and there remains confusion about the actual numbers of Soviet prisoners of war and the death toll among them. The tendency to underestimate and under-register battlefield losses, reportedly by a factor of one-third, is adduced in order to question the 'objectivity' of archive data. If the archive data, utilising wartime front-line formation and unit nominal rolls (*po spisku*), is suspect there is evidently yet another source, the card-indexes of the former Soviet (now Russian) Ministry of Defence.

Major S. A. Il'enko has recently supplied detailed information on the wartime and post-war history of the Department for the Individual Registration of Irrecoverable Losses/Soviet Army Sergeants and Soldiers and its alphabetical card-indexes—'a priceless treasure of history'. He reserves judgement about Army General I.

Gerasimov's assertion in the *Ukrainian Historical Journal* (*Ukrains'kii istorichnii zhurnal*), October 1990, based on card-indexes, that the true loss (sergeants and men) was 16.2 million plus 1.2 million officers. On the other hand he implicitly challenges 'the official figure of army losses, which was equivalent to 8.6 million men'.

The question of methodology, the genuineness and objectivity of data, the manner of its interpretation and much else have all been called into question with respect to the compilation and investigation of Soviet war losses from 1941 to 1945. When the context is the entire gamut of Soviet military operations from 1918 to 1989, as it is in *Soviet Casualties and Combat Losses of the Twentieth Century*, then they assume even greater significance. Under the editorship of Colonel-General G. F. Krivosheev, the book is described as 'statistical research', covering human losses in 'wars, military actions and military conflicts', beginning with the Civil War and ending with 'rendering military aid to the government of Afghanistan, 1979–1989'. Though concerned primarily with manpower, the lengthy chapter devoted to the Great Patriotic War 1941–1945 includes, nevertheless, substantial data on Soviet losses in weapons and equipment.

Whatever the reservations, of which there are many, it would be hard to dispute that *Soviet Casualties and Combat Losses* marks an undertaking as unique as it is ambitious, even revolutionary, given previous reticence and persistent distortion. Statistics apart, here is nothing short of a 'military biography' of the Soviet Union, beginning with the Civil War and ending with the Cold War, spanning the years 1918–89. The total human cost, according to this reckoning, was 39,641,479, just under 10 million killed, missing and prisoners who never returned, a shade below 30 million wounded or sick. All Soviet military life is here, whether it was fighting the insurgent *Basmachi*, supplying military assistance to the Spanish Republic and China between 1936 and 1939, the 'liberation march' into the Western Ukraine and Byelorussia in 1939, Soviet aviation divisions in Korea, military interventions in Hungary and Czechoslovakia, border clashes in the Far East and Kazakhstan in 1969, 'military-technical assistance' in Asia, the Middle East and Africa.

The second key feature is the presentation of manpower strengths for Soviet forces committed in major wars and conflicts. In the case of the Great Patriotic War this includes both the *boevoi sostav*, force composition, and numerical strength for Fronts in defensive and offensive operations. For those interested in the profile of Front operations, duration and loss tables have been assembled into a separate set of statistical tables, followed by numerical strength/personnel losses for operational units of the Soviet navy and independent flotillas. Due to ships sunk and submarines lost, naval losses displayed a higher proportion of 'missing in action' to those killed in action.

The temptation is to dwell at inordinate length on the Great Patriotic War to the excursion of all else. However, this would be to neglect some rich findings relating to the Civil War. Manpower mobilised for the Red Army between 1918 and 1920, including *voenspets*, reached a total of 6,707,588 men. Over the contentious issue of total losses in the Civil War, the editors display caution and discretion. In the absence of 'the necessary data' they offer no figure for losses in the White Army and

Intervention forces. Professor Yu. A. Polyakov's asserts that both sides, Red and White, suffered more or less equal losses, of the order of 2,500,000. The editors conclude that White losses were 'not less than those in the Red Army'.

Colonel-General Krivosheev and his colleagues reject the curiously diminished totals suggested by the demographer-historian B. Urlanis and take care to present differentiated loss figures for two periods of the Civil War, 1918–20 and the 'concluding period' 1921–22. For the first period the irrecoverable loss was 701,847, for the closing period 237,908, giving a final irrecoverable loss of 939,755, medical casualties, wounded and sick amounting to 6,791,783. Those figures do not wildly contradict previous estimates, which even as approximations mentioned Red Army battle casualties, killed and missing, to be 'in the order of one million'. Obviously as much work will be involved in interpreting these figures as went into compiling them. Worthy of a mention also are two interesting sections, one dealing with desertion, the other with the incidence of infectious diseases, the scourge of soldier and civilian alike in this pitiless and ferocious war.

Lack of precise documentation prevented an analysis of loss figures differentiated with respect to Red Army offensive or defensive operations. A similar dearth of documentation ruled out any reliable analysis of losses in the Soviet partisan operations, numerous and widespread as they were, for example in Siberia and the Far East.

If the figures for overall losses in the Civil War can be accepted as generally accurate, can the same be said for those presented with respect to the Great Patriotic War? There seems to be no appreciable disagreement over the figure for total mobilised manpower—34,476,000, including 4,826,907 men already under arms in June 1941. Vast movements of men into and out of the armed forces occurred during the war. Wartime mobilisation accounted for 29,574,900 men. The turnover in manpower during the war amounted to 21,700,000, 62.9% of all mobilised personnel. Of those 21 million, 'more than half were irrecoverable losses', namely 11,285,057. As for the rest, more than 3.8 million were wounded, sick or invalided out, 3½ million were released into industry or transferred to local air defence and 1,425,000 were assigned to the NKVD and other establishments. Almost one million men were variously convicted, 436,600 imprisoned, and 422,700 sentenced to penal battalions, the *strafbats*, assigned the most dangerous tasks in the most dangerous sectors. Almost one-third of those convicted, 376,300, were charged with desertion.

Why, one may reasonably ask, are there three sets of figures supplied for irrecoverable losses—11,444,100, 8,668,400 and 12,400,900? The first figure represents the wartime 'military-operational' environment, the Soviet armed forces between 1941 and 1945 'irrecoverably' deprived of men killed in action, died of wounds and illness or shot for cowardice, the missing and prisoners of war in enemy hands, all removed from the battlefield. The second figure is the 'demographic' loss—dead soldiers, dead prisoners of war never to return, offset by the recovery of soldiers in liberated Soviet territory previously 'written off' as missing in action or untraced in encircled units and those 1,836,000 prisoners returned from German captivity. The third figure, which apparently added a further million to the loss total, was derived from the records of the local military commissariats, the *voenkomaty*, or military registration offices. Due to evacuation or displacement of the population, one enquiry for a named individual was often directed to several of these offices. Each enquiry resulted in the registration of a name, the geographic dispersal resulting in many instances of 'multiple counting'. Losses during the Soviet blitzkrieg in the Far East, operations lasting from August to 2 September 1945, amounted to 12,031 (9,780 killed in action or died of wounds, 911 missing, 1,340 non-combat losses).

The challenges to these figures and the methodology associated with them have been vigorous, to say the least. There is, for example, the charge that loss figures for the chaotic months following the German attack in June 1941—'unrecorded losses in the first months of the war'—are too low. There are problems with both methodology and data, many of them freely acknowledged and discussed by the editors, but that these are of an order to render the figures 'unsound' or 'untrustworthy' and the implications drawn from them 'groundless' is open to doubt.

Losses for NKVD and Border Troops have been included, figures supplied at the request of the General Staff. Some have suggested the inclusion of militia, fire-fighting units and railway workers, sailors of the merchant marine and the fishing fleets. Losses among 'these active participants in the war' were unavoidable but they are not counted here. The figure of 4 million is cited for those who volunteered for the militia, *narodnoe opolchenie*, 2 million of whom comprising 40 divisions were incorporated into the Red Army. Those badly armed and poorly trained militia divisions defending Leningrad, Smolensk, Tula and Moscow suffered grievous losses facing the Wehrmacht.

The Soviet partisan movement was both widespread and numerically significant. German reports arrive at a final figure of 4–500,000, Soviet sources cite a figure of 360,000 in Byelorussia and 220,000 in the Ukraine. According to the editors, lack of reliable documentation has prevented them from presenting 'a full picture of losses' among Soviet partisans. The converse, anti-Soviet armed military collaboration with the Germans, receives a brief mention, specifically that 150,000 former Soviet citizens served with the SS. But this was the tip of the iceberg.

What cannot be disputed is the enormous contribution women made to the Soviet war effort and the front-line role of many of the women in the Soviet armed forces. Their numbers have been variously estimated, ranging from 800,000 to 490,235, the latter figure used in this volume. Losses among women were by no means negligible and clearly deserve more than the perfunctory note they have received at the hands of the editors. This distressing omission cannot be due to lack of records. Party and *Komsomol* mobilisations of women and young girls presumably involved records and documentation. Soviet air force records must contain details of women air crew, operations and losses.

Stalin himself predicted a future war of machines in which victory would be won in the machine-shops. A singular feature of this volume is a compilation of the production figures and loss rates for all types of weapons and equipment. From the mass of data, a suitable accompaniment to the huge numbers of men involved, certain salient features of 'loss profiles' emerge. The heaviest losses in small arms occurred in 1941–42, those in tanks and self-propelled guns in 1941, 1943 and 1944, the latter years marked by an increase in the German anti-tank capabilities in heavily defended positions.

The enforced retreats of 1941–42 accounted for the greatest loss in guns and mortars, many abandoned only slightly damaged due to the shortage or unrepaired state of gun-tows. Harsh words are reserved for Soviet aircraft losses, of which half (43,100 out of 88,300) were non-combat accidents due to the curtailment of pilot training, especially introducing new aircraft types, the 'indiscipline' of air crews, lax flight procedures during training flights, structural failures and manufacturing defects in the aircraft produced. Ship and submarine losses of the Soviet Navy are tabulated separately, submarine losses totalling 102, though an alternative source puts them at 111, six in the Pacific, 23 in the Northern Fleet, 34 in the Black Sea and 48 in the Baltic.

Grif sekretnosti snyat, an exceptional contribution to the history of the Second World War, arguably in a category all its own, is now to hand in translation, complete with text, tables and graphs. The like of it was never seen in the former Soviet Union. Such mention and discussion of Red Army strengths and battlefield losses as did exist had to be derived piecemeal from widely disparate materials. The other resource has long been the haul of captured German military documents, Wehrmacht wartime compilations and estimates of Soviet 'irrecoverable losses' (*Unwiederbringliche Verluste*), tank losses (*Feindliche Panzer-Verluste, Ost*), captured weapons and prisoners of war. These have by no means been superseded, and it may be that their value is further enhanced by having confirmed Soviet wartime data to hand.

The key to this volume revolves round reliability and credibility. To dismiss it as 'unsound' is too negative. It is conservative and in parts selective, which the authors themselves do not conceal. On the other hand, the criteria for compilation and interpretation have been overtly set out. The casualty information does generally accord with previous estimates in 'round figures', but, given the vast scale of losses and the complexity of the material, revision will and must continue. The editors themselves advance just such a proposition, inviting the aid of foreign specialists.

Thanks to the Herculean labours and commendable enterprise of Greenhill Books, this translation opens up a whole world, a tragic and bloodied world, hitherto hermetically sealed in secrecy. I wonder at this distance what Marshal of the Soviet Union Ivan Koniev and his fellow commanders would have made of these disclosures.

John Erickson
Edinburgh, 1997

List of Abbreviations

Archive references

TsAMO	Central Archive of the Ministry of Defence
TaGA	Central State Archive
TsGAOR	Central State Archive of the October Revolution
TsGASA	Central State Archive of the Soviet Army
TsGAVMF	Central State Archive of the Navy
TsPAIM	Institute of Marxism-Leninism Central Party Archive
TsVMA	The Central Naval Archive
f.	*fond* (= collection)
op.	*opis'* (= catalogue)
d.	*delo* (= file, dossier)
l.	*list* (= page, sheet)

Other Russian (and German) Abbreviations

BMP	battalion medical aid post
ChON	special purpose units
CPSU	Communist Party of the Soviet Union
GRU	Intelligence Directorate
KGB	Committee for State Security
MD	Military District
MVD	Ministry of Internal Affairs
NKVD	People's Commissariat for Internal Affairs
NRA	People's Revolutionary Army
ODVA	Special Far Eastern Army
OKH	*Oberkommando des Heeres* (= Army High Command) (German)
OKW	*Oberkommando der Wehrmacht* (= Wehrmacht High Command) (German)
RKKA	Workers' and Peasants' Red Army
RKP(B)	Russian Communist Party (Bolshevik)
RSFSR	Russian Soviet Federation of Socialist Republics
RVSR	Revolutionary Military Council of the Republic
STO	Labour and Defence Council

TsVMU (MO)   (Ministry of Defence) Central Military Medical Directorate
VNUS   internal service troops
VOKhR   internal security troops of the republic

English Military Abbreviations

AAG   anti-aircraft gun
AAV   air assault vehicle
APC   armoured personnel carrier
ATG   anti-tank gun
G   gun
GH   gun-howitzer
H   howitzer
IFV   infantry fighting vehicle
M   mortar
SP   self-propelled (gun)

Introduction

This book represents the results of the authors' statistical research into personnel and material losses of the Soviet Armed Forces in wars, military actions and conflicts from 1918 to 1989.

During this time the USSR was subjected to repeated attack, most significantly the attack by Nazi Germany in 1941. Millions of Soviet people were called upon to take up arms to defend their country, and many sacrifices were made for the sake of its freedom and independence.

Behind the casualty figures are revealed the courage and heroism of the men and women who gave their lives fighting for their country, who defended it against attack by the many interventionists, bravely resisted the Nazis, perished in battle at Minsk, Kiev, Moscow and Leningrad, marched from the Volga to Berlin and fell at the walls of the Reichstag, died from wounds in hospitals or remained true to their country until their final hour in the hellish conditions of Nazi prison camps.

Until recently, statistical information on war losses was classified secret. Many countries temporarily adopted the practice of classifying this kind of information. However, the process of declassification 'dragged on' somewhat in the USSR. Therefore several historians and commentators started trying independently to determine the scale of war losses. Their calculations were, however, based on fragmentary information and subjective arguments not backed up by documents. In some of the mass media, calculations of losses appeared which had been taken from foreign sources which were also a long way from the historical truth. All this has led to a distortion of the actual state of affairs and sometimes to attempts to undervalue the Soviet victory in the Great Patriotic War and to belittle the moral spirit of the Soviet troops, the organisational and fighting skill of the Army and Navy command and their loyalty to their country.

Now that the documents on the Soviet armed forces' losses have been declassified, the authors have for the first time carried out research into all categories of personnel losses (also material losses from 1941 to 1945) incurred by the Army and Navy during the years of Soviet power.

The main objective of the present work is to give historians, current affairs commentators, military personnel and the general reader objectively presented and factual statistical information.

The information on war losses given in the book will, we hope, contribute to an objective understanding of the tangled web of complexities which characterise the different stages of the civil war and the Great Patriotic War, the strengths and weaknesses of the army's military preparedness when confronted by an enemy, the country's defence capability and the strength of spirit of the Soviet people. This research will also make it possible to assess more realistically Soviet military skill in battles and operations. The authors hope that the material will prove useful for the study of the military history of the USSR.

In the course of carrying out this research, over several years thousands of separate documents and reports from different archives were examined and compared and figures calculated. The authors' search revealed that, unfortunately, statistics from the war years are far from complete. The years of the civil war and phase one of the Great Patriotic War are marked by a lack of precise information. The explanation for this is the very difficult conditions under which the Red Army fought. Often information on casualties was lost, and sometimes there was simply no one to report it to (this is also true of information on casualties in Nazi Germany in 1945, when the precise system of reporting and recording casualties had completely broken down). In cases where it did not prove possible to find the missing documents, the authors have calculated the number of casualties.

The main part of the book is taken up with an analysis of fighting troop and Navy losses, and also those among the various forces, formations and units which were directly involved in different armed conflicts. It also gives figures for border troop and internal service troop losses during casualty evacuation. In 1988, at the request of the General Staff, the KGB and USSR Interior Ministry made the necessary calculations of irrecoverable losses among border and internal service troops. These figures are summarised in tables giving irrecoverable losses in the Soviet Armed Forces during the Great Patriotic War.

In order that the scale of casualties may be evaluated, a number of tables contain information on the numerical strength of the armed forces at various stages. Information on losses is given in standardised tables and diagrams. These show loss categories and casualty numbers by year of the war (quarter-year), by front, operation, service and arm of service, except where this was not possible because of lack of information.

The ranks of servicemen, regardless of what they were called at the time, are mostly in modern terminology. 'Officers' includes Intermediate, Senior and Higher Command personnel and staff officers, students at military educational establishments, generals and admirals; 'sergeants' includes Junior Command personnel and officers, sergeant-majors and warrant officers; 'men' includes Red Army and Red Navy men, seamen and also officer cadets at military educational establishments.

Fighting troop (Navy) personnel losses are divided into:

(a) Irrecoverable losses. These include deaths in action, deaths from wounds during casualty evacuation and men missing in action or taken prisoner (the number of deaths in hospital from wounds or disease is only shown as part of total armed forces casualties). Irrecoverable losses among the fighting troops also include non-combat losses not directly connected with military actions—deaths in accidents, those sentenced to death by military tribunal for various offences, suicides and deaths from disease in hospital.

(b) Sick and wounded. These figures include servicemen suffering from wounds, concussion, burns, sickness and frostbite evacuated from combat zones to army, front and rear-area hospitals. When assessing the total number of sick and wounded it must be borne in mind that many servicemen were wounded twice or more in the course of a war or repeatedly underwent treatment for disease and therefore appear in the casualty figures more than once.

It should also be borne in mind that there may have been incidences of repeat counting with combat losses in general. For example, if a serviceman who returned to duty after being wounded was subsequently killed, he would have appeared twice in the casualty figures, once as wounded, the second time as killed. Unfortunately it is not possible to determine the number of such incidences.

Losses are given in the tables in figures and as a percentage of total losses. In addition, the ratio of total and average monthly losses to average monthly listed personnel strength is given for fronts, fleets or the fighting troops as a whole for the war, and also for each year and quarter-year.

All losses of arms and equipment are counted as irrecoverable losses, i.e. beyond economic repair or no longer serviceable: although some repaired equipment was returned to service, the number of incidences were few and difficult to calculate.

The book is divided in four chapters. Chapter 1 concentrates on Red Army losses during the civil war and period of foreign military intervention. It covers losses (by year, front and arm of service) during the main civil war period and while the army was putting down subsequent anti-Soviet uprisings. The chapter concludes with the final stage of the war in the Far East. As a rule the casualty figures have been determined on the basis of archive domuments. In some cases, however, where precise information was lacking, they have been calculated.

Chapter 2 investigates Red Army personnel losses in military actions and armed conflicts in the inter-war period. This includes information on losses in the Sino-Soviet military conflict over the Chinese Eastern Railway (1929), among Soviet volunteers in Spain (1936–39) and China (1937–39), in military actions at Lake Khasan (1938) and on the Khalkhin Gol river (1939), in the campaigns in the Western Ukraine and Western Byelorussia (1939) and in the war between Finland and the USSR (November 1939–March 1940).

Chapter 3 is the longest chapter and covers the Soviet Armed Forces' losses in the Great Patriotic War from 1941 to 1945, giving State Statistics Committee data on personnel losses. Casualty numbers have been calculated for servicemen of different ranks. There is a summary of information on irrecoverable losses (killed in action, died of wounds, missing in action, prisoners of war, died in accidents or from other causes) for the whole period of the war, and also an analysis of the medical statistics relating to the number of sick and wounded, the outcome of their treatment and the number returned to duty or invalided out of the armed forces.

Army and Navy combat losses are given by year and phase of the war, arm of service, strategic operation or battle, front or fleet. Total officer casualties are given, with a breakdown by rank and position. One section is devoted to Soviet servicemen who were missing in action or prisoners of war. Another gives material losses, both in figures and as percentages, with a breakdown by year and phase of the war and by operation.

There are several pages on irrecoverable personnel losses incurred by the armed forces of Nazi Germany and its allies on the German-Soviet front. There are figures for the number killed in action, dying of wounds, missing in action or taken prisoner. The irrecoverable losses of Germany's allies and foreign Wehrmacht units (Vlasovite, Muslim, Baltic and other sub-units) are given, as are Japanese losses between August and September 1945.

Chapter 4 gives the casualty figures for Soviet Armed Forces' personnel who took part in local wars and other incidents outside the USSR. This includes the war in Korea (1950–53), events in Hungary in 1956, the sending of troops into Czechoslovakia (1968) and the war in Afghanistan (1979–89).

In preparing this book documents were used from the military establishment and from a number of archives in the former Soviet Union: those of the Armed Forces' General Staff, the Central Party Archive of the CPSU Central Committee Institute of Marxism-Leninism (TsPAIML), the Central State Archive of the October Revolution (TsGAOR), the Central Archive of the Ministry of Defence (TsAMO), the Central State Archive of the Soviet Army (TsGASA; since June 1992 known as the *Ros. gos. voen. arkhiv*, RGVA), the Central State Archive of the Navy (TsGAVMF) and the Central Naval Archive (TsVMA).

In this research work, for the first time full and systematised information is given on the Soviet Armed Forces' losses in wars, military actions and conflicts from 1918 to 1989. A summary of the figures is given in Table 111, from which it can be seen that, during this period, as a result of military actions irrecoverable losses came to 9,763,326 and there were 29,878,153 sick or wounded.

The greatest number of irrecoverable losses were incurred during the two major wars, the civil war (1918–22) and the Great Patriotic War (1941–45). In the former they came to 939,755, in the latter to 8,668,400.

The Great Patriotic War was inflicted on the Soviet Union as a result of German fascism and was unprecedented in scale and for the bitterness of the fighting. The Soviet people succeeded in withstanding unprecedentedly violent strikes by the enemy, putting paid to their plans, inflicting very heavy losses on them and then, together with the Allies, routing the enemy hordes and finally winning a historic victory.

In the period between the civil war and the Great Patriotic War, the Soviet Armed Forces were involved in several conflicts, fighting *Basmachestvo*, defending the Soviet border at Lake Khasan and on the Khalkhin Gol river, in the war with Finland and in other military conflicts. In the post-war years Soviet forces gave assistance to many friendly developing countries under the terms of inter-governmental agreements. All this as a rule called for considerable human sacrifice. In the inter-war period (1923–40), Red Army irrecoverable losses came to 139,100, and in the post-war period (1950–89) the armed forces lost 16,100 men.

The figures presented in this book may not only be used for research purposes but may also be used in various ways to commemorate those servicemen who died.

The authors are continuing their research on the subject treated in this monograph. Their main efforts are directed towards finding new documents and material which would enable them, first, to fill in a number of gaps in the figures for the Soviet Armed Forces' casualties, and second, to discover fuller, more adequate information on enemy losses in past wars and military conflicts. This concerns losses of the Wehrmacht and its allies on the German-Soviet front, of the Japanese Armed Forces in the Far East, the Finnish Army in 1939–40 and 1941–44 and of foreign interventionists during the civil war. Studying the losses of the White Armies will require serious effort.

Historians in Austria, Britain, Bulgaria, Hungary, Germany, Spain, Italy, Canada, China, Poland, Romania, the USA, Finland, France, Czechoslovakia, Yugoslavia, Japan and other interested countries are being invited to carry out research as co-authors of a future book, as are custodians of overseas archives of the White Russian Movement and researchers working therein.

It seems to the authors of the present book that producing a unique work on the losses incurred by all the warring sides in all the wars and military conflicts of recent times, and also losses during the major battles and operations, can only be achieved through the joint efforts of an international group of authors with access to the necessary documents in the various countries' archives.

In preparing the manuscript of this book, the authors made use of material by the following people:

I. A. Arkhiereev, S. S. Berezhnoi, V. A. Bogdanov, Yu. V. Borgunov, I. N. Venkov, Yu. A. Gorkov, N. N. Dmitriev, A. F. Klushin, Yu. V. Petrov, A. K. Samartsev, N. A. Samoilov, A. S. Sapozhnikov, A. P. Sergeev, A. N. Tamrazov and K. K. Shilov.

The Publishers are grateful to Colonel John Sloan and Micha Mihailo Jelisavcic for their review of the English translation and assistance with special terms and explanatory information.

Chapter One

Red Army Losses during the Civil War and Foreign Military Intervention

The civil war in Soviet Russia began soon after the October Revolution. It was in essence an armed struggle between supporters of the new regime and its opponents. It lasted for five years, from October 1917 to October 1922.

The war meant several years of intensive fighting which brought great suffering to millions of people. It was aggravated by foreign military interference and intervention.

It should be added, however, that life in the republic was dominated by war only from May 1918, when the rebellion of the Czechoslovak Corps began, until November 1920, when Wrangel's army was defeated in the Crimea.

In those two and a half years, the country's fate was decided purely on the battle-fields of the civil war. During that period the regular Soviet armed forces, consisting of the Red Army and Navy, were formed and their maximum strength was reached (5,427,273 men as of 1 November 1920),[1] the most important operations to defeat the interventionists and White Guards were fought and the greater part of the country's territory was liberated.

The defeat of the combined forces of interventionists and White Guards by the young Red Army meant that at the end of 1920 the Soviet republic was able to begin the transition from war to peace. By this time most of the civil war fronts had been eliminated and, although in a number of places individual pockets of military resistance remained (in the Trans-Caucasus, Central Asia and the Far East), it was no longer these which determined the basic policy direction of the Soviet state. The solution of military problems now took second place.

The fact that the civil war can be divided into two distinct periods is reflected in this book. All the statistical data on Red Army losses[2] is divided into two parts: losses for the period 1918–20, which saw the worst of the armed struggle, and losses from 1921 to 1922, when the Red Army was conducting military operations mostly against individual armed bands sent from abroad, also against local anti-Soviet resistance and *basmachestvo*, the anti-Soviet movement in Central Asia.

RED ARMY LOSSES, 1918–20

The civil war and military intervention brought widespread destruction to Soviet Russia and caused very heavy losses. The cost to the economy in financial terms was about fifty billion gold roubles. As a result of the war industrial production fell to

7

between 4% and 20% of the level in pre-revolutionary Russia (compared with 1913 figures). Both the working class population and agricultural production were reduced by about half. Total demographic losses on the various fronts and in the rear (in battle, from hunger, epidemics and the terror) reached eight million.[3] This figure also includes Red Army personnel killed or dying from wounds or disease between 1918 and 1922.

There are considerable discrepancies in the source literature regarding the number of casualties among the men and officers of the Workers' and Peasants' Red Army (RKKA) in the civil war. Modern encyclopedias (*The Great Soviet Encyclopedia*, *The Soviet Historical Encyclopedia* and *The Civil War and Military Intervention in the USSR: an Encyclopedia*), all give the same figure of about one million for the number of servicemen who died.[4]

The well-known Soviet researcher B. Ts. Urlanis quotes different figures in his book *Wars and Population in Europe*. According to him, about 125,000 were killed at the front and about 300,000 died with the field army or in military districts.[5] Thus, in all, 425,000 died or were killed, which is about half the number given in the encyclopedias mentioned.

There are also many discrepancies in the statistical material from the central organs of the Red Army, which collated information on battle losses in the civil war. For example, according to calculations made by the Revolutionary Military Council of the Republic (RVSR) Field Staff Mobilisation Administration, 85,343 commanders and men were killed and 502,016 were wounded up to December 1920.[6]

Different figures for Red Army personnel losses between 1918 and 1920 are given in a report dated 26 July 1924 from the Red Army Chief Directorate's records and statistics department:

Irrecoverable losses	
Killed in action, died of wounds	40,000
Missing in action	96,000
Prisoners of war	24,000
Deserted	20,000
Sick and wounded	
Wounded or concussed	360,000
Sick	1,040,000
Total	1,580,000[7]

Thus, according to these calculations, irrecoverable losses came to 180,000 and sick and wounded to 1,400,000.

The following year the same Red Army Chief Directorate, in its letter of 11 June 1925 to the Budgets Department of the RSFSR People's Commissariat for Finance, gave somewhat different figures for total personnel casualties over the same period:

Irrecoverable losses

Killed in action, died of wounds	60,000
Missing in action	150,000

Sick and wounded

Wounded or concussed	260,000
Sick	1,000,000
Total	1,470,000 [8]

Here, irrecoverable losses come to 210,000 and sick and wounded to 1,260,000.

If one compares the two sets of figures, the 1925 figures show 20,000 more in the category 'killed in action, died of wounds' and 100,000 fewer in the category 'wounded or concussed'.

That same year information on Red Army losses for 1918–22 was published in the book *The Economy of the USSR in Figures* (based on information from the Red Army Chief Directorate's statistics department). It is given in Table 1 below.[9]

Table 1

Loss category	Year of the war					Total
	1918	1919	1920	1921	1922	
Combat losses	8,292	131,396	300,059	171,185	20,826	631,758
Sick and wounded (including evacuated casualties)	5,127	150,324	212,580	194,758	18,277	581,066
Total	13,419	281,720	512,639	365,943	39,103	1,212,824

This table is a very important statistical document and is particularly useful for research into civil war casualties. However, as its compilers did not specify what was meant by 'combat losses' or 'sick and wounded', various interpretations of the document have appeared. Thus, for some reason in the Urlanis book mentioned above, *Wars and Population in Europe*, only the figures for combat losses in this table are taken and analysed. Urlanis states that 'both the actual figures and a comparison of the figures give one grounds to assume that "combat losses" denotes *killed and wounded* [our emphasis—Authors].'[10]

Yu. A. Polyakov, in his book *The Soviet Land After the End of the Civil War: Territory and Population*,[11] disagrees with Urlanis and gives a different interpretation of 'combat losses' and 'sick and wounded' (literally, in Russian, 'medical losses') in this table. 'It is logical to assume,' he says, 'that in both cases what is meant is resulting fatalities: it says "medical losses", not "cases of sickness"' (i.e., in the author's opinion the figures for combat losses and sick and wounded given in the table should be interpreted as the number of servicemen who were killed or who died).[12] He also proposes that the figures in this table be taken as the statistical basis for the total, and that this total of 1,212,824 be taken as the total number of all Red Army servicemen killed between 1918 and 1922.[13]

The contradictions and discrepancies in the published figures for exactly the same loss categories in the civil war are primarily explained by the fact that information on losses in many of the reports sent from the field to the higher and central military bodies was incomplete or even lacking altogether. There were also frequent instances of army headquarters failing to attach due significance to casualty figures and reports, or being unable to deal with this important matter because of an unexpected deterioration in the operational situation. As a result, civil war archive collections suffer from a lack of the primary source materials needed to work out statistical data such as casualty figures. Such gaps are especially common in archive material relating to 1918–19.

The situation began to improve somewhat only after the Records and Statistics Information Department was set up as part of the All-Russian Supreme Staff in September 1919.[14] The work done by this department helped to regulate the reporting and recording of all types of losses in the subsequent period of the civil war from 1920 onwards. On the basis of information on combat losses collected by this department between 1918 and 1920, in 1926 the 'Roll of Casualties at the Fronts in the Workers' and Peasants' Red Army During the Civil War' (*Imennoi spisok poter' na frontakh v Raboche-Krest'yanskoi Krasnoi Armii za vremya grazhdanskoi voiny*, Moscow, 1926) was drawn up by the Red Army Chief Directorate's Directorate for the Organisation of Troops. On it are the names of about 51,000 servicemen who were killed at the front (including those who died during casualty evacuation), and also a small number who died of disease. Even though the roll is far from complete and contains the names of only a minority of the servicemen who died, it is still valuable today both as a historical document and as a memorial to these soldiers.

Bearing in mind the experience of earlier researchers who have investigated civil war casualty figures, and as they are working on virtually the same problem but under new conditions, the authors of this book have drawn mainly on archive documents. For example, the figures for servicemen killed or missing in action or taken prisoner were established on the basis of documents from the Operations Directorate of the RVSR Field Staff, which received information on casualties from front and army headquarters as recorded in the Report Priority Log.[15] The figures for sick and wounded are based on information from the Chief Military Medical Directorate, where reports on cases of wounding, concussion, sickness and frostbite were sent from front and army medical units. Documents from other military departments were also used.

Unfortunately, in the archive collections mentioned, there are long stretches when there were no reports from the field on casualty figures, and this undoubtedly had an adverse effect on the reliability of statistical data. All such instances are noted in the footnotes to the tables which give casualty figures.

Statistical material on the average monthly personnel strength of both the fighting troops and the Red Army as a whole for each year of the war is important when assessing casualty figures for this period. These figures, given in Tables 2 and 3, were used to calculate relative numbers of casualties (as a percentage).

Table 2. Personnel Strength of the Fighting Troops, 1918–20, taken as Average Monthly Figures[1]

Year	Numerical strength in/as of:	Numerical strength
1918	July	225,000
1919	July	1,307,376
1920	1 June	1,539,667
Average annual numerical strength		1,024,014

1. As it was not possible to calculate the average monthly personnel strength of the fighting troops because of incomplete data, the total numerical strength for July 1918, July 1919 and 1 June 1920 is given.

Table 3. Personnel Strength of the Armed Forces of the Soviet Republic, 1918–20[1]

Numerical strength as of:			By Service and arm of service			
Year	Date and month	Total personnel strength of armed forces	Ground forces	Navy	Admin. and logistic support units	Construction units
1918	1 June	374,551	326,335	48,216	—	—
1919	1 June	2,320,542[2]	2,212,047[3]	33,520[4]	60,808[5]	14,167[6]
1920	1 June	4,424,317[7]	3,875,257[8]	46,405	261,415	241,240[9]
Average annual numerical strength		2,373,137	2,137,880	42,714	161,112	127,704

1. As it was not possible to calculate the average monthly strength of the armed forces from 1918 to 1920, total personnel strength is given as of 1 June or 1 July for each year of the war.
2. In addition 112,000 workers at defence industry factories were receiving Red Army rations.
3. The figure given for the Ground Forces includes 187,000 who were sick, wounded or at transit centres.
4. The personnel strength of the Navy was down by 14,696 compared with 1918 because almost a third of the men and officers were sent to the land fronts.
5. The 'administrative and logistic support units' column includes figures for the following Ground Forces services: supplies, military communications, medical (including nursing) and veterinary, also animal-drawn transport services, which were directly subordinated to fronts, military districts and the centre.
6. Indicates the numerical strength of military field construction units under central command.
7. In addition, by this time 189,801 workers at defence industry factories and 12,090 peasants who were involved in transporting military stores were receiving Red Army rations, as were a certain number of entertainers and other persons.
8. Including 201,282 temporary personnel at medical treatment centres, 343,365 servicemen who were in transit (at backloading points, halting places, distribution points and feeding centres) and 222,328 Internal Security troops (VOKhR).
9. Construction units included labour armies, military field construction units and various construction and timber cutting detachments. Labour armies were formed in accordance with the Council of People's Commissars' decree of 15 January 1920 'On the serious economic situation in the country and the impossibility of demobilising the Red Army because of the continuing military threat from the imperialist powers'. In accordance with this decree labour armies could be brought in to reinforce the regular field army at any time.

A comparison of the figures in these tables shows that the total numerical strength of the Red Army at the middle of each year of the war is significantly higher (by 1.6–2.3 times) than the numerical strength of the fighting troops for the same period.

This is because the total strength of the army and navy included a large number of rear, reserve and auxiliary formations, military establishments and institutions (replacement, reserve and training units, district and local military directorates, military educational establishments, railway security troops and other auxiliary troops, military district hospitals with a large number of sick and wounded servicemen, etc). In 1919–20 such major troop formations as the republic's reserve army and the reserve armies of several fronts, and also the labour armies which were under the command of the RVSR, were added to the troops deployed in the Red Army's rear area.

It should be said that the various structures making up the Red Army rear were constantly developing and growing as the war and military construction progressed. Nonetheless, throughout almost the whole of this period of the civil war there was a severe shortage of commanders and men at the front. At the beginning of 1919, for example, the Red Army's fighting troops were at least 280,000 bayonets and sabres short.[16] It was thought that this shortfall would be made up in two to three months, but in fact in this space of time the Russian Supreme Staff was only able to detail a maximum of 157,000 men from available reserves, and only 111,900 men actually arrived at the front, i.e. 71% of the number anticipated.

As a result the situation deteriorated still further. The reinforcements the armies received, as was noted in the High Command report of 9 May 1919, 'were not even sufficient to replace casualties at the front and the losses caused by the high number of desertions, and at present the number of bayonets and sabres both among the fighting troops and in units in interior districts is down by 85,000, i.e. about 20%'.[17]

In the High Command memorandum of 26 May 1919 on the shortage of fighting troops it was stated that 'Armies and fronts are down by about 400,000 bayonets and sabres alone. Southern Front has been particularly weakened by constant battles, some armies being up to 10,000 bayonets short. Reinforcements arrive extremely slowly and many short of the number of reinforcements detailed to the front.'[18]

There were several main reasons for the unsatisfactory state of affairs with regard to maintaining front-line fighting troops at full strength. The process of calling up and training those liable for military service and dispatching them to their place of duty was badly organised; desertion by conscripts was now on a mass scale; there was a lack of weapons, particularly rifles, with which formations bound for the front were supposed to be provided; rail transport was poor; and many state and military organs were ignorant as to what the needs and requirements of the fighting troops were. All these factors were mentioned time and again in reports from the Commander-in-Chief to the Defence Council on the situation at the front. Here are some excerpts from these:

'Up to the present time we do not have the right to claim that our Republic has paid due attention to its armed forces. Until now, things have been done in the time-honoured fashion, with the War Department waging war and other departments occupied with their own concerns.'[19] As a result, 'it was not uncommon for citizens called up for military service to rebel, dispersing and going back home simply because they had not been allotted any barrack accommodation, supposedly because there was none. There were such incidences almost everywhere, yet the reason there was a shortage of places was because suitable premises, even barracks which had belonged to the old army, cadet corps buildings and religious seminary buildings, were occupied by other commissariats. Often call-up had to be abandoned because there were no boots, no uniforms. One often had to witness mutinies and discontent in Red Army units because the interests of those fighting for the good of the revolution and the socialist Republic were not taken into account by the authorities in the localities.'[20]

Considerable alarm was expressed in one report from the Commander-in-Chief in May 1919 about the catastrophic shortage of rifles and cartridges in the field army and about the ignorance in the rear in both military and non-military circles as to front-line needs: 'The problem with supplies of rifles and cartridges is particularly acute ... in two to three months with decisive front-line actions taking place we could be left without a single cartridge at the front or in the rear.'[21]

It continues: '... High Command orders [concerning troop reinforcements—Authors] over the past two-and-a-half months have not been carried out, not only because of conditions prevailing in the Republic, but partly also because our system suffers from a lack of communication between the front and the rear not only in the country as a whole but also ... within the War Department'.[22]

The problem of keeping fighting troop numbers up to strength and replacing personnel losses remained unsolved almost throughout the whole of the civil war, thus in the majority of instances the fighting strength of the Red Army's front-line forces was less than the number of enemy bayonets and sabres. Only by mid-1920 did the situation begin to change for the better, as is shown by the figures relating to the numerical strength and relative numbers of fighting troops on each side from 1918–20. See Table 4.[23] In this table only the numerical strength of Red Army troops fighting at the front during the civil war is given, and therefore the total figures here are less than those in Table 2, which give the total strength of the fighting troops.

Table 4. Numerical Strength of Red Army and Enemy Troops Engaged in Fighting at the Front, 1918–20[1]

Year	Numerical strength as of:	Front: (independent army)	Numerical strength Red Army	Numerical strength Enemy forces	Ratio
1918	1–10 December[2]	Northern Front	20,010	34,053	1 : 1.7
		Independent Western Army (16th Army)	7,840	93,350	1 : 11.9
		Southern Front	105,910	220,000	1 : 2.1
		Eastern Front	86,850	118,662	1 : 1.4
		Total	220,610	466,065	1 : 2.1

Year	Numerical strength as of:	Front: (independent army)	Numerical strength		Ratio
			Red Army	Enemy forces	
1919	Latter half of June[3]	6th Independent Army (formerly Northern Front)	13,820	39,500	1 : 2.9
		Western Front	139,595	378,600	1 : 2.7
		Southern Front	76,194	109,500	1 : 1.4
		Eastern Front	125,240	129,000	1 : 1
		Total	354,849	656,600	1 : 1.8
1920	First half of May[4]	7th Independent Army	21,986	114,090	1 : 5.2
		Western Front	88,952	74,850	1.2 : 1
		South-Western Front	42,877	97,360	1 : 2.3
		Caucasian Front	66,448	63,800	1 : 1
		Turkestan Front	30,685	10,900	2.8 : 1
		Total	250,948	361,000	1 : 1.4
1920	1 November[5]	7th Independent Army	33,934	102,900	1 : 3
		Western Front	86,726	87,000	1 : 1
		South-Western Front	72,192	45,500	1.6 : 1
		Southern Front (against Wrangel)	186,068	about 41,000	4.5 : 1
		Caucasian Front	85,902	28,400	3 : 1
		Turkestan Front	34,069	about 13,000	2.6 : 1
		Total	498,891	317,800	1.6 : 1

1. The figures given here for the numerical strength of Red Army and enemy troops include only the number of bayonets and sabres among the troops fighting at the front (they exclude the numerical strength of HQs, administrative and logistic units and army and front reserves). They have been taken from the collections of civil war documents *Direktivy Glavnogo komandovaniya* and *Direktivy komandovaniya frontov Krasnoi Armii 1917–22*.
2. *Direktivy Glavnogo komandovaniya*, p.132; *Direktivy komandovaniya frontov*, vol. 4, pp. 51, 468–73.
3. *Direktivy komandovaniya frontov*, vol. 4, pp. 70–1, 480–2.
4. *Direktivy Glavnogo komandovaniya*, p. 327; *Direktivy komandovaniya frontov*, vol. 4, pp. 142–9, 160, 510–14.
5. *Direktivy komandovaniya frontov*, vol. 4, pp. 220–7, 525–6.

A comparison of the figures in Tables 2 and 3 shows that in the course of the war there was a change in the balance in numbers of combat and non-combat troops (administration and logistics, internal service, auxiliary, reserve and replacement troops, etc), with an increase in numbers of the latter. This was evidence on the one hand of the steady increase in the provision of logistical support to the front, and on the other hand of the overwhelming increase in the number of rear structures to the detriment of the front line, as the former swallowed up a large number of those who were conscripted and mobilised.

In turn, the fighting troops included troops fighting in the front line and HQs, rear services, administrative and logistic units, and reserve and replacement troops. The proportion of troops in each category is given in Table 5, which shows the listed strength of the troops at the front and of the fighting troops as a whole, as of 15 October 1920.

Table 5. Composition and Numerical Strength of the Field Armies as of 15 November 1920[1]

Strategic formation	Total numerical strength of fighting troops	Made up of:					
		Troops in the front line		Reserve and replacement troops		HQs, rear services, admin. and logistic units	
		No of men	% of total numerical strength	No of men	% of total numerical strength	No of men	% of total numerical strength
7th Independent Army	117,282	72,432	61.8	—	—	44,850	38.2
Western Front	431,591	151,399	35.1	146,864	34.0	133,328	30.9
South-Western Front	296,713	110,429	37.2	18,513	6.3	167,771	56.5
Southern Front	468,472	290,738	62.1	43,601	9.3	134,133	28.6
1st Cavalry Army	49,822	33,898	68.0	—	—	15,924	32.0
Caucasian Front	304,437	158,961	52.2	43,393	14.3	102,083	33.5
Turkestan Front	73,470	46,511	63.3	—	—	26,959	36.7
Troops of 2i/c Siberia	124,526	55,158	44.3	—	—	69,368	55.7
Total	1,866,313	919,526	49.3	252,371	13.5	694,416	37.2

1. The table was compiled from statistical material on the fighting and numerical strength of the field armies as of 15 October 1920 (*Direktivy komandovaniya frontov*, vol. 4, pp. 200–17).

From the summer of 1918 higher strategic formations (fronts) began to be formed as part of the army's active forces. They were set up by decree of the Central Committee of the Russian Communist Party (Bolsheviks) and the Soviet government and by resolution of the Defence Council; these were then implemented by order of the RVSR. These fronts were considered to be the most important formations.[24] Table 6 shows the order in which they were set up and the dates when they existed.

Table 7 shows the average monthly numerical strength of each front (independent army) for 1920, and Table 8 gives their casualty figures for the same year. It has not proved possible to find similar information on the fronts' (independent armies') casualties for 1918 and 1919.

Of particular interest are the figures for the total number of irrecoverable losses and sick and wounded in the Red Army from 1918 to 1920 (see Table 9), which are made up of fighting troop and military district losses. The latter figures mainly represent the number of sick who were treated in hospital and the number of deaths from wounds or disease in military district hospitals.

Table 6. Dates when the Different Fronts (Independent Armies, Defended Areas) Existed during the Civil War, 1918–22

Front (independent army, defended area)	Existed (from – to)
Eastern Front	13.6 1918–15.1 1920
Northern Front	11.9 1918–19.2 1919
Southern Front (against Denikin)	11.9 1918–10.1 1920
Western Defended Area	11.9–15.11 1918
Independent Western Army	15.11 1918–19.2 1919
Caspian–Caucasian Front	8.12 1918–13.3 1919
Ukrainian Front	4.1–15.6 1919
Western Front	19.2 1919–18.4 1924
6th Independent Army	19.2 1919–15.4 1920
11th Independent Army	19.3–12.6 1919
Turkestan Front	14.8 1919–6 1926
South-Eastern Front	1.10 1919–16.1 1920
South-Western Front	10.1–31.12 1920
5th Independent Army	15.1 1920–6.9 1922
Caucasian Front	16.1 1920–29.5 1921
7th Independent Army	10.5 1920–10.5 1921
Southern Front (against Wrangel)	21.9–10.12 1920

Year and month of the war

1918 · 1919 · 1920 · 1921 · 1922 (months 1 2 3 4 5 6 7 8 9 10 11 12)

Table 7. Average Monthly Personnel Strength of Fronts and Independent Armies in 1920

Front (Independent army)	Numerical strength			Numerical strength in (month):
	Commanders	NCOs and men	Total	
7th Independent Army	13,583	141,070	154,653	July–August
Western Front	26,272	355,799	382,071	July–August
South-Western Front	17,231	265,276	282,507	July–August
Southern Front (against Wrangel)	26,576	395,731	422,307	October
Caucasian Front	32,336	307,862	340,198	July–August
Turkestan Front	10,688	150,167	160,855	July–August
5th Independent Army	9,432	104,778	114,210	July–August

Note. The table shows the total average monthly numerical strength of the active formations of fronts (independent armies), together with their HQs, logistic and reserve units. However, the number of commanders and men directly involved in combat missions was significantly lower. The following list gives the fighting strength of the fronts and independent armies as of 1 August 1920: 7th Independent Army 49,188; Western Front 136,292; South–Western Front 147,875; Caucasian Front 76,563; Turkestan Front 29,758; Southern Front (on 15 October 1920) 114,787; 5th Independent Army 42,187. See *Direktivy komandovaniya frontov*, vol. 4, pp.180–4, 210.

Table 8. The Fronts' Personnel Losses for 1920

		7th Independent Army (formerly Northern Front)		Western Front		South-Western Front		Southern Front		Caucasian Front		Turkestan Front		5th Independent Army (formerly Eastern Front)		Total losses	
Loss categories		Total	No of commanders	Total	No of commanders	Total	No of commanders	Total	No of commanders	Total	No of commanders	Total	No of commanders	Total	No of commanders	Total	No of commanders
Irrecoverable losses — Killed in action, died during casualty evacuation	No	245	23	6,989	763	10,653	1,292	811	115	3,139	245	333	15	218	14	22,388	2,467
	% of losses	3.1	7	4.8	10.2	12.2	16.9	3.4	9.2	8.8	14.1	22.2	23.4	1.1	2.4	7	12.9
Missing in action, POWs	No	1,155	43	53,805	1,864	41,075	1,905	14,819	562	9,576	423	97	—	1,588	—	122,115	4,797
	% of losses	14.5	13.1	37.3	24.8	46.9	24.8	62.3	44.8	26.9	24.4	6.5	—	7.8	—	38	25.1
Non-combat losses	No	1,065	31	11,597	381	5,949	135	599	32	657	12	—	—	151	3	20,018	594
	% of losses	13.4	9.4	8	5.1	6.8	1.8	2.5	2.6	1.9	0.7	—	—	0.7	0.5	6.2	3.1
Total irrecoverable losses	No	2,465	97	72,391	3,008	57,677	3,332	16,229	709	13,372	680	430	15	1,957	17	164,521	7,858
	% of losses	31	29.5	50.1	40.1	65.9	43.5	68.2	56.6	37.6	39.2	28.7	23.4	9.6	2.9	51.2	41.1
	% of average monthly numerical strength	1.6	0.7	18.9	11.5	20.4	19.3	3.8	2.7	3.9	2.1	0.3	0.1	1.7	0.2	8.9	5.8
Sick and wounded — Wounded, burns and concussion cases	No	608	52	38,861	3,203	6,653	3,237	3,548	340	6,846	642	292	5	667	65	57,475	7,544
	% of losses	7.6	15.8	26.9	42.7	7.6	42.2	14.9	27.1	19.3	37.0	19.5	7.8	3.3	11.3	17.9	39.4
Sick	No	4,878	180	33,171	1,296	23,234	1,100	4,019	204	15,318	413	777	44	17,698	494	99,095	3,731
	% of losses	61.4	54.7	23	17.2	26.5	14.3	16.9	16.3	43.1	23.8	51.8	68.8	87.1	85.8	30.9	19.5
Total sick and wounded	No	5,486	232	72,032	4,499	29,887	4,337	7,567	544	22,164	1,055	1,069	49	18,365	559	156,570	11,275
	% of losses	69	70.5	49.9	59.9	34.1	56.5	31.8	43.4	62.4	60.8	71.3	76.6	90.4	97.1	48.8	58.9
	% of average monthly numerical strength	3.6	1.7	18.9	17.1	10.6	25.2	1.8	2	6.5	3.3	0.6	0.5	16.1	5.9	8.4	8.3
Total losses	No	7,951	329	144,423	7,507	87,564	7,669	23,796	1,253	35,536	1,735	1,499	64	20,322	576	321,091	19,133
	% of losses	100	100	100	100	100	100	100	100	100	100	100	100	100	100	100	100
	% of average monthly numerical strength	5.2	2.4	37.8	28.6	31	44.5	5.6	4.7	10.4	5.4	0.9	0.6	17.8	6.1	17.3	14.1

Note. The fronts' casualty figures for 1920 are incomplete, and they do not include the figures for January. Therefore the totals for irrecoverable losses and sick and wounded do not tally with other figures for casualties in the armed forces in 1920. (TsGASA—Central State Archive of the Soviet Army—f. 7, op. 6, d. 802, l. 86, 86a, 99). Individual fronts' casualty figures for January 1920 are as follows: Western Front 174 killed, 1,094 died of wounds or disease, 952 wounded and 19,772 sick; South-Western Front 15 killed, 1,053 died of wounds or disease, 1,768 wounded and 37,022 sick; 6th Independent Army 3 killed, 278 died of wounds or disease, 40 wounded and 2,860 sick. Casualty figures for January for the other fronts were not found (TsGASA, f. 6, op. 6, d. 308, l. 65, 66, 84).

Table 9. Total Personnel Losses of the Soviet Armed Forces in the Civil War, 1918–20[1]

| | No of losses, by year | | | | | | | | | | | Total losses, 1918–20 | | |
| | 1918 | | | 1919 | | | 1920 | | | | | | | | |
Loss category	No of losses during year	% of average monthly personnel strength	% of losses	No of losses during year	% of average monthly personnel strength	% of losses	No of losses during year	% of average monthly personnel strength	% of losses			No of losses over the 3 years	% of average monthly personnel strength	% of losses
Irrecoverable losses														
Fighting troops (naval forces):														
Killed in action, died during casualty evacuation	1,662[2]	0.7	1.1	22,569[9]	1.7	1.7	122,257[16]	7.9	3.8			146,488[23]	14.3	3.1
Missing in action, POWs	2,060[3]	0.9	1.5	37,839[10]	2.9	2.8	122,130[17]	7.9	3.8			162,029[24]	15.8	3.4
Died as result of accident, condemned by military tribunal, deserted, committed suicide	199[4]	0.1	0.1	7,343[11]	0.6	0.4	20,018[18]	1.3	0.6			27,560[25]	2.7	0.6
Military districts: Died of wounds or disease	4,258[5]	—	2.9	18,395[12]	—	1.4	17,539[19]	—	0.6			40,192[26]	—	0.9
Total irrecoverable losses	8,179	—	5.6	86,146	—	6.3	281,944	— —	8.8			376,269	—	8
Sick and wounded														
Fighting troops (naval forces):														
Wounded, concussion, burns and frostbite cases	15,335[6]	6.9	10.5	202,293[13]	15.5	14.9	319,097[20]	20.7	10			536,725	52.4	11.4
Sick	45,542[7]	20.2	31.1	819,617[14]	62.7	60.2	2,203,078[21]	143.1	69.1			3,068,237	299.6	65.3
Military districts: sick	77,322[8]	—	52.8	253,502[15]	—	18.6	386,455[22]	—	12.1			717,279	—	15.3
Sick and wounded, total	138,199	—	94.4	1,275,412	—	93.7	2,908,630	—	91.2			4,322,241	—	92
Total losses	146,378	—	100	1,361,558	—	100	3,190,574	—	100			4,698,510	—	100

1. Personnel losses are shown in the table without any breakdown as to rank or Service, as it has not proved possible to obtain full or reliable information on this. Percentages of losses have been calculated taking the average monthly numerical strength of the field armies on active service given in Table 2.

2. 962 killed (TsGASA, f. 6, op. 4, d 739, 1. 369) and 681 deaths from wounds and disease (in the 6th Army alone from August to December 1918 and the 8th and 9th Armies from November to December 1918) (TsGASA, f. 6, op. 6, d. 308, 1 65, 66); 19 deaths in the navy (TsGAVMF—Central State Archive of the Navy—f. R-715, op. 1, d. 137, 1. 229). Figures incomplete.

3. 1,479 missing in action and 181 prisoners of war (TsGASA, f. 6, op. 4, d. 739, 1. 369); 400 navy personnel taken prisoner on 25 December 1918 on the destroyers *Spartak* and *Avtroil* (TsGAVMF, f. R-55, op. 1, d. 18, 1. 63).

4. TsGASA, f. 6, op. 4, d. 739, 1. 369.

5. This represents the number of deaths from wounds and disease in the Moscow, Orel and Volga Military Districts for the period May–December 1918 (TsGASA, f. 6, op. 6, d. 308, 1. 57, 63, 73).

6. Eastern Front, September–November 1918: 8,470; South-Western Front, November–December 1918: 5,334; 6th Army, August–November 1918: 1,439 (TsGASA, f. 6, op. 6, d. 308, 1. 65, 66, 82); navy losses: 92 (TsGAVMF, f. R-715, op. 1, d. 137, 1. 229). Figures incomplete.

7. Eastern Front, September 1918: 3,394; 6th Army, August–September 1918: 1,536 (TsGASA, f. 6, op. 6,

d. 308, l. 57, 82); fronts and independent armies, second half of 1918: 40,585 (TsGASA, f. 6, op. 4, d. 739, l. 383); navy losses: 27 (highly contagious disease cases in the Baltic Fleet) (TsGAVMF, f. R-588, op. 1, d. 263, l. 1).

8. This figure includes 24,174 cases of sickness in Moscow Military District, March–June 1918; 5,951 cases in Orel Military District, May–June; also cases of sickness in all military districts in the second half of 1918 (TsGASA, f. 6, op. 6, d. 308, l. 73; op. 4, d. 739, l. 383).

9. Losses of fronts: 7,311 killed (TsGASA, f. 6, op. 4, d. 739, l. 369), 898 deaths from wounds and 13,387 deaths from disease (TsGASA, f. 6, op. 4, d. 739, l. 383); navy losses: 757 killed and 216 deaths from disease (source: see note 14).

10. Losses of fronts: 30,799 missing in action and 6,830 prisoners of war (TsGASA, f. 6, op. 4, d. 739, l. 367–9); navy losses: 101 missing in action and 109 prisoners of war (source: see note 14).

11. TsGASA, f. 6, op. 4, d. 739, l. 367–9.

12. This represents the number of deaths from wounds and disease in Moscow and Volga Military Districts 1 January 1919–1 January 1920 and Orel Military District 1 January 1919–1 July 1919 (TsGASA, f. 6, op. 6, d. 308, l. 57, 63, 73).

13. Losses of fronts: 201,269 cases (TsGASA, f. 6, op. 4, d. 739, l. 383); navy losses: 1,024 (source: see note 14).

14. Losses of fronts: 818,244 cases (TsGASA, f. 6, op. 4, d. 739, l. 383); navy losses: 1,373 (highly contagious disease cases at the Kronstadt and Petrograd Baltic Fleet Naval Hospitals and the Astrakhan-Caspian Flotilla Hospital).

According to a report from the head of the Chief Directorate for Navy Personnel, there were about 4,000 casualties in the navy in 1919 (TsGAVMF, f. R-1, op. 1, d. 288, l. 18–19). It has not proved possible, however, to find documented figures corroborating this or to give a breakdown by loss category. Documents were found confirming 3,580 of the casualties. Of these, 757 were killed, 216 died of disease, 1,024 were wounded and 210 were missing in action, and there were 1,373 highly contagious disease cases. These corroborated figures have been included in this book.

Documentary sources for navy losses are as follows: Baltic Fleet: TsGAVMF, f. R-1, op. 1, d. 604, l. 25–67; f. R-55, op. 1, d. 23; f. R-187, op. 1, d. 324, 343; f. R-307, op. 1, d. 10; d. 11, l. 12, 13, 26; d. 13; d. 16, l. 24; f. R-588, op. 1, d. 263, 271, 273, 283. Astrakhan-Caspian Flotilla: TsGAVMF, f. R-1, op. 1, d. 203; f. R-55, op. 1, d. 26; f. R-562, op. 2, d. 316, l. 1-8; d. 345; f. R-588, op. 1, d. 273, l. 112–13. Dnieper Flotilla: TsGAVMF, f. R-1, op. 1, d. 208, l. 29, 32; op. 3, d. 396, l. 19, 25; f. R-139, op. 1, d. 42, l .41; f. R-187, op. 1. d. 343. Onega Flotilla: TsGAVMF, f. R-55, op. 1, d. 26, l. 95; f. R-124, op. 1, d. 141, l. 303; f. R-342, op. 1, d. 776, l.9. Northern Dvina Flotilla: TsGAVMF, f. R-1, op. 3, d. 55, l. 6–9. Chudskoye (Lake Peipus) Flotilla: TsGAVMF, f. R-1, op. 3, d. 196, l. 81; f. R-187, op. 1, d. 138, l. 20.

15. This shows the total number of cases of sickness in military districts in 1919 (TsGASA, f. 6, d. 739, l. 383).

16. 192 killed, January 1920, Western and South-Western Fronts and 6th Army (TsGASA, f. 6, d. 308, l. 65, 66, 84); losses of fronts: 21,965 killed (2,334 of them commanders), February–December 1920 (TsGASA, f. 7, op. 6, d. 802, l. 99) and 99,522 died from wounds or disease (TsGASA, f. 6, op. 4, d. 739, l. 383; f. 4, op. 8, d. 177, 387); navy losses: 578 killed or died from wounds and disease (source: see note 21).

17. Includes 4,797 commanders (TsGASA, f. 8, op. 6, d. 802, l. 99) and 15 navy casualties (source: see note 21).

18. Shows non-combat losses (number of deserters), 15 February–31 December 1920 (TsGASA, f. 6, op. 4, d. 739, l. 159–62, 303, 354, 355, 377, 378; d. 824). Figures incomplete.

19. Shows deaths from wounds and disease during 1920 in all military districts (TsGASA, f. 4, op. 8, d. 177, 387). Figures incomplete. Throughout 1920 at the front and in the rear 174,000 died from disease alone. (Bol'shaya meditsinskaya entsiklopediya—Greater Medical Encyclopedia, 1st edition, vol. 5, p. 450).

20. Number of wounded taken from the Encyclopedic Dictionary of Military Medicine (Entsiklopedicheski slovar' voennoi meditsiny), Moscow, 1947, vol. 2, p. 228, plus 290 navy casualties.

21. Includes 1,454 highly contagious disease cases in the navy (figures for the Petrograd Baltic Fleet Naval Hospital for 1920 and the Volga-Caspian Flotilla for January–March and November–December 1920) (TsGASA, f. 6, op. 4, d. 739, l. 383).

The column showing losses for 1920 includes 2,337 in the navy, comprising 169 killed, 409 deaths from disease, 15 missing in action, 290 wounded and 1,454 sick.

Documentary sources for navy losses: Baltic Fleet: TsGAVMF, f. R-1, op. 1, d. 245; d. 60, l. 25–67; f. R-641, op. 1, d. 195, 212, 213. Amu Darya River Flotilla: TsGAVMF, f. R-1, op. 1, d. 183, l. 12. Aral, Azov and Siberian Flotillas: TsGAVMF, f. R-55, op. 1, d. 69. Volga-Caspian Flotilla: TsGAVMF, f. R-1, op. 3, d. 574; f. R-562, op. 3, d. 139, l. 104; d. 380, l. 1–12; op. 2, d. 604. Dnieper Flotilla: TsGAVMF, f. R-1, op. 1, d. 137, l. 39; op. 3, d. 704. Western Dvina Flotilla: TsGAVMF, f. R-187, op. 1, d. 343. Northern Dvina Flotilla: TsGAVMF, f. R-1, op. 1, d. 241, l. 35. Onega Flotilla: TsGAVMF, f. R-1, op. 1, d. 141.

22. Shows the total number of cases of sickness in military districts for 1920 (TsGASA, f. 4, op. 8, d. 177, 387).

23. Shows the total number killed in action or dying during casualty evacuation, comprising 31,375 killed and 115,113 deaths from wounds and disease. Figures for those killed during these three years of the war are incomplete.

Even the far from complete list of Red Army casualties at the front during the civil war, which on the whole only includes those killed on the field of battle, contains the names of 51,000 men killed in these three years of the war, i.e. almost 20,000 more than the above figure.

According to the Mobilisation Directorate, Red Army Staff report of 14 December 1920, approximately 159,858 were killed in action or died of wounds and disease during the civil war (or 13,370 more than is shown in the table), and 48,896 died of wounds or disease in military districts (or 8,704 more than is shown in the table). It has not proved possible to find documented information confirming these different figures. (TsGASA, f. 7, op. 7, d. 1158, l. 14).

24. About half of the number shown in the table as missing in action or POWs were commanders and men of Western Front who were taken prisoner in 1920 during the war with Poland. Moreover, older servicemen who had no desire to fight simply surrendered. In a number of South-Western Front formations, 'Natives of the Don and Kuban areas all without exception went over to the enemy' (TsGASA, f. 6, op. 2, d. 17, l. 16).

According to reports from the Mobilisation Directorate, Red Army Staff, on 21 November 1921 75,699 prisoners of war were returned from Poland and 40,986 internees from Germany, a total of 116,685 Red Army servicemen. This figure comprised 3,713 command personnel, 412 administrative personnel, 1,296 political staff, 712 medical personnel, 100,434 Red Army men and NCOs and 10,118 servicemen, category unspecified (TsGASA, f. 7, op. 7, d. 89, l. 287, 288; d. 1,158, l. 14).

Those interned were Western Front troops—formations and units of the 4th Army (including the 3rd Cavalry Corps, which was part of it) and two divisions of the 15th Army. In August 1920 during the retreat from the Vistula area they were unable to break through to the east and had to withdraw to East Prussian territory. There they were interned by the German authorities and, in 1921, returned to Russia.

According to Mobilisation Directorate, Red Army Staff figures, as of 1 December 1920 there were 38,153 missing in action and 107,173 prisoners of war, in all 145,326 men (or 16,703 fewer than is shown in the table). It has not proved possible to find documented information confirming these different figures.

Of the 162,029 missing in action or prisoners of war as shown in the table, 45,344 are believed to have died or been killed (representing irrecoverable demographic losses).

25. Figures for non-combat losses for 1918–20 (27,560) comprised only deserters from the fighting troops, which henceforth will not be included with irrecoverable (demographic) losses.

26. Represents the total number of deaths from wounds and disease in military districts from 1918 to 1920.

The figures are incomplete as many reports and dispatches from the troops on the number of deaths in military districts from 1918 to 1920 are missing from the archives.

The figures in the table reflect the steady increase in all types of losses year by year throughout the war, which was one reason for the shortage of fighting troops. There was a particularly large number of sick and wounded, especially in 1919 and 1920. If in 1918 there were 138,000 sick and wounded, by 1919 this number had increased to 1,275,000 and by 1920 to 2,908,000 (figures rounded down). These figures are explained by the high incidence of epidemics among troops at the front and in the rear (there were three or four strains of typhus, and dysentry, cholera, smallpox, etc). In 1918–20 over half of all cases of sickness among servicemen were due to these. Epidemics, especially typhus, proved disastrous for the Red Army during the civil war.

One of the main causes of typhus epidemics and epidemics of other highly contagious diseases among personnel was the poor sanitary conditions in which the troops lived, while at the same time there was a universal shortage of medical personnel, medicines, medical equipment, etc. Bearing in mind that in a number of regions across which the front line moved there were already pockets of typhus, cholera, plague, smallpox, malaria and other dangerous diseases in pre-Revolutionary times, it is understandable that epidemics, including typhus fever, spread as they did. In 1912 in Russia there were 13,000,000 recorded cases of contagious disease. World War I, famine, chaos, civil war and intervention led to a dramatic worsening of sanitary conditions in the country, so that in 1918–23 over 7,500,000 people were registered as having typhus fever alone, of whom over 700,000 died. These figures are incomplete, however, as it was not possible to count all those who fell sick.

Another source of epidemics among Red Army personnel was the enemy troops. For example, it is well known that, because of appalling sanitary conditions, almost all the White Guard armies were infected with typhus, which spread via prisoners of war and defectors to the Red Army. This was particularly true of the fronts fighting Denikin's and Kolchak's armies. One such contemporary testimony, taken from the notes of the People's Commissar for Healthcare, N. A. Semashko, reads: 'When our troops advanced beyond the Urals and into Turkestan, a whole avalanche of epidemics (all three strains of typhus) swept through our army from the Kolchak and Dutov troops. Suffice it to say that of the 60,000-strong enemy army which went over to our side in the very first days after the defeat of Kolchak and Dutov, 80% were infected with typhus. Typhus fever on the Eastern Front and recurring fever mainly on the South-Eastern Front bore down on us in a veritable flood-tide. Even typhoid fever, which is a sure sign that even elementary preventive measures such as inoculation have not been taken, swept through Dutov's army and on to ours.'[25]

The situation worsened still further with the unceasing hardships of wartime and severe food shortages, all of which led to a weakening of the human organism which in turn became less resistant to infection.

The fight against the epidemics which raged through both the army and the civilian population was waged on a country-wide scale. For this purpose authorised commissions, including the Emergency Military Medical Commission, were set up centrally, in the regions where epidemics were spreading and on the various fronts. The Council of People's Commissars published a number of decrees aimed at combating the epidemics—'On measures for combating typhus fever' (28 January 1919), 'On compulsory vaccination' (10 April 1919), 'On measures for combating epidemics' (10 April 1919), etc.

The Military Medical Department, set up as part of the People's Commissariat for Health, was in charge of matters concerning medicine and sanitation in the Red

Army. On its recommendation a decree was issued on the mobilisation of medical personnel, which when enacted helped reduce the shortage of medical personnel in the Red Army from 40–50% in 1919 to 20–22% in 1920.

Emergency counter-measures were taken among the troops. A system of quarantine, check points and front-line hospital centres for contagious disease victims was instigated. On the initiative of the Military Medical Department, mass vaccination of army and navy personnel was begun. Whereas in 1918 only 140 out of a thousand servicemen had been immunised, by 1920 the figure was 700 per thousand and by 1921 847 per thousand, while by 1922 almost all front-line troops and those in the rear had been inoculated. These figures reflect the scale of the operation.

Figures for the incidence of contagious disease among Red Army personnel from 1918 to 1920 are given in Table 10, which is based on documents and reports from the Chief Military Medical Directorate of the Soviet Armed Forces.[26]

Table 10. Cases of Contagious Disease in the Red Army (1918–20)[1]

Year	Disease and no of cases									Total contagious disease cases
	Typhus fever	Recurring fever	Unidentified strain of typhus	Typhoid fever	Cholera	Dysentry	Malaria	Scurvy	Small-pox	
1918[2]	2,022	225	—	3,296	176[3]	90	—	49[4]	82	5,940
1919	319,765	182,391	—	25,990	1,392	10,581	39,773	4,154	3,434	587,480
1920	512,776	787,083	92,910	46,455	4,336	67,780	78,910	66,187	3,548	1,659,985
Total	834,563	969,699	92,910	75,741	5,904	78,451	118,683	70,390	7,064	2,253,405

1. TsGASA, f. 4, op. 5, d. 19, l. 140.
2. 1918 figures for the number of contagious disease cases (excluding cholera) are from July onwards.
3. 1918 cholera figures are from April onwards.
4. The figure for scurvy cases in 1918 is only for fronts.

From this table it can be seen that cases of contagious disease in the army and navy in 1918–20 (2,253,405) accounted for more than half of all sick and wounded in the Red Army for that period (4,322,241: see Table 9).

Table 11 shows the number of deaths from contagious diseases among Red Army personnel.[27]

Table 11. Deaths from Contagious Diseases among Red Army Personnel

Loss category	Year of war			Total
	1918	1919	1920	
No of contagious disease cases	5,940	587,480	1,659,985	2,253,405
No of fatalities	756	73,804	208,519	283,079

As a result of the wide-ranging measures taken, after 1922 there was a marked decrease in the number of cases of contagious disease in the Red Army. If in 1920 there were 1,659,985 cases, in 1921 there were 580,548 and from January to October

1922 164,973 cases, i.e. many times fewer. Epidemics of contagious diseases were finally eradicated by 1926.

To return to Table 9, the main statistical document on Red Army personnel losses for 1918–20, figures for the total number of sick and wounded show that the largest number of cases was in 1920 (2,908,630 men). This represents an increase of more than double compared with 1919 and is mainly attributable to the increase in epidemics. Because of this the number of hospital beds available in military medical facilities was increased in 1920 from 158,000 to 397,000.[28]

Calculations based on the number of cases treated in each hospital show that on average each serviceman was in hospital for a month to a month and a half. At the same time 407,209, or 9.4% of the total number of sick and wounded, died in hospitals between 1918 and 1920.[29] A total of 578,468, or 13.4%, were invalided out of the Red Army or sent on sick leave until they had fully recovered.[30] Over the three years a total of 3,336,564, or 77.2%, returned to their posts after treatment.

Of all the categories of irrecoverable losses given in Table 9, particular attention should be paid to so-called non-combat losses among Red Army personnel. As a general rule, these cover all deaths among servicemen as a result of non-combat injuries, accidents, suicides, murder, executions after courts martial, and deserters. However, our statistics on non-combat losses for 1918–20 only include deserters. Information on other types of non-combat losses has not been found. It may be assumed that these losses are included in the number killed or dying of wounds.

The figures given in the table for the number of deserters do not reflect the full picture, as the official reports only included the most serious cases of desertion from fighting units. The specific circumstances of the civil war were an important reason for the situation, and more needs to be said about this.

Desertion[31] started occurring in the Red Army soon after the Soviet government was obliged in May–June 1918 to abandon the principle of using only volunteers in the armed forces and go over to universal conscription. Most deserters at that time were prosperous and middle peasants, because they were politically uncommitted and discontented with the policies of war communism, especially the requisitioning of farm produce. This was most typical in the Ukraine, the North Caucasus, Tambov province and certain other areas.

The fact that people were growing more and more weary of the war and the innumerable burdens it imposed also led to an increase in the number of desertions. This was particularly emphasised by Lenin in a letter to the Petrograd Party organisations, in which he wrote that 'Signs of the masses' weariness (100,000 desertions) grow ever more frequent'.[32]

To this it should be added that, as mentioned previously, military conscription and mobilisation of the population in 1918–19 were often badly organised and conducted without any accurate information as to the numbers liable for call-up. There was also a lack of clear leadership at local level. As a result there was a lack of coordination, and confusion at call-up centres, in the system for training, allocating and dispatching drafts of reinforcements and checking that these arrived at their destinations. The system for informing people that they were to be called up or mobilised was also seriously flawed.

Moreover, the Red Army itself was not yet a single, clearly defined, functioning military body, and this too had a negative effect on the functioning of all military bodies at all levels. As M. N. Tukhachevski wrote later in his memoirs, 'Hundreds and thousands of detachments, differing widely in numerical strength, character, level of discipline and fighting efficiency—these were the distinguishing features of our Red Army before autumn 1918. Only after that comes the turning point, when detachments start being re-formed into regiments and regiments into brigades and divisions.'[33]

In view of the situation, in 1918 the Soviet authorities and the War Department began taking more decisive measures against desertion. Thus in December 1918 the Temporary Central Commission for Combating Desertion was set up, with representatives from the All-Russia Main Staff, the All-Russia Bureau of Military Commissars and the NKVD. On a local level provincial commissions were set up and these were, on 29 March 1919, granted the right to investigate desertion cases and impose punishments. Punishment measures were also established, ranging from a suspended prison sentence to execution by firing squad. Other punishments which revolutionary tribunals and provincial commissions were granted the right to impose were the confiscation of deserters' property and the confiscation of some or all of their land allocation.

There was a general tightening of checks on all those liable for call-up, especially on the railways and at railway junctions. As a result, 2,846,000 men were found and returned to duty between 1 January 1919 and 1 December 1920. Of these, 1,543,000 reported voluntarily and 837,000 were rounded up.[34]

The following are figures for the most serious cases of desertion from the fighting troops: 1918—199 men; 1919—7,343 men; 1920—20,018 men (including 59 commanding officers).

Desertion from the fighting troops continued after 1920, too. Thus in 1921 231,000 men deserted,[35] including 32,773 (1,704 of them commanders) from units which were engaged in putting down anti-Soviet uprisings. In 1922 there were 112,224 desertions, including 3,763 commanders.[36]

As the proportion of very serious cases was relatively small for that period (desertions soon after call-up amounted to 18–20% and from troop units 5–7%), severe punishment measures for desertion were not used particularly often. This is borne out by the fact that of the total number detained over seven months in 1919 (1,500,000 men), only 95,000 were found guilty of desertion in aggravated circumstances. Of these, 55,000 were sent to penal units, 6,000 were given custodial sentences (suspended or otherwise), 4,000 were sentenced to death (the vast majority having the sentence suspended) and 600 were actually shot.[37]

Thus the question of desertion as a loss category in the civil war was a fairly complex one. In the tables 'irrecoverable losses' only include those listed deserters who did not return to Red Army ranks either voluntarily or after being ordered to do so.

As mentioned before, the documented information on losses among Soviet troops between 1918 and 1920 used in this book is incomplete. The authors have therefore calculated more accurate total figures. These adjusted figures, with the necessary explanatory notes, are given in Table 12.

Table 12. Adjusted Total Figures for Red Army Personnel Losses, 1918–20

Loss category	Total losses	% of average annual personnel strength	% of losses
Irrecoverable losses			
Fighting troops (naval forces):			
Killed in action, died during casualty evacuation	249,294[1]	10.5	4.9
Missing in action, POWs who failed to return	45,344[2]	1.9	0.9
Non-combat losses[3]	—	—	—
Fighting troops (naval forces) and military districts:			
Died of wounds or disease	407,209[4]	—	8.2
Total irrecoverable losses	701,847	—	14
Sick and wounded			
Fighting troops (naval forces):			
Wounded; concussion, burns and frostbite cases	536,725	22.6	10.7
Sick	3,068,237	129.3	61
Military districts: sick	717,279	—	14.3
Sick and wounded, total	4,322,241	—	86
Total losses	5,024,088	—	100

1. Figure obtained as follows: taking the total number of wounded shown in the table (536,725) and the ratio of killed to wounded calculated for the civil war (1:4), the number killed between 1918 and 1920 was arrived at (134,181). After adding this figure to the number of deaths among the field armies taken from archive sources (115,113), the final figure in the table of 249,294 was obtained.
2. Of the total number missing in action or taken prisoner between 1918 and 1920, the table only gives the number who failed to return after being held captive or who were were killed (45,344), i.e. purely demographic losses.
3. Among non-combat losses for 1918–20 the documents list only 27,560 deserters (from the fighting troops). These do not count as irrecoverable demographic losses.
4. Figures worked out by calculation (see notes 27 and 29 to Chapter 1).

As is evident from the table, more accurate figures have been worked out only for certain categories of irrecoverable losses. The number who were killed in action or who died during casualty evacuation was calculated to give a more precise total; of a total of 162,029 missing in action or prisoners of war, the table only shows those who were killed or who died, i.e. purely demographic losses; 'irrecoverable losses' does not include non–combat losses of 27,560, as in this instance they only cover de-serters, which do not count as demographic losses. The figures for sick and wounded have not been adjusted even though they are incomplete, as it proved impossible to do so on the basis of the archive material available. In any case the fact that the figures are incomplete is in effect compensated for by the inflated figure caused by 'double counting' in the medical statistics, thanks to which servicemen who were admitted to military medical facilities for treatment on more than one occasion were counted as new cases each time. This means that one can take the figures given here as correct without being guilty of gross inaccuracy.

By looking at the adjusted casualty figures for 1918–20 and at the information available on the total number called up and mobilised by the Red Army during those years, one can calculate 'intake' and 'wastage' in the armed forces for that period of the civil war. Figures showing these are given in Table 13.

Table 13. Numbers Enlisting and Men Lost, 1918–20

Reinforcements and losses: categories	No
No on roll as of 1 June 1918 (end of period of voluntary enlistment, beginning of transition to universal compulsory military service)	374,551[1]
Mobilised by Red Army:	
Those born 1879–1901	4,449,383[2]
Under special orders (military specialists, Party and other workers)	1,883,654[3]
Total joining Red Army over the 3 years (including those already in army on 1 June 1918)	6,707,588
Men lost (total)	1,280,315[4]
Comprising:	
Irrecoverable losses	701,847[5]
Invalided out or on sick leave	578,468[6]
No on roll as of 1 November 1920	5,427,273[7]

1. The total personnel strength of the Red Army as of 1 June 1918 is taken from Table 3.
2. See *Direktivy komandovaniya frontov*, vol. 4, pp. 275–6.
3. Those mobilised under special orders include the following categories of persons joining the Red Army between 12 June 1918 and 15 June 1920: 35,502 former officers and generals; 3,441 former military administrative staff; 178,139 former NCOs and senior NCOs; 3,494 former doctors and veterinary surgeons; 13,481 former medical and veterinary auxiliaries; 366,718 persons of particular ages drafted into the Red Army in local and combat zone mobilisation drives; 71,559 specialists; 24,364 *volost'* dwellers (10–20 men per *volost'*, a peasant community of several villages); 63,334 previously declared unfit for active service; 47,287 railway workers; 26,780 members of the RKP(B); 12,573 trade union members; 40,938 RKP(B) and trade union members; 2,355 postal workers; 40,024 blue- and white-collar workers in trade, industry and transport; 5,528 students in further and higher education; 32,671 after undergoing (medical) re-examination; 39,407 soldiers from the old army who were returned prisoners of war; 37,530 former prisoners of war born in 1898–99; 502,873 selected during training sessions (under the Defence Council decree of 27 August 1919); 214,387 mobilised in the Ukraine in 1919–20; 2,648 refugees from Lithuania, Latvia, Byelorussia and the Ukraine; 101,831 remaining after call-up completed; and 16,790 home guard—total 1,883,654. These figures are taken from document number 67, 'The Number of Citizens Drafted into the Red Army between 12 June 1918 and 15 June 1920' (see *Direktivy komandovaniya frontov*, vol. 4, p. 274). Only the figures as of 15 June 1920 were used, or, if these were lacking, as of 1 September 1919. Information on call-up by year of birth contained in the document has been omitted as it has already been included in the table (under 'Mobilised by the Red Army: those born 1879–1901').
4. The figure for Red Army personnel losses for 1918–20 represents the difference between the total number of all personnel called up, mobilised or volunteering for the Red Army during this period (6,707,588) and total listed personnel strength at the end of 1920 (5,427,273).
5. The number of irrecoverable losses is taken from Table 12.
6. The figure for those invalided out of the Red Army or sent on sick leave in the three years of the war represents the difference between total losses (1,280,315) and irrecoverable losses (701,847) as shown in the table.
7. See *Direktivy komandovaniya frontov*, vol. 4, p. 227.

The table shows that, during the period of voluntary enlistment, by the beginning of June 1918 the numerical strength of the Soviet armed forces was 374,551. This was, however, insufficient to repel attacks by enemy troops numbering about 700,000. The interventionist and White Guard forces outnumbered the Red Army by almost two to one, and their fronts were able to form a ring round the Soviet republic. In view of this situation the Soviet government went over to a general mobilisation of working people (in the first instance of workers and peasants) in order to bring the army and navy up to strength. Therefore, on 29 May 1918 the Central Executive Committee's Decree on Compulsory Conscription was announced, which marked the beginning of a new phase of military development. Recruitment into the Red Army was by means of call-up of citizens of a particular age, the right to defend the revolution with arms being granted only to the working masses. 'Non-working elements' were taken on to perform various auxiliary tasks (fatigue duties, construction of fieldworks, repair of equipment, etc).

The fifth All-Russian Congress of Soviets which took place in July 1918 approved measures to create a regular Red Army. The Congress established universal compulsory military service for citizens aged between eighteen and forty, abolished the appointment of officers by election and also acknowledged that there was a need for former officers and generals to be brought in to serve as military specialists in the army and navy. The resolution passed by the Congress particularly emphasised that every fighter who was given arms must obey his commanders and superiors unquestioningly.

In August 1918 a special decree was issued by the Council of People's Commissars transferring to the jurisdiction of the People's Commissariat for Military Affairs all troops organised by various other People's Commissariats: railway defence troops (the Commissariat for Railways), frontier guards (the Commissariat for Trade and Industry) and food requisitioning brigades (the Commissariat for Food). Some time later the scope of the decree was extended to cover Cheka troops. At the same time a government decree was issued under which all fighting troops made up of independent detachments and units began to be combined into armies and fronts. All these measures were aimed at achieving greater central control of the armed forces, at regulating the mobilisation process and at increasing its efficiency.

From Table 13 it can be seen that once the Law on Universal Compulsory Military Service was put into practice, 4,449,383 in the age group liable for mobilisation were drafted into the Red Army over the three years of the war. This number, which represented those called up by year of birth, did not, however, include all categories of persons drafted. Therefore others within that age group who had not been called up by year of birth were mobilised under special orders, for example during training sessions and local and front-line zone mobilisation drives. In addition, administrative, medical and command personnel were drafted into the Red Army, together with a significant number who joined through trade union, communist party or Komsomol mobilisation drives. These included volunteers, those who had undergone medical re-examination, former prisoners of war and refugees. In all, 1,883,654 citizens were called up under special orders.

Between 1918 and 1920 a total of 6,707,588 were called up and mobilised by the Red Army, as can be seen from Table 13, while 1,280,315 were lost, or 19% of those mobilised. This number represents irrecoverable losses plus those invalided out or sent on sick leave from the army and navy.

RED ARMY LOSSES 1921–22,
WHEN THE LAST POCKETS OF COUNTER-REVOLUTION
AND INTERVENTION WERE ELIMINATED

With the defeat of Wrangel's troops in the autumn of 1920, the main period of the civil war came to an end and most of the fronts had been eliminated. Military questions ceased to dominate the Soviet government's policies and actions. The period saw the start of a gradual changeover to a time of peaceful construction. The economic and political situation at that time was very complex, however, and in a number of places there were armed uprisings against the new order.

Many foreign governments supported the remaining pockets of White Guard resistance, peasant uprisings and rebellions of various kinds. Because armed formations mainly of White emigrés were being sent into Soviet territory, there was constant tension on the country's borders.

It was also at this time that the Socialist Revolutionaries and *Mensheviks* began their anti-Soviet activities. In 1921 a whole series of armed rebellions flared up in Tambov province, Siberia, the North Caucasus, the Ukraine, Byelorussia and elsewhere. These were partly the result of economic collapse and famine (when the harvest failed in 1921) and the fact that demobilisation had started, leading to unemployment. The difficulties and privations experienced and accepted during the war now gave rise to discontent not only among the peasants but also among a section of the working class. The middle peasants' lack of political commitment which was now on a mass scale also told on the mood of the personnel in certain army and navy units. The most acute manifestation of this was the Kronstadt mutiny in March 1921.

The fight against rebellions was difficult and long drawn-out. Significant numbers of Red Army forces took part, as did internal service[38] and Cheka troops, special purpose units[39] and other formations which in the end broke the resistance of the rebels. With the introduction of the New Economic Policy (NEP), the number of rebellions fell sharply everywhere. By spring 1922 they had generally died out in the Ukraine and in central parts of the Russian Federation. In Central Asia, because of national, religious, political, geographical and social factors and because the leaders of opposition formations had links with foreign governments, the fight against *Basmachestvo*, the anti-Soviet movement there, dragged on until 1925–26. Individual *Basmachi* formations were active until 1931.

It should be noted that as the last pockets of counter-revolution were eliminated and the interventionists were finally driven out, there was a major reduction in the Red Army's forces. The changes in its average monthly and annual numerical strength from 1921 to 1922 are given in Table 14.

29

Table 14. Average Monthly Personnel Strength of the Soviet Armed Forces, 1921–22[1]

			By Service and arm of Service					
Numerical strength as of:		Total strength of armed forces	Army	Navy	Air Force	Admin. and logistic support units	Construction units	Units not part of the Services
Year	Date, month							
1921	1 July	2,009,321	1,571,856	67,273	24,251	272,507[2]	73,434[3]	—
1922	1 January	1,354,516	1,195,945	47,238	12,904[4]	97,868[5]	—	561[6]
Average annual numerical strength		1,681,918	1,383,400	57,255	18,577	185,187	73,434	561

1. As the figures necessary to calculate the average monthly numerical strength of the armed forces for 1921–22 were lacking, the table shows instead numerical strength as of 1 July (1921) and 1 January (1922).
2. Administrative and logistic support units include railway troops who, together with military communications establishments, numbered 57,870.
3. Only the numerical strength of construction units is given. In accordance with the Labour and Defence Council (STO) decree of 30 March 1921 (RVSR order No 864 of 18 April 1921) and as the demobilisation of the Red Army got under way, labour armies, which were previously part of the construction units, were transferred to the jurisdiction of the People's Commissariat for Labour and by 1 February 1922 had been disbanded (STO decree of 2 December 1921).
4. Numbers for the air force do not include training establishments, which are included under 'Army'.
5. Includes railway troops who, together with military communications establishments, numbered 23,753.
6. The column 'Units not part of the Services' gives personnel numbers for units and establishments of the military topographical service.

Table 15. Front, Military District and Independent Army or Operations Group Personnel Losses during Combat Operations to Defeat the Counter-Revolutionary Forces and Put Down Anti-Soviet Uprisings, 1921–22[1]

	No of losses		
Fronts and military districts	Irrecoverable losses	Sick and wounded	Total
Western Front[2]	14,602	26,372	40,974
Caucasian Front[3]	9,338	29,617	38,955
Turkestan Front (the struggle against the *Basmachi*, January 1921–July 1922)[4]	926	867	1,793
The Ukrainian and Crimean Armed Forces[5]	14,935	37,860	52,795
Trans-Volga Military District[6]	4,164	3,192	7,356
Orel Military District (suppression of revolt in Tambov province in 1921)[7]	6,096	4,142	10,238
Petrograd Military District (suppression of Kronstadt rebellion in 1921)[8]	1,912	1,208	3,120
Troops under command of 2i/c Siberia[9]	3,485	11,295	14,780
Urals Military District[10]	259	156	415
Independent Red Banner Caucasian Army[11]	2,328	8,206	10,534
Operations group in Karelia (defeat of White Finnish troops who invaded Soviet Karelia, 1921–22)[12]	352	1,042	1,394
Total	58,397★	123,957	182,354★★

★ Includes 32,773 deserters.
★★ Casualty figures are incomplete.

1. The figures in the table were calculated using the following archive sources:
   (a) Combat operations against anti-Soviet forces in the Ukraine, Byelorussia, the Volga region, Siberia and other regions (TsGASA, f. 7, op. 6, d. 802, l. 71, 101, 120, 183, 256; d. 803, l. 60, 103, 194, 238, 266);
   (b) The crushing of the Kronstadt mutiny (TsGASA, f. 263, op. 1, d. 27, l. 49; d. 51, l. 56–60; f. 264, op. 1, d. 28, l. 31; d. 29, l. 48, 66);
   (c) The crushing of the rebellion in Tambov province (TsGASA, f. 5, op. 1, d. 176; f. 7, op. 6, d. 802, l. 120; f. 235, op. 2, d. 254, l. 87, 182, 334, 523, 644, 695; d. 567, l. 15);
   (d) Battles fought in Georgia and Armenia (TsGASA, f. 6, op. 4, d. 641; f. 7, op. 6, d. 802, l. 71, 101, 120, 183);
   (e) Combat operations against the White Finnish troops who invaded Soviet Karelia (TsGASA, f. 7, op. 2, d. 837, l. 17);
   (f) Losses on the Turkestan Front among troops taking part in the fight against the *Basmachi*, 1921–22 (TsGASA, f. 110, op. 4, d. 605, l. 3–5).

2. Western Front troops (together with Cheka units, special purpose units, militia detachments and others) took part in operations against countless armed formations (led by Bulak-Balakhovich, Pavlovsk, Prudnikov, Pimenov, etc) sent from Poland into Byelorussia and the western regions of Russia .

3. At the request of the Georgian Revolutionary Committee, in February–March 1921 troops of the Caucasian Front's 9th and 11th Armies took part in armed uprisings against rule by *Mensheviks* and their foreign patrons. At the same time, in February–July 1921, 11th Army troops fought with Armenian revolutionary detachments to defeat *Dashnak* (Armenian nationalist party) forces throughout Armenian territory.

4. Infantry and cavalry units of the Turkestan Military District (Bukhara Troop Group) fought with Bukhara Red Army units in 1921–22 against massive *Basmachi* forces in the Bukhara People's Soviet Republic.

5. Significant numbers in the Ukrainian and Crimean armed forces engaged in combat operations against the countless Petlura-ite formations sent into the Ukraine from Poland. The largest of these, led by Nelgovski, Palia-Chernyi and Tyutyunik, had been defeated by the end of 1922. In 1921 a number of operations were carried out in which Makhno and his followers were finally routed.

6. In 1921 Trans-Volga Military District troops stationed in Samara, Tsaritsyn, Astrakhan, Orenburg and Saratov provinces and the Volga Germans' area, and also on the territory of Turgai and Urals regions, conducted combat operations against rebels led by Sapozhnikov.

7. Between January and July 1921 Orel Military District troops carried out combat operations in Tambov province and part of Voronezh province to put down the rebellion led by Antonov. From February 1921 these troops were under the direct command of the Commander-in-Chief. In March 1922 Orel Military District was disbanded.

8. In March 1921 troops of the Petrograd Military District's 7th Army under the command of M. N. Tukhachevski put down the Kronstadt mutiny among the Kronstadt garrison and several ships' crews (in all, about 27,000 soldiers and sailors took part in the uprising).

9. Between February and June 1921 troops under the command of the second-in-command for Siberia put down the anti-Soviet rebellion in Western Siberia.

10. The troops of the Urals Military District, which covered the territory of Chelyabinsk, Vyatka, Northern Dvina and Tyumen provinces and the Bashkirian autonomous republic, helped put down the Western Siberian rebellion (February–June 1921).

11. The Independent Red Banner Caucasian Army was formed in May 1921 when the Caucasian Front's 11th Army was abolished on 29 May 1921 and re-formed. Caucasian Army troops helped eliminate banditry and anti-Soviet uprisings in the North Caucasus in 1921–22.

12. In November 1921 an operations group was formed in Karelia to put a stop to the so-called 'Karelian adventure' (the invasion of Soviet Karelia by White Finnish troops between October 1921 and February 1922). The operations group which defeated the anti-Soviet forces in Karelia was headed by the Commander-in-Chief of the Armed Forces of the Republic, S. S. Kamenev, and the commander of the group, A. I. Sedyakin.

Red Army combat operations to defeat the counter-revolutionary forces and put down anti-Soviet uprisings led to considerable personnel losses among the Soviet troops. Information on these is given in Tables 15 and 16, which show losses among the fighting troops of fronts, military districts and operations groups as well as giving figures for the different categories of losses.

Table 16. Losses among Red Army Troops which Took Part in the Armed Struggle against Anti-Soviet Uprisings, 1921–22

	No of casualties			
Loss categories	Total	% of losses	No of commanders[1]	% of losses
Irrecoverable losses				
Killed in action, died during casualty evacuation	9,454	6.3	926	9.1
Missing in action, POWs who failed to return	14,481	9.7	473	4.6
Non-combat losses (died as result of accident, condemned by military tribunal, committed suicide	1,689[2]	1.1	1,733	17.1
Total irrecoverable losses	25,624	17.1	3,132	30.8
Sick and wounded				
Wounded; concussion, burns and frostbite cases	10,711	7.2	956	9.4
Sick	113,246	75.7	6,091	59.8
Total sick and wounded	123,957	82.9	7,047	69.2
Total losses	149,581	100	10,179	100

1. The column headed 'No of commanders' shows losses among senior and command personnel from platoon commander and equivalent ranks upwards (TsGASA, f. 7, op. 6, d. 802, l. 71, 101, 120, 183, 256; d. 803, l. 60, 103, 238, 266).
2. The figure for non-combat losses does not include 32,773 deserters (from fighting units), as these do not count as irrecoverable demographic losses.

The fight against interventionists and White Guards in the Far East in 1921–22 merits particular attention, as it was here that the Far Eastern Republic was created in April 1920 because of the military and political situation there. It was bourgeois-democratic in form and was situated on the territory of Trans-Baikal, Amur and Maritime (Primorski) regions. The Far Eastern Republic had its own People's Revolutionary Army (NRA).[40]

The NRA was formed in March–October 1920 from partisan formations and rebel detachments. From the start it was essentially part of the Red Army. It followed RVSR directives and was under the command of the Commander-in-Chief and Second-in-Command for Siberia. In July 1922 the NRA numbered 45,594,[41] 6,832 commanders and 38,762 men.

The NRA's first operation was to drive Semenov's White Guards and the Japanese occupiers out of Chita and the Trans-Baikal region in April–November 1920, as a result of which the Trans-Baikal and Amur regions could now be merged into one. By the summer of 1921 the Maritime region remained occupied. The White Guards, who were the puppets of the Japanese occupiers, had seized power there on 26 May.

Their White rebel army tried to mount an offensive against the NRA, but the attack was stopped and then repelled in February 1922.

In September 1922 NRA troops stopped an advance by White Guard Zemstvo forces from the Maritime region towards Khabarovsk, then in October 1922 launched the Maritime operation which culminated in the liberation of the Far East. When the Far Eastern Republic became part of the Russian Federation on 15 November 1922 the NRA was renamed the 5th Army of the RKKA.

It has only proved possible to obtain information on NRA losses for the period 1 January–15 June 1922[42] (see Table 17). There were 7,791 casualties—2,888 irrecoverable losses and 4,903 sick and wounded.

Table 17. The People's Revolutionary Army of the Far Eastern Republic: Losses in Battles against the White Guards and Japanese Invaders, 1 January–15 June 1922

Loss categories		Com-manders	NCOs	Men	Total
Killed in action, died during casualty evacuation	No	74		391	465
	% of losses	13.6		5.4	6
Missing in action	No	3		230	233
	% of losses	0.6		3.2	3
POWs	No	1			1
	% of losses	0.1			
Non-combat losses	No	43		2,146	2,189
	% of losses	7.9		29.6	28.1
Total irrecoverable losses	No	121		2,767	2,888
	% of losses	22.2		38.2	37.1
	% of personnel strength:				
	All losses	1.8		7.1	6.3
	Average monthly losses	0.27		1.10	0.97
Wounded; burns and concussion cases	No	145		1,276	1,421
	% of losses	26.7		17.6	18.2
Sick	No	278		3,204	3,482
	% of losses	51.1		44.2	44.7
Frostbite cases	No				
	% of losses				
Total sick and wounded	No	423		4,480	4,903
	% of losses	77.8		61.8	62.9
	% of personnel strength:				
	All losses	6.20		11.6	10.8
	Average monthly losses	0.95		1.78	1.66
Total losses	No	544		7,247	7,791
	% of losses	100		100	100
	% of personnel strength:				
	All losses	8		18.7	17.1
	Average monthly losses	1.22		2.88	2.63

Row group labels (left margin): "Irrecoverable losses" spans the first five loss categories; "Sick and wounded (including those evacuated to hospitals)" spans the Wounded, Sick, Frostbite and Total sick and wounded categories.

Table 18. Total Losses for the Red Army and the People's Revolutionary Army of the Far Eastern Republic in the Final Period of the Civil War (1921–22)

Loss categories	Number of casualties								
	Red Army			People's Revolutionary Army, Far Eastern Republic			Total losses, 1921–22		
	Personnel losses	% of average annual troop strength	% of losses	Personnel losses	% of average annual troop strength	% of losses	Personnel losses	% of average annual troop strength[4]	% of losses
Irrecoverable losses									
Fighting troops:									
Killed in action, died during casualty evacuation	9,454	0.6	0.3	465	1	6	9,919	0.6	0.4
Missing in action, POWs who failed to return	14,481	0.8	0.5	234	0.5	3	14,715	0.8	0.5
Died as result of accident, condemned by military tribunal, committed suicide	1,689[1]	0.1	0.1	2,189	4.8	28.1	3,878	0.2	0.1
Fighting and non-combatant troops (deaths in hospital from wounds and disease)	209,396[2]	12.5	7.8	—	—	—	209,396	12.1	7.8
Total irrecoverable losses	235,020	14	8.7	2,888	6.3	37.1	237,908	13.7	8.8
Sick and wounded									
Wounded; concussion, burns and frostbite cases	10,711	0.6	0.4	1,421	3.1	18.2	12,132	0.7	0.5
Sick (fighting troops)	113,246	6.7	4.2	3,482	7.6	44.7	116,728	6.8	4.3
Sick (non-combatant troops)	2,340,682[3]	139.2	86.7	—	—	—	2,340,682	135.5	86.4
Sick and wounded, total	2,464,639	146.5	91.3	4,903	10.7	62.9	2,469,542	143	91.2
Total losses	2,699,659	160.5	100	7,791	17	100	2,707,450	156.7	100

1. The figure for non-combat losses does not include the 230,000 who deserted in 1921 (including 32,773 who deserted from the fighting troops), or 112,224 who deserted in 1922, as they do not come into the category of irrecoverable demographic losses.

2. The figure for those dying in hospital from wounds and disease was calculated as follows. In 1921 there were 580,548 contagious disease cases, resulting in 77,901 deaths (TsGASA, f. 4, op. 5, d. 19, l. 122; d. 63, l. 105; op. 8, d. 528, l. 18; d. 479, l. 81). In 1922 (from 1 January to 1 October) there were 164,973 contagious disease cases, with 28,368 deaths (TsGASA, f. 4, op. 5, d. 77, l. 33). By subtracting the number of cases of contagious disease for 1921–22 (745,521) from the total number of sick and wounded for the same period (2,464,639), the number of wounded and non-contagious disease cases (1,719,118) has been calculated. Taking a fatality rate of 6%, it has been possible to work out the number of deaths (103,147) from the number of wounded and non-contagious disease cases. By adding this figure to the number of deaths in hospital from contagious diseases (106,249), the number of deaths in hospital from wounds and disease (209,396) shown in the table was arrived at.

3. The figure for cases of sickness among non-combatant Red Army troops in 1921–22 (2,340,682) includes those hospitalised during 1921 (1,822,832; TsGASA, f. 4, op. 5, d. 19, l. 122) and 1922 (517,850; figure arrived at by calculation).

4. Average annual personnel strength, which was used to work out the proportion of personnel losses for 1921–22, is made up of the average annual numerical strength of the Red Army (1,681,918; see Table 14), plus the average monthly numerical strength of the NRA (45,594), and comes to 1,727,512.

34

The bloodiest battles were during the Chita operations (1–13 April, 2 April–5 May and 1–31 October 1920), the Volochaevsk operation (1–12 February 1922) and the Maritime (Primorski) operation (4–25 October 1922). During the last, the Spassk operation was notable for the determination of the opposing forces. Over 1,000 enemy troops were killed or wounded and about 280 were taken prisoner.[43] NRA losses were no doubt also considerable, but no documented information on these has been found. The same can be said of NRA losses in other operations.

The total figures for Red Army losses from 1921 to 1922 are given in Table 18. Separate figures are given for the Red Army and the NRA, with a breakdown of the total figures according to loss categories.

The total Red Army personnel losses throughout the whole period of the civil war (1918–22) are given in Table 19. From this it can be seen that irrecoverable demographic losses during the war amounted to 939,755 persons (killed in action, died of wounds or disease, missing in action, or died while being held prisoner or in other circumstances).

When evaluating the figure for the number of sick and wounded during the war, it should be borne in mind that the total number given here for cases of wounding, concussion and disease (6,791,783) was inevitably affected by so-called double counting (a significant number of servicemen were admitted to hospitals or other medical facilities on more than one occasion and each time were listed as new cases). Furthermore, a significant number who were listed as sick and wounded later died, and so were also listed under 'irrecoverable losses'.

Table 19. Total Red Army Personnel Losses throughout the Period of the Civil War (1918–22)

	Total losses throughout the civil war	Stage of war	
Loss category		1918–1920	1921–1922
Irrecoverable losses			
Killed in action, died during casualty evacuation	259,213	249,294	9,919
Missing in action, POWs who failed to return	60,059	45,344[1]	14,715[2]
Died as result of accident, condemned by military tribunal, committed suicide	3,878	—	3,878
Died of wounds or disease in treatment centres	616,605	407,209	209,396
Total irrecoverable losses	939,755	701,847	237,908
Sick and wounded			
Wounded; concussion, burns and frostbite cases	548,857	536,725	12,132
Sick	6,242,926	3,785,516	2,457,410
Sick and wounded, total	6,791,783	4,322,241	2,469,542

1. TsGASA, f. 7, op. 7, d. 89, l. 287, 288.
2. TsGASA, f. 7, op. 6, d. 802, l. 71, 101, 120, 183, 256; d. 805, l. 60, 103, 194, 238, 266; op. 2, d. 527, l. 6; f. 235, op. 2, d. 564, l. 87, 182, 334, 523, 644, 695; f. 263, op. 1, d. 51, l. 55–60; f. 264, op. 1, d. 29, l. 48, 66.

Chapter 1 sets out the conclusions of the authors' wide-ranging research into Red Army personnel losses during the civil war. Total figures are given for these, with a breakdown for each year of the war (1918, 1919 and 1920) and for the two phases of the war (1918–20 and 1921–22). Because the necessary information is lacking or incomplete, it has not proved possible to show Soviet troop casualties in individual defensive or offensive operations.

Also lacking are casualty figures for the Red Guards, who consituted the Soviet republic's main defence force after the October Revolution. It is well known that Red Guard detachments played a decisive role in eliminating counter-revolutionary uprisings along the Don, in the Southern Urals, in the Ukraine and in the Far East at the end of 1917. Together with the first Red Army units, Red Guard detachments fought a decisive battle against German invaders at Pskov and Narva and fought successfully against German and Austro-Hungarian troops in the Ukraine.

In the period after the Revolution and before the formation of the Red Army, the Red Guards numbered 253,000.

The question of casualty numbers among partisans who fought with rifles in their hands behind interventionist and White Guard lines in 1918–22 also remains unsolved.

The partisan movement was on the largest scale in Siberia, the Trans-Baikal and Amur regions and the Far East. Incomplete figures show that partisan detachments in Siberia alone numbered 140,000–150,000, and in Amur region the partisan detachments 'grew into a real partisan army, numbering over 100,000 active fighters under a single command by the spring of 1919. The partisans were responsible for inflicting heavy losses on the White Guards and interventionists, killing up to 17,600 men.'[44]

There is only limited information on partisan casualties. We know, for example, that of the Amur partisans about 4,300 were killed in battles, engagements, ambushes and raids.[45]

Enemy losses (White Guards, interventionist and other forces) were not researched because the relevant information was lacking. It is only possible to obtain an idea of casualty numbers from the approximate figures given in a number of works on the history of the civil war in different publications on demographic and population problems. Thus B. Ts. Urlanis, in *Wars and Population in Europe* mentioned earlier in the chapter, puts the number of front-line casualties among the Whites in the civil war (the number killed in action or dying of wounds during evacuation) at 175,000,[46] and the number of deaths from disease at 150,000.[47] Yu. A. Polyakov notes in his monograph *The Soviet Land After the End of the Civil War: Territory and Population* that losses on both sides in 1918–22 were about the same and totalled about 2½ million.[48] It should, however, be said that the foregoing figures are in both cases conjectural, as they are not strictly based on documented evidence. We can agree, though, that enemy losses in the civil war were not less than those of the Red Army.

In conclusion, it should be emphasised that the statistical material on Soviet troop losses presented in Chapter 1 will mean that mistakes and inaccuracies in this field can be avoided in future and will help shed more light on many incidents in the civil war.

NOTES

1. See *Direktivy komandovaniya frontov Krasnoi Armii (1917–22)* (*Red Army Fronts' Command Directives*), Moscow, 1978, vol. 4, p. 227. Any further references to this publication will be designated *Direktivy komandovaniya frontov*.

2. Throughout the book the term 'losses' is used to mean personnel losses only.

3. See *Grazhdanskaya voina v SSSR* (*The Civil War in the USSR*), 2 vols, Moscow, 1986, vol. 2, p. 406.

4. See *Bol'shaya Sovetskaya Entsiklopediya*, Moscow, 1972, vol. 7, p. 234; *Sovetskaya istoricheskaya enstiklopediya*, Moscow, 1965, vol. 6, p. 79; *Grazhdanskaya voina i voennaya interventsiya: Entsiklopediya*, Moscow, 1983, p. 14.

5. See B. Ts. Urlanis, *Voiny i narodonaselenie Evropy*, Moscow, 1960, pp. 183, 305.

6. TsGASA (*Tsentral'nyi gosudarstvennyi arkhiv Sovetskoi armii*—Central State Archive of the Soviet Army), f. 7, op. 7, d. 1158, l. 14.

7. TsGASA, f. 51/36, op. 5, d. 8, l. 13.

8. TsGASA, f. 54, op. 6, d. 493, l. 3–4.

9. See *Narodnoe khozyaistvo SSSR v tsifrakh*, Moscow, 1925, p. 110.

10. B. Ts. Urlanis, op. cit., p. 181.

11. Yu. A. Polyakov, *Sovetskaya strana posle okonchaniya grazhdanskoi voiny: territoriya i naselenie*, Moscow, 1986.

12. Yu. A. Polyakov, op. cit., p. 102. (Looking at the figures, 'combat losses' are greater than 'sick and wounded' which, if it meant all sick and wounded, would logically have to be far higher than combat losses; hence Polyakov's conclusion that what is meant is ultimate fatalities.—Editor)

13. Ibid., p. 103.

14. The Records and Statistics Information Department was set up as part of the All-Russia Supreme Staff's Command Personnel Directorate, by RSVR order number 1488, issued 17 September 1919. It was given the task of recording and registering all categories of Red Army losses at the front in the civil war, and of recording Russian Army losses during World War I. The Department also had the task of processing statistical material on combat losses and answering requests for information which came in.

15. Report Priority Log records started being used in May 1919 (RVSR order no 909 of 22 May 1919).

16. See *Direktivy Glavnogo komandovaniya Krasnoi Armii, 1917–20* (*Red Army High Command Directives*), Moscow, 1969, p. 164. Any further references to this publication will be designated *Direktivy Glavnogo komandovaniya*

17. *Direktivy Glavnogo komandovaniya*, p. 319.

18. Ibid., p. 423.

19. Ibid., p. 171.

20. Ibid.

21. Ibid., p. 322.

22. Ibid., p. 323.

23. The numerical strength of fighting troops is the actual number of bayonets and sabres in units, formations and forces directly assigned to combat tasks.

24. Apart from the main fronts there were also local fronts which were formed by decision of local soviet, Party and military organisations. They were brought up to prescribed strength by recruiting men from the local area. The fronts in question were the Semirechensk, Trans-Caspian, Fergana, Aktyubinsk and other local fronts. Sometimes separate battle areas and regions where there were combat operations involving Soviet troops were unofficially called

fronts, which were part of the main fronts or independent armies (for example the Georgievsk, Kuban-Black Sea, Tsaritsyn, Steppe, Kamyshin, Urals-Orenburg, Northern Siberia, Arkhangelsk, Petrograd and other regions).

25. *Izvestiya Narodnogo komissariata zdravookhraneniya (The People's Commissariat for Healthcare News)*, 1920, no 1–2, p. 11.

26. TsGASA, f. 4, op. 5, d. 19, l. 140.

27. Calculated using the incomplete information available on the number of deaths from contagious disease for 1919–22, taking a fatality rate which was calculated at 13% (average) for typhus epidemics, 28% for cholera and 14% for dysentery and other contagious diseases (TsGASA, f. 6, op. 6, d. 294; f. 5, op. 1, d. 36; f. 4, op. 8, d. 177, 387; op. 5, d. 19, 77; op. 8, d. 479, 528).

28. See *Grazhdanskaya voina i voennaya interventsiya v SSSR*, p. 341.

29. The total number of deaths has been calculated as follows. To the 283,079 deaths from contagious disease (see Table 11) have been added the 124,130 deaths among the remaining 2,068,836 sick and wounded. The figure of 124,130 was obtained taking a fatality rate of 6%, which is the rate calculated for wounded and ordinary sick in the civil war (see B. Ts. Urlanis, op. cit., pp. 170, 189, 305, 306).

30. The figure given for those invalided out of the Services or sent on sick leave was obtained by subtracting the number of irrecoverable losses for 1918–20 (701,847) from the total number of men lost by the Red Army in the same period (1,280,315). See Table 13.

31. During the civil war the term 'desertion' was used widely to mean all forms of evasion of service in the Red Army, including servicemen going absent without leave from their unit or place of duty with the purpose of avoiding military service or avoiding participation in combat actions, and also those liable for military service failing to report to call-up centres or to their place of duty on being called up or mobilised.

32. V. I. Lenin, *Polnoe sobranie sochinenii (Complete Collected Works)*, vol. 50, p. 296.

33. M. N. Tukhachevskii, *Izbrannye proizvedeniya (Collected Works)*, Moscow, 1964, vol. 1, p. 73.

34. See *Grazhdanskaya voina 1918–21 (The Civil War)*, Moscow, 1928, vol. 2, p. 83.

35. This figure was calculated as follows. Over five months in 1921 (August–December) 96,255 men deserted, which is on average 19,251 per month. This gives a rounded-down figure of 231,000 for the year (TsGASA, f. 7, op. 7, d. 285, l. 253–9).

36. TsGASA, f. 7, op. 7, d. 285, l. 246–8.

37. See *Grazhdanskaya voina 1918–21*, vol. 2, p. 84.

38. Internal Service troops (VNUS) were special military formations which fulfilled the function of guarding the interior of the Soviet state. They were also given the task of guarding state borders. They were formed by decree of the Labour and Defence Council (STO), issued on 1 September 1920. They included the Internal Security Troops of the Republic (VOKhR), guard units, combat zone railway defence troops and transport militia (railways and waterways). They were subordinate to the NKVD and the Commander-in-Chief. By the end of 1920 they numbered 360,000 men (14 divisions and 18 brigades). By STO decree of 19 January 1921 the Internal Service troops, excluding the Cheka troops and the railway and waterways militia, were transferred completely to the military establishment.

39. Special purpose units (ChON) were Party detachments. They were formed by Party branches in factories and in district, urban, *uezd* and provincial Party committees (*uezd*: an administrative subdivision of a *guberniya* or province), on the basis of the RKP(B) Central Committee decree of 17 April 1919, in order to assist the organs of Soviet power in the fight against counter-revolution, to keep order and to defend state property. Members of these units were trained under the universal military training system or, from July 1921, within the system of military educational establishments and Red Army training courses. In March 1921 ChON

detachments became part of the Red Army militia units. In December 1921 ChoN had 39,673 regular and 323,373 temporary personnel.

40. Here and henceforth any references to the People's Revolutionary Army of the Far Eastern Republic shall be taken to include the People's Revolutionary Navy of the Far Eastern Republic.

41. This number is taken as being the average monthly and average annual numerical strength of the NRA for 1921–22.

42. TsGASA, f. 7, op. 6, d. 991, l. 15, 38.

43. See *Grazhdanskaya voina i voennaya interventsiya v SSSR*, p. 565.

44. S. N. Shishkin, *Grazhdanskaya voina na Dal'nem vostoke* (*The Civil War in the Far East*), Moscow, 1957, p. 66.

45. See S. Kurguzov, *Amurskie partizany* (*The Amur Partisans*), Khabarovsk, 1929, p. 55.

46. See B. Ts. Urlanis, op. cit., p. 188.

47. Ibid., p. 307.

48. See Yu. A. Polyakov, op. cit., p.104.

Chapter Two

Red Army Personnel Losses
in Combat Operations and Military
Conflicts in the Inter-War Period

On several occasions in the inter-war period Soviet troops were called upon to repulse aggressors and insurgents of various kinds and to take up arms to defend their country's interests. The Soviet Armed Forces suffered significant losses in these actions. Details of these losses will be given for each conflict, based on the documents available.

The chapter also includes Soviet troop losses during the campaigns in the Western Ukraine and Western Byelorussia in 1939, and casualties among Soviet volunteers in Spain from 1936 to 1939 and in China from 1937 to 1939.

THE ROLE OF TURKESTAN FRONT
(TURKESTAN MILITARY DISTRICT) TROOPS
IN THE FIGHT AGAINST *BASMACHESTVO*, 1923–31

As a result of active combat operations by Turkestan Front troops against the *Basmachi* in 1921–22, most of the armed *Basmachi* groupings in Central Asia had been destroyed. By October 1922 there were only 63 bands left numbering 6,707 men in all, compared with the 26,061 there had been in mid-May 1922.[1] In subsequent years the level of combat activity and *Basmachi* numbers fluctuated according to the military and political situation in the republic of Turkestan (the Central Asian republics).[2]

In 1923 Turkestan Front units were specially detailed to continue pursuing the remaining uncoordinated *Basmachi* detachments, inflicting significant losses on them in the course of various clashes.

Between October 1922 and February 1923 the *Basmachi* lost 1,749 killed and wounded, of whom 21 were *kurbashi* (commanders); 127, of whom 14 were *kurbashi*, were taken prisoner. A total of 628 laid down their arms voluntarily, including 56 *kurbashi*.[3] Turkestan Front losses for the same period were 327 killed and wounded and 43 taken prisoner.[4]

In 1924–25, because of severe drought and popular discontent at the actions of certain Soviet authorities (they had failed to arrange for cotton seed to be delivered to peasant farmers on time, as a result of which many fields remained unsown, and had acted against the interests of the poorest peasants over the matter of state insurance), the *Basmachestvo* again flared up in many parts of Central Asia. This was particularly true in Tadjikistan, where the overall head of the movement was Ibrahim-bek, the puppet of the former Emir of Bukhara. He received active support in the form of supplies of arms, ammunition and equipment from foreign intelligence services, especially the British.

Before launching a decisive attack, Ibrahim-bek reorganised his forces and set up a special group to spread anti-Soviet propaganda and carry out acts of sabotage. He even tried to levy taxes and duties on the people. However, in the spring of 1925 his grouping suffered a massive defeat at the hands of Red Army units. As a result only 30 small bands numbering a little over 400 in total were left in Tadjikistan (formerly Eastern Bukhara).

From 1 May 1924 to 1 December 1925, the *Basmachi* lost 2,104 killed and 638 taken prisoner; 2,279 surrendered of their own accord.

In 1926 the Turkestan Front troops detailed to fight the *Basmachi* numbered 18,477 men and officers. In the course of the year they had 190 clashes with *Basmachi* bands, who lost 140 men killed and 70 taken prisoner between 1 April and 10 July alone, including 14 *kurbashi* in each case; 142, of whom 16 were *kurbashi*, surrendered of their own accord. During this period there was much wider support than before from the local population for the Red Army units, and by the end of summer 1926 the main pockets of *Basmachestvo* had been wiped out. At the same time the Uzbek republic had been more or less cleared of armed bands, while in the Turkmen and Tadjik republics nine *Basmachi* groups remained, numbering about a hundred men in all.[5] The task of eliminating these was given to the militia and local defence detachments, while the military units which had been detailed to fight the *Basmachi* were returned to their permanent places of duty.

As part of this reorganisation the Turkestan Front was re-formed, becoming the Central Asian Military District.[6]

The revolutionary reforms and the establishment of Soviet power in Turkestan did not go smoothly, however, and were beset by difficulties. This was because of the general cultural backwardness of the whole Central Asian region, the fairly strong influence of feudalism and a fanatical Muslim clergy, and also because of the fact that the central and local authorities in the republics were bureaucratic and unreliable, between 60 and 80% of their staff having been functionaries in the old feudal administration. The fact that Party organisations in the republic were small and insufficiently active was also regarded as a weak point.

It should be added that, with the forced collectivisation of agriculture taking place at this time, the internal political situation in the country was very tense, especially in Central Asia.

Thus in August and September 1929 *Basmachi* activity flared up again in the eastern part of the Uzbek republic (Fergana region) and in southern Kirgizia (Osh region). At the same time several *Basmachi* bands which had come up from Afghanistan appeared on Tadjik territory.[7] The heads of these bands knew how to derive maximum advantage from mistakes made by the local ruling authorities and from discontent among the people at the methods used in collectivising peasant holdings, procuring grain, etc.

The leadership of the *Basmachestvo* this time concentrated on stirring up religious fanaticism among the Muslim population. The *Basmachi* killed Party and Soviet workers and collective farm activists and robbed and burned state- and cooperative-owned property.

From September 1929, at the request of the republic's leaders, entire units of the 2nd Turkestan Division were called upon to fight the *Basmachi*, and by the end of 1929 these had wiped out most of the active *Basmachi* formations. The survivors managed to escape abroad.

Soviet troop losses from September to December 1929 were 11 killed, six wounded and two missing in action.[8]

The final stage of the Turkestan Military District troops' actions against *Basmachi* bands was in 1931, when they helped defeat the large *Basmachi* grouping headed by Ibrahim-bek, which in March and April 1931 broke through in small sub-units from Afghanistan and dispersed around the Uzbek republic. In the first half of May that year their numbers reached 2,823.[9]

The *Basmachi* tried to foment uprisings in several regions of Uzbekistan and to seize power. They did not succeed, however. It was not only Red Army units which joined the fight against them, but also the local population, including volunteer anti-*Basmachestvo* detachments consisting mainly of villagers, whose strength was 7,213 by the end of May 1931.[10]

As a result of political and military measures taken, Ibrahim-bek's *Basmachi* bands had been eliminated by mid-1931.

In actions against the *Basmachi* between 20 March and 2 June 1931 the Turkestan Military District fighting troops lost 106 killed, 90 wounded and three missing in action.[11] In the same period the enemy lost 1,224 killed and 75 taken prisoner; 314 surrendered voluntarily. *Basmachestvo* was finally eliminated without the help of regular Red Army units (a few *Basmachi* bands were active until 1933).

Table 20 gives figures from archive sources for Soviet troop losses during the fight against *Basmachestvo* in Central Asia between October 1922 and June 1931. It should be noted here that information on total personnel losses during these combat operations is incomplete, nor has it proved possible to obtain full information on losses by rank. The proportion of losses compared with average monthly personnel strength is not given, as it has not proved possible to determine this.

THE SINO-SOVIET CONFLICT, 1929

On 10 July 1929, in contravention of existing Sino-Soviet agreements on the joint operation of the Chinese Eastern Railway, detachments of Manchurian troops and White Guards seized the railway, crushed the trade unions and arrested over 200 Soviet citizens. At the same time Manchurian troops started massing on the Soviet border and shooting at border posts and villages. The Soviet government's repeated

Table 20. Personnel Losses among the Troops of the Turkestan Front (Central Asian Military District) in the Fight against Basmachestvo, October 1922–June 1931

Period losses relate to	Total losses	Losses by category							
		Irrecoverable losses				Sick and wounded			
		Killed in action, died during casualty evacuation	Missing in action	Prisoners of war	Total irrecoverable losses	Wounded; burns and concussion cases, etc.	Sick[8]	Frostbite cases	Sick and wounded, total
October 1922–February 1923	370[1]	109	7	43	152	218	—	—	218
May 1923	56[2]	28	7	—	35	21	—	—	21
May 1924–December 1925	719[3]	239	—	—	239	480	—	—	480
April–August and November–December 1926	12[4]	4	—	—	4	8	—	—	8
January–December 1927	66[5]	19	2	1	22	44	—	—	44
September–December 1929	19[6]	11	2	—	13	6	—	—	6
March–June 1931	199[7]	106	3	—	109	90	—	—	90
Total	1,441	516	14	44	574	867	—	—	867

1. From a report by the commander of the Turkestan Front (TsGASA, f. 7, op. 2, d. 466, l. 66). This document gives the total number of killed and wounded (327). The separate figures of 109 and 218 given in the table for these two categories were calculated on the basis of a ratio of killed to wounded of 1:2 among Turkestan Front personnel during actions against the *Basmachi* in 1921–22.

2. TsGASA, f. 5, op. 1, d. 144, l. 14–18. Casualty figures for the year 1923 are incomplete.

3. TsGASA, f. 25895, op. 14, d. 170, l. 239. This document gives the total number of killed and wounded for this period (719). The individual figures for the two categories were calculated using the same formula as in note 1.

4. TsGASA, f. 25895, op. 14, d. 3, l. 112–20. This document gives the total number of killed and wounded (12). The individual figures for each of these were calculated using the same formula as in note 1. The 1926 casualty figures are incomplete.

5. TsGASA, f. 25895, op. 14, d. 19, l. 59.

6. TsGASA, f. 25895, op. 14, d. 53.

7. TsGASA, f. 25835, op. 15, d. 11, l. 37; op. 12, d. 230, l. 201–4: op. 14, d. 178, l. 78.

8. Either cases of sickness in the units which took part in combat operations against *Basmachi* bands were not counted as losses or the figures were included with the total number of wounded and concussion cases.

protests against these acts of provocation by the Manchurian authorities did not bring the hoped-for results, and additional measures were taken to defend the border and repulse the aggressors.

By the beginning of October 1929 the Manchurian government under Chang Hsueh-liang had at its disposal the so-called Mukden Army numbering about 300,000 men, White Guard detachments of up to 70,000 men and the Sungari Flotilla of 11 warships. These forces were mainly concentrated in four sectors: Trans-Baikal (Manchouli, Hailar and Tsitsihar stations), with about 59,000 men, 107 machine guns, 70 guns, 100 bomb-throwers,[12] two armoured trains and three aircraft; Blagoveshchensk, with up to 5,000 men; Sungari, with over 5,500 men, 26 machine guns, 20 guns and 16 bomb-throwers; and Maritime (Primorski), with 63,000 men, 200 machine guns, 120 guns and 110 bomb-throwers.

The Soviet troop grouping in the Far East consisted of two rifle corps transferred there urgently from the Siberian Military District (one to the Trans-Baikal region, the other to the Maritime region) and from several other units and formations. It was from these troops that the Special Far Eastern Army (ODVA) was formed under the command of V. K. Blyukher, by order of the Revolutionary Military Council of the USSR issued on 7 August 1929. It included the Far Eastern Flotilla.[13]

It should be noted that in every sector the 18,521 Soviet fighting troops were outnumbered by enemy troops by between three and five to one, but they had military and technical superiority and their morale was better.

The Manchurian troop groupings were defeated by the ODVA between 12 October and 20 November 1929 in three successive offensive operations: the Sungari offensive operation, from 12 October to 2 November, the Mishan offensive operation of 17 and 18 November, and the Manchouli-Chalainor offensive operation of 17–20 November. The enemy suffered heavy losses during these actions in terms of numbers killed, wounded and taken prisoner. For example, near Manchouli and Chalainor stations Soviet troops captured over 8,000 men and 300 officers of the Mukden Army. The 35th Rifle Division alone captured 42 enemy officers and 998 men in the battles fought between 17 and 19 November 1929. After the operation was over, 1,035 Manchurian troops killed in the conflict were buried.[14]

On 1 December 1929 the Manchurian government under Chang Hsueh-liang was obliged to begin peace talks, and on 22 December the Sino-Soviet agreement restoring the former status of the Chinese and Eastern Railway was signed at Khabarovsk. After this the Soviet troops were withdrawn from Manchurian territory.

On the Soviet side, the following forces took part in combat operations against the Manchurian troops: in October, the 2nd Amur Division, the Far Eastern Flotilla and two air force squadrons from the Maritime region group; and in November, the 21st, 35th and 36th Rifle Divisions, the 5th Cavalry Brigade, the Buryat Cavalry Division and the 6th and 25th Air Force Detachments from the Trans-Baikal group.

The average monthly strength of the Soviet troops taking part in combat operations during the 1929 Sino-Soviet conflict was as shown in Table 21; losses on the Soviet side during the conflict are shown in Table 22.

Table 21. Average Monthly Strength of Soviet Troops Taking Part in Combat Operations during the 1929 Sino-Soviet Conflict

Numerical strength as of	Commanders	NCOs	Men	Total
October–November 1929	1,334	3,097	14,090	18,521

Table 22. Soviet Losses Incurred during the 1929 Sino-Soviet Conflict

Loss category	Total	Commanders		NCOs		Men	
		No of losses	% of total losses in this category	No of losses	% of total losses in this category	No of losses	% of total losses in this category
Killed	143	10	7	15	10.5	118	82.5
Missing in action	4	—	—	1	25	3	75
Wounded and concussed	665	59	8.9	124	18.7	482	72.4
Total	812	69	8.5	140	17.2	603	74.3

The archive documents show that the rifle troops suffered the heaviest losses. Losses in other arms of the services were negligible: out of a total of 812 casualties, in the cavalry there were only 11 men killed and seven wounded, in the Far Eastern Flotilla there were four wounded, three of these when their gun exploded on firing on board ship, and in the air force detachments which took part in the actions there was only one man wounded.

The information available on the types of wounds suffered by ODVA personnel during combat operations also merits attention. The figures show that the majority of wounds and cases of concussion were caused by artillery shells. For example, in the 36th Rifle Division, of the 250 wounded in battle (100%), sixteen were wounded by shrapnel shells (6.4%), 118 were wounded by HE shells (47.2%), 10 suffered concussion (4%) and 106 received bullet wounds (42.4%).

Table 23 gives both actual and relative casualty figures for the ODVA.

Table 23. Special Far Eastern Army (ODVA): Losses during the Sino-Soviet Military Conflict, 12 October–20 November 1929.[1]

	Loss category		Commanders	NCOs	Men	Total
Irrecoverable losses	Killed in action, died during casualty evacuation	No	10	15	118	143
		% of losses	14.5	10.7	19.5	17.6
	Missing in action	No		1	3	4
		% of losses		0.7	0.5	0.5
	Prisoners of war	No				
		% of losses				
	Non-combat losses	No				
		% of losses				
	Total irrecoverable losses	No	10	16	121	147
		% of losses	14.5	11.4	20	18.1
		% of personnel strength:				
		All losses	0.7	0.5	0.8	0.8
		Average monthly losses	0.54	0.38	0.62	0.62

	Loss category		Com-manders	NCOs	Men	Total
Sick and wounded (including those evacuated to hospitals)	Wounded, concussion and burns cases	No	59	124	482	665
		% of losses	85.5	88.6	80	81.9
	Sick	No				
		% of losses				
	Frostbite cases	No				
		% of losses				
	Sick and wounded, total	No	59	124	482	665
		% of losses	85.5	88.6	80	81.9
		% of personnel strength:				
		All losses	4.4	4	3.4	3.6
		Average monthly losses	3.38	3.08	2.61	2.76
	Total losses	No	69	140	603	812
		% of losses	100	100	100	100
		% of personnel strength:				
		All losses	5.1	4.5	4.2	4.4
		Average monthly losses	3.92	3.46	3.23	3.38

1. TsGASA, f. 35083, op. 1, d. 60, l. 6, 10; f. 37977, op. 1, d. 1, l. 75; TsAMO, f. 5, op. 176703, d. 27, l. 48, 49.

MILITARY ASSISTANCE TO THE SPANISH REPUBLIC, 1936–39

In July 1936, with the support of Hitler and Mussolini, reactionary forces in Spain led by General Franco mounted a fascist uprising against the Spanish republic and its government. They also won most of the army over to their side (about 100,000 men).

The international solidarity movement and democratic forces throughout the world played an important role in supporting Spanish resistance to fascism. In response to a request from the Spanish government, the Soviet Union agreed to supply arms and military equipment to the republic. In all, between October 1936 and January 1939 the Soviet Union supplied Spain with 648 aircraft, 347 tanks, 60 armoured vehicles, 1,186 artillery pieces, 20,486 machine guns and 497,813 rifles.[15]

At the request of the republican government, the Soviet Union also sent about 3,000 volunteers to Spain. These were military advisers, pilots, tank crews, sailors and various specialists who fought and worked alongside the republicans. 158 volunteers were killed.[16]

Table 23a. Soviet Volunteers Killed or Missing in Action in Spain, 1936–39

Loss category		Commanders	NCOs	Total
Killed	No	95	37	132
	% of losses	82.6	86	83.5
Missing in action	No	20	6	26
	% of losses	17.4	14	16.5
Total	No	115	43	158
	% of losses	100	100	100

Table 23a shows the number of Soviet volunteers killed or missing in action in Spain, with a breakdown by loss category and by rank.

MILITARY ASSISTANCE TO CHINA, 1937–39

In July 1937 a war of national liberation started in China against the Japanese, who were occupying north-eastern and central China. On the initiative of the Chinese Communist Party, which formed an alliance with the ruling Kuomintang,[17] a united anti-Japanese front was created. A few areas in Japanese-occupied territory were liberated and the Chinese Red Army concentrated considerable forces there.

The Chinese were greatly assisted in their national liberation struggle by the Soviet Union, which responded under the terms of the 1937 Sino-Soviet non-aggression treaty and the 1939 treaties on trade and the granting of credits. Between October 1937 and September 1939 the Soviet Union supplied China with a total of 985 aircraft, 82 tanks, over 1,300 artillery pieces, over 14,000 machine guns, 50,000 rifles and 1,550 lorries and tractors, plus ammunition, equipment and supplies.[18]

At the request of the Nanking government, from autumn 1937 Soviet military specialists and advisers were sent to China as volunteers. By mid-February 1939, 3,665 Soviet volunteers were working there and joining in the fight against the Japanese occupiers.[19] In all, 195 of them died fighting for the liberation of the Chinese people.[20]

Table 23b shows the number of Soviet volunteers killed or missing in China, with a breakdown by loss category and rank.

Table 23b. Soviet Volunteers Killed or Missing in China, 1937–39

Loss category		Commanders	NCOs	Men	Total
Killed	No	146	33	7	186
	% of losses	95.4	94.3	100	95.4
Missing in action	No	7	2	—	9
	% of losses	4.6	5.7	—	4.6
Total	No	153	35	7	195
	% of losses	100	100	100	100

THE SOVIET-JAPANESE
MILITARY CONFLICT NEAR LAKE KHASAN, 1938

When the Japanese seized Manchuria in 1931–32 and turned it into the puppet state of Manchoukuo, a bridgehead was created for an attack on the USSR and the Japanese Kwantung Army started making intensive preparations for war. In the latter half of the 1930s, with encouragement from the US, British and French governments and the support of Nazi Germany, Japan started launching direct attacks on the Soviet Union.

Having amassed three infantry divisions, a mechanised brigade, a cavalry regiment, three machine gun battalions and 70 aircraft near the Posyet section of the Soviet frontier in mid-July 1938, on 29 July two companies of Japanese troops attacked the Soviet border post at Bezymyannaya hill, which was defended by eleven border guards, and penetrated into Soviet territory. However, sub-units of regular Red Army troops came to the assistance of the border guards and drove out those Japanese troops which had broken across the frontier.

On 31 July the enemy again invaded Soviet territory, penetrating 4km inside the border and taking the tactically important Zaozernaya and Bezymyanaya hills near Lake Khasan.

Far Eastern Front's command[21] assigned the mission of defeating the Japanese invaders to the newly formed 39th Rifle Corps, which was made up of the 40th and 32nd Rifle Divisions, the 2nd Mechanised Brigade and reinforcement units—a total of 22,950 men.[22] On 2 and 3 August the Corps' command made an attempt to dislodge the enemy from the heights they were occupying using only one rifle division, the 40th, before its troops had finished concentrating. The operation was not a success as by this time the Japanese had managed to consolidate and bring in substantial reinforcements.

The Soviet command hurriedly moved reinforcements into the battle area. On 6 August they went over to the offensive and within three days had ousted the Japanese invaders from Soviet territory. New attacks were repulsed, the enemy suffering heavy losses in the process. As a result, on 10 August the Japanese government proposed to the Soviet government that a settlement be negotiated, and on 11 August combat operations between Soviet and Japanese troops ceased.

Japanese sources put Japanese casualties during the fighting near Lake Khasan at 500 killed and 900 wounded.[23] Table 24 gives the basic figures for Soviet personnel losses during the two weeks of fighting in the Lake Khasan area.

Table 24. Soviet Personnel Losses during the Soviet-Japanese Military Conflict near Lake Khasan, 1938

Loss category	Commanders	NCOs	Men	Total
Irrecoverable losses				
Killed in action, died during casualty evacuation	129	191	397	717
Missing in action	5	8	62	75
Total irrecoverable losses	134	199	459	792
Sick and wounded				
Wounded, concussion and burns cases	290	406	2,056	2,752
Sick	37	79	411	527
Sick and wounded, total	327	485	2,467	3,279

The figures given in Table 24 make it possible to determine the ratio of killed to wounded among the Soviet troops, which works out at approximately one to four, i.e. for every person killed there were about four wounded. A higher than usual proportion of casualties, especially of those killed, were command personnel (18%).

It should be added here that, of the 2,752 wounded, 66 (2.4%) died in hospital during the period 30 July–12 August 1938.[24] Information on types of wounds is given in Tables 25 and 26.

Table 25. Types of Wounds Suffered by Personnel during the Lake Khasan Conflict, 1938[1]

Type of wounds	No of cases	% of total no of cases
Bullet	869	31.6
Shrapnel	1,498	54.4
'Cold steel'	110	4
Various	275	10
Total	2,752	100

1. TsAMO, f 5, op. 176703, d. 27, l. 56.

Table 26. Types of Wounds Suffered by Personnel during the Lake Khasan Conflict, 1938[1]

Head wounds	Facial wounds	Neck wounds	Chest wounds	Stomach wounds	Arm wounds	Leg wounds	Total
86	78	53	252	72	1,122	1,146	2,809
3.1%	2.8%	1.9%	9%	2.6%	39.8%	40.8%	100%

1. TsGASA, f. 37299, op. 2, d. 559, l. 134.

The figures in Tables 25 and 26 show that shrapnel wounds and arm and leg wounds predominated (54.4% and 80.6% of wounds respectively). Turning now to the sickness figures, 56.1% of cases were due to gastric and intestinal disorders caused by the lack of clean drinking water, 18.9% were catarrhal infections, 13.3% were cases of malaria and 11.7% fell into other categories.[25] Also of some interest are figures relating to the outcome of treatment for Red Army men and officers who were wounded or fell sick during the fighting near Lake Khasan (see Table 27).

Table 27. Outcome of Treatment for Red Army Officers and Men Wounded or Falling Sick during the Fighting near Lake Khasan

Sick and wounded		Total no admitted to medical facilities	Breakdown		
			Returned to active duty	Discharged to the reserve and taken off strength, granted sick leave	Died
Wounded, concussion and burns cases[1]	No	2,752	1,973	470	93
	%	100	71.7	17	3.4
Sick[2]	No	527	271	115	1
	%	100	51.4	21.8	0.2
Total	No	3,279	2,244	585	94
	%	100	68.4	17.9	2.9

1. The table only gives figures for those who were treated in hospital. There is no information on the number of sick, wounded, burns and concussion cases or on those returned to active duty who were treated at regimental and divisional medical aid posts.
2. Columns 4, 5 and 6 exclude 216 wounded, concussion and burns cases (7.9% of cases) and 140 sick (26.6% of cases) for whom the outcome of treatment is not known.

Something should be said here regarding the administering of first aid to personnel who were wounded or concussed during the Lake Khasan operation. At first it was intended that casualties would be treated at battalion medical aid posts (BMPs), as at that time battalions had their own doctors. However, in the first days of the fighting it became apparent that the BMPs, which had been set up in the open, were sitting targets for enemy artillery fire. Therefore, in the majority of battalions, instead of BMPs being set up, battalion doctors and medical auxiliaries together administered first aid on the spot, dressed wounds and arranged for casualty evacuation.

In conclusion, Table 28 gives the average monthly strength of the Soviet troops, Table 29 casualty figures with a breakdown by arm of service, and Table 30 a breakdown of the casualty figures by rank.

Table 28. Average Monthly Strength of Soviet Troops who Took Part in Combat Operations at Lake Khasan

Total strength of fighting troops	Comprising			Numerical strength as of:
	Commanders	NCOs	Men	
22,950	1,636	3,442	17,872	August 1938

Table 29. Losses by Arm of Service at Lake Khasan

Arm of service	Rank	Loss category		
		Killed[1]	Wounded	Missing in action
Rifle troops	Commanders	55	268	5
	NCOs	68	391	1
	Men	243	2,056	7
	Total	366	2,715	13
	%	91.1	98.7	72.2
Tank troops	Commanders	10	22	—
	NCOs	23	15	5
	Men	—	—	—
	Total	33	37	5
	%	8.2	1.3	27.8
Corps artillery	Commanders	—	—	—
	NCOs	1	—	—
	Men	1	—	—
	Total	2	—	—
	%	0.5	—	—
Communications	Commanders	1	—	—
	NCOs	—	—	—
	Men	—	—	—
	Total	1	—	—
	%	0.2	—	—
	Overall total	402	2,752	18
	%	100	100	100

1. Figures for the number killed are incomplete.

**Table 30. Soviet Losses during Fighting near Lake Khasan,
29 July–11 August 1938[1]**

	Loss categories		Com-manders	NCOs	Men	Total
Irrecoverable losses	Killed in action, died during casualty evacuation	No	129	191	397	717
		% of losses	28	27.9	13.6	17.6
	Missing in action, POWs	No	5	8	62	75
		% of losses	1.1	0.1	2.1	1.8
	Non-combat losses	No				
		% of losses				
	Irrecoverable losses, total	No	134	199	459	792
		% of losses	29.1	29.1	15.7	19.4
		% of personnel strength: All losses Average monthly losses	8.2	5.8	2.6	3.4
Sick and wounded (including those evacuated to hospitals)	Wounded, concussion and burns cases	No	290	406	2,056	2,752
		% of losses	62.9	59.4	70.3	67.7
	Sick	No	37	79	411	527
		% of losses	8	11.5	14	12.9
	Frostbite cases	No				
		% of losses				
	Sick and wounded, total	No	327	485	2,467	3,279
		% of losses	70.9	70.9	84.3	80.6
		% of personnel strength: All losses Average monthly losses	20	14.1	13.8	14.3
	Total losses	No	461	684	2,926	4,071
		% of losses	100	100	100	100
		% of personnel strength: All losses Average monthly losses	28.2	19.9	16.4	17.7

1. TsGASA, f. 35083, op. 1, d. 60, l. 6, 10; d. 105, l. 1–22; f. 37977, op. 1, d. 1, l. 75.

THE DEFEAT OF THE JAPANESE
INVADERS AT THE KHALKHIN GOL RIVER, 1939

In May 1939, it having been proved during the Lake Khasan conflict in 1938 that the Soviet frontier was secure and that their military ambitions in the Maritime region had little prospect of success, the Japanese military orchestrated several serious acts of provocation against the Mongolian People's Republic, at the same time sending Japanese troops to invade Mongolian territory near the Khalkhin Gol river. However, the Japanese were conclusively repulsed in a joint operation by Soviet troops, who were there under the terms of the 1936 Protocol on Mutual Assistance,[26] and troops of the Mongolian People's Revolutionary Army.[27] After this the Kwantung Army command concentrated a larger grouping of troops on the Mongolian border.

By the end of June this grouping consisted of 38,000 officers and men with 310 guns, 135 tanks and 225 aircraft. The Soviet and Mongolian troops, from June 1939 under the command of Division Commander (from 31 July Corps Commander) Zhukov, numbered 12,500 men and officers supported by 109 guns, 266 armoured vehicles, 186 tanks and 82 aircraft.

On 2 July the enemy took advantage of his superiority of forces and went over to the offensive, his aim being to surround and wipe out the Soviet-Mongolian units and seize an operational bridgehead on the west bank of the Khalkhin Gol from which to carry out further offensives in Soviet Trans-Baikal. However, in the course of the bloody, three-day battle, those Japanese troops who succeeded in forcing the river were all either killed or driven back to the east bank. Subsequent attacks by the Japanese which went on for most of July also failed, as everywhere they were repulsed.

In spite of the failures and heavy losses, the Japanese command stuck determinedly to their plan. They started preparing for a general offensive timed to coincide with the unleashing of war by Nazi Germany in Europe. With this aim, the 6th Japanese Army was formed at the beginning of August under the command of General Rippoh. It numbered 75,000 men, with 500 guns, 182 tanks and air support from over 300 aircraft.

The Soviet and Mongolian troops, which by that time had been combined to form the 1st Army Group under Corps Commander Zhukov, numbered 57,000 men and commanding officers. They were supported by 542 guns and mortars, 498 tanks, 385 armoured vehicles and 515 aircraft. Anticipating the enemy's actions, on 20 August, after heavy air strikes and almost three hours of artillery bombardment, the Soviet and Mongolian troops went over to the offensive, attacking in two groups, northern and southern. As a result of these two groups' decisive and skilful manoeuvring on the enemy's flanks, on 23 August the entire Japanese grouping was surrounded. By the evening of 31 August it had been completely routed. At Japan's request combat operations ceased,[28] and on 15 September a Soviet-Japanese agreement was signed putting an end to the conflict.

During the fighting at the Khalkhin Gol river about 61,000 Japanese were killed, wounded or captured, about 45,000 of them in July and August 1939. The number killed in the course of the conflict was about 25,000.

On the Soviet side the following were directly involved in the fighting: the 36th Motor Rifle Division, the 57th and 82nd Rifle Divisions, the 5th Machine-Gun and Rifle Brigade, the 6th and 11th Tank Brigades, the 7th, 8th and 9th Motor-Armoured Brigades, the 56th Fighter Regiment, the 185th Artillery Regiment, the 85th Anti-Aircraft Regiment and logistic support units.[29] On the Mongolian side, the 6th and 8th Cavalry Divisions were directly involved in actions against the Japanese invaders at Khalkhin Gol. Their total strength was about 2,260, including 862 commanders.[30]

Table 31 lists the figures for the average monthly strength of the Soviet troops who took part in the fighting at Khalkhin Gol. Soviet losses during the fighting at Khalkhin Gol up to mid-September 1939 are shown in Table 32.

Table 31. Average Monthly Strength of Soviet Troops at Khalkhin Gol

Average monthly strength calculated by taking numerical strength in months:	Commanders	NCOs	Men	Total
June, July, August and September 1939	8,457	12,583	48,061	69,101

Table 32. Soviet Losses during the Fighting at Khalkhin Gol, up to mid-September 1939

Loss category	Commanders	NCOs	Men	Total
Irrecoverable losses				
Killed in action, died during casualty evacuation	1,063	1,313	4,455	6,831
Missing in action	71	120	952	1,143
Total irrecoverable losses	1,134	1,433	5,407	7,974
Sick and wounded				
Wounded, concussion and burns cases	1,335	2,123	11,793	15,251
Sick	85	127	489	701
Sick and wounded, total	1,420	2,250	12,282	15,925

The sick and wounded who were in hospitals on Mongolian territory were sent to military hospitals in the Trans-Baikal Military District, mostly to Chita. About half of the sick and wounded from Tamsagbulag Hospital were evacuated by air.[31]

There is some information on battle casualties among command and senior personnel during the fighting in August 1939, with a detailed breakdown by designation. In the 57th, 82nd and 36th Motor Rifle Divisions there were 180 casualties, excluding political workers and artillerymen, made up as follows:[32] division commanders—1; rifle regiment commanders—4; regiment chiefs of staff—1; regiment deputy chiefs of staff—2; battalion commanders—4; battalion deputy commanders—2; battalion chief transport officers—1; battalion chiefs of staff—8; rifle company commanders—36; company deputy commanders—2; rifle and machine-gun platoon leaders—116; battalion deputy chiefs of staff—1; battalion ammunition supplies officers—1; transport platoon leaders—1.

In the tank and motor-armoured brigades in the same period (August), 130 command personnel were killed, excluding political workers. A breakdown of these is as follows:[33] tank brigade commanders—1; brigade chiefs of staff—1; brigade chief operations officers—1; armoured battalion commanders—1; brigade deputy chief operations officers—1; rifle regiment and brigade commanders—2; tank battalion deputy commanders—1; battalion chiefs of staff—4; battalion deputy chiefs of staff—7; company commanders—19; battalion chief transport officers—2; deputy company commanders—13; platoon leaders—66; battalion chief signals officers—3; brigade assistant military administrative officers—1; brigade chief signals officers—1; battalion ammunition supplies officers—1; artillery battery commanders—1;

CW platoon leaders—1; brigade chief logistics officers—1; brigade radio technicians—1; anti-tank battery commanders—1.

These figures show that command personnel of almost all ranks were killed during the Khalkhin Gol conflict.

Table 33 gives the percentage of rifle and tank unit and sub-unit commanders killed in relation to the total number of command personnel killed.

Table 33. Percentage of Rifle and Tank Unit and Sub-Unit Commanders Killed during the Fighting at Khalkhin Gol

Officer rank	Rifle divisions and motor rifle divisions, %	Tank and motor-armoured brigades, %
Platoon commanders	65	58.8
Company commanders	20	14.6
Battalion commanders	2.2	0.8
Regiment commanders	2.2	1.5

Table 34. Breakdown by Type of Wound during the Fighting at Khalkhin Gol[1]

Type of wounds	Rank			Total	%
	Commanders	NCOs	Men		
Skull	56	80	344	480	3.1
Eye	14	28	94	136	0.9
Jaw and facial	50	78	438	566	3.7
Neck	23	26	139	188	1.2
Chest	91	122	613	826	5.4
Stomach	26	37	301	364	2.4
Uro-genital system	5	8	29	42	0.3
Arm	272	530	3,539	4,341	28.5
Leg	343	529	3,125	3,997	26.2
Joints	38	62	276	376	2.5
Back and spinal	36	44	246	326	2.1
Various	261	436	1,970	2,667	17.5
Concussion	90	104	476	670	4.4
Burns	14	17	24	55	0.4
Not known	16	22	179	217	1.4
Total	1,335	2,123	11,793	15,251	100

1. TsGASA, f. 32113, op. 2, d. 56, l. 71.

Table 32 shows that the total number of wounded was 15,251. The breakdown by cause of wound is as follows:[34] bullet wounds—44.2%; shrapnel wounds (from shells, mines and grenades)—48.4%; shrapnel wounds (from aerial bombs)—6.5%; 'cold steel' wounds 0.9%.

When looking at the number of arm and leg wounds, it should be borne in mind that in July 1939, among the men and some NCOs of the 603rd Rifle Regiment, which was made up of reserve personnel, there were a significant number of cases of self-inflicted wounds, mostly to the arms.[35] This stopped after the 1st Army Group's military council took decisive measures to combat this disgraceful practice.

Finally, Table 35 gives the available (incomplete) figures showing the outcome of treatment for sick and wounded personnel who were treated in hospitals.

Table 35. Outcome of Treatment for Sick and Wounded Personnel Treated in Hospitals

| Wounded personnel | Total no admitted to military medical facilities | Of these:[1] | | |
		Returned to duty	Discharged to the reserve, taken off strength, sent on leave	Died
Wounded, burns and concussion cases	15,251	3,964 (figures incomplete)	355 (figures incomplete)	720[2] (figures incomplete)

1. Figures in the table concerning the outcome of treatment for servicemen who were wounded or who suffered burns or concussion are as of November 1939. By this time it had not yet been determined what the outcome of treatment was for 10,212 servicemen who were treated in military medical facilities.
2. This figure includes 543 who died in field hospitals and hospitals for evacuated personnel, plus 104 who died in hospitals in Trans-Baikal Military District (TsGASA, f. 32113, op. 2, d. 59, l. 37; f. 37462, op. 2, d. 1, l. 147).

Something more should be said here about the 701 Soviet servicemen who fell sick during the Khalkhin Gol conflict.[36] The overwhelming majority of cases were due to catarrhal, gastric and intestinal disorders and eye infections.[37]

From an analysis of the figures available, in the 36th Motor Rifle Division, in the 57th Rifle Division and in Military Unit 9355 in the period between 1 April and 1 October 1939, gastro-intestinal and catarrhal infections on average accounted for 56% of cases (19.6% and 36.4% respectively).[38]

It should be noted that, because of the shortage of doctors at regimental medical aid posts, battalion doctors were transferred to these and in their place medical assistants were sent to the battalions.

Systematised data on all categories of Soviet troop losses at Khalkhin Gol are given in Tables 36 and 37.

Table 36. Personnel Losses by Arm of Service at Khalkhin Gol[1]

| Arm of service | Rank | Loss categories | | |
		Killed	Missing in action	Wounded
Rifle troops	Commanders	283	6	857
	NCOs	575	48	1,405
	Men	2,533	405	7,807
	Total	3,391	459	10,069
	%	68.2	79.7	82.9
Tank troops	Commanders	120	3	165
	NCOs	195	15	225
	Men	344	18	474
	Total	659	36	864
	%	13.2	6.3	7.1

Arm of service	Rank	Loss categories		
		Killed	Missing in action	Wounded
Artillery (incl. divisional)	Commanders	17	—	65
	NCOs	33	—	91
	Men	127	14	310
	Total	177	14	466
	%	3.6	2.4	3.8
Air force	Commanders	85	44	88
	NCOs	13	15	14
	Men	2	—	—
	Total	100	59	102
	%	2	10.2	0.8
Other	Commanders	36	1	32
	NCOs	109	2	128
	Men	502	5	498
	Total	647	8	658
	%	13	1.4	5.4
	Overall total	4,974	576	12,159
	%	100	100	100

1. Figures are incomplete.

Table 37. Soviet Personnel Losses at Khalkhin Gol, 11 May–15 September 1939[1]

	Loss categories		Commanders	NCOs	Men	Total
Irrecoverable losses	Killed in action, died during casualty evacuation	No	1,063	1,313	4,455	6,831
		% of losses	41.6	35.6	25.2	28.6
	Missing in action, POWs	No	71	120	952	1,143
		% of losses	2.8	3.3	5.4	4.8
	Non-combat losses	No				
		% of losses				
	Irrecoverable losses, total	No	1,134	1,433	5,407	7,974
		% of losses	44.4	38.9	30.6	33.3
		% of personnel strength: All losses Average monthly losses	13.4	11.4	11.2	11.5
Sick and wounded (including those evacuated to hospitals)	Wounded, concussion and burns cases	No	1,335	2,123	11,793	15,251
		% of losses	52.3	57.7	66.7	63.7
	Sick	No	85	127	489	701
		% of losses	3.3	3.4	2.7	2.9
	Frostbite cases	No				
		% of losses				
	Sick and wounded, total	No	1,420	2,250	12,282	15,952
		% of losses	55.6	61.1	69.4	66.7
		% of personnel strength: All losses Average monthly losses	16.8	17.9	25.6	23.1

Loss categories		Com-manders	NCOs	Men	Total
Total losses	No	2,554	3,683	17,689	23,926
	% of losses	100	100	100	100
	% of personnel strength: All losses Average monthly losses	30.2	29.3	36.8	34.6

1. TsGASA, f. 32113, op. 2, d. 56, l. 71; d. 59, l. 71–6; f. 37977, op. 1, d. 101, l. 17, 20, 99–101; d. 104, l. 91–4; d. 589, l. 1–205.

THE WESTERN UKRAINIAN
AND BYELORUSSIAN CAMPAIGN, 1939

On 1 September 1939 Nazi Germany suddenly attacked Poland, moving in a large troop force whose strength by far exceeded that of the Polish Army: Poland's infantry was outnumbered by 1.5 to 1, its artillery by 2.8 to 1 and its tank force by 5.3 to 1.[39] On 17 September the Polish government fled, having been unable to organise the country's defence, leaving its people and a demoralised army to the mercy of fate.

Soon after the start of World War II, the Soviet government took the decision to send Soviet troops into Western Ukraine and Western Byelorussia.

On 17 September 1939 Ukrainian and Byelorussian Front troops crossed the Soviet-Polish frontier and by 25 September had reached their report line along the Western Bug and San rivers. On their line of march the Soviet troops met isolated pockets of resistance consisting of remnants of army formations, nationalist para-militaries and gendarmes, which were quickly neutralised in the armed clashes which occurred. The main Polish forces, however, did not take part in these clashes. Whole units and formations surrendered: between 17 September and 2 October 1939 the Ukrainian Front took 392,334 prisoners, of whom 16,723 were officers;[40] between 17 and 30 September 1939 the Byelorussian Front took 60,202 prisoners, including 2,066 officers.[41] Table 38 gives the total strength of the two Fronts individually and combined.

Table 38. Total Strength of the Ukrainian and Byelorussian Fronts, September 1939[1]

Front	Commanders	NCOs	Men	Total	Numerical strength in (month):
Ukrainian Front	25,740	34,980	204,994	265,714	September 1939
Byelorussian Front	36,243	45,169	119,390	200,802	September 1939
Total during campaign	61,983	80,149	324,384	466,516	

1. TsGASA, f. 37977, op. 1, d. 187, l. 85–128; d. 193, l. 146; d. 215, l. 72, 82; d. 217, l. 26.

Ukrainian and Byelorussian Front losses in the campaign are shown in Table 39.

Table 39. Ukrainian and Byelorussian Front Losses in the Western Ukrainian and Byelorussian Campaign, 1939[1]

Loss category	Commanders	NCOs	Men	Total
Irrecoverable losses				
Killed in action, died during casualty evacuation	127	150	575	852
Missing in action	20	18	106	144
Total irrecoverable losses	147	168	681	996
Sick and wounded				
Wounded, concussion and burns cases	186	298	1,518	2,002
Sick	26	11	344	381
Total sick and wounded	212	309	1,862	2,383

1. TsGASA, f. 35084, op. 1, d. 22, l. 22, 23; d. 23, l. 21; d. 24, l. 108; d. 25, l. 45, 46; f. 37977, op. 1, d. 193, l. 146, 188; f. 35086, op. 1, d. 213, l. 33; d. 244, l. 907; d. 396, l. 99, 100; d. 435, l. 31, 32; d. 447, l. 84; TsAMO, f. 16, op. 204, d. 3, l. 7, 35, 54, 63, 64.

Table 40 gives losses by arm of service.

Table 40. Ukrainian and Byelorussian Front Losses in the Western Ukrainian and Byelorussian Campaign by Arm of Service, 1939

Arm of service[1]	Loss category	Rank			Total
		Commanders	NCOs	Men	
Rifle troops[2]	Killed in action, died of wounds during casualty evacuation	66	121	528	715
	Missing in action	20	18	106	144
	Wounded	164	270	1,442	1,876
	Total	250	409	2,076	2,735
Cavalry	Killed in action, died of wounds during casualty evacuation	2	10	16	28
	Wounded	4	4	14	22
	Total	6	14	30	50
Tank troops	Killed in action, died of wounds during casualty evacuation	9	17	26	52
	Wounded	18	22	41	81
	Total	27	39	67	133
Artillery	Killed in action, died of wounds during casualty evacuation	1	2	5	8
	Wounded	—	1	21	22
	Total	1	3	26	30
Air force	Killed in action, died of wounds during casualty evacuation	4	—	—	4
	Wounded	—	1	—	1
	Total	4	1	—	5
	Total, all arms of the services	288	466	2,199	2,953

1. TsGASA, f. 35084, op. 1, d. 22, l. 22, 23; d. 23, l. 21; d. 24, l. 108; d. 25, l. 45, 46; f. 35086, op. 1, d. 213, l. 33; d. 235, l. 40; d. 244, l. 907; d. 396, l. 98; d. 435, l. 31, 32; d. 447, l. 84; f. 37977, op. 1, d. 193, l. 188; d. 217, l. 58, 63, 86. The figures for losses by arm of service are incomplete.

2. Rifle troop losses include losses among communications troops, engineers, etc., based on the information available.

Table 41. Total Soviet Personnel Losses in the Western Ukrainian and Byelorussian Campaign, 17–25 September 1939[1]

	Loss categories		Com- manders	NCOs	Men	Total
Irrecoverable losses	Killed in action, died during casualty evacuation	No	127	150	575	852
		% of losses	35.4	31.4	22.6	25.2
	Missing in action, POWs	No	20	18	106	144
		% of losses	5.6	3.8	4.2	4.3
	Non-combat losses	No				
		% of losses				
	Irrecoverable losses, total	No	147	168	681	996
		% of losses	41	35.2	26.8	29.5
		% of personnel strength: All losses Average monthly losses	0.2	0.2	0.2	0.2
Sick and wounded (including those evacuated to hospitals)	Wounded, concussion and burns cases	No	186	298	1,518	2,002
		% of losses	51.8	62.5	59.7	59.2
	Sick	No	26	11	344	381
		% of losses	7.2	2.3	13.5	11.3
	Frostbite cases	No				
		% of losses				
	Sick and wounded, total	No	212	309	1,862	2,383
		% of losses	59	64.8	73.2	70.5
		% of personnel strength: All losses Average monthly losses	0.3	0.4	0.6	0.5
	Total losses	No	359	477	2,543	3,379
		% of losses	100	100	100	100
		% of personnel strength: All losses Average monthly losses	0.6	0.6	0.8	0.7

1. TsGASA, f. 35086, op. 1, d. 396, l. 98; f. 35084, op. 1. d. 22, l. 22, 23; d. 23, l. 21; d .24, l. 108; d. 25, l. 45, 46; f. 35086, op. 1, d. 213, l. 33; d. 235, l. 40; d. 244, l. 907; d. 396, l. 98; d. 435, l. 31, 32; d. 447, l. 84; f. 37977, op. 1, d. 193, l. 188; d. 217, l. 58, 63, 86; Archive of the USSR Ministry of Defence Chief Personnel Directorate, ref. no 22 (roll of command personnel casualties).

Table 42. Byelorussian Front Losses, 17–25 September 1939[1]

	Loss category		Commanders	NCOs	Men	Total
Irrecoverable losses	Killed in action, died during casualty evacuation	No	32	63	221	316
		% of losses	39.5	39.9	30.6	32.9
	Missing in action	No	1		2	3
		% of losses	1.2		0.3	0.3
	Prisoners of war	No				
		% of losses				
	Non-combat losses	No				
		% of losses				
	Total irrecoverable losses	No	33	63	223	319
		% of losses	40.7	39.9	30.9	33.2
		% of personnel strength: All losses Average monthly losses	0.1	0.1	0.2	0.2
Sick and wounded (including those evacuated to hospitals)	Wounded, concussion and burns cases	No	48	95	499	642
		% of losses	59.3	60.1	69.1	66.8
	Sick	No				
		% of losses				
	Frostbite cases	No				
		% of losses				
	Sick and wounded, total	No	48	95	499	642
		% of losses	59.3	60.1	69.1	66.8
		% of personnel strength: All losses Average monthly losses	0.1	0.2	0.4	0.3
	Total losses	No	81	158	722	961
		% of losses	100	100	100	100
		% of personnel strength: All losses Average monthly losses	0.2	0.3	0.6	0.5

1. TsGASA, f. 35086, op. 1, d. 213, l. 33; d. 244, l. 907; d. 396, l. 99, 100; d. 435, l. 31, 32; d. 447, l. 84. Figures for command personnel losses are incomplete.

THE WAR WITH FINLAND, 30 NOVEMBER 1939–13 MARCH 1940

Just before the outbreak of World War II there was a rapid *rapprochement* between Nazi Germany and Finland which saw the start of military collaboration between the two countries. The Nazi leadership's determination to turn Finland into a bridgehead for an attack on the USSR went unopposed by a sizeable section of Finnish society. Military bases, arsenals and various kinds of fortifications were hastily erected on Finnish territory. Specialists from abroad, including Germans, helped with the construction work. Many of the military installations built were designed for far greater numbers than those commanded by Finland's armed forces. For example, the

Table 43. Ukrainian Front Losses, 17–25 September 1939[1]

	Loss category		Com-manders	NCOs	Men	Total
Irrecoverable losses	Killed in action, died during casualty evacuation	No	50	87	354	491
		% of losses	21.5	27.3	19.4	20.7
	Missing in action	No	19	18	104	141
		% of losses	8.2	5.6	5.7	5.9
	Prisoners of war	No				
		% of losses				
	Non-combat losses	No				
		% of losses				
	Total irrecoverable losses	No	69	105	458	632
		% of losses	29.7	32.9	25.1	26.6
		% of personnel strength: All losses Average monthly losses	0.3	0.3	0.2	0.2
Sick and wounded (including those evacuated to hospitals)	Wounded, concussion and burns cases	No	138	203	1,019	1,360
		% of losses	59.2	63.6	56	57.3
	Sick	No	26	11	344	381
		% of losses	11.1	3.5	18.9	16.1
	Frostbite cases	No				
		% of losses				
	Sick and wounded, total	No	164	214	1,363	1,741
		% of losses	70.3	67.1	74.9	73.4
		% of personnel strength: All losses Average monthly losses	0.6	0.6	0.7	0.7
	Total losses	No	233	319	1,821	2,373
		% of losses	100	100	100	100
		% of personnel strength: All losses Average monthly losses	0.9	0.9	0.9	0.9

1. TsGASA, f. 35084, op. 1, d. 22, l. 22, 23; d. 23, l. 21; d. 24, l. 108; d. 25, l. 45, 46; f. 37977, op. 1, d. 193, l. 146, 188; TsAMO, f. 16-A, op. 204, d. 3, l. 35, 54, 63, 64. Figures for command personnel losses are incomplete.

military airfields built by the beginning of 1939 with the help of German specialists had capacity for ten times more aircraft than were operated by the Finnish air force.[42] With financial and technical assistance from several Western countries, a powerful system of permanent fortifications 135km long and up to 90km deep (the Mannerheim Line) was erected on the Karelian isthmus.

Naturally, the Soviet government was alarmed by these military preparations. Its attempts to improve relations with its neighbour were unsuccessful, however, as the latter was unwilling to reciprocate. Talks with Finland in 1939 on matters of mutual security which were held at the initiative of the Soviet Union ended in failure.

By the end of November 1939 the Finnish armed forces were deployed along the border with the Soviet Union. Including trained reserves, they numbered about 600,000 men supported by approximately 900 guns of various calibres. They also had 270 operational aircraft and 29 ships. Almost half of their ground forces, consisting of seven infantry divisions, four independent infantry brigades, a cavalry brigade and several independent infantry battalions which were combined to form the Karelian Army, were concentrated on the Karelian isthmus. In the Murmansk, Kandalaksha, Ukhta, Reboly and Petrozavodsk sectors, special troop forces or other tactical formations were created.

The Finnish armed forces' aim was to contain and isolate the main grouping of Soviet troops at the Mannerheim Line, then to move into Soviet territory once reinforcements of troops and arms had arrived from other Western countries.

On the Soviet side, by the start of the conflict the north-western frontier from the Barents Sea to the Gulf of Finland was covered by four armies which came under Leningrad Military District: the 14th Army, consisting of two rifle divisions supported by the Northern Fleet, in the Arctic; the 9th Army, with three rifle divisions, in northern and central Karelia; the 8th Army, with four rifle divisions, to the north of Lake Ladoga; and, on the Karelian Isthmus, the 7th Army with nine rifle divisions, a tank corps and three tank brigades. The 7th Army also had support from air force and Baltic Fleet units. It should be said, however, that of the four armies mentioned, only the 7th was fully prepared for mobilisation by the time combat operations commenced.

The Soviet command's plan in case of war was for the Leningrad Military District troops in central and northern Finland to contain the Finnish troops and to prevent troops sent by the Western powers from landing on the Barents Sea coast, while the 7th Army was to deliver an attack on the Karelian isthmus, breach the Mannerheim Line and destroy the Finnish troops' fortified bridgehead near Leningrad.

It should be noted here that the forces placed at the disposal of the commander of Leningrad Military District, Army Commander 2nd Class K. A. Meretskov, to carry out this mission were clearly inadequate. Stalin and Voroshilov had underestimated the fighting efficiency of the Finnish Army and so rejected the plan by the head of the General Staff, Army Commander 1st Class B. M. Shaposhnikov, to create a more powerful troop grouping.

The war with Finland started because of a number of incidents on and around 26 November in which Soviet troops were shelled from Finnish territory, as a result of which several Soviet soldiers were killed.[43] Who carried out the attacks and who sanctioned them is now hard to say, as the incidents were never investigated.

On 28 November the Soviet government declared the joint non-aggression treaty of 1932 null and void and recalled its diplomatic representatives from Finland. On 30 November Leningrad Military District troops received orders to drive the Finnish troops back from near Leningrad. At the same time the USSR again proposed to Finland that the two countries should sign a pact of friendship and mutual assistance. The Finnish government failed to respond to this proposal and on the same day declared war on the Soviet Union.

With the commencement of combat operations, the Finnish government sent a message via the Swedish ambassador in Moscow to the effect that they were prepared to renew negotiations. This time, however, the proposal was rejected by the Soviet leadership.

Soviet combat operations in the war with Finland can be divided into two stages: from 30 November 1939 until 10 February 1940 and from 11 February until 13 March 1940. During stage one, in December, 14th Army troops supported by the Northern Fleet took control of the Rybachi and Sredni peninsulas and the town of Petsamo, cutting off Finland's access to the Barents Sea. At the same time 9th Army troops, attacking further south, penetrated 35–45km into the enemy's defences. 8th Army troops pushed forwards up to 80km, but some units found themselves surrounded and were forced to retreat.

The toughest and bloodiest battles took place on the Karelian isthmus, where the 7th Army was advancing. By 12 December, with naval and air support, its troops crossed a strong security zone and penetrated the forward layers of the main defences along the entire 110km width of the Mannerheim Line. Their attempt to break through the defences was unsuccessful, however, as they had insufficient forces.

There was also a severe shortage of manpower in the 9th, 8th and 14th Armies. Losses among the Soviet troops were high, too. There were 69,986 casualties in December 1939,[44] which break down as follows: 11,676 killed in action or died of wounds or disease; 5,965 missing in action; 35,800 wounded; 1,164 cases of concussion; 493 burns cases; 5,725 frostbite cases; and 9,163 sick.

At the end of December the Red Army High Command decided to call a halt to the unsuccessful attacks and begin careful preparations for a breakthrough. With this in view, the North-Western Front was formed on the Karelian isthmus, led by Army Commander 1st Class S. K. Timoshenko and A. A. Zhdanov, who was Secretary of the Leningrad Regional and Urban Committees of the All-Union Communist Party (Bolsheviks) and a member of the military council. The Front was made up of the 7th Army, which from 7 December 1939 was under the command of Army Commander 2nd Class Meretskov, and the 13th Army, which had been formed at the end of December and was commanded by Corps Commander V. D. Grendal. Both armies had air force back-up as well as support from artillery, tank and engineer units.[45]

At this time the total strength of the fighting troops was being rapidly increased. If on 1 January 1940 they numbered 550,757 (46,776 commanders, 79,520 NCOs and 424,461 men),[46] by the beginning of March the strength of the fighting troops had reached 760,578 (78,309 commanders, 126,690 NCOs and 555,579 men)— in other words it had increased by about 1.4 times. Meanwhile the establishment strength of the troops was 916,613.[47] On 12 February 1940 certain of the 8th Army forces were detached to form the 15th Army.

The Finnish command hurriedly brought in reinforcements of personnel, and also military equipment, arms and ammunition from abroad. During the war the Western powers provided Finland with a total of 350 aircraft, 500 guns, over 6,000 machine guns, about 100,000 rifles, 650,000 hand grenades, 2.5 million shells and 160 million cartridges. 11,500 volunteers came from Scandinavia, the USA and elsewhere.[48]

On 11 February the second and final stage of the war with Finland began. After intense artillery bombardment, the North-Western Front troops went over to the offensive and in the course of a bitter, three-day battle broke through the main defences on the Mannerheim Line.

Battles developed all along the front, with the 7th Army attacking in the direction of Vyborg and the 13th Army in the direction of Keksholm. The Soviet troops effectively breached the Mannerheim Line's system of permanent fortifications in the first ten days of March, destroying the enemy's guns in the process. Also at this time the Soviet advance on Vyborg began. The main forces of Finland's Karelian Army were routed.

In spite of opposition from Britain, France and the United States, after brief negotiations a peace treaty between the USSR and Finland was signed in Moscow on 12 March 1940. Under the terms of the treaty, military operations were to cease all along the front from 1200 hours on 13 March, the border to the north of Leningrad was moved back to the level of Vyborg and Sortavala, and the Karelian isthmus, several islands in the Gulf of Finland, a small area around the town of Kuolayarvi and part of the Rybachi and Sredni peninsulas became part of the USSR. The Hango peninsula was leased to the Soviet Union for a thirty-year period, giving it the right to set up a naval base there which would control access to the Gulf of Finland and cover the sea approaches to Leningrad.

In conclusion it should be said that although the Soviet troops had won a victory, achieved their objectives and acquired combat experience, the victory was far from glorious. Moreover, the failure of the Leningrad Military District troops to break through the Mannerheim Line during the December offensive because of miscalculations by the Red Army High Command led a number of Western countries to underestimate Soviet military capabilities. 'The frontal attack by the Russians on the Karelian Isthmus with forces which were at first too weak,' notes the West German military historian K. Tippelskirch, 'was stopped in the forward area of the Mannerheim Line by the skilful and obstinate defence put up by the Finns. The whole of December passed, yet the Russians, in spite of … attacks, were unable to gain any substantial victories.'[49] He goes on to speak of the heavy casualties suffered by the Soviet troops during the fighting at the Mannerheim Line, about their 'lack of tactical manoeuvrability' and 'poor leadership' by their commanders, as a result of which 'the whole world received an unfavourable impression of the Red Army's fighting efficiency. Undoubtedly, in consequence this also had a considerable influence on Hitler's plans.'[50]

Especially during the first stage of the war with Finland, the Soviet troops found themselves in very difficult circumstances, as they were not prepared for combat in harsh winter conditions in temperatures of 40–45 degrees of frost and in deep snow. At the outbreak of war they had not been trained to negotiate densely planted minefields or for the kind of decisive action required to break through the complex system of permanent fortifications on the Karelian isthmus.

Other serious weaknesses became apparent, in the handling of troops, in the operational and tactical coordination between troops and in the organisation of supplies of food and winter uniforms and of medical assistance. As a result, the military operation dragged on for over three months and entailed heavy casualties.

At the end of 1940 the People's Commissar for Defence, Marshal of the Soviet Union S. K. Timoshenko, analysing the weaknesses in the training of Soviet troops which became apparent in the war with Finland at a meeting with the Red Army leadership, noted that 'The war with the White Finns revealed the fatal flaws in our system of military training which were the result of conducting purely theoretical training in the classroom. Our commanders and staffs had no practical experience and so were unable to organise the efforts of the arms of the services properly or achieve close coordination between them or, most importantly, to command effectively.'[51]

The enemy was better prepared for war, although enemy losses were also considerable. The Finnish Army, its weapons, equipment and tactics were well adapted for fighting in a location where there were large expanses of forest and numerous lakes, in harsh winter conditions and in heavy snow. Another strength of the Finns' defence was the skill with which they made use of the many natural obstacles.

Let us now examine the statistical information on the strength of the Soviet fighting troops and on losses suffered during the war. Table 44 shows the average monthly strength of the Soviet troops which took part in the war with Finland.

Table 44. Average Monthly Strength of Soviet Fighting Troops in the War with Finland, 30 November 1939–13 March 1940

Name of army or Front	Total no of troops	Average monthly strength as in:
North-Western Front	422,640	December 1939–March 1940
7th Army, N. Western Front	254,290	December 1939–March 1940
13th Army, N. Western Front	145,640	January–March 1940
8th Army	153,710	December 1939–March 1940
9th Army	93,610	December 1939–March 1940
14th Army	56,953	December 1939–March 1940
15th Army	117,770	February–March 1940
Red Banner Baltic Fleet	62,780	November 1939–January 1940
Average monthly strength of whole troop grouping	848,570	December 1939–March 1940

In the 105 days of the war, the Soviet troops suffered 333,084 casualties (according to reports on total casualties submitted by units and formations; figures as of 15 March 1940): killed in action, died during casualty evacuation—65,384; missing in action—19,610; wounded, burns and concussion cases—186,584; frostbite cases—9,614; sick—51,892.

It should be noted here that some of the 19,610 missing in action were prisoners of war. After the signing of the peace treaty, 5,468 prisoners of war were returned (301 commanders, 787 NCOs and 4,380 men) and about 99 (eight commanders, one NCO and 90 men) opted to remain in Finland.[52] It should be assumed that the remaining 14,043 (71.6% of all those listed as missing in action) were killed.

Figures are also available which show the outcome of treatment for those treated for wounds, concussion, burns, frostbite and disease, a total of 248,090 cases (figures as of 1 March 1941): returned to active service—172,203 (69.4%); transferred to the reserve and taken off strength, sent on sick leave—46,925 (18.9%); died of wounds and disease in medical service facilities—15,921 (6.4%); wounded, concussed, etc., for whom the outcome of treatment in medical service facilities had not been determined by this date—13,041 (5.3%).

Figures for the total number of irrecoverable personnel losses during the war are as follows: killed in action, died of wounds during casualty evacuation—65,384; missing declared dead—14,043; died in hospital from wounds or concussion—5,921 (as of 1 March 1941). The total number of irrecoverable losses was 95,348.

Of the armies which were not part of North-Western Front, the heaviest losses were suffered by the 15th Army during their brief participation in the war between 12 February and 13 March 1940 (49,795 casualties, of whom 18,065 were killed or missing in action). This was because of incompetent leadership by the Army's command, as a result of which many units of the 18th and other rifle divisions found themselves surrounded during the offensive by columns of enemy troops and came under heavy fire.

Table 45 gives casualty figures by arm of service (for the 7th, 13th, 14th and 15th Armies only).

Given below are the existing figures for losses among the Soviet fighting troops' intermediate and senior command personnel in December 1939. Of the 3,500 commanders who were killed in December 1939, the breakdown by arm of service is as follows: rifle units—2,170 (62%); artillery—490 (14%); air force—175 (5%); political staff—525 (15%); engineers—53 (1.5%); signallers—35 (1%); administrative, medical and veterinary service personnel—35 (1%); other arms of the services—17 (0.5%).

Among the 2,170 rifle troop commanders who were killed, there were:[53] 28 staff officers (1.3%); 52 rifle battalion commanders (2.4%); 340 rifle company commanders (15.7%); and 1,750 rifle platoon leaders (80.6%).

With regard to North-Western Front troops who were sent to Leningrad for treatment between 7 January and 13 March 1940, the breakdown by cause of wound is as follows:[54] bullet wounds 68%; artillery shell wounds 31.6%; wounds caused by mines 0.3%; 'cold steel' wounds 0.1%. Of these, 80.8% of wounds were serious or moderately serious and 19.2% were minor wounds.

The breakdown by type of wound was as follows:[55] head and neck wounds 10.2%; wounds to the thorax: 7.4%; wounds to the abdomen and pelvis 4.6%; wounds to the upper limbs 45.5%; wounds to the lower limbs 27.4%; and multiple wounds 4.9%.

There were some cases of typhoid and typhus during the war with Finland, but these diseases were not widespread among the troops. Existing figures show that between 1 January and 13 March 1940, 20 cases of typhus fever and 59 cases of typhoid fever were recorded among the North-Western Front forces.[56] Among units of the

Table 45. Casualty Figures by Arm of Service[1]

Arm of service[2]	Rank	Loss category			
		Killed	Wounded	Missing in action	Sick; frostbite cases
Rifle troops	Commanders	3,082	8,346	245	434
	NCOs	6,417	17,313	765	927
	Men	34,405	112,824	7,188	8,853
	Total	43,904	138,483	8,198	10,214
	%	94.4	97.4	92.6	94.7
Tank troops	Commanders	269	337	57	19
	NCOs	469	614	105	19
	Men	775	932	261	73
	Total	1,513	1,883	423	111
	%	3.3	1.3	4.8	1
Artillery	Commanders	27	81	2	11
	NCOs	42	134	4	31
	Men	188	479	9	182
	Total	257	694	15	224
	%	0.6	0.5	0.1	2.2
Communications troops	Commanders	4	6	14	1
	NCOs	6	14	19	3
	Men	50	70	138	21
	Total	60	90	171	25
	%	0.1	0.1	1.9	0.2
Engineers	Commanders	18	20	—	6
	NCOs	15	80	5	4
	Men	63	329	20	69
	Total	96	429	25	79
	%	0.2	0.3	0.3	0.7
Airborne forces	Commanders	59	71	1	19
	NCOs	130	107	6	41
	Men	469	469	15	72
	Total	658	647	22	132
	%	1.4	0.4	0.3	1.2
	Overall total	46,488	142,226	8,854	10,785
	%	100	100	100	100

1. TsGASA, f. 34980, op. 10, d. 548, l. 109; d. 552, l. 288–308; op. 14, d. 249, l. 182; op. 16, d. 81, l. 244–52; op. 17, d. 194, l. 302, 307; f. 39777, op. 1, d. 572, l. 132; TsVMA (Central Naval Archive), f. 92, op. 25, d. 14, l. 2 31; f R-1877, op. 1, d 675, l. 519, 652; f. R-1701, op. 1, d. 57, l. 326; f. R-1881, op. 1, d. 1, l. 69. Figures are for the 7th, 13th, 14th and 15th Armies
2. It has not proved possible to find separate figures for air force unit losses during the war with Finland which were complete. According to figures from the operational headquarters of the Red Army General Staff (TsGASA, f. 39777, op. 1, d. 572, l. 132), in the air force units attached to the 7th, 8th, 9th, 13th, 14th and 15th Armies and the special group and air force group attached to North-Western Front, there were 785 killed or missing in action and 144 wounded. Of the 642 who were confirmed killed or missing, 40% were pilots, 28% were navigators and radio operator gunners and about 3% came under other categories, while of the 106 wounded 24% were pilots and 76% other categories (TsGASA, f. 37977, op. 1, d. 441).

Red Banner Baltic Fleet, three cases of typhoid fever were recorded in December 1939 and a further 17 cases between 1 January and 15 March 1940.[57]

Table 46. Summary of Soviet Personnel Losses during the War with Finland, 30 November 1939–13 March 1940

Loss category		Com-manders	NCOs	Men	Total
Irrecoverable losses Killed in action, died during casualty evacuation	No	5,027	9,741	48,010	65,384[1]
	% of losses				19.6
Missing in action	No	830	2,042	16,024	19,610[2]
	% of losses				5.9
Prisoners of war	No				
	% of losses				
Non-combat losses	No				
	% of losses				
Total irrecoverable losses	No	5,857	11,783	64,034	84,994[3]
	% of losses				25.5
	% of personnel strength: All losses				10
	Average monthly losses				2.95
Sick and wounded (including those evacuated to hospitals) Wounded, concussion and burns cases	No	11,780	23,675	145,755	186,584[4]
	% of losses				56
Sick	No	335	635	5,792	51,892[5]
	% of losses				15.6
Frostbite cases	No	257	729	8,315	9,614[6]
	% of losses				2.9
Total sick and wounded	No	12,372	25,039	159,862	248,090[7]
	% of losses				74.5
	% of personnel strength: All losses				29.2
	Average monthly losses				8.6
Total losses	No	18,229	36,822	223,896	333,084[8]
	% of losses				100
	% of personnel strength: All losses				39.3
	Average monthly losses				11.55

1. Includes 2,606 for whom there is no breakdown by rank.
2. Includes 714 for whom there is no breakdown by rank.
3. Includes 3,320 for whom there is no breakdown by rank.
4. Includes 5,374 for whom there is no breakdown by rank.
5. Includes 45,130 for whom there is no breakdown by rank.
6. Includes 313 for whom there is no breakdown by rank.
7. Includes 50,817 for whom there is no breakdown by rank.
8. Includes 54,137 for whom there is no breakdown by rank. The figures in the table are incomplete as they do not include non-combat losses, nor do they include sickness cases in the 14th Army.

The figures in the table were arrived at by analysing the reports from the field, including those which were not at first taken into account when the final lists of irrecoverable losses and sick and wounded were drawn up by the General Staff when combat operations ceased (TsGASA, f. 40442, op. 1, d. 1875, l. 116–18).

Summaries of the figures for losses in the war between Finland and the Soviet Union, both for the fighting troops as a whole and individually for North-Western Front, each of the armies and the Red Banner Baltic Fleet, are given in Tables 46–54 (based on reports from the field). Table 46 gives an overall summary of personnel losses during the war. It not only includes casualty figures for the 7th, 8th, 9th, 13th, 14th and 15th Combined Arms Armies, the Red Banner Baltic Fleet, other units which were under the command of North-Western Front and a number of special formations which were under central command, but also for the operations group led by Corps Commander Grendal, which operated independently on the Karelian isthmus until 26 December 1939. The Northern Fleet, which supported the 14th Army offensive, did not suffer any casualties.

In 1949–51, after lengthy and painstaking work to reach a more accurate figure for the number of losses, the USSR Ministry of Defence Chief Personnel Directorate and the Ground Forces Main Staff drew up a roll of the Red Army servicemen killed or missing in action or who died during the war with Finland in 1939–40.[58] In all, the names of 126,875 commanders and men, manual and white collar workers were listed. A summary of the totals calculated on the basis of this roll is given in Table 54a.

Table 47. North-Western Front Personnel Losses, 7 January–13 March 1940[1]

	Loss category		Com- manders	NCOs	Men	Total
Irrecoverable losses	Killed in action, died during casualty evacuation	No	2,791	5,217	25,712	33,720
		% of losses				17.7
	Missing in action	No	321	658	5,131	6,110
		% of losses				3.2
	Prisoners of war	No				
		% of losses				
	Non-combat losses	No				
		% of losses				
	Total irrecoverable losses	No	3,112	5,875	30,843	39,830
		% of losses				20.9
		% of personnel strength: All losses Average monthly losses				9.4 4.28
Sick and wounded (including those evacuated to hospitals)	Wounded, concussion and burns cases	No	7,558	15,390	95,036	119,122[2]
		% of losses				62.7
	Sick	No	199	318	2,475	27,242[3]
		% of losses				14.3
	Frostbite cases	No	153	366	3,403	3,922
		% of losses				2.1
	Total sick and wounded	No	7,910	16,074	100,914	150,286[4]
		% of losses				79.1
		% of personnel strength: All losses Average monthly losses				35.6 16.16

69

Loss category		Com-manders	NCOs	Men	Total
Total losses	No	11,022	21,949	131,757	190,116[4]
	% of losses				100
	% of personnel strength: All losses Average monthly losses				45 20.44

1. The North-Western Front was set up by order No 0977/017 of the USSR People's Commissariat for Defence dated 7 January 1940 and was made up of the 7th and 13th Armies. The figures in the table include losses in the 7th and 13th Armies and in units under the command of the Front.
2. Includes 1,138 for whom there is no breakdown by rank.
3. Includes 24,250 for whom there is no breakdown by rank.
4. Includes 25,388 for whom there is no breakdown by rank. TsGASA, f. 34980, op. 10, d. 540, l. 81; f. 37977, op. 1, d. 572, l. 132, 140–3. TsAMO, f. 15-A, op. 2245, d. 48, l. 38, 61–73; f. 5, op. 176705, d. 67, l. 44–53; d. 68, l. 430.

The troops of the North-Western Front (the 7th and 13th Armies) had the highest proportion of sick and wounded, which accounted for 79.1% of their losses. In other strategic formations which took part in the war (the 8th, 9th, 14th and 15th Armies) the proportion was lower (70.9%, 70.6%, 68.8% and 63.7% respectively).

The main reason for this was the fact that conditions on the Karelian isthmus (limited troop manoeuvrability, concentrated fire from the enemy who took cover in numerous permanent and earth-and-timber pillboxes and other fortified emplacements) meant that the fighting there resulted in heavy casualties. Another factor was the proximity of major Red Army medical service facilities in Leningrad and other nearby towns, and the fact that medical treatment and the evacuation of the wounded were well organised. This meant that there were fewer deaths from wounds, and, in consequence, the ratio of sick and wounded to irrecoverable losses was on average 4 to 1 (calculated on the basis of the figures in Tables 47–49).

Table 48. Personnel Losses of North-Western Front's 7th Army, 30 November 1939–13 March 1940[1]

	Loss category		Com-manders	NCOs	Men	Total
Irrecoverable losses	Killed in action, died during casualty evacuation	No % of losses	1,320	2,649	12,453	16,422 16.4
	Missing in action	No % of losses	86	189	1,762	2,037 2
	Prisoners of war	No % of losses				
	Non-combat losses	No % of losses				
	Total irrecoverable losses	No % of losses	1,406	2,838	14,215	18,459 18.4
		% of personnel strength: All losses Average monthly losses				7.3 2.14

Loss category		Com-manders	NCOs	Men	Total
Sick and wounded (including those evacuated to hospitals) Wounded, concussion and burns cases	No	4,021	8,240	48,392	61,481[2]
	% of losses				61.5
Sick	No	119	174	1,464	19,256[3]
	% of losses				19.3
Frostbite cases	No	25	45	653	723
	% of losses				0.8
Total sick and wounded	No	4,165	8,459	50,509	81,460[4]
	% of losses				81.6
	% of personnel strength:				
	All losses				32
	Average monthly losses				9.42
Total losses	No	5,571	11,297	64,724	99,919[4]
	% of losses				100
	% of personnel strength:				
	All losses				39.3
	Average monthly losses				11.56

1. The 7th Army was involved in combat operations between these dates.
2. Includes 828 burns cases for whom there is no breakdown by rank.
3. Includes 17,499 for whom there is no breakdown by rank.
4. Includes 18,327 for whom there is no breakdown by rank. TsGASA, f. 34980, op. 10, d. 540, l. 76–8; d. 552, l. 288–308; op. 12, d. 73, l. 35, 148; d. 128, l. 62–77. TsAMO, f. 15-A, op. 2245, d. 48, l. 5, 202–309.

Throughout the war with Finland the 7th Army (under Army Commander 2nd Class V. F. Yakovlev and from 26 December 1939 under Army Commander 2nd Class Meretskov) had the greatest troop strength compared with the other armies involved in the war (see Table 44), as it was attacking in the main (Vyborg) sector. As the figures show, it suffered considerably fewer casualties than the 13th Army or a number of other armies.

Table 49. Personnel Losses of North-Western Front's 13th Army, 26 December 1939–13 March 1940[1]

Loss category		Com-manders	NCOs	Men	Total
Irrecoverable losses Killed in action, died during casualty evacuation	No	1,239	2,430	13,209	16,878
	% of losses				18.9
Missing in action	No	106	376	3,344	3,826
	% of losses				4.3
Prisoners of war	No				
	% of losses				
Non-combat losses	No				
	% of losses				
Total irrecoverable losses	No	1,345	2,806	16,553	20,704
	% of losses				23.2
	% of personnel strength:				
	All losses				14.2
	Average monthly losses				5.47

	Loss category		Com-manders	NCOs	Men	Total
Sick and wounded (including those evacuated to hospitals)	Wounded, concussion and burns cases	No	3,476	7,009	46,476	57,271[2]
		% of losses				64.2
	Sick	No	80	144	1,011	7,986[3]
		% of losses				9
	Frostbite cases	No	128	321	2,750	3,199
		% of losses				3.6
	Total sick and wounded	No	3,684	7,474	50,237	68,456[4]
		% of losses				76.8
		% of personnel strength:				
		All losses				47
		Average monthly losses				18.08
	Total losses	No	5,029	10,280	66,790	89,160[4]
		% of losses				100
		% of personnel strength:				
		All losses				61.2
		Average monthly losses				23.55

1. The 13th Army was formed on 26 December 1939 from the troops of Corps Commander Grendal's operations group and certain units which were detached from the 7th Army. It took part in combat operations from 26 December 1939 until 13 March 1940.
2. Includes 310 burns cases for whom there is no breakdown by rank.
3. Includes 6,751 for whom there is no breakdown by rank.
4. Includes 7,061 for whom there is no breakdown by rank. TsGASA, f. 34980, op. 10, d. 546, l. 165–77; d. 540, l. 78–80; d. 548, l. 109–13. TsAMO, f. 15-A, op. 2245, d. 48, l. 13, 316–35.

The 13th Army (under Grendal, then from 2 March 1940 under Corps Commander F. A. Parusinov), was part of North-Western Front. It suffered the heaviest losses of all the armies (61.2% of average monthly troop strength). During the offensive on the Karelian isthmus the 13th Army was advancing at a much slower pace than the 7th Army on its left flank, which was the reason for the change of commander.

Table 50. 8th Army Personnel Losses, 30 November 1939–13 March 1940[1]

	Loss category		Com-manders	NCOs	Men	Total
Irrecoverable losses	Killed in action, died during casualty evacuation	No	654	1,273	6,173	8,100
		% of losses				18
	Missing in action	No	129	446	4,396	4,971
		% of losses				11.1
	Prisoners of war	No				
		% of losses				
	Non-combat losses	No				
		% of losses				
	Total irrecoverable losses	No	783	1,719	10,569	13,071
		% of losses				29.1
		% of personnel strength:				
		All losses				8.5
		Average monthly losses				2.5

	Loss category		Com-manders	NCOs	Men	Total
Sick and wounded (including those evacuated to hospitals)	Wounded, concussion and burns cases	No	1,524	2,582	17,222	21,723[2]
		% of losses				48.4
	Sick	No				7,296
		% of losses				16.3
	Frostbite cases	No	45	154	2,598	2,797
		% of losses				6.2
	Total sick and wounded	No	1,569	2,736	19,820	31,816[3]
		% of losses				70.9
		% of personnel strength: All losses				20.7
		Average monthly losses				6.09
	Total losses	No	2,352	4,455	30,389	44,887[3]
		% of losses				100
		% of personnel strength: All losses				29.2
		Average monthly losses				8.59

1. The 8th Army took part in combat operations between these two dates.
2. Includes 395 for whom there is no breakdown by rank (231 concussion and 164 burns cases).
3. Includes 7,691 for whom there is no breakdown by rank. TsGASA, f. 34980, op. 13, d. 1272, l. 18–20, 25; d. 1276, l. 24–7. TsAMO, f. 15-A, op. 2245, d. 48, l. 5, 47, 385–7.

Until 12 February the 8th Army, led by Division Commander I. N. Khabarov, was active in two main sectors, Ilomantsi and Sortavala, with a front which stretched over 200km. It was made up of six rifle divisions and several reinforcement units. The numerical strength of the opposing sides started out the same, but the Finnish units' combat training gave them the advantage.

The 8th Army's losses were among the lowest, amounting to 29.2% of its average monthly strength. Only the 14th Army had fewer casualties.

Table 51. 9th Army Personnel Losses, 30 November 1939–13 March 1940[1]

	Loss category		Com-manders	NCOs	Men	Total
Irrecoverable losses	Killed in action, died during casualty evacuation	No	634	1,214	5,770	8,540[2]
		% of losses				18.6
	Missing in action, POWs	No	208	566	3,895	4,996[3]
		% of losses				10.8
	Non-combat losses	No				
		% of losses				
	Total irrecoverable losses	No	842	1,780	9,665	13,536[4]
		% of losses				29.4
		% of personnel strength: All losses				14.5
		Average monthly losses				4.25

	Loss category		Com-manders	NCOs	Men	Total
Sick and wounded (including those evacuated to hospitals)	Wounded, concussion and burns cases	No	1,280	2,635	13,070	17,674[5]
		% of losses				38.3
	Sick	No				12,250
		% of losses				26.6
	Frostbite cases	No	52	177	2,107	2,649[6]
		% of losses				5.7
	Total sick and wounded	No	1,332	2,812	15,177	32,573[7]
		% of losses				70.6
		% of personnel strength:				
		All losses				34.8
		Average monthly losses				10.24
	Total losses	No	2,174	4,592	24,842	46,109[8]
		% of losses				100
		% of personnel strength:				
		All losses				49.3
		Average monthly losses				14.49

1. The 9th Army was involved in combat operations between these dates.
2. Includes 922 for whom there is no breakdown by rank.
3. Includes 327 for whom there is no breakdown by rank.
4. Includes 1,249 for whom there is no breakdown by rank.
5. Includes 689 for whom there is no breakdown by rank.
6. Includes 313 for whom there is no breakdown by rank.
7. Includes 13,252 for whom there is no breakdown by rank.
8. Includes 14,501 for whom there is no breakdown by rank. TsGASA, f. 34980, op. 14, d. 246, l. 1; d. 249, l. 182; d. 253, l. 41; d. 255, l. 40; f. 37977, op. 1, d. 572, l. 146. TsAMO, f. 15-A, op. 2245, d. 48, l. 9; f. 5, op. 176705, d. 69, l. 137–42, 378–81.

The advance of the 9th Army under Corps Commander M. P. Dukhanov in the Kuolayarvi, Suomussalmi and Karpisalmi sectors involved heavy casualties, particularly as a result of unsuccessful actions by the 44th and 163rd Rifle Divisions and the 54th Mountain Rifle Division. In February 1940 the number of irrecoverable losses in these divisions was as much as 20–30% of their strength (TsGASA, f. 34980, op. 10, d. 658).

Table 52. 14th Army Personnel Losses, 30 November 1939–13 March 1940[1]

	Loss category		Com-manders	NCOs	Men	Total
Irrecoverable losses	Killed in action, died during casualty evacuation	No	40[2]	22	119	181
		% of losses	71.4	26.8	26.6	30.9
	Missing in action, POWs	No			2	2
		% of losses			0.4	0.3
	Non-combat losses	No				
		% of losses				
	Total irrecoverable losses	No	40	22	121	183
		% of losses	71.4	26.8	27	31.2
		% of personnel strength:				
		All losses	0.7	0.2	0.3	0.3
		Average monthly losses	0.16	0.04	0.07	0.09

	Loss category		Com-manders	NCOs	Men	Total
Sick and wounded (including those evacuated to hospitals)	Wounded, concussion and burns cases	No	14	36	251	301
		% of losses	25	43.9	56.2	51.5
	Sick	No				
		% of losses				
	Frostbite cases	No	2	24	75	101
		% of losses	3.6	29.3	16.8	17.3
	Total sick and wounded	No	16	60	326	402
		% of losses	28.6	73.2	73	68.8
		% of personnel strength:				
		All losses	0.3	0.7	0.7	0.7
		Average monthly losses	0.07	0.16	0.16	0.21
	Total losses	No	56	82	447	585
		% of losses	100	100	100	100
		% of personnel strength:				
		All losses	1	0.9	1	1
		Average monthly losses	0.23	0.20	0.23	0.3

1. The 14th Army was involved in combat operations between these two dates.
2. Including 19 air force officers. Figures for the number of cases of sickness have not been found. TsGASA, f. 34980, op. 10, d. 551, l. 197, 199, 313, 368; op. 16, d. 81, l. 244–52. TsAMO, f. 15-A, op. 2245, d. 48, l. 11, 426, 427, 430; f. 5, op. 176705, d. 66, l. 606, 607.

The 14th Army under Division Commander V. A. Frolov, which consisted of two divisions plus reinforcement units, fought successful actions in the Petsamo and Nautsi sectors in the Arctic. The 14th Army had the lowest number of casualties (a mere 0.3% of average monthly strength). Of the sick and wounded, a significant number were frostbite victims (about 25% of cases).

The 15th Army was formed during the war from the left-flank formations and units of the 8th Army fighting between Lake Ladoga and the village of Laimola. It had

Table 53. 15th Army Personnel Losses, 12 February–13 March 1940[1]

	Loss category		Com-manders	NCOs	Men	Total
Irrecoverable losses	Killed in action, died during casualty evacuation	No	860	1,976	10,169	14,689[2]
		% of losses				29.5
	Missing in action	No	127	339	2,523	3,376[3]
		% of losses				6.8
	Prisoners of war	No				
		% of losses				
	Non-combat losses	No				
		% of losses				
	Total irrecoverable losses	No	987	2,315	12,692	18,065[4]
		% of losses				36.3
		% of personnel strength:				
		All losses				15.3
		Average monthly losses				15.34

	Loss category		Com-manders	NCOs	Men	Total
Sick and wounded (including those evacuated to hospitals)	Wounded, concussion and burns cases	No % of losses	1,350	2,977	19,984	27,463[5] 55.2
	Sick	No % of losses	136	317	3,317	4,259[6] 8.5
	Frostbite cases	No % of losses				
	Total sick and wounded	No % of losses	1,486	3,294	23,301	31,722[7] 63.7
		% of personnel strength: All losses Average monthly losses				 26.9 26.94
	Total losses	No % of losses	2,783	6,576	40,428	49,787[8] 100
		% of personnel strength: All losses Average monthly losses				 42.2 42.28

1. Troops were detached from the 8th Army to form the 15th Army, which took part in the fighting between these dates.
2. Includes 1,684 for whom there is no breakdown by rank.
3. Includes 387 for whom there is no breakdown by rank.
4. Includes 2,071 for whom there is no breakdown by rank.
5. Includes 3,152 for whom there is no breakdown by rank.
6. Includes 489 for whom there is no breakdown by rank. The sickness figures include frostbite cases; it has not proved possible to find separate figures for these because the relevant information was not available.
7. Includes 3,641 for whom there is no breakdown by rank.
8. Including 18th Rifle Division losses for the period 25 December 1939–13 March 1940, for whom there is no breakdown by loss category. TsGASA, f. 34980, op. 17, d. 190, l. 116–21, 175–344; d. 194, l. 210, 214, 302, 307, 308, 310, 311. TsAMO, f. 5, op. 176705, d. 67, l. 258.

Table 54. Red Banner Baltic Fleet Personnel Losses, 30 November–13 March 1940

	Loss category		Com-manders	NCOs	Men	Total
Irrecoverable losses	Killed in action, died during casualty evacuation	No % of losses	48	39	67	154 9.6
	Missing in action, POWs	No % of losses	45	33	77	155 9.7
	Non-combat losses	No % of losses				
	Total irrecoverable losses	No % of losses	93	72	144	309 19.3
		% of personnel strength: All losses Average monthly losses				 0.5 0.15

	Loss category		Com-manders	NCOs	Men	Total
Sick and wounded (including those evacuated to hospitals)	Wounded, concussion and burns cases	No	54	55	192	301
		% of losses				18.8
	Sick	No				845
		% of losses				52.8
	Frostbite cases	No	5	8	132	145
		% of losses				9.1
	Total sick and wounded	No	59	63	324	1,291[1]
		% of losses				80.7
		% of personnel strength: All losses				2
		Average monthly losses				0.6
	Total losses	No	152	135	468	1,600[1]
		% of losses				100
		% of personnel strength: All losses				2.5
		Average monthly losses				0.75

1. Includes 845 sickness cases for whom there is no breakdown by rank. TsGAVMF, f. R-92, op. 25, d. 14, l. 2–31; f. R-1701, d. 56, l. 1–64, 90; d. 57, l. 326, 329; f. 1877, op. 1, d. 164, l. 183, 222; d. 675, l. 519, 652. TsVMA, f. 2, op. 0356360, d. 2, l. 5, 6, 8, 9.

a higher proportion of irrecoverable losses than the other armies involved in the war (15.3% of its average monthly strength). This was mainly because of heavy casualties in the 18th Rifle Division and the 34th Light Tank Brigade which in February 1940, because of bungling by the command, were cut off and block-aded by the enemy and came under intensive fire (TsGASA, f. 34980, op. 10, d. 210, l. 12, 15).

Table 54a. Adjusted Totals for the Number of Irrecoverable Losses in the War between the USSR and Finland

Loss category	Com-manders	NCOs	Men	Rank not known	Total
Killed or died of wounds during evacuation	6,000	9,611	54,215	1,388	71,214
Died in hospital of wounds or disease	802	1,436	12,185	1,869	16,292
Missing in action	1,010	2,998	33,827	1,534	39,369
Total	7,812	14,045	100,227	4,791	126,875

The figures for the number of irrecoverable losses given in Table 54a are very different from the totals given in Table 46, which have been calculated on the basis of reports from the field which had come in before the end of March 1940. The difference in the figures is shown in Table 54b overleaf.

The reason for the discrepancy was that the roll of casualties included air force losses which had not previously been taken into account (see Table 45), servicemen

Table 54b. Differences in Figures between Tables 46 and 54a

Loss category	Total irrecoverable losses		Difference
	According to reports from the field	According to roll of casualties	
Killed in action, died of wounds during casualty evacuation	65,384	71,214	5,830
Died in hospital from wounds or disease	15,921	16,292	371
Missing in action	14,043	39,369	25,326
Total	95,348	126,875	31,527

who died in hospital after March 1940, and border guards and other servicemen who were not part of the Red Army who died of wounds or disease in those same hospitals. In addition, the roll included a large number of servicemen who failed to return home (included on the basis of statements by relatives), especially from among those called up in 1939–40 with whom contact had been lost during the war with Finland. After many years' unsuccessful searching they were listed as missing in action (it should be noted that this roll was drawn up ten years after the war with Finland ended). This explains why the roll contains such a large number of MIAs—39,369 men, which represents 31% of all irrecoverable losses in the war with Finland. According to the reports from the field, only 14,093 men were missing in action during combat operations, or about 15% of the irrecoverable losses given in these reports.

In this book the authors have presented both the figures calculated on the basis of the roll of casualties and those which were calculated by analysing the reports from the field and the full report of the General Staff which was drawn up at the end of March 1940 immediately after hostilities ceased. However, the figure of 126,875 has been taken as representing the final total for irrecoverable losses in the war between the USSR and Finland. This is based on the roll of casualties and includes all those who were killed or missing in action or who died of wounds or disease. In the authors' opinion this figure reflects more accurately the country's irrecoverable demographic losses in the war with Finland.

According to Finnish sources, Finland's losses in the war were 48,243 killed and 43,000 wounded (see the journal *Za rubezhom*, No 48, 1989).

A summary of the Soviet armed forces' total losses in military conflicts and combat operations between 1923 and 1940 is given in Table 55. The table shows that the Red Army's irrecoverable combat losses in this period (killed in action, died of wounds or disease, missing in action, POWs who failed to return) amounted to 139,100 men. The largest number of these was during the war with Finland in 1939–40 (126,875), followed by the Khalkhin Gol conflict in 1939 (8,931).

Table 55. Summary of the Soviet Armed Forces' Total Personnel Losses in Combat Operations and Military Conflicts, 1923–1940

Military conflict/ combat operation	Irrecoverable losses								Sick and wounded							
	Killed in action, died during evacuation or as result of accident		Missing in action, POWs who failed to return		Died in hospital of wounds or disease[1]		Total		Wounded, concussion and burns cases		Sick		Frostbite cases		Total	
	No	%	No	%	No	%	No	%	No	%	No	%	No	%	No	%
The fight against Basmachestvo, 1923–31	516	82.4	58	9.3	52	8.3	626	100	867	100	—	—	—	—	867	100
The Sino-Soviet conflict, 1929	143	76.5	4	2.1	40	21.4	187	100	665	100	—	—	—	—	665	100
Military assistance to the Spanish republic, 1936–39	132	83.5	26	16.5	—	—	158	100	—	—	—	—	—	—	—	—
Military assistance to China, 1937–39	186	95.4	9	4.6	—	—	195	100	—	—	—	—	—	—	—	—
Repelling of Japanese aggressors at Lake Khasan, 1938	717	72.5	75	7.6	197	19.9	989	100	2,752	83.9	527	16.1	—	—	3,279	100
Defeat of Japanese invaders at the Khalkhin Gol river, 1939	6,831	76.5	1,143	12.8	957	10.7	8,931	100	15,251	95.6	701	4.4	—	—	15,952	100
The W. Ukrainian and W. Byelorussian campaign, 1939	852	74.8	144	12.6	143	12.6	1,139	100	2,002	84	381	16	—	—	2,383	100
The war with Finland, 30.11.1939–13.3.1940	71,214	56.1	39,369	31.1	16,292	12.8	126,875	100	188,671[2]	71.2	58,370[2]	22	17,867[2]	6.8	264,908[2]	100
Total	80,591	57.9	40,828	29.4	17,681	12.7	139,100	100	210,208	73	59,979	20.8	17,867	6.2	288,054	100

1. Figures for deaths in hospital from wounds and disease during each military conflict (with the exception of the war with Finland) have been calculated taking a fatality rate of 6% of the total number of sick and wounded.
2. Amended figures based on information from the Central Military Medical Directorate of the USSR Ministry of Defence (TsVMU MO).

From the information included in Chapter 2 it can be seen that during the inter-war period the largest number of military conflicts and the greatest number of casualties occurred at the end of the 1930s. At the time this was taken by the Soviet Union as a clear sign that the military threat to the USSR from Nazi Germany and its Anti-Comintern Pact allies represented an increasing danger.[59]

Because of the deteriorating military and political situation on the USSR's borders in the years leading up to the war, the Soviet government took measures to increase the country's defence capability and strengthen its eastern and western borders. In 1939 Soviet troops were sent into the Baltic states under the terms of treaties signed.

The Soviet troops sent into the Baltic states were as follows:

Estonia: 25,000 men (the HQ of the 65th Rifle Corps, the 16th Rifle Division, the 18th Tank Brigade, the HQ of the 55th Air Brigade, the 25th and 38th Fighter Regiments, the 35th and 44th Medium-Range Bomber Regiments, MT and other units). The first troops entered Estonia on 18 October 1939.

Latvia: About 25,000 men (the HQ of the 2nd Rifle Corps, the 67th Rifle Division, the 6th Tank Brigade, the 10th Tank Regiment, the HQ of the 18th Air Brigade, the 31st and 15th Fighter Regiments, the 39th Medium-Range Bomber Regiment and other units). The first troops entered Latvia on 3 November 1939.

Lithuania: About 20,000 men (the HQ of the 16th Rifle Corps, the 5th Rifle Division, the 2nd Tank Brigade, the 10th Fighter Regiment, the 31st Medium-Range Bomber Regiment and other units). The first troops entered Lithuania on 3 November 1939.

By 1 January 1940 Red Army ground and air formations and units numbering 58,055 men[60] had actually been sent into the Baltic republics. Of these, 20,954, including 2,371 officers, were sent to Estonia, 19,339, including 2,210 officers, to Latvia and 17,762, including 2,009 officers, to Lithuania.

No hostile actions were recorded when the Soviet troops entered the Baltic republics. There is no information on combat losses among Soviet servicemen.

After the new legislative bodies of these republics passed resolutions on joining the USSR as union republics, their national armies were re-formed by the USSR Council of People's Commissars' decree of August 1940 into territorial rifle corps each numbering 15,000–16,000 men.

The experience gained by the Soviet armed forces in combat operations in the inter-war period, especially in 1938–40, was made use of when the army and navy were reorganised, the training of troops and staff was improved and new regulations were drawn up.

NOTES

1. TsGASA, f. 7, op. 2, d. 466, l. 58.
2. The Turkestan Autonomous Soviet Socialist Republic, which was part of the RSFSR, was created in April 1918 at the Fifth *Krai* (Territory) Congress of Turkestan Soviets. Between its

eastern and western parts lay the territories of two despotically ruled, feudal Muslim states, the Khiva khanate and the Bukhara emirate. After successful popular democratic revolutions in these territories in 1920, the Khorezm People's Soviet Republic was created in June 1920 and the Bukhara People's Soviet Republic in October 1920. Both of these were incorporated into the Turkestan Autonomous Republic.

3. TsGASA, f. 7, op. 2, d. 466, l. 65.

4. Ibid., l. 66.

5. TsGASA, f. 25895, op. 14, d. 3, l. 112–20.

6. Order no 304 of the Revolutionary Military Council of the USSR, issued 4 June 1926.

7. In 1929–31, as in some preceding years, it was made easier for the *Basmachestvo* movement to re-emerge because there were large *Basmachi* groupings who retreated periodically into neighbouring Afghanistan from the Central Asian republics. They were in communication with relatives and supporters in these republics and were able to carry out bloody raids into Soviet territory almost unimpeded across state borders which at that time were poorly guarded.

8. TsGASA, f. 25895, op. 14, d. 53.

9. TsGASA, f. 25895, op. 14, d. 178, l. 144.

10. TsGASA, f. 25835, op. 15, d. 12.

11. TsGASA, f. 25835, op. 15, d. 11, l. 37; op. 12, d. 230, l. 201–4; op. 14, d. 178, l. 78.

12. A breech-loading mortar used in World War I.

13. The Far Eastern Flotilla was the name given to the Amur Military Flotilla from September 1926 until January 1931.

14. TsGASA, f. 33879, op. 6, d. 1, l. 15.

15. See *Istoriya vtoroi mirovoi voiny 1939–45* (*History of World War II*), Moscow, 1974, vol. 2, p. 54.

16. GRU (Chief Intelligence Directorate) memorandum of 30 July 1991, ref. no 24/243.

17. Kuomintang: a Chinese political party founded in 1912 and the ruling party from 1927. The Kuomintang were overthrown in 1949.

18. See *Istoriya vtoroi mirovoi voiny 1939–45*, vol. 2, p. 72.

19. See *Istoriya vtoroi mirovoi voiny 1939–45*, vol. 2, p. 73.

20. GRU memorandum of 30 July 1991, ref. no 24/243.

21. The Far Eastern Front was formed in June 1938 from troops of the Special Red Banner Eastern Army, in order to repulse Japanese aggression. After an end to the fighting near Lake Khasan in August 1938 the Front's headquarters was disbanded. The Far Eastern Front was re-established in July 1940 and existed until August 1945.

22. TsGASA, f. 35083, op. 1, d. 60, l. 60.

23. See *1939 god: Uroki istorii* (*1939: Lessons of History*), Moscow, 1990, p. 291.

24. TsGASA, f. 37299, op. 2, d. 561, l. 163.

25. TsGASA, f. 37299, op. 5, d. 560, l. 19–21.

26. In January 1936, at a time when there was a growing threat of attack on Mongolia by Japan, the Mongolian government approached the Soviet government with a request for military assistance. In February that year the Soviet government announced that the Soviet Union would help Mongolia repel Japanese aggression. Soon after this, on 12 March, a ten-year Soviet-Mongolian Protocol on Mutual Assistance was signed at Ulan Bator, replacing the agreement of 1934. Under the terms of this Protocol, Soviet troops were stationed on Mongolian territory. By 25 May 1939 these troops numbered 5,544, including 523 commanders and 996 NCOs (TsGASA, f. 37977, op. 1, d. 101, l. 20); they were part of the 57th Independent Rifle Corps and took part in the first battles at Khalkhin Gol. After this Soviet troop numbers were increased because of the increase in the scale of Japanese aggression.

27. The Mongolian troops in the combat area were made up of three cavalry divisions whose total strength was 4,860, including 1,293 commanders (TsGASA, f. 37977, op. 1, d. 101).

28. Air battles between the Soviet and Japanese air forces continued until 15 September 1939.
29. TsGASA, f. 32113, op. 2, d. 59, l. 37.
30. TsGASA, f. 37977, op. 1, d. 101, l. 17.
31. See Ye. I. Smirnov, *Frontovoe miloserie* (*Medical Care at the Front*), Moscow, 1991, p. 24.
32. TsGASA, f. 32113, op. 2, d. 185, l. 179, 180.
33. TsGASA, f. 32113, op. 2, d. 56, l. 71.
34. TsGASA, f. 32113, op. 2, d. 56, l. 61.
35. Ibid., l. 71.
36. This represents the number of sick who were treated in military district hospitals. There are no figures for those who were treated at regimental and divisional medical aid posts.
37. Catarrhal infections were mainly caused by the unaccustomed contrast between day- and night-time temperatures, which went from +35° to −15°. The main cause of gastric and intestinal disorders was the lack of clean drinking water. Eye infections were caused by exposure to bright sunlight, which irritated the mucous membrane of the eye. In many cases the problem was aggravated by the strong wind blowing into the eyes, which caused the mucous membrane to become inflamed.
38. TsGASA, f. 32113, op. 2, d. 386, l. 1032, 1085–92.
39. See *1939 god: Uroki istorii*, p. 373.
40. TsGASA, f. 35084, op. 1, d. 22, l. 21; d. 24, l. 103; d. 25, l. 44; d. 28, l. 31.
41. TsGASA. f. 37977, op. 1, d. 217, l. 69. In June 1940, under the terms of a Soviet-Romanian agreement, the old national border between the USSR and Romania along the rivers Prut and Danube was restored. Troops of the Southern Front, which was formed from personnel of the Kiev Special Military District, were moved into Bessarabia and Northern Bukovina, which had been seized from the Soviet state in 1918. There were no casualties.
42. *Istoriya vtoroi mirovoi voiny 1939–45*, vol. 3, p. 359.
43. See *Istoriya vtoroi mirovoi voiny 1939–45*, vol.3, p. 361.
44. TsAMO (Central Archive of the Ministry of Defence), f. 15-A, op. 2245, d. 48, l. 16.
45. The North-Western Front and the 14th, 9th, 8th and 15th Armies were directly subordinate to the USSR People's Commissariat for Defence until the end of the war.
46. TsAMO, f. 15, op. 2245, d. 48, l. 5, 7, 9, 11, 13.
47. TsAMO, f. 15, op. 2248, d. 48, l. 35, 37.
48. See *Istoriya vtoroi mirovoi voiny 1939–45*, vol. 2, p. 363.
49. K. Tippelskirch, *Istoriya vtoroi mirovoi voiny*, Moscow, 1956, p. 48.
50. Ibid., p. 50.
51. *Voenno-istoricheski zhurnal* (*Journal of Military History*), 1989, No 11, p. 17.
52. TsGASA, f. 37977, op. 1, d. 428, l. 237–40.
53. TsAMO, f. 15-A, op. 2245, d. 48, l.19.
54. TsGASA, f. 34980, op. 10, d. 1855, l. 93.
55. Ibid.
56. TsGASA, f. 34980, op. 10, d. 1855, l. 93.
57. TsVMA, f. R-1701, op. 7, d. 57, l. 326; f. R-1881, op. 1, d. 1, l. 69.
58. TsGASA, f. 34980, op. 15, d. 200, 203, 204, 206, 208, 211, 213, 215, 217, 219; Archive of the USSR Ministry of Defence Chief Personnel Directorate, ref. nos 21, 22.
59. The Anti-Comintern Pact was a treaty between Germany and Japan which was concluded on 25 November 1936, with the aim of fighting for world hegemony under the flag of anti-communism. In 1937–39 Franco's Spain and Italy joined the pact, as did the reactionary governments of Hungary, Finland, Romania, Denmark and several other countries.
60. TsGASA, f. 39977, op. 1, d. 638, l. 116, 127, 138, 139.

Chapter Three

The Soviet Armed Forces' Losses in the Great Patriotic War, 1941–45

The Great Patriotic War was the greatest ordeal in the history of the Soviet state. Nazi Germany's objective in invading the USSR was the rapid defeat of the Red Army and the destruction of the Soviet state, with the mass extermination and enslavement of its peoples

The first blows were struck against the country's border posts and those divisions which were stationed near the border. Bitter fighting broke out. The Soviet troops were at a severe disadvantage when the Germans attacked suddenly. In military districts along the border, troops had not been fully deployed and were fewer in number than those of their attackers. The enemy divisions were at full strength, well armed and highly mobile. In some sectors enemy troops outnumbered Soviet troops by three or four to one.[1] Italy, Romania, Finland and Hungary also joined the forces hostile to the USSR.

The Soviet troops showed exceptional courage, heroism and self-sacrifice in the face of very difficult circumstances. However, defeat in the border battles meant that they were forced to retreat. The unfavourable conditions at the start of the war led to heavy Red Army casualties in this initial phase, and there were many more casualties in the push to drive the Nazis from Soviet soil and as the Red Army helped to liberate Europe. Over eleven million on both sides were involved in the bitter fighting at any one time.

The sophisticated equipment, tremendous fire-power and destructive power on both sides all had a direct bearing on casualty numbers. The fighting spread over a vast area from the Barents to the Black Sea and lasted 1,418 days. At first the fatal storm raged from the frontier as far as Moscow and the Volga then, gathering force, it turned westwards towards Berlin.

Tens of millions of Soviet soldiers went through this terrible ordeal. Millions failed to return from the field of battle.

IRRECOVERABLE LOSSES

Research carried out by the USSR State Statistics Committee Central Office of Population Statistics and the Centre for the Study of Population Problems at Moscow University shows that the total number of deaths during the Great Patriotic War can be estimated at almost 27 million. This includes servicemen and partisans who were killed in action or died of wounds, ordinary civilians who died of hunger or disease or were killed during air raids, artillery shelling and punitive actions, and prisoners of war and underground fighters who were tortured and shot in concentration camps.

Red Army and Navy losses have been determined by analysing statistical material from the General Staff, reports from the fronts (army groups), fleets, armies and military districts and from the Central Military Medical Directorate (TsVMU). Other documents in the Ministry of Defence and central state archives have also been examined. Casualty figures for the border troops and NKVD internal service troops were obtained from the KGB and the USSR Ministry of Internal Affairs. The number of casualties suffered by armies and fronts in the theatre of operations in the first months of the war, and in cases where casualty reports failed to arrive (during the fighting in border areas and during the Kiev, Crimean and Kharkov defensive operations and certain others), have had to be estimated by calculation.

Casualty numbers in the first days of the war were high, but because the tragedy was unexpected there was a breakdown in both administration and communications, which meant that HQs were not always able to keep a record of casualties. Therefore, in compiling this data the authors have used information on the listed personnel strength of the forces and formations which were routed by the enemy or which were encircled as territory was occupied, and also archive material from the German military command.

The authors' calculations show that in the years of the Great Patriotic War (including the campaign in the Far East against Japan in 1945), the Soviet armed forces' total irrecoverable demographic losses (killed or missing in action, POWs who failed to return, deaths from wounds, disease or as a result of accidents), including border troop and internal service troop casualties, came to 8,668,400: the army and navy lost 8,509,300, the internal services lost 97,700, the border troops and state security services lost 61,400.

The figure does not include 939,700 servicemen listed as missing in action at the beginning of the war but who were called up again between 1942 and 1945 once territory which had been occupied was liberated, nor does it include 1,836,000 former servicemen who returned from captivity after the end of the war. These 2,775,700 servicemen are not included under total irrecoverable losses.

All irrecoverable losses for the Red Army, the navy and border and internal service troops are given in Table 56 (figures are in thousands).

'Unrecorded casualties' shown in section 3 of Table 56 are grouped together with 'missing in action' and are included with the casualty figures for those fronts and independent armies which did not submit reports in the third and fourth quarters of 1941. They have been grouped together with the extensive category of 'missing in action' because full information on the fate of several of formations and forces which found themselves encircled or defeated in the unequal battles is not available. These figures have been calculated and are not entirely accurate, although on the whole they do give a true picture of the scale of losses in the first months of the war.

Table 56. Irrecoverable Losses for the Red Army, Navy and Border and Internal Service Troops, 1941–45 (in thousands)

	Loss category	Total	Comprising:		
			Red Army and Navy	Border troops*	Internal service troops
1	Killed in action, died of wounds during evacuation (based on reports from troops)	5,226.8	5,187.2	18.9	20.7
	Died in hospital of wounds (based on TsVMU MO figures)	1,102.8	1,100.3		2.5
	Total	6,329.6	6,287.5	18.9	23.2
2	Died of disease, as result of incident or accident, sentenced to be shot (non-combat losses)	555.5	541.9	7.1	6.5
3	Missing in action, POWs (based on reports from troops and figures from repatriation organisations)	3,396.4	3,305.6	22.8	68
	Unrecorded casualties from first months of war: killed, missing in action at time when reports not received from fronts and armies (taken from individual archive documents including those of German military command)	1,162.6	1,150	12.6	
	Total	4,559	4,455.6	35.4	68
	Total losses during war	11,444.1	11,285	61.4	97.7
Not included in casualty figures	Servicemen who were encircled or missing in action in occupied areas who were reconscripted once areas liberated	939.7			
	Returned from captivity at end of war (based on figures from repatriation organisations)	1,836			
	Total	2,775.7			
	Actual number of irrecoverable losses (from listed strength)	8,668.4	8,509.3	61.4	97.7
	Plus reservists captured by the enemy after being conscripted but before being taken on strength	500.0			

* Including state security service organs and troops.

Table 56 shows that the actual number of irrecoverable (demographic) losses was 8,668,400. However, from a military-operational point of view, taking into account missing in action and POWs, 11,444,100 servicemen were put permanently out of action in the course of the war.[2] Henceforth, in order to make calculations and estimates as accurate as possible, when comparing and analysing the scale of losses by quarter-year, year, phase and campaign of the war, strategic operation, front, fleet, etc., the higher figure which reflects actual losses during the war has been taken. All subsequent calculations of numbers and percentages of casualties reflect this.

The proportion of irrecoverable losses by category is shown in Table 57.

Table 57. Total Irrecoverable Losses for the Red Army and Navy in the War with Germany (22 June 1941–9 May 1945) and with Japan (9 August– 2 September 1945)

Loss category	No	% of losses
Killed in action, died during casualty evacuation	5,187,190	46
Died in hospital of wounds	1,100,327	9.8
Died of disease or as result of incident or accident, sentenced to be shot (non-combat losses)	541,920	4.8
Missing in action, POWs (including unrecorded casualties from first months of war)	4,455,620	39.4
Total irrecoverable losses (excluding border and internal service troops)	11,285,057	100

If one looks at casualty numbers in the war with Japan alone, the proportion is rather different. In the 25 days of fighting in the Far East, of the 12,031 casualties sustained by the three eastern fronts and the Pacific Fleet, 80% were killed in action or died of wounds.

Table 58. Casualties in the War with Japan (9 August–2 September 1945)

Loss category	No	% of losses
Killed in action, died during casualty evacuation	9,780	81.3
Died of disease or as result of accident (non-combat losses)	1,340	11.1
Missing in action	911	7.6
Total irrecoverable losses	12,031	100

Table 59. Total Irrecoverable Losses in the Navy during the War with Germany (22 June 1941–9 May 1945) and with Japan (9 August–2 September 1945)

Loss category	No	% of losses
Killed in action, died during casualty evacuation	47,699	30.8
Died of disease or as result of accident (non-combat losses)	11,807	7.6
Missing in action, POWs	95,265	61.6
Total irrecoverable losses	154,771	100

The nature of the job performed by the navy is reflected in the relative number of losses in each category. Whereas the largest number of ground force casualties were killed in action or died of wounds, in the navy there were twice as many missing in action as killed. These were mainly ships' and aircraft crews who failed to return from missions and whose fate is unknown.

In conclusion to this analysis of total irrecoverable losses, it should be noted that in preparing this book the authors also studied sources such as military commissariats' record books, where incoming information on servicemen who were killed in action, who died or who were listed as missing was recorded. These list 12,400,900 names,

956,800 more than the number determined on the basis of reports from the field (11,444,100). Our research has shown that this discrepancy is explained by the 'double reporting' of casualties in cases when two or more notices concerning the same person who had been killed in action, died or been listed as missing were sent to different military commissariats (on inquiries being made by relatives when they moved or were evacuated).

Moreover, all incoming notices were entered in the record books of the military commissariats (in districts where servicemen were called up or their relatives lived), including information on those serving in the people's militia, in partisan detachments or in special formations coming under different departments, reports on whose numerical strength and casualty numbers were not submitted to the General Staff. Furthermore, the books were not amended when servicemen who had been considered missing in action were subsequently called up again in areas which had been liberated, or if they returned from prison camps after the war.

For these reasons the casualty figures recorded by the military commissariats were inflated, and therefore the authors have taken only the reports from the field and other archive documents as the basis for their research.

SICK AND WOUNDED

According to reports from the fronts, fleets, independent armies and flotillas, there were 18,344,148 sick and wounded on the Soviet side, of whom 15,205,592 were wounded or sustained burns and concussion, 3,047,675 were sick and 90,881 suffered from frostbite. However, the military medical statistics show the actual scale of these losses to be significantly higher (see Table 60).

Table 60. Sick and Wounded

| | | Comprising | |
| | | Wounded, concussion, burns and frostbite cases | Sick |
Year of war	Losses		
1941 (in 6 months)	2,118,666	1,712,981	405,685
1942	5,573,484	3,625,351	1,948,133
1943	6,299,955	4,124,093	2,175,862
1944	5,901,524	3,520,203	2,381,321
1945	2,433,276	1,702,965	730,311
Total	22,326,905	14,685,593	7,641,312

As can be seen from Tables 60 and 69, most of the large number of sick and wounded recorded by military medical establishments were in fact sickness cases. The figure is 4,593,600 higher than in the reports from the field. This is explained by the fact that the sick and wounded figures include all sick personnel, including those admitted to treatment facilities from forces which did not take part in the fighting, from troop convoys and sub-units of reinforcements en route to the front, and also from military formations coming under civilian departments, formations and units of the people's militia, partisan detachments and other units and services, reports on whose numerical strength and casualties were not submitted to the General Staff.

The discrepancy in the number of wounded, concussion and frostbite cases (of whom there were 610,900 more listed in the reports from the field than recorded by the hospitals) may be because a substantial number of wounded remained with their units after being treated at regimental or divisional medical aid posts and were not taken off the unit's roll.

When calculating and analysing the number of sick and wounded it must be borne in mind that a large number of servicemen were wounded or concussed on between two and seven occasions while serving at the front, and as a result appear in casualty reports more than once.

As has already been mentioned, it is possible that double counting occurred not only of wounded but of battle casualties in general. If, for example, a serviceman returned to duty after being wounded but was later killed, his name would appear twice on the lists of battle casualties, first on the lists of wounded, then on the lists of fatalities. The following figures give a full picture of the situation.

As of 1 October 1945 there were over a million Red Army servicemen who remained in the ranks after having been wounded several times (see Table 61).

Table 61. Number of Wounded Red Army Servicemen

No of times wounded	No of servicemen wounded				Times recorded	Included in the number of wounded
	Officers	Sergeants	Men	Total		
Twice	135,352	230,164	374,646	740,162	×2	1,480,324
3 times	64,613	106,698	137,762	309,073	×3	927,219
4 times	23,104	35,119	40,780	99,003	×4	396,012
5 times	7,864	10,759	11,334	29,957	×5	149,785
6 times	2,496	3,395	3,234	9,125	×6	54,750
7 or more times	1,226	1,552	1,200	3,978	×7	27,846
Total	234,655	387,687	568,956	1,191,298		3,035,936
Wounded once	242,422	398,839	836,318	1,477,579		

As can be seen from the table, the 1,191,298 servicemen who were wounded more than once appear in the casualty figures as 3,035,936 cases, i.e. on average each of them was included on the lists of wounded 2.5 times. In so far as probably only a small number of those who were wounded in battle more than once still remained in the ranks by 1 October 1945, it may be assumed that in fact the number of servicemen wounded in the course of the war was considerably lower than 15,205,592. This applies equally to the number who fell sick.

The figures show that of the number of sick, wounded and frostbite cases admitted to medical establishments for treatment right through the war, 72% returned to duty, 20.8% were declared unfit for service and discharged from the army or sent on long-term sick leave, while about 7.5% died. Those who died in hospital were listed both under 'sick and wounded' and under 'total irrecoverable losses'.

Table 62 gives an idea of the number of sick and wounded, with a breakdown by category and by outcome of treatment for the period 1941–45, including the war with Japan.

Table 62. Numbers of Sick and Wounded by Category

Loss category and outcome of treatment	No	%
Wounded, concussion, burns and frostbite cases	14,685,593	100
Of these:		
returned to active duty	10,530,750	71.7
discharged and taken off strength or sent on sick leave	3,050,733	20.8
died[1]	1,104,110	7.5
Sick	7,641,312	100
Of these:		
returned to active duty	6,626,493	86.7
discharged and taken off strength or sent on sick leave	747,425	9.8
died[2]	267,394	3.5
Sick and wounded, total	22,326,905[3]	100
Of these:		
returned to active duty	17,157,243	76.9
discharged and taken off strength or sent on sick leave	3,798,158	17
died	1,371,504	6.1

1. Included with irrecoverable combat losses under 'died in hospital from wounds'.
2. Included with irrecoverable non-combat losses.
3. Henceforth calculations of the scale of losses by year, phase of the war, strategic operation and front will be based on the number of sick and wounded recorded in reports from the field (18,344,148).

An analysis of over 14 million case histories of wounded personnel has revealed information on the incidence of wounds to different parts of the body. See Table 63.

Table 63. Incidence of Wounds to Different Parts of the Body

Part of the body	Wounded	
	No of men	%
Skull	773,500	5.4
Eyes	214,861	1.5
Face	501,342	3.5
Neck	157,565	1.1
Chest	1,289,166	9
Stomach	444,046	3.1
Spine	143,241	1
Pelvis	630,259	4.4
Genitals	28,648	0.2
Upper limbs	5,042,074	35.2
Lower limbs	5,099,369	35.6
Total	14,324,071	100

The average amount of time spent in medical service facilities by sick and wounded personnel is shown in Table 64.

Table 64. Average Time Spent in Medical Service Facilities by Sick and Wounded Personnel

Category of wounded or sick	Average number of days spent in medical service facilities
Wounded	76.4
Concussed	49.4
Suffered hidden combat injuries (broken bones etc.)	69.4
Burns cases	51.8
Frostbite cases	89
Sick	34.5

The huge number of sick and wounded is an indication of how hard the job of the medical services was, both at the front and in the rear. Over 22 million men and commanders from the army and navy passed through their hands. Thanks to them, over 17 million servicemen who fell sick or were injured in battle were able to return to duty, over 10.5 million wounded returning to fight the enemy after treatment.

The Colonel-General of the medical service, Ye. I. Smirnov, who was head of the Red Army Main Military Medical Administration during the war, is right when he states in his book *Frontovoe miloserdie* (*Medical Care at the Front*) that 'from being a care service for those injured in battle and for the sick as in previous wars, military medicine became one of the main sources of reinforcements for the field army, providing soldiers and officers with combat experience who were able to return to duty after treatment'.

The country placed a high value on the work of the medical profession. Eight medical battalions and 39 military hospitals were awarded orders, over 116,000 doctors, medical assistants, nurses and medical auxiliaries were awarded either orders or medals and 43 doctors were awarded the title Hero of the Soviet Union.

NUMERICAL STRENGTH AND LOSSES

In reckoning up total army and navy losses we see that in all phases of the war there were a large number of casualties who had to be replaced promptly and in equal numbers.

Millions of people were called up to replace casualties, make up new formations and, from 1943 until the end of the war, maintain the total strength of the armed forces at 11.5 million, including 6.5 million with the fighting troops (operational fleet). This was necessary primarily in order to provide men for active combat operations on the different fronts, to form a specific grouping for the Far East, to cover the state borders in Central Asia and the Trans-Caucasus and also to bring reserve and training units up to full strength in military districts in the interior where drafts of reinforcements were undergoing intensive training for the front.

The war had a devastating effect on various aspects of life in the country, especially on the economy. A significant proportion of the working population was taken out of jobs in industry, which meant that workers, especially qualified ones, had to be sought for military production and other branches of the economy. The very difficult task of redistributing human resources between the army and the economy was embarked upon, but the first priority was to bring front-line troops up to prescribed strength and to replace casualties.

The figures in Table A, showing the increase in personnel strength of the Red Army and Navy in the Great Patriotic War, reflect the displacement of a vast mass of people.

Table A. Use of Human Resources Called Up (Mobilised) during the Great Patriotic War, 1941–45 (in thousands)

Numerical strength at start of war:	
—army and navy	4,826.9
—formations coming under other departments on People's Defence Commissariat ration strength	74.9
Called up/mobilised during war (excluding those called up twice)	29,574.9
Total drafted during war into army, navy (including those already serving before war), formations coming under other departments or for work in industry	34,476.7
Number lost during war (total):	21,636.9
—killed in action, died of wounds, disease, in accidents, committed suicide, shot after court martial	6,885.1
—missing in action, POWs (including 500,000 reservists called up but taken prisoner before being taken on strength)	5,059.0
—sent on sick leave (no who became invalids: 2,576,000)	3,798.2
—transferred to work in industry, local AA defence and sub-units of armed guards	3,614.6
—sent to bring up to strength troops and organs of NKVD and formations coming under civilian departments	1,174.6
—transferred to Polish, Czechoslovak or Romanian units and formations	250.4
—imprisoned after sentencing	436.6
—discharged for various reasons	206.0
—not found after deserting, becoming detached from troop convoy or missing in military districts in interior	212.4
Remaining in army and navy after end of war:	12,839.8
—on active service	11,390.6
—in hospital undergoing treatment	1,046.0
—in formations coming under civilian departments on People's Commissariat of Defence ration strength	403.2

At the beginning of the war (as of 22 June 1941) there were 4,826,907 servicemen on the Red Army and navy roll. Also on People's Commissariat for Defence ration strength were 74,945 servicemen and military construction workers who were serving in formations which came under civilian departments.

In the four years of the war a further 29,574,900[3] men were mobilised (excluding those who were called up for a second time), while altogether, including regular personnel, 34,476,700 men were drafted into the army, navy and military formations coming under other departments. In other words, millions of the country's most active and able-bodied citizens were mobilised, equal in number to the entire population of Denmark, the Netherlands, Norway, Sweden and Finland combined. In order to give a better idea of the numbers involved, suffice it to say that over half of all manual workers, white collar workers and collective farmers[4] employed in production and in non-industrial branches of the economy were drafted into the army, over two million of them being called up twice.

What use was made of this large section of the country's population? Of the 34,476,700 men who donned military uniform during the war, over one-third annually were available for duty (10.5–11.5 million were on the roll). Half of these (5.0–6.5 million) served with the fighting troops, i.e. fought at the front against the Germans.

During the war a total of 21.7 million men were lost or left the armed forces for various reasons, which represents 62.9% of all those who were called up and who served in the forces. Over half of these were irrecoverable losses.

Table 65.

| | | | % |
| | | | |
Loss category	Total, 000s	of losses	of total number called up
Killed in action, died of wounds or disease, as result of accident etc.	6,885.1	31.7	19.9
Missing in action, POWs	4,559	21	13.2

In addition in the initial phase of the war the enemy captured about 500,000 reservists who had been called up but had not yet been taken on strength (1.5% of the total number called up).

The breakdown for other personnel who left the armed forces is given in Table 66.

Table 66. Other Personnel who Left the Armed Forces

| | | | % |
| | | | |
Loss category	Personnel, 000s	of losses	of total number called up
Invalided out	3,798.2	17.5	11
Of these, permanently disabled	2,576	11.9	7.5
Transferred to work in industry or to military formations coming under other departments	3,614.6	16.7	10.5
Sentenced by court martial	994.3[1]	4.6	2.9
Including those sentenced for desertion	376.3		

1. Of these, 422,700 had the carrying out of their sentences postponed until the end of the war and were sent to join penal sub-units at the front.

The figure for those who left the armed forces also covers servicemen who were discharged from the army or navy because they were politically unreliable (these were mainly persons who were suspected at the time of treason, spying or sabotage, together with servicemen of various nationalities whose families were forcibly removed from their place of permanent residence to the eastern part of the country) and a significant number of deserters who were not caught. The listed strength of the troops (forces) did not include sick and wounded personnel undergoing hospital treatment (see Tables 60 and 64) or personnel who, when the records were being compiled, were en route to their place of duty in units and sub-units of reinforcements, including those returning from hospitals.

After the end of the war, as of 1 July 1945 11,390,600 remained on the armed forces' roll, 403,200 in military formations which came under other departments who were on People's Commissariat of Defence ration strength and 1,046,000 who were in hospital.

GENERAL APPRAISAL OF THE SCALE OF LOSSES

To return to an analysis of total army and navy losses, it should be noted that the statistical material available means that losses by year and phase of the war, by campaign, strategic operation, major battle and individual engagement, can be assessed accurately from a military-operational point of view.

An objective picture of the scale of Soviet losses during the war may be obtained from a careful examination of Table 69. Cold statistics serve as a reminder of the first heroic, tragic days of the war and of the position those defending the country were in during the memorable year of 1941: the heavy fighting against a more numerous and better-armed enemy on the country's borders, the defence of the Brest fortress, the first successful counter-attacks and the desperate attempts to break out from encirclement or from captivity. In the six months and nine days of 1941 there were 4,473,820 casualties. Of these, 465,400 were killed in action or died during casualty evacuation, 101,500 died in hospital of wounds, 235,300 died of disease, as a result of accident, etc., 2,335,500 were missing in action or prisoners of war, 1,256,400 were wounded or sustained concussion, 66,100 fell sick and 13,600 suffered from frostbite. A particularly high proportion were missing in action or prisoners of war (52.2% of total losses).

It cannot be said that any one year was harder or easier than another for the troops. The number of irrecoverable losses in 1942 was also considerable, a conclusion reinforced by the figures in the table. Organised resistance by the Soviet Army was growing as the Nazi troops continued their offensive, while the enemy suffered his first major defeat at Moscow. The intensity of the fighting is reflected in the number of losses for that year—3,258,200 irrecoverable losses and 4,111,100 sick and wounded.

The quarterly casualty figures in subsequent years of the war reflect the scale of the major battles fought by the Red Army in driving out the Nazi invaders.

Table 67. Red Army and Navy Losses in the Great Patriotic War, 1941–45, by Rank, Year and Quarter-Year

Period	Irrecoverable losses (killed or missing in action, died of wounds or disease, POWs, non-combat losses)					Sick and wounded (wounded, concussion, burns and frostbite cases, sick etc.)					Total				
	Officers	Sergeants	Men	Total	%	Officers	Sergeants	Men	Total	%	Officers	Sergeants	Men	Total	%
1941															
3rd quarter	142,043	310,955	1,676,679	2,129,677	18.9	48,192	81,560	557,874	687,626	3.8	190,235	392,515	2,234,553	2,817,303	9.5
4th quarter	61,040	137,002	809,954	1,007,996	8.9	42,748	84,257	521,516	648,521	3.5	103,788	221,259	1,331,470	1,656,517	5.6
Total for 1941	203,083	447,957	2,486,633	3,137,673	27.8	90,940	165,817	1,079,390	1,336,147	7.3	294,023	613,774	3,566,023	4,473,820	15.1
1942															
1st quarter	45,678	92,728	536,909	675,315	6	72,324	152,578	954,555	1,179,457	6.4	118,002	245,306	1,491,464	1,854,772	6.3
2nd quarter	60,185	135,006	647,707	842,898	7.5	45,684	94,036	566,927	706,647	3.9	105,869	229,042	1,214,634	1,549,545	5.2
3rd quarter	101,429	222,404	900,662	1,224,495	10.8	102,136	217,845	963,081	1,283,062	7	203,565	440,249	1,863,743	2,507,557	8.5
4th quarter	47,969	94,151	373,388	515,508	4.6	75,451	162,866	703,579	941,896	5.1	123,420	257,017	1,076,967	1,457,404	4.9
Total for 1942	255,261	544,289	2,458,666	3,258,216	28.9	295,595	627,325	3,188,142	4,111,062	22.4	550,856	1,171,614	5,646,808	7,369,278	24.9
1943															
1st quarter	63,169	141,781	521,764	726,714	6.4	128,416	250,600	1,046,676	1,425,692	7.8	191,585	392,381	1,568,440	2,152,406	7.2
2nd quarter	21,523	33,850	136,531	191,904	1.7	36,877	70,708	383,052	490,637	2.7	58,400	104,558	519,583	682,541	2.3
3rd quarter	77,262	192,069	534,525	803,856	7.1	149,714	460,238	1,450,853	2,060,805	11.2	226,976	652,307	1,985,378	2,864,661	9.7
4th quarter	40,451	107,259	442,245	589,955	5.3	107,769	254,326	1,205,845	1,567,940	8.5	148,220	361,585	1,648,090	2,157,895	7.3
Total for 1943	202,405	474,959	1,635,065	2,312,429	20.5	422,776	1,035,872	4,086,426	5,545,074	30.2	625,181	1,510,831	5,721,491	7,857,503	26.5
1944															
1st quarter	50,556	113,731	406,474	570,761	5	114,468	284,108	1,174,166	1,572,742	8.6	165,024	397,839	1,580,317	2,143,503	7.2
2nd quarter	38,815	66,035	239,408	344,258	3.1	70,665	165,666	728,877	965,208	5.3	109,480	231,701	968,608	1,309,466	4.4
3rd quarter	46,673	105,457	358,660	510,790	4.5	122,830	300,419	1,122,193	1,545,442	8.4	169,503	405,876	1,480,853	2,056,232	7
4th quarter	28,762	61,861	247,459	338,082	3	76,606	183,155	771,597	1,031,358	5.6	105,368	245,016	1,019,056	1,369,440	4.6
Total for 1944	164,806	347,084	1,252,001	1,763,891	15.6	384,569	933,348	3,796,833	5,114,750	27.9	549,375	1,280,432	5,048,834	6,878,641	23.2
1945															
1st quarter	49,661	121,812	386,048	557,521	4.9	125,932	339,103	1,129,600	1,594,635	8.7	175,593	460,915	1,515,648	2,152,156	7.3
2nd quarter	23,502	48,502	171,292	243,296	2.2	52,480	123,697	441,878	618,055	3.4	75,982	172,199	613,170	861,351	2.9
Total for 1945	73,163	170,314	557,340	800,817	7.1	178,412	462,800	1,571,478	2,212,690	12.1	251,575	633,114	2,128,818	3,013,507	10.2
Total during war with Germany	898,718	1,984,603	8,389,705	11,273,026	99.9	1,372,292	3,225,162	13,722,269	18,319,723	99.9	2,271,010	5,209,765	22,111,974	29,592,749	99.9
Campaign in the Far East (09.08–02.09 1945)	1,470	3,568	6,993	12,031	0.1	2,019	7,123	15,283	24,425	0.1	3,489	10,691	22,276	36,456	0.1
Total during Great Patriotic War	900,188	1,988,171	8,396,698	11,285,057	100	1,374,311	3,232,285	13,737,552	18,344,148	100	2,274,499	5,220,456	22,134,250	29,629,205	100
%	7.98	17.62	74.40	100		7.49	17.62	74.89	100		7.68	17.62	74.70	100	

Notes

1. Losses in the period 22–30 June 1941 are included in the third quarter of 1941; losses between 1 April and 9 May 1945 and subsequently (in fighting against the remaining Nazi troops and various armed bands), and also deaths in hospital from wounds between May and July 1945, are included in the second quarter of 1945.

2. Acting officers who did not hold officer rank have been included with sergeants; manual and white collar workers are included with men.

3. 'Irrecoverable losses' includes all those who died of wounds or disease, both during evacuation and in hospital.

Total casualty figures for the army and navy during the Great Patriotic War, including the campaign in the Far East, were 11,285,000 irrecoverable losses and 18,344,000 sick and wounded (according to reports from the field).

Tables 67 and 68 give a breakdown of casualties by rank. Of the total number of casualties (100%), 7.68% were officers, 17.62% were sergeants and 74.7% men. The heaviest losses were among the last category.

Table 68. Correlation between Average Monthly Strength and Losses in the Red Army and Navy, by Rank

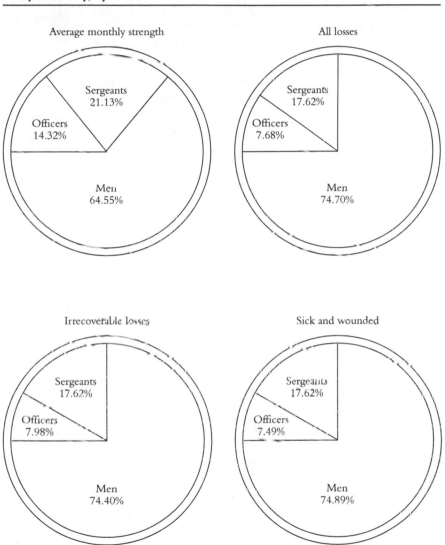

Table 69. Red Army and Navy Losses in the Great Patriotic War, 1941–45, by Loss

		Irrecoverable losses							
		Killed in action, died during casualty evacuation		Died in hospital of wounds		Died of disease, as result of accident etc. (non-combat losses)		Missing in action, POWs, incl. unrecorded casualties from first months	
	Period	No	%	No	%	No	%	No	%
1941	3rd quarter	236,372	8.4	40,680	1.4	153,526	5.5	1,699,099	60.3
	4th quarter	229,009	13.8	60,791	3.7	81,813	4.9	636,383	38.4
	Total for year	465,381	10.4	101,471	2.3	235,339	5.2	2,335,482	52.2
1942	1st quarter	413,681	22.3	45,651	2.4	34,328	1.9	181,655	9.8
	2nd quarter	232,388	15	55,761	3.6	26,294	1.7	528,455	34.1
	3rd quarter	416,569	16.6	69,470	2.8	53,689	2.1	684,767	27.3
	4th quarter	310,978	21.3	49,344	3.4	34,842	2.4	120,344	8.3
	Total for year	1,373,616	18.6	220,226	3	149,153	2	1,515,221	20.6
1943	1st quarter	486,912	22.6	65,474	3	30,200	1.4	144,128	6.8
	2nd quarter	100,967	14.8	53,254	7.8	15,231	2.2	22,452	3.3
	3rd quarter	562,604	19.6	111,125	3.9	14,413	0.5	115,714	4
	4th quarter	418,225	19.3	70,903	3.3	15,315	0.7	85,512	4
	Total for year	1,568,708	20	300,756	3.8	75,159	1	367,806	4.6
1944	1st quarter	414,298	19.3	95,021	4.4	8,779	0.4	52,663	2.5
	2nd quarter	206,193	15.8	86,901	6.6	12,787	1	38,377	2.9
	3rd quarter	374,817	18.2	75,017	3.6	15,491	0.8	45,465	2.2
	4th quarter	216,754	15.8	72,907	5.3	17,363	1.3	31,058	2.3
	Total for year	1,212,062	17.6	329,846	4.8	54,420	0.8	167,563	2.4
1945	1st quarter	410,066	19.1	78,017	3.6	17,979	0.8	51,459	2.4
	2nd quarter	147,577	17.1	70,011	8.1	8,530	1	17,178	2
	Total for year	557,643	18.5	148,028	4.9	26,509	0.9	68,637	2.3
Total during war with Germany		5,177,410	17.5	1,100,327	3.7	540,580	1.8	4,454,709	15.1
Campaign in Far East (09.08–02.09.1945)		9,780	26.8			1,340	3.7	911	2.5
Total during Great Patriotic War		5,187,190	17.5	1,100,327	3.7	541,920	1.8	4,455,620	15.1

Table 69, which gives casualty numbers by loss category, and the graph showing comparative losses by year, quarter-year and stage of the war (Table 70) reflect the situation at the front throughout the war. Casualty numbers increase or decrease strictly in line with the intensity of the fighting. For example, if one takes the line representing the percentage of prisoners of war and missing in action, the line's highest point is in 1941: the Soviet armed forces were at a severe disadvantage when Nazi Germany suddenly attacked, and military districts adjoining the frontier immediately lost the main bulk of their people. Because the recording of casualties was badly organised and often there was in any case no means of reporting them, superior HQs were unable to determine precisely the true state of affairs at the front. Units and

96

Category, Year and Quarter-Year

Sick and wounded (including those evacuated to hospitals)											
Total		Wounded, concussion and burns cases		Sick		Frostbite cases		Total		Total losses	
No	%	No	%	No	%	No	%	No	%	No	%
2,129,677	75.6	665,961	23.6	21,665	0.8	—	—	687,626	24.4	2,817,303	100
1,007,996	60.8	590,460	35.7	44,504	2.7	13,557	0.8	648,521	39.2	1,656,517	100
3,137,673	70.1	1,256,421	28.1	66,169	1.5	13,557	0.3	1,336,147	29.9	4,473,820	100
675,315	36.4	1,011,040	54.5	117,007	6.3	51,410	2.8	1,179,457	63.6	1,854,772	100
842,898	54.4	552,437	35.6	154,210	10	—	—	706,647	45.6	1,549,545	100
1,224,495	48.8	1,146,667	45.7	136,395	5.5	—	—	1,283,062	51.2	2,507,557	100
515,508	35.4	765,577	52.5	169,461	11.6	6,858	0.5	941,896	64.6	1,457,404	100
3,258,216	44.2	3,475,721	47.2	577,073	7.8	58,268	0.8	4,111,062	55.8	7,369,278	100
726,714	33.8	1,181,338	54.9	230,055	10.6	14,299	0.7	1,425,692	66.2	2,152,406	100
191,904	28.1	252,954	37.1	237,683	34.8	—	—	490,637	71.9	682,541	100
803,856	28.1	1,829,666	63.9	231,139	8	—	—	2,060,805	71.9	2,864,661	100
589,955	27.3	1,349,890	62.6	217,607	10.1	443	—	1,567,940	72.7	2,157,895	100
2,312,429	29.4	4,613,848	58.7	916,484	11.7	14,742	0.2	5,545,074	70.6	7,857,503	100
570,761	26.6	1,289,049	60.2	280,714	13.1	2,979	0.1	1,572,742	73.4	2,143,503	100
344,258	26.3	677,318	51.7	287,890	22	—	—	965,208	73.7	1,309,466	100
510,790	24.8	1,261,089	61.4	284,353	13.8	—	—	1,545,442	75.2	2,056,232	100
338,082	24.7	748,725	54.7	282,385	20.6	248	—	1,031,358	75.3	1,369,440	100
1,763,891	25.6	3,976,181	57.8	1,135,342	16.5	3,227	0.1	5,114,750	74.4	6,878,641	100
557,521	25.9	1,341,025	62.3	252,523	11.7	1,087	0.1	1,594,635	74.1	2,152,156	100
243,296	28.2	522,834	60.7	95,221	11.1	—	—	618,055	71.8	861,351	100
800,817	26.6	1,863,859	61.9	347,744	11.5	1,087	—	2,212,690	73.4	3,013,507	100
11,273,026	38.1	15,186,030	51.3	3,042,812	10.3	90,881	0.3	18,319,723	61.9	29,592,749	100
12,031	33	19,562	53.7	4,863	13.3	—	—	24,425	67	36,456	100
11,285,057	38.1	15,205,592	51.3	3,047,675	10.3	90,881	0.3	18,344,148	61.9	29,629,205	100

formations which had been encircled as territory was occupied were unable to report their situation. Many who were killed on the battlefield were listed as missing in action or were not listed at all.

Such was the overall picture in the first months of the war. Subsequently, when the situation at the front had stabilised somewhat, the number missing in action or taken prisoner fell substantially and by the first quarter of 1942 had been reduced to 10% of total losses. There then followed a number of unsuccessful defensive operations and the number of prisoners of war and missing in action again rose to almost 35%. By the end of the year the number in this category had fallen again, and it remained at a minimal level until the end of the war.

Table 70. Relative Casualty Numbers in the Red Army and Navy in the Great Patriotic War, by Loss Category, Year, Quarter-Year and Phase of the War (% of Total Losses)

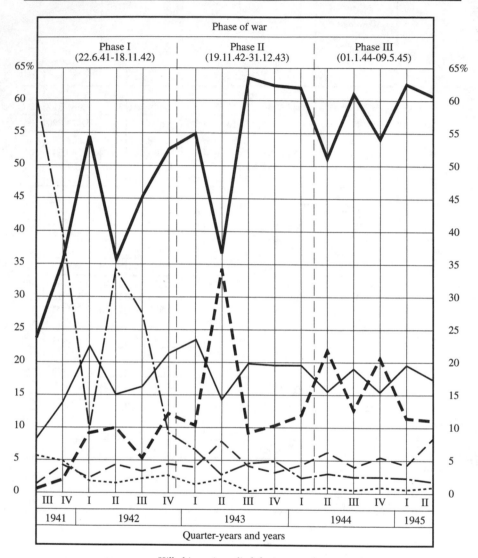

Killed in action, died during casualty evacuation

Died in hospital of wounds

Died of disease or as result of accident etc. (non-combat losses)

Missing in action, POWs, including unrecorded losses

Wounded, concussion and burns cases

Sick, frostbite cases

The number of wounded, concussion and burns cases also reflects events at the front. There was always a high proportion of these, but particularly so in summer 1943 when 65% of all losses were in this category. At this time, of course, there was fierce fighting at Kursk, where the Nazi Command was trying to exact revenge for Stalingrad, but their troops were nonetheless defeated. Both sides suffered heavy losses, the number of Soviet troops killed in action or dying of wounds reaching almost 20%.

Conversely, when the level of fighting was less there were fewer killed or wounded in action but the number of cases of sickness and frostbite increased. Numbers in this category reached their peak of about 35% in the second quarter of 1943, when there was something of a lull at the front. There was a similar pattern in 1944 and 1945.

Changes in the number of casualties in each loss category are given in the form of a graph (Table 70), and reflect the direct link between the number of losses and the situation at the front in different campaigns or stages of the war.

Table 71 shows the relative numbers of irrecoverable losses and sick and wounded, by year of the war.

Table 71. Relative Numbers of Irrecoverable Losses and Sick and Wounded, by Year

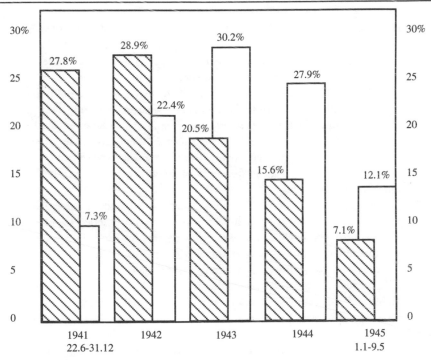

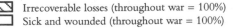 Irrecoverable losses (throughout war = 100%)
Sick and wounded (throughout war = 100%)

In 1941 the Soviet troops were fighting bitter defensive battles, forced to retreat and often finding themselves encircled. This explains the high proportion of killed and missing in action (27.8%) and the relatively low proportion of sick and wounded (7.3%). There were of course in reality a large number of sick and wounded, but it was not possible to record them properly. Many wounded remained on battlefields which were taken by the enemy and so were listed as missing in action. This explains the radical difference in length between the two columns.

The proportion altered somewhat in 1942. Irrecoverable losses remained high (28.9%), but the number of sick and wounded increased, even though at the beginning of the year a significant number of wounded were still listed as missing.

The proportion of irrecoverable losses was rather lower in 1943, mainly because there were fewer missing in action and prisoners of war. The evacuation of wounded was better organised and the recording of casualty numbers improved, including recording by the medical services. The proportion of sick and wounded increased to 30.2%.

The year 1944 was one of major offensive operations by the Red Army. In this year there were fewer irrecoverable losses, but sick and wounded exceeded irrecoverable losses by almost double. The situation was similar in 1945.

THE FIELD ARMY: NUMERICAL STRENGTH AND LOSSES

The fighting troops and operational fleet were those parts of the armed forces directly involved in fighting during the war. In accordance with a decree by the USSR Council of People's Commissars, the following were attached to the fighting troops for the duration of the Great Patriotic War: field headquarters of fronts (army groups) and HQ elements of fleets which were directing operations and the preparations for them; and formations, forces, units (ships), logistic and other units and services which formed part of those fronts and fleets while they were engaged in operations within the operational zone of the front or fleet, including on the coast at a distance of up to 100km from the shore line.

Air defence troops, formations and units of the long-range air force and other troops which were not part of operational fronts were only attached to the fighting troops (operational fleet) while they were directly involved in combat actions or giving combat support within the operational zones of fronts.

The fighting strength and numerical strength of the field army were not constant. They changed depending on the scale of the strategic task and the degree of intensity of the fighting. Thus at the start of the war the personnel strength of operational fronts stood at a little over 3 million, but by the end of 1944 it had increased to 6.7 million.

Table 72 gives a comparison of troop losses and the numerical strength of the field army.[5] It gives the average monthly strength for each quarter-year during the war and personnel losses for the same periods. By comparing these figures one can see what

Table 72. Average Monthly Listed Strength and Losses of Operational Fronts and Independent Armies for the Period 22 June 1941–9 May 1945

Period	Average monthly listed strength	Irrecoverable losses				Sick and wounded				All losses			
		No of men	% of losses	% of numerical strength All losses	% of numerical strength Average monthly losses	No of men	% of losses	% of numerical strength All losses	% of numerical strength Average monthly losses	No of men	% of losses	% of numerical strength All losses	% of numerical strength Average monthly losses
1941 3rd quarter	3,334,400	2,067,801	75.34	62.01	18.79	676,964	24.66	20.30	6.15	2,744,765	100	82.31	24.94
4th quarter	2,818,500	926,002	59.23	32.85	10.95	637,327	40.77	22.61	7.54	1,563,329	100	55.46	18.49
Total for the year	3,024,900	2,993,803	69.49	98.97	15.71	1,314,291	30.51	43.45	6.90	4,308,094	100	142.42	22.61
1942 1st quarter	4,186,000	619,167	34.56	14.79	4.93	1,172,274	65.44	28	9.33	1,791,441	100	42.79	14.26
2nd quarter	5,060,300	776,578	52.52	15.35	5.12	702,150	47.48	13.87	4.63	1,478,728	100	29.22	9.75
3rd quarter	5,664,600	1,141,951	47.21	20.16	6.72	1,276,810	52.79	22.54	7.51	2,418,801	100	42.70	14.23
4th quarter	6,343,690	455,800	32.75	7.19	2.40	936,031	67.25	14.76	4.92	1,391,831	100	21.95	7.32
Total for the year	5,313,600	2,993,536	42.28	56.34	4.69	4,087,265	57.72	76.92	6.41	7,080,801	100	133.26	11.10
1943 1st quarter	5,892,800	656,403	31.60	11.14	3.71	1,421,140	68.40	24.12	8.04	2,077,543	100	35.26	11.75
2nd quarter	6,459,800	125,172	20.97	1.94	0.65	471,724	79.03	7.30	2.43	596,896	100	9.24	3.08
3rd quarter	6,816,800	694,465	25.27	10.19	3.40	2,053,492	74.73	30.12	10.04	2,747,957	100	40.31	13.44
4th quarter	6,387,200	501,287	24.31	7.84	2.62	1,560,164	75.69	24.43	8.14	2,061,251	100	32.27	10.76
Total for the year	6,389,200	1,977,127	25.42	30.95	2.58	5,506,520	73.58	86.18	7.18	7,483,647	100	117.13	9.76
1944 1st quarter	6,268,600	470,392	23.11	7.51	2.51	1,565,431	76.89	24.97	8.32	2,035,823	100	32.48	10.83
2nd quarter	6,447,000	251,745	20.83	3.91	1.30	956,828	79.17	14.84	4.95	1,208,573	100	18.75	6.25
3rd quarter	6,714,300	430,432	21.82	6.41	2.13	1,541,965	78.18	22.97	7.66	1,972,397	100	29.38	9.79
4th quarter	6,770,100	259,766	20.19	3.84	1.28	1,026,645	79.81	15.16	5.05	1,286,411	100	19	6.33
Total for the year	6,550,000	1,412,335	21.72	21.57	1.80	5,090,869	78.28	77.72	6.48	6,503,204	100	99.29	8.28
1945 1st quarter	6,451,100	468,407	22.84	7.25	2.42	1,582,517	77.16	24.49	8.16	2,050,924	100	31.74	10.58
2nd quarter	6,135,300	153,226	21.13	2.66	2.05	609,231	78.87	3.93	7.63	772,457	100	12.59	9.68
Total for the year	6,330,880	631,633	22.37	9.98	2.32	2,191,748	77.63	34.62	8.05	2,823,381	100	44.60	10.37
Total for the war	5,778,500	10,008,434	35.49	173.20	3.72	18,190,693	64.51	314.80	6.77	28,199,127	100	488	10.49

Notes
1. Losses between 22 and 30 June 1941 are included in the third quarter of 1941, losses between 1 April and 9 May 1945 in the second quarter of 1945.
2. Sick and wounded who later died in hospital are included under 'sick and wounded'.

proportion of personnel was out of action each quarter throughout the war, both in numerical and percentage terms. The way these proportions changed over time is represented as a graph in Table 73.

The average monthly listed strength as shown in Table 72 has been calculated by adding the numerical strength for each month (normally as of the 1st of the month), quarter, year and the war as a whole and dividing it by the appropriate number of months.

The figures presented here on the whole give a true picture of the scale of total and average monthly losses. They show that there were thousands of casualties every day in the bitter fighting which took place.

Bearing in mind that front-line losses were constantly being replaced, listed strength was maintained as far as possible at a steady level, while the percentage of average monthly losses changed in accordance with the intensity of the fighting. If one adds together all losses during a particular phase of the war, their total number will often be considerably higher than the average listed strength of the field army (front, arm of service) for that period, sometimes several times higher. For example, if a company with an average monthly strength of 100 men suffered average monthly losses of 25%, over the year, if its listed strength remained the same (100%), total losses would be 300%.

The average monthly strength of the Western Front in 1941 was 501,120, for example,[6] while its irrecoverable losses for the year were 956,293.[7] In 1941 the Front therefore lost 190.8% of its listed strength, with 30.3% of its personnel killed or missing in action every month. Including sick and wounded, in the same period 259% of the Front's average monthly strength became casualties. Taking into account replacements, in 1941 41.1% of the Western Front's personnel were lost every month.

Table 72, which gives a summary of numerical strength and losses for the whole fighting army, shows that in 1941 alone the fronts' and independent armies' irrecoverable losses were 98.9% of average monthly strength and sick and wounded 43.5%. In all in 1941, 142.4% of personnel became casualties. In 1942 the fronts' irrecoverable losses decreased to 56.3%, while the number of sick and wounded increased to 76.9% of average monthly strength. In all in 1942, 133.2% of personnel became casualties.

In subsequent years total losses were somewhat less than at the start of the war. In all during the war with Germany, 488% of the fighting troops' average monthly strength became casualties; 173.2% of these were irrecoverable losses and 314.8% sick and wounded.

The graph showing the correlation between losses and numerical strength (Table 73) illustrates the sharp changes in the number of casualties in both categories during the course of the war. In the first months of 1941 there are more killed and missing in action than sick and wounded. Later, when the situation at the front stabilised and the recording of casualty numbers improved, irrecoverable losses decreased and the number of sick and wounded increased. As can be seen from the graph, the proportion of total losses to listed strength alters sharply, reflecting the intensity of fighting at the front. There is also a sharp fall in casualty numbers in the second quarter of 1943, when there was a lull in operations (1 April–30 June 1943).

Table 73. Proportion of Average Monthly Losses to Average Monthly Listed Strength in the Army's Active Combat Formations, by Quarter, Year and Stage of the War (%)

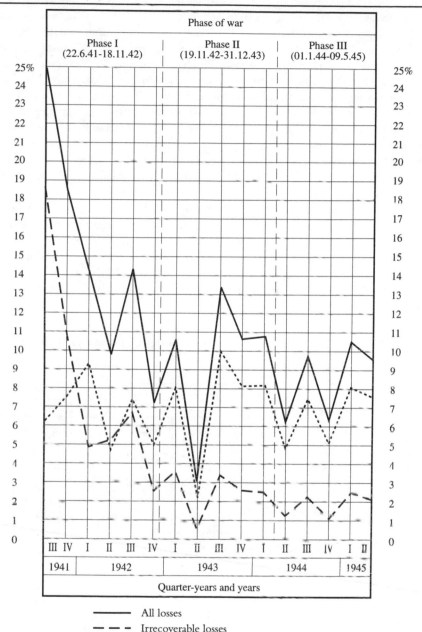

———— All losses

– – – Irrecoverable losses

‑‑‑‑‑‑‑ Sick and wounded

LOSSES BY PHASE OF THE WAR AND BY CAMPAIGN

From the strategic point of view the Great Patriotic War can be divided into three phases, with several campaigns in each. During phase one, which lasted from 22 June 1941 to 18 November 1942, there were three campaigns: the summer and autumn campaign of 1941, the winter campaign of 1941–42 and the summer and autumn campaign of 1942. In phase two, from 19 November 1942 to 31 December 1943, there were two campaigns: the winter campaign of 1942–43 and the summer and autumn campaign of 1943. In phase three, from 1 January 1944 to 9 May 1945, there were three campaigns: the winter and spring campaign of 1944, the summer and autumn campaign of 1944 and the campaign in Europe in 1945. In the war with Japan there was a separate Far Eastern campaign. Thus during the war the Soviet armed forces conducted nine campaigns, of which seven were offensives. In terms of time, the latter accounted for 70% of all combat operations in the war with Germany and Japan.

Total casualty figures by phase and campaign of the war are given in Table 74 and show that the Soviet armed forces suffered the greatest number of casualties during phase one of the war (37.7% of total losses and 54.6% of irrecoverable losses for the entire war). The greatest number of irrecoverable losses occurred during the summer and autumn defensive campaigns of 1941 and 1942 (25.2% and 18.3% respectively), as fronts and armies retreated fighting deep into the interior of the country.

Table 74. Proportion of Red Army and Navy Losses by Phase and Campaign of the Great Patriotic War

Phase of war	Campaign	Casualties, in 000s					
		Irrecoverable losses		Sick and wounded		Total	
		No	%	No	%	No	%
First (22.06.41–18.11.42)	Summer–autumn (22.06–04.12.41)	2,841.9	25.2	1,145.8	6.2	3,987.7	13.5
		17.1	0.15	6.9	0.04	24	0.08
	Winter (05.12.41–30.04.42)	1,249	11.1	1,602.7	8.7	2,851.7	9.6
		8.5	0.08	10.9	0.06	19.4	0.07
	Summer–autumn (01.05–18.11.42)	2,064.1	18.3	2,258.5	12.3	4,322.6	14.6
		10.2	0.09	11.2	0.06	21.4	0.07
	Total during phase one	6,155	54.6	5,007	27.2	11,162	37.7
		12	0.11	9.7	0.05	21.7	0.07
Second (19.11.42–31.12.43)	Winter (19.11.42–31.03.43)	967.7	8.6	1,865.9	10.2	2,833.6	9.5
		7.3	0.06	14	0.08	21.3	0.07
	Strategic lull (01.04–30.06.43)	191.9	1.7	490.6	2.7	682.5	2.3
		2.1	0.02	5.4	0.03	7.5	0.03
	Summer–autumn (01.07–31.12.43)	1,393.8	12.3	3,628.8	19.8	5,022.6	17
		7.6	0.07	19.7	0.11	27.3	0.09
	Total during phase two	2,553.4	22.6	5,985.3	32.7	8,538.7	28.8
		6.3	0.06	14.7	0.08	20.9	0.07

Phase of war	Campaign	Casualties, in 000s					
		Irrecoverable losses		Sick and wounded		Total	
		No	%	No	%	No	%
Third (01.01.44–09.05.45)	Winter–spring (01.01–31.05.44)	801.5	7.1	2,219.7	12.1	3,021.2	10.2
		5.3	0.05	14.6	0.08	19.9	0.07
	Summer–autumn (01.06–31.12.44)	962.4	8.5	2,895	15.8	3,857.4	13
		4.5	0.04	13.5	0.07	18	0.06
	Campaign in Europe (01.01–09.05.45)	800.8	7.1	2,212.7	12.1	3,013.5	10.2
		6.2	0.05	17.2	0.09	23.4	0.08
	Total during phase three	2,564.7	22.7	7,327.4	40	9,892.1	33.4
		5.2	0.05	14.8	0.08	20	0.07
Total during war with Germany		11,273.1	99.9	18,319.7	99.9	29,592.8	99.9
		7.9	0.07	12.9	0.07	20.9	0.07
Campaign in Far East (09.08–02.09.45)		12	0.1	24.4	0.1	36.4	0.1
		0.5	—	0.97	—	1.5	—
Total during Great Patriotic War		11,285.1	100	18,344.1	100	29,629.2	100
		7.8	0.07	12.7	0.07	20.5	0.07

Note: The top number gives all losses, the lower number gives average daily losses.

In these campaigns there were over a million more killed or missing in action than sick and wounded. In later phases of the war the number of killed and missing in action decreased and was 2–2.5 times lower than the number of sick and wounded.

As for total casualties (irrecoverable losses and sick and wounded) in military campaigns, the greatest number was in the summer and autumn campaign of 1943 (17%) and the smallest number in the winter campaigns of 1941–42 and 1942–43 (9.6% and 9.5% of all losses during the war respectively).

Soviet troop and naval force losses were relatively small in the Far East campaign: in 25 days of fighting there were 36,400 casualties, of whom 12,000 were killed, died or were missing in action.

The figures for average daily losses merit particular attention. In the war with Germany, there were on average 20,869 casualties every day; about 8,000 of these represented irrecoverable losses. The highest daily losses were during the summer and autumn campaigns of 1941 (24,000) and 1943 (27,300).

LOSSES IN STRATEGIC OPERATIONS

In the course of the war the Soviet armed forces conducted various operations in order to achieve their operational and strategic goals. These operations represented a combination of battles, engagements and strikes by combined-arms forces which were coordinated and interconnected in their aim, purpose, timing and location and which were carried out simultaneously or consecutively at a given period of time. According to the scale of the action, the operations subdivide into strategic, army group and army operations and, according to the nature of the action, into offensive or defensive operations.

As a rule, strategic operations were made up of army group operations and army group operations of army operations. Each differed in scale and duration, the number of participating forces,[8] the size of the area covered, the distance advanced (or retreated, if the operation was defensive) and the rate of advance (retreat).

During the war the Soviet armed forces conducted over 50 strategic, about 250 army group and over 1,000 army operations. Some army and army group operations were carried out as part of strategic operations and some were carried out independently.

In the last war, 'strategic operation' meant one in which one of the most important tasks in an entire campaign or stage of a campaign in a strategic sector or theatre of operations was undertaken. In carrying out such operations it was usual to use troops from one or more fronts (army groups), long-range air force formations, air defence troops and, in maritime sectors, naval forces (flotillas).

As a rule the troops of several fronts were used for strategic operations. This was because it was not easy to accomplish a task of military and political importance in a strategic sector or theatre of operations with the forces of a single front. Therefore, this new form of strategic operation using several fronts was developed and successfully adopted: a front would carry out tasks of strategic importance, operating in one strategic or operational sector. Thus 82.3% of all strategic operations by Soviet troops were conducted by the combined forces of two or more fronts, 9.8% by the forces of one front and one fleet combined and only 7.9% by the forces of one front alone.

The tables which follow give not only casualty figures but also information on the scale of each operation and fighting strength and numerical strength at the start of the operation. This means that the outcome of different operations may be compared and evaluated.

An analysis of the casualty figures for specific strategic operations reveals that the greatest number of irrecoverable losses on the Soviet side were in defensive operations in the initial phase of the war, a total of 3,580,000 men or 31.8% of all irrecoverable losses during the war. 616,300 of these were during the Kiev operation, 486,200 during the Smolensk operation, 514,300 during the Moscow operation, 370,500 during the Voronezh-Voroshilovgrad operation and 323,800 during the Stalingrad defensive operation.

In the strategic defensive operations in phase two of the war, irrecoverable losses on the Soviet side were far fewer, for example 45,200 in the Kharkov defensive operation in March 1943 and 70,300 in the Kursk operation in July 1943.

In phase three of the war, the Soviet armed forces did not conduct any planned defensive operations apart from the Balaton army group defensive operation. In this operation total losses were 32,900, with irrecoverable losses of 8,500.

In strategic offensive operations a decline can be seen in the number of irrecoverable losses and an increase of 2–2.5 times in the number of sick and wounded. Thus in the Rzhev-Vyazma operation of 1942 there were irrecoverable losses of 272,300, with 504,600 sick and wounded (1:1.8); in the Stalingrad operation the figures were 154,900 and 330,900 (1:2.1) and in the Orel operation 112,500 and 317,400 (1:2.8) respectively. This change in the proportion of irrecoverable losses to sick and wounded is particularly marked in the offensive operations of phase three of the war. Thus in the Leningrad-Novgorod operation the ratio was 1:3, in the Lvov-Sandomierz operation it was 1:3.4, in the Baltic, Vistula-Oder and Berlin operations it was 1:3.5 in each case and in the Manchurian operation it was 1:2.

When looking at the scale of total losses in strategic operations, it should be borne in mind that this depended on the number of forces involved (fronts and armies) and on the duration of the operation. For example, as is shown in the tables, the highest casualty numbers were in the Dnieper-Carpathian (1,109,500), Byelorussian (765,800) and East Prussian (584,800) offensive operations. However, these operations did not have the highest daily casualty figures, rather the figures reflect the fact that they were long drawn out operations.

The tables relating to strategic operations give only the fighting and numerical strength at the start of each operation (that is, they exclude troops and drafts of reinforcements brought in during the operation). Casualty figures are given for all troops (forces) which took part in the operation concerned.

Table 75 gives the casualty figures for some of the army group operations, including unsuccessful ones, which influenced the course of the war.

Table 75. Casualty Figures for Selected Army Group Operations

No	Operation, dates, forces involved	Numerical strength at start of operation	Irrecoverable	Sick and wounded	Total	Average daily losses
	PHASE ONE OF WAR (22.06.41–18.11.42)					
1	Defensive operation in Moldavia (01.07–26.07.41). Southern Front	364,700	8,519	9,374	17,893	688
2	Defence of Odessa (05.08–16.10.41). Odessa defended area (Maritime Army, Black Sea Fleet)	34,500	16,578	24,690	41,268	565
3	Yelnya offensive operation (30.08–08.09.41). Reserve Front (24th Army)	103,200	10,701	21,152	31,853	3,185
4	Tikhvin defensive operation (16.10–18.11.41). Leningrad Front's 54th Army, 4th and 52nd Independent Armies	135,700	22,743	17,846	40,589	1,194
5	Crimean defensive operation (18.10–16.11.41). Maritime and 51st Independent Armies, Black Sea Fleet	235,600	48,438	15,422	63,860	2,129
6	Defence of Sevastopol (30.10.41–04.07.42). Sevastopol defended area (Black Sea Fleet, Maritime Army)	52,000	156,880	43,601	200,481	808

No	Operation, dates, forces involved	Numerical strength at start of operation	Losses			
			Irrecoverable	Sick and wounded	Total	Average daily losses
7	Lyuban offensive operation (07.01–30.04.42). Volkhov Front, Leningrad Front's 54th Army	325,700	95,064	213,303	308,367	2,705
8	Demyansk offensive operation (07.01–20.05.42). N.W. Front (1st Shock Army, 11th, 34th and 53rd Armies)	105,700	88,908	156,603	245,511	1,832
9	Bolkhov offensive operation (08.01–20.04.42). Bryansk Front	317,000	21,319	39,807	61,126	593
10	Toropets-Kholm offensive operation (09.01–06.02.42). N.W. Front's 3rd and 4th Shock Armies (from 21.01.42 transferred to Kalinin Front)	122,100	10,400	18,810	29,210	1,007
11	Barvenkovo–Lozovaya offensive operation (18.01–31.01.42). S.W. and Southern Fronts	204,000	11,095	29,786	40,881	2,920
12	Kerch defensive operation (08.05–19.05.42). Crimean Front, part of Black Sea Fleet	249,800	162,282	14,284	176,566	14,714
13	Battle of Kharkov (12.05–29.05.42). S.W. Front, Southern Front's 9th and 57th Armies	765,300	170,958	106,232	277,190	15,399
14	Operation to rescue Volkhov Front's 2nd Shock Army from encirclement (13.05–10.07.42). Volkhov Front's 2nd Shock Army and 52nd and 59th Armies	231,900	54,774	39,977	94,751	1,606
15	Rzhev-Sychevka offensive operation (30.07–23.08.42). Kalinin Front (29th and 30th Armies, 3rd Air Army); Western Front (20th and 31st Armies, 1st Air Army)	345,100	51,482	142,201	193,683	7,747
16	Sinyavino offensive operation (19.08–10.10.42). Leningrad Front (Neva operations Group, 13th Air Army); Volkhov Front (2nd Shock and 14th Air Armies, 8th Army), part of Baltic Fleet and Ladoga Flotilla	190,000	40,085	73,589	113,674	2,145
	PHASE TWO OF WAR (19.11.42–31.12.43)					
17	Velikiye Luki offensive operation (24.11.42–20.01.43). Kalinin Front (3rd Shock and 3rd Air Armies)	86,700	31,674	72,348	104,022	1,793
18	Krasnodar offensive operation (09.02–24.05.43)[1]. N. Caucasus Front	390,000	66,814	173,902	240,716	2,293
19	Demyansk offensive operation (15.02–28.02.43). N.W. Front	327,600	10,016	23,647	33,663	2,405

No	Operation, dates, forces involved	Numerical strength at start of operation	Irrecoverable	Sick and wounded	Total	Average daily losses
			Losses			
20	Rzhev-Vyazma offensive operation (02.03–31.03.43). Kalinin and Western Fronts	876,000	38,862	99,715	138,577	4,619
21	Mga offensive operation (22.07–22.08.43). Leningrad Front (67th Army, 13th Air Army); Volkhov Front (8th Army, 14th Air Army)	253,300	20,890	59,047	79,937	2,498
22	Bryansk offensive operation (01.09–03.10.43). Bryansk Front	530,000	13,033	43,624	56,657	1,717
23	Melitopol offensive operation (26.09–05.11.43). Southern (4th Ukrainian) Front	555,300	42,760	155,989	198,749	4,847
24	Nevel-Gorodok offensive operation (06.10–31.12.43). Kalinin (1st Baltic) Front: 3rd and 4th Shock, 11th Guards and 3rd Air Armies, 43rd Army	198,000	43,551	125,351	168,902	1,941
25	Zaporozhye offensive operation (10.10–14.10.43). S.W. Front (3rd and 8th Guards and 17th Air Armies, 12th Army)	150,500	3,443	14,265	17,708	3,542
26	Kerch-Eltingen amphibious operation (31.10–11.12.43). N. Caucasus Front (from 20.11.43: Independent Maritime Army), part of Black Sea Fleet and Azov Flotilla	150,000	6,985	20,412	27,397	652
27	Gomel-Rechitsa offensive operation (10.11–30.11.43). Byelorussian Front	761,300	21,650	66,556	88,206	4,200
28	Kiev defensive operation (13.11–22.12.43). 1st Ukrainian Front	730,000	26,443	61,030	87,473	2,187
	PHASE THREE OF WAR (01.01.44–09.05.45)					
29	Zhitomir-Berdichev offensive operation (24.12.43–14.01.44). 1st Ukrainian Front	831,000	23,163	76,855	100,018	4,546
30	Kalinkovichi-Mozyr offensive operation (08.01–30.01.44). Byelorussian Front	232,600	12,350	43,807	56,157	2,442
31	Korsun-Shevchenkovski offensive operation (24.01–17.02.44). 1st Ukrainian Front (27th and 40th Armies, 6th Tank and 2nd Air Armies, 2nd Ukrainian Front (52nd and 53rd Armies, 4th Guards, 5th Tank, 5th Air Armies)	336,700	24,286	55,902	80,188	3,208

No	Operation, dates, forces involved	Numerical strength at start of operation	Losses			Average daily losses
			Irrecover- able	Sick and wounded	Total	
32	Rogachev-Zhlobin offensive operation (21.02–26.02.44). Byelo- russian (from 24.02 1st Byelorussian) Front (3rd, 48th and 50th Armies, 16th Air Army)	232,000	7,164	24,113	31,277	5,213
33	Rezhitsa-Dvinsk offensive operation (10.07–27.07.44). 2nd Baltic Front	391,200	12,880	45,115	57,995	3,222
34	Pskov-Ostrov offensive operation (11.07–31.07.44). 3rd Baltic Front	258,400	7,663	25,951	33,584	1,599
35	Madona offensive operation (01.08– 28.08.44). 2nd Baltic Front, part of Baltic Fleet	390,000	14,669	50,737	65,406	2,336
36	Tartu offensive operation (10.08– 06.09.44). 3rd Baltic Front	272,800	16,292	55,514	71,806	2,564
37	Debrecen offensive operation (06.10– 28.10.44). 2nd Ukrainian Front	698,200	19,713	64,297	84,010	3,653
38	Goldap offensive operation (16.10– 30.10.44). 3rd Byelorussian Front	377,300	16,819	62,708	79,527	5,302
39	Lower Silesian offensive operation (08.02–24.02.45). 1st Ukrainian Front	980,800	23,577	75,809	99,386	5,846
40	Balaton defensive operation (06.03– 15.03.45). 3rd Ukrainian Front	465,000	8,492	24,407	32,899	3,290
41	Upper Silesian offensive operation (15.03–31.03.45). 1st Ukrainian Front	408,400	15,876	50,925	66,801	3,929
42	Moravska Ostrava offensive operation (10.03–05.05.45). 4th Ukrainian Front	317,300	23,964	88,657	112,621	1,976
43	Bratislava-Brno offensive operation (25.03–05.05.45). 2nd Ukrainian Front, Danube Flotilla	272,200	16,933	62,663	79,596	1,895

1. The length of the operation takes into account the time the North Caucasus Front was involved in combat operations until they reached the enemy's fortified line of defence (the 'blue line').

The Defensive Operation in Lithuania and Latvia
(Baltic Strategic Defensive Operation), 22 June–9 July 1941

The operation was conducted by the troops of North-Western Front and part of the Baltic Fleet forces. An additional 14 divisions and one brigade were brought in during the operation. It lasted 18 days. The fighting ranged over a front 350–450km wide. The Soviet troops retreated 400–450km.

Fighting Strength, Numerical Strength and Losses

Name of force, period involved in operation	Fighting strength and numerical strength of troops at start of operation		Losses during the operation				
	No of formations	Numerical strength	Irrecoverable losses	Sick and wounded	Total	Average daily losses
N.W. Front (whole period)	rifle divisions—19 motorised divisions—2 tank divisions—4 rifle brigades—1 airborne brigades—3 fortified areas—1	440,000	73,924	13,284	87,208	4,845
Baltic Fleet (part of; whole period)	—	58,000	1,278	—	1,278	71
Total	Divisions—25 Brigades—4 Fortified areas—1	498,000	75,202	13,284	88,486	4,916

Outcome of the operation. In repelling the sudden attack by superior enemy forces, the North-Western Front troops were forced to retreat into the interior amid heavy fighting, dispersing in different directions—into Estonia and eastwards to the River Velikaya. The Soviet troops, supported by the Baltic Fleet, put up a stubborn resistance. Fighting with courage and determination, they slowed the advance of Army Group North and inflicted considerable losses on its assault grouping.

The Defensive Operation in Byelorussia
(Byelorussian Strategic Defensive Operation), 22 June–9 July 1941

The operation was conducted by the troops of Western Front with support from the Pina Flotilla. An additional 45 divisions were brought in during the operation, which lasted 18 days. The fighting ranged over a front 450–800km wide. The Soviet troops retreated 450–600km.

Fighting Strength, Numerical Strength and Losses

Name of force, period involved in operation	Fighting strength and numerical strength of troops at start of operation		Losses during the operation				
	No of formations	Numerical strength	Irrecoverable losses	Sick and wounded	Total	Average daily losses
Western Front (whole period)	rifle divisions—24 cavalry divisions—2 motorised divisions—6 tank divisions—12 airborne brigades—3 fortified areas—8	625,000	341,012	76,717	417,729	23,207

111

Name of force, period involved in operation	Fighting strength and numerical strength of troops at start of operation		Losses during the operation			
	No of formations	Numerical strength	Irrecoverable losses	Sick and wounded	Total	Average daily losses
Pina Flotilla (whole period)	—	2,300	61	—	61	3
Total	Divisions—44 Brigades—3 Fortified areas—8	627,300	341,073	76,717	417,790	23,210

Outcome of the operation. In spite of tremendous sacrifices by the Red Army during this operation, it did not prove possible to contain the enemy troops. Attacks by superior enemy forces forced the Western Front troops to retreat eastwards. Nonetheless, they put up a stubborn resistance in the border areas, launching counterstrikes and inflicting appreciable losses on Army Group Centre, the main Wehrmacht grouping, slowing its advance on Smolensk and Moscow. This enabled the Soviet High Command to deploy a second strategic echelon on the Western Dvina-Dnieper line.

The Defensive Operation in the Western Ukraine (Lvov-Chernovitsy Strategic Defensive Operation), 22 June–6 July 1941

The operation was conducted by the troops of South-Western Front, with an additional 12 divisions, six brigades and the headquarters of the 18th Army brought in during the operation. It lasted 15 days. The fighting ranged over a front 600–700km wide. The Soviet troops retreated 300–350km.

Fighting Strength, Numerical Strength and Losses

Name of force, period involved in operation	Fighting strength and numerical strength of troops at start of operation		Losses during the operation			
	No of formations	Numerical strength	Irrecoverable losses	Sick and wounded	Total	Average daily losses
SW Front (whole period)	rifle divisions—32 cavalry divisions—2 motorised divisions—8 tank divisions—16 airborne brigades—3 fortified areas—14	864,600	165,452	65,755	231,207	15,414
Southern Front's 18th Army (25.06–06.07.41)	—	—	6,871	3,516	10,387	866
Total	Divisions—58 Brigades—3 Fortified areas—14	864,600	172,323	69,271	241,594	16,106

Outcome of the operation. In the course of active fighting in the frontier regions and in intermediate defensive positions, the South-Western Front troops inflicted heavy losses on the enemy. They slowed the main enemy grouping's advance on Kiev with counterstrikes by the mechanised corps and combined-arms formations in the Dubno, Lutsk and Rovno areas, which meant that the Front was able to pull back its main forces and occupy defences in fortified areas on the old state border.

The Strategic Defensive Operation
in the Arctic and Karelia, 29 June–10 October 1941

The operation was conducted by the troops of the Northern Front (from 23 August 1941 split into Karelian and Leningrad Fronts) and the 7th Independent Army, supported by the Northern Fleet. In addition 10 divisions, five brigades and the White Sea Flotilla were brought in during the operation. It lasted 104 days. The fighting ranged over a front 800km wide. The Soviet troops retreated 50–150km.

The strategic defensive operation included a number of army group and army operations—by the Northern (Karelian) Front's 14th Army in the Murmansk and Kandalaksha sectors and by the 7th Independent Army on the Ladoga-Onega isthmus.

Fighting Strength, Numerical Strength and Losses

Name of force, period involved in operation	Fighting strength and numerical strength of troops at start of operation		Losses during the operation				
	No of formations	Numerical strength	Irrecoverable losses	Sick and wounded	Total	Average daily losses
Northern Front (29.06–23.08.41)	rifle divisions—8 tank divisions—1 rifle brigades—1 fortified areas—7	358,390	36,822	35,714	72,536	1,295
Karelian Front (23.08–10.10.41)	—	—	29,856	32,336	62,192	1,269
7th Independent Army (25.09–10.10.41)	Fighting strength, numerical strength and losses listed in reports from Northern and Karelian Front					
Part of Northern Fleet; White Sea Flotilla (01.09–01.10.41)	—	—	587	398	985	32
Total	Divisions—9 Brigades—1 Fortified areas—7	358,390	67,265	68,448	135,713	1,305

Outcome of the operation. The Soviet troops put up a stubborn defence, stopping the German and Finnish advance on Murmansk, Kandalaksha, Petrozavodsk and Svir and thwarting the enemy's plans to capture Murmansk and the Kirov railway and take Leningrad from the north and north-west.

The Kiev Strategic Defensive Operation, 7 July–26 September 1941

The operation was conducted by the troops of the South-Western Front and part of the Pinsk Flotilla. In addition, the Central Front's 21st Army, the Southern Front's 6th and 12th Armies and also the 37th, 38th and 40th Armies, newly formed as part of the South-Western Front, were brought in during the operation—in all, 28 divisions and four brigades. The operation lasted 82 days. Fighting ranged over a front 300km wide. The Soviet troops retreated 600km.

Fighting Strength, Numerical Strength and Losses

Name of force, period involved in operation	Fighting strength and numerical strength of troops at start of operation		Losses during the operation			
	No of formations	Numerical strength	Irrecoverable losses	Sick and wounded	Total	Average daily losses
S.W. Front (whole period)	rifle divisions—26 cavalry divisions—1 motorised divisions—4 tank divisions—13 airborne brigades—6 fortified areas—12	627,000	531,471	54,127	585,598	7,141
Central Front's 21st Army (10.08–30.08.41)	—	—	31,792	3,793	35,585	1,695
Southern Front's 6th and 12th Armies (20.08–26.09.41)	—	—	52,900	26,320	79,220	2,085
Part of Pina Flotilla (10.08–20.09.41)	—	—	141	—	141	3
Total	Divisions—44 Brigades—6 Fortified areas—12	627,000	616,304	84,240	700,544	8,543

Outcome of the operation. In over two and a half months of uninterrupted heavy fighting, the Soviet troops abandoned Kiev and a number of regions in the left-bank Ukraine (to the east of the Dnieper), incurring many casualties. However, the prolonged and stubborn defence put up by the South-Western Front's troops and the heavy losses inflicted on the Germans' Army Group South forced the enemy command to transfer troops away from Army Group Centre which was advancing on Moscow in the main sector. This played a major part in frustrating Hitler's plans for a blitzkrieg and a continuous offensive against Moscow.

The Leningrad Strategic Defensive Operation, 10 July–30 September 1941

The operation was conducted by the troops of the Northern Front (from 23 August 1941 Leningrad Front) and North-Western Front, supported by the Baltic Fleet. From 1 September 1941 the 52nd Independent Army also took part in the operation. An additional five army headquarters and 20 divisions were brought in during the operation.

The Leningrad strategic operation included a number of army group and army operations: the Tallin defensive operation, defensive operations in the western and south-western approaches to Leningrad and on the Karelian isthmus, counterstrikes by North-Western Front troops in the Soltsy area, at Staraya Russa and Kholm, and the Demyansk defensive operation.

The operation lasted 83 days. The fighting ranged over a front 450km wide. The Soviet troops retreated 270–300km. The operation marked the start of the heroic battle for Leningrad.

Fighting Strength, Numerical Strength and Losses

Name of force, period involved in operation	Fighting strength and numerical strength of troops at start of operation		Losses during the operation				
	No of formations	Numerical strength	Irrecoverable losses	Sick and wounded	Total	Average daily losses
Northern Front (10.07–23.08.41)	rifle divisions—7 tank divisions—2 motorised divisions—1 rifle brigades—1 fortified areas—5	153,000	40,491	15,044	55,535	1,234
N.W. Front (10.07–30.09.41)	rifle divisions—23 motorised divisions—4 tank divisions—5 rifle brigades—3 airborne brigades—3 fortified areas—3	272,000	96,953	47,835	144,788	1,744
Leningrad Front (23.08–30.09.41)	—	—	65,529	50,787	116,316	2,982
52nd Independent Army (01.09–30.09.41)	—	—	1,721	2,389	4,110	137
Baltic Fleet (whole period)	—	92,000	9,384	14,793	24,177	291
Total	Divisions—42 Brigades—7 Fortified areas—8	517,000	214,078	130,848	344,926	4,155

Outcome of the operation. Although they put up a stubborn defence, the Soviet troops were unable to stop the enemy advance in the distant approaches to Leningrad. The enemy succeeded in taking Estonia and much of the Leningrad region and breaking through towards the city. Their losses were heavy, however, and the German Command's assumption that they would be able to march on Leningrad unhindered and use the freed forces of Army Group North to advance on Moscow proved somewhat over-optimistic. By the end of September 1941 the front outside Leningrad had stablilised and the long battle for the city began. It lasted for over three years.

The Battle of Smolensk, 10 July–10 September 1941

The battle of Smolensk was a complex defensive and offensive operation conducted by the Soviet forces with the aim of preventing the enemy from breaking through to the strategic Moscow sector. In addition the headquarters of the Central, Reserve and Bryansk Fronts, nine army headquarters, 59 divisions and two brigades were brought in during the operation, which included a number of army group and army operations. These were the Smolensk defensive and offensive operations by the Western Front, the Western Front's offensive in the Bobruisk sector, the Gomel-Trubchevsk defensive operation by the Central Front and the Yelnya offensive by the Reserve Front.

The operation lasted 63 days. The fighting ranged over a front 600–650km wide and the Soviet troops retreated 200–250km.

Fighting Strength, Numerical Strength and Losses

Name of force, period involved in operation	Fighting strength and numerical strength of troops at start of operation		Losses during the operation			
	No of formations	Numerical strength	Irrecoverable losses	Sick and wounded	Total	Average daily losses
Western Front (10.07–10.09.41)	rifle divisions—49 motorised divisions—6 tank divisions—11 airborne brigades—2 fortified areas—6	579,400	309,959	159,625	469,584	7,454
Central Front (26.07–25.08.41)	—	—	79,216	28,009	107,225	3,459
Reserve Front (30.07–10.09.41)	—	—	45,774	57,373	103,147	2,399
Bryansk Front (16.08–10.09.41)	—	—	50,972	28,603	79,575	3,061
Pina Flotilla (10.07–10.09.41)	—	2,200	250	193	443	7
Total	Divisions—66 Brigades—2 Fortified areas—6	581,600	486,171	273,803	759,974	12,063

Outcome of the operation. Bloody defensive and offensive battles were fought, during which the Soviet troops succeeded in thwarting the Germans' plans for a continuous offensive against Moscow. Army Group Centre, the strongest German grouping, suffered very heavy losses and was forced to go over to the defensive, delaying their plans for an advance on Moscow by almost two months. The Battle of Smolensk played an important part in frustrating Hitler's plans for a blitzkrieg against the Soviet Union.

The Donbass-Rostov Strategic
Defensive Operation, 29 September–16 November 1941

The operation was conducted by the troops of the Southern Front and South-Western Front's 6th Army, supported by the Azov Flotilla. In addition the head-quarters of the 56th Independent Army and eight divisions were brought in during the operation.

The Donbass-Rostov strategic defensive operation included the Donbass and Rostov defensive army group operations. It lasted 49 days. The fighting ranged over a front 400–670km wide. The Soviet troops retreated 150–300km.

Fighting Strength, Numerical Strength and Losses

Name of force, period involved in operation	Fighting strength and numerical strength of troops at start of operation		Losses during the operation			
	No of formations	Numerical strength	Irrecoverable losses	Sick and wounded	Total	Average daily losses
Southern Front (29.09–16.11.41)	rifle divisions—20 cavalry divisions—3 fortified areas—1 tank brigades—4	491,500	132,014	15,356	147,370	3,007
S.W. Front's 6th Army (29.09–16.11.41)	rifle divisions—3 cavalry divisions—2 tank brigades—2	45,000	11,201	1,862	13,063	267
Azov Flotilla (29.09–01.11.41)	—	5,100	98	45	143	4
Total	Divisions—28 Brigades—6 Fortified areas—1	541,600	143,313	17,263	160,576	3,277

Outcome of the operation. In spite of heavy defensive fighting, the Southern Front troops did not succeed in stopping the enemy advance. They were forced to abandon the south-western Donbass and retreat to the approaches to Rostov. The German Command's plan to encircle and destroy the Southern Front troops and press home their attack on the Caucasus was unsuccessful, however. The Germans suffered heavy losses and, finding themselves in an unfavourable operational position, went over to the defensive. The Soviet Command took advantage of this to go over to the counter-offensive at Rostov.

The Moscow Strategic Defensive
Operation, 30 September–5 December 1941

The operation was conducted by the troops of the Western, Reserve, Bryansk and Kalinin Fronts. In addition, the headquarters of the Kalinin Front, of the 1st Shock Army and of the 5th, 10th and 16th Armies, together with 34 divisions and 40 brigades, were brought in during the operation.

During the Moscow strategic defensive operation, the Orel-Bryansk, Vyazma, Kalinin, Mozhaisk-Maloyaroslavyets, Tula, Klin-Solnechnogorsk and Naro-Fominsk army group defensive operations were carried out.

The operation lasted 67 days. The fighting ranged over a front 700–1,110km wide and the Soviet troops retreated 250–300km. The operation was the first stage in the battle for Moscow.

Fighting Strength, Numerical Strength and Losses

Name of force, period involved in operation	Fighting strength and numerical strength of troops at start of operation		Losses during the operation				
	No of formations	Numerical strength	Irrecoverable losses	Sick and wounded	Total	Average daily losses
Western Front (01.10–05.12.41)	rifle divisions—31 motor rifle divisions—2 cavalry divisions—3 rifle brigades—1 tank brigades—4 fortified areas—2	558,000	254,726	55,514	310,240	4,700
Reserve Front (01.10–12.10.41)	rifle divisions—28 cavalry divisions—2 tank brigades—5	448,000	127,566	61,195	188,761	15,730
Bryansk Front (30.09–10.11.41)	rifle divisions—25 cavalry divisions—4 tank divisions—1 tank brigades—4	244,000	103,378	6,537	109,915	2,617
Kalinin Front (20.10–05.12.41)	—	—	28,668	20,695	49,363	1,050
Total	Divisions—96 Brigades—14 Fortified areas—2	1,250,000	514,338	143,941	658,279	9,825

Outcome of the operation. There was heavy fighting in the near and distant approaches to Moscow during which the Soviet troops stopped the advance of the main German grouping, Army Group Centre, which was heavily defeated. This paved the way for going over to the counter-offensive and defeating the enemy at Moscow.

The Tikhvin Strategic Offensive Operation
(Tikhvin Counter-Offensive), 10 November–30 December 1941

The operation was conducted by the 4th and 52nd Independent Armies (from 17 December 1941 they were incorporated into the newly formed Volkhov Front), the Leningrad Front's 54th Army and the North-Western Front's Novgorod Army Group. In addition, the headquarters of the Volkhov Front and of the 59th Army, and 16 divisions and two brigades, were brought in during the operation.

It lasted 51 days. The fighting ranged over a front 300–350km wide. The Soviet troops advanced 100–120km, the average rate of advance being 2–2.5km a day.

Fighting Strength, Numerical Strength and Losses

Name of force, period involved in operation	Fighting strength and numerical strength of troops at start of operation		Losses during the operation				
	No of formations	Numerical strength	Irrecoverable losses	Sick and wounded	Total	Average daily losses
Leningrad Front's 54th Army (whole period)	rifle divisions—4 tank divisions—1 rifle brigades—2 tank brigades—2	55,600	6,065	11,486	17,551	344
4th Independent Army (whole period)	rifle divisions—6 cavalry divisions—1 tank divisions—1	62,700	8,916	16,018	24,934	489
52nd Independent Army (whole period)	rifle divisions—4	42,660	871	1,769	2,640	52
N.W Front's Novgorod Army Group (whole period)	rifle divisions—2 tank divisions—1	31,990	2,072	1,704	3,776	74
Total	Divisions—20 Brigades—4	192,950	17,924	30,977	48,901	959

Outcome of the operation. The Soviet troops defeated 10 enemy divisions, liberated several important areas and completely thwarted the German Command's plans to isolate Leningrad. The way was paved for continuing the advance in the North-Western sector and going over to the counter-offensive at Moscow.

The Rostov Strategic Offensive Operation
(Rostov Counter-Offensive), 17 November–2 December 1941

The operation was conducted by the troops of the Southern Front and the 56th Independent Army (from 23 November 1941 incorporated into the Southern Front). An additional five brigades were brought in during the operation.

The operation lasted 16 days and the fighting ranged over a front 140–180km wide. The Soviet troops advanced 60–80km, the rifle formations' average rate of advance being 4–5km a day.

Fighting Strength, Numerical Strength and Losses

Name of force, period involved in operation	Fighting strength and numerical strength of troops at start of operation		Losses during the operation				
	No of formations	Numerical strength	Irrecoverable losses	Sick and wounded	Total	Average daily losses
Southern Front (whole period, minus the 12th Army)	rifle divisions—16 cavalry divisions—5 tank brigades—7	262,500	11,163	12,758	23,921	1,495
56th Independent Army (whole period)	rifle divisions—5 cavalry divisions—5 tank brigades—1	86,500	4,101	5,089	9,190	574
Total	Divisions—31 Brigades—8	349,000	15,264	17,847	33,111	2,069

Outcome of the operation. In the course of the offensive the Germans' Army Group South was heavily defeated by the Soviet troops. Its formations were driven back from Rostov to the River Mius and prevented from breaking through to the Caucasus. The situation on the southern wing of the Soviet-German front stabilised, which contributed to the success of the Red Army counter-offensive near Moscow in the winter of 1941–42.

The Moscow Strategic Offensive Operation (Moscow Counter-Offensive), 5 December 1941–7 January 1942

The operation was conducted by the troops of the Western and Kalinin Fronts and the right wing of the South-Western Front. From 24 December 1941 the Bryansk Front also took part in the operation. In addition, the headquarters of the Bryansk Front and of the 39th and 61st Armies, and also 22 divisions and 11 brigades, were brought in during the operation.

It lasted 34 days. The fighting ranged over a front 1,000km wide, the Soviet troops advancing 100–250km. The rifle formations' average rate of advance was 3–6km a day. The Moscow strategic offensive operation included the Kalinin, Klin-Solnechnogorsk, Tula, Yelets and Kaluga army group operations.

Fighting Strength, Numerical Strength and Losses

Name of force, period involved in operation	Fighting strength and numerical strength of troops at start of operation		Losses during the operation				
	No of formations	Numerical strength	Irrecoverable losses	Sick and wounded	Total	Average daily losses
Western Front (whole period)	rifle divisions—50 motor rifle divisions—1 cavalry divisions—16 tank divisions—3 rifle brigades—16 airborne brigades—2 tank brigades—22	748,700	101,192	160,038	261,230	7,683
Kalinin Front (whole period)	rifle divisions—15 cavalry divisions—1 rifle brigades—1	192,200	27,343	54,944	82,287	2,420
Right wing of S.W. Front: 3rd and 13th Armies, Gen. Kostenko's operations group (06.12–31.12.41)	rifle divisions—12 cavalry divisions—7 motor rifle brigades—1 tank brigades—2	80,800	9,709	12,186	21,895	842
Bryansk Front (24.12.41– 07.01.42)	—	—	1,342	4,201	5,543	370
Total	Divisions—105 Brigades—44	1,021,700	139,586	231,369	370,955	10,910

Outcome of the operation. The Soviet troops routed the battle groups of Army Group Centre which had tried to envelop Moscow from the north and south, thereby removing the threat to Moscow, the Moscow industrial area and the Soviet state as a whole. It was on the battlefields near Moscow that the German Army suffered its first major defeat in World War II and the myth that it was invincible was dispelled. The Red Army seized the strategic initiative from the enemy, paving the way for going over to a general offensive.

The Kerch-Feodosia Amphibious Operation, 25 December 1941–2 January 1942

The operation was conducted by the troops of Trans-Caucasus Front (from 30 December 1941 the Caucasus Front), with support from part of the Black Sea Fleet and Azov Flotilla.

It lasted nine days. The fighting ranged over a front 250km wide. The Soviet troops advanced 100–110km and the rifle formations' average rate of advance was 10–12km a day.

Fighting Strength, Numerical Strength and Losses

Name of force, period involved in operation	Fighting strength and numerical strength of troops at start of operation		Losses during the operation			
	No of formations	Numerical strength	Irrecoverable losses	Sick and wounded	Total	Average daily losses
Trans-Caucasus (from 30.12.41 Caucasus) Front (25.12.41–02.01.42)	rifle divisions—8 rifle brigades—2	62,000	30,547	7,714	38,261	4,251
Part of Black Sea Fleet and Azov Flotilla (25.12.41–02.01.42)	—	20,500	1,906	1,768	3,674	408
Total	Divisions—8 Brigades—2	82,500	32,453	9,482	41,935	4,659

Outcome of the operation. The Soviet troops liberated the Kerch peninsula and took control of the sea ports of Kerch and Feodosia, which meant that the Soviet Command was able to deploy Crimean Front troops there. The defeat of the enemy's Kerch Group forced the German Command to abandon their advance on Sevastopol and transfer some of their forces to the Kerch peninsula area. With the peninsula cleared of enemy forces, the threat of a German invasion of the Caucasus via the Taman peninsula was averted.

The Rzhev-Vyazma Strategic Offensive Operation, 8 January–20 April 1942

The operation was conducted by the troops of the Western and Kalinin Fronts. In addition, the headquarters of the 3rd and 4th Shock Armies, and also 29 divisions and 33 brigades, were brought in during the operation.

It lasted 103 days. The fighting ranged over a front 650km wide. The Soviet troops advanced 80–250km. The rifle formations' average rate of advance was 1–2.5km a day. The Rzhev-Vyazma strategic operation included the Sychevka-Vyazma, Vyazma and Rzhev army group offensive operations.

Fighting Strength, Numerical Strength and Losses

Name of force, period involved in operation	Fighting strength and numerical strength of troops at start of operation		Losses during the operation			
	No of formations	Numerical strength	Irrecoverable losses	Sick and wounded	Total	Average daily losses
Kalinin Front (08.01–20.04.42)	rifle divisions—32 cavalry divisions—5 tank brigades—4	346,100	123,380	217,847	341,227	3,313

Name of force, period involved in operation	Fighting strength and numerical strength of troops at start of operation			Losses during the operation			
	No of formations	Numerical strength	Irrecoverable losses	Sick and wounded	Total	Average daily losses
Western Front (08.01–20.04.42)	rifle divisions—45 cavalry divisions—12 tank divisions—1 rifle brigades—26 airborne brigades—2 tank brigades—14	713,100	148,940	286,722	435,662	4,230
Total	Divisions—95 Brigades—46	1,059,200	272,320	504,569	776,889	7,543

Outcome of the operation. The Soviet Command was not entirely successful in carrying out its intended plan. In spite of this the operation was still of military and political significance. In the course of the Soviet advance the enemy was heavily defeated and pushed back 80–250km. The whole of the Moscow and Tula regions were liberated, as were many parts of the Kalinin and Smolensk regions. Army Group Centre was enveloped on two sides by the Soviet forces, which left it in an unfavourable operational position. The Germans were only able to avoid total defeat by transferring additional forces from Western Europe.

The Voronezh-Voroshilovgrad Strategic Defensive Operation, 28 June–24 July 1942

The operation was conducted by the troops of the Voronezh, South-Western and Southern Fronts, part of the Bryansk Front and part of the Azov Flotilla. In addition, the headquarters of the Voronezh Front and of three armies, and also four tank corps and 20 divisions, were brought in during the operation.

It lasted 27 days. The fighting ranged over a front 900km wide, the Soviet troops retreating 150–400km. The Voronezh-Voroshilovgrad strategic defensive operation included the Kastornoye, Valuiki-Rossosh and Voroshilovgrad-Shakhty army group defensive operations.

Fighting Strength, Numerical Strength and Losses

Name of force, period involved in operation	Fighting strength and numerical strength of troops at start of operation			Losses during the operation			
	No of formations	Numerical strength	Irrecoverable losses	Sick and wounded	Total	Average daily losses
Bryansk Front: 13th and 40th Armies, 5th Tank Army (28.06–24.07.42)	rifle divisions—12 rifle brigades—4 tank corps—2 ind. tank brigades—4	169,400	36,883	29,329	66,212	2,452

Name of force, period involved in operation	Fighting strength and numerical strength of troops at start of operation		Losses during the operation				
	No of formations	Numerical strength	Irrecoverable losses	Sick and wounded	Total	Average daily losses
S.W. Front (28.06–12.07.42)	rifle divisions—33 cavalry divisions—6 rifle brigades—6 fortified areas—5 tank corps—4 motor rifle brigades—3 ind. tank brigades—10	610,000	161,465	71,276	232,741	15,516
Southern Front (28.06–24.07.42)	rifle divisions—23 rifle brigades—4 fortified areas—1 tank brigades—6	522,500	128,460	64,753	193,213	7,156
Voronezh Front (09.07–24.07.42)	—	—	43,687	32,442	76,129	4,758
Azov Flotilla (Don Detachment)	—	8,900	27	25	52	2
Total	Divisions—74 Tank corps—6 Brigades—37 Fortified areas—6	1,310,800	370,522	197,825	568,347	21,050

Outcome of the operation. The Bryansk, South-Western and Southern Front troops found themselves in the position of having to repel attacks by superior enemy forces before they had replenished their own forces after previous heavy fighting and before they had consolidated their defences. They were unable to hold their defensive positions and retreated to the Voronezh area and the River Don, incurring heavy casualties. The 6th and 60th Armies, which were brought in from the Supreme Command HQ reserve, and the counterstrike by the 5th Tank Army against the enemy's Northern Group, weakened the German onslaught but failed to change the overall outcome of the situation. The enemy was able to continue his advance on Rostov and Stalingrad.

The Stalingrad Strategic Defensive Operation, 17 July–18 November 1942

The operation was conducted by the troops of the Stalingrad (Don) and South-Eastern (Stalingrad) Fronts, with support from the Volga Flotilla. In addition, the headquarters of the South-Eastern Front, of five combined-arms armies and of two tank armies, and also 56 divisions and 33 brigades, were brought in during the operation.

It lasted 125 days. The fighting ranged over a front 250–520km wide. The Soviet troops retreated 150km.

Fighting Strength, Numerical Strength and Losses

Name of force, period involved in operation	Fighting strength and numerical strength of troops at start of operation		Losses during the operation			
	No of formations	Numerical strength	Irrecoverable losses	Sick and wounded	Total	Average daily losses
1st and 2nd Formations' Stalingrad Front (whole period)	rifle divisions—34 cavalry divisions—3 tank corps—3 rifle brigades—8 ind. tank brigades—14	540,300	194,685	215,305	409,990	3,280
S.E. Front (07.08–30.09.42)	—	—	110,636	62,440	173,076	3,147
Don Front (30.09–18.11.42)	—	—	18,028	41,941	59,969	1,200
Volga Flotilla (25.07–18.11.42)	—	6,700	507	300	807	7
Total	Divisions—37 Tank corps—3 Brigades—22	547,000	323,856	319,986	643,842	5,151

Outcome of the operation. In the bitter defensive battles and engagements which were fought in the area of the large bend in the River Don, then in the area surrounding Stalingrad and in the city itself, not only was the enemy's attacking strength decimated and the German Army's main battle group on the southern wing of the Soviet-German front incapacitated, but the way was paved for the Soviet troops to go over to a decisive counter-offensive.

The North Caucasus Strategic
Defensive Operation, 25 July–31 December 1942

The operation was conducted by the troops of the North Caucasus, Trans-Caucasus and, until 28 July 1942, Southern Front, supported by the Black Sea Fleet and the Azov Flotilla. In addition, the headquarters of the Trans-Caucasus Front, of the Northern Group and of the 44th and 46th Armies, and also 31 divisions and 27 brigades, were brought in during the operation.

It lasted 160 days. The fighting ranged over a front 320–1,000km wide. The Soviet troops retreated 400–800km. The North Caucasus strategic defensive operation included the following army group operations: the defensive operation in the Stavropol and Krasnodar sectors; and the Armavir-Maikop, Novorossiysk, Mozdok-Malgobek, Tuapse and Nalckik-Ordzhonikidze defensive operations.

Fighting Strength, Numerical Strength and Losses

Name of force, period involved in operation	Fighting strength and numerical strength of troops at start of operation		Losses during the operation				
	No of formations	Numerical strength	Irrecoverable losses	Sick and wounded	Total	Average daily losses
Southern Front (25.07–28.07.42)	rifle divisions—26 cavalry divisions—1 rifle brigades—8 tank corps—1 tank brigades—5 fortified areas—2	300,000	15,317	1,412	16,729	4,182
N. Caucasus Front (28.07–31.08.42; 01.09.42, re-formed as Black Sea Group)	rifle divisions—2 cavalry divisions—4 rifle brigades—3 fortified areas—1	216,100	35,245	8,748	43,993	1,257
Trans-Caucasus Front's Northern Group (10.08–31.08.42)	—	—	7,324	5,132	12,456	566
Trans-Caucasus Front: Northern and Black Sea Groups, 46th Army (01.09–31.12.42)	—	—	132,020	163,723	295,743	2,424
Black Sea Fleet and Azov Flotilla (25.07–31.12.42)	—	87,100	2,885	2,105	4,990	31
Total	Divisions—33 Tank corps—1 Brigades—16 Fortified areas—3	603,200	192,791	181,120	373,911	2,337

Outcome of the operation. Under attack by superior enemy forces, the Soviet troops had to abandon the North Caucasus and retreat to the passes across the main Caucasian Ridge and to the River Terek. In November–December 1942 the enemy advance was stopped. The German Command's plans to take the oil-rich lands of the Caucasus and draw Turkey into the war did not succeed.

The Stalingrad Strategic Offensive Operation, 19 November 1942–2 February 1943

The operation was conducted by the troops of the South-Western, Don and Stalingrad Fronts, supported by the Volga Flotilla. In addition, the headquarters of the 1st and 2nd Guards Armies, of the 5th Shock Army and the 6th Army, and also five tank and three mechanised corps and six brigades, were brought in during the operation.

It lasted 76 days. The fighting ranged over a front 850km wide. The Soviet troops advanced 150–200km. The average daily rate of advance was 1.5–2.5km (rifle formations) and 4–4.5km (tank and mechanised formations).

The Stalingrad strategic offensive operation included the following army group operations: the November offensive operation to encircle the enemy's Stalingrad Group (Operation 'Uranus'), the Kotelnikovo and Middle Don ('Little Saturn') operations, and Operation 'Koltso' ('Ring') to eliminate the encircled enemy troops at Stalingrad.

Fighting Strength, Numerical Strength and Losses

Name of force, period involved in operation	Fighting strength and numerical strength of troops at start of operation		Losses during the operation			
	No of formations	Numerical strength	Irrecoverable losses	Sick and wounded	Total	Average daily losses
S.W. Front (19.11–31.12.42)	rifle divisions—18 cavalry divisions—6 rifle brigades—2 mechanised corps—1 tank corps—3 tank brigades—1	398,100	64,649	148,043	212,692	4,946
Don Front (19.11.42–02.02.43)	rifle divisions—24 tank corps—1 tank brigades—6 fortified areas—2	307,500	46,365	123,560	169,925	2,236
Stalingrad Front (19.11–31.12.42)	rifle divisions—24 cavalry divisions—2 rifle brigades—17 mechanised corps—1 tank corps—1 tank brigades—8 fortified areas—7	429,200	43,552	58,078	101,630	2,363
Voronezh Front's 6th Army and 2nd Air Army (16.12–18.12.42)	—	—	304	1,184	1,488	496
Volga Flotilla (19.11.42–02.02.43)	—	8,700	15	27	42	0.5
Total	Corps—7 Divisions—74 Brigades—34 Fortified areas—9	1,143,500	154,885	330,892	485,777	6,392

Outcome of the operation. The Soviet troops encircled and destroyed the main forces of the Germans' 4th Panzer and 6th Field Armies and routed the 3rd and 4th Romanian and 8th Italian Armies. Enemy losses exceeded 800,000; 32 enemy divisions and three brigades were completely destroyed, while 16 suffered heavy losses. In Operation

'Koltso' alone, between 10 January and 2 February 1943 over 91,000 prisoners were taken, including 2,500 officers and 24 generals. The Stalingrad victory proved to be the turning point in the war and had a decisive effect on its future course. The Red Army seized the strategic initiative and maintained it until the end of the war.

The North Caucasus Strategic Offensive Operation, Code-Named 'Don', 1 January–4 February 1943

The operation was conducted by the troops of the Trans-Caucasus, Southern and North Caucasus Fronts, supported by the Black Sea Fleet. In addition, the head-quarters of the 5th Shock Army, and also five divisions and six brigades, were brought in during the operation. The North Caucasus strategic operation included the Rostov, Mozdok-Stavropol, Novorossiysk-Maikop and Tikhoretsk army group offensive operations.

The operation lasted 35 days. The fighting ranged over a front 840km wide. The Soviet troops advanced 300–600km, the average rate of advance being 9–17km per day.

Fighting Strength, Numerical Strength and Losses

Name of force, period involved in operation	Fighting strength and numerical strength of troops at start of operation		Losses during the operation			
	No of formations	Numerical strength	Irrecoverable losses	Sick and wounded	Total	Average daily losses
Southern Front (01.01–04.02.43)	rifle divisions—13 cavalry divisions—2 rifle brigades—7 fortified areas—3 mechanised corps—3 tank corps—2 tank brigades—3	393,800	54,353	47,364	101,717	2,906
Trans-Caucasus Front (01.01–04.02.43)	rifle divisions—37 cavalry divisions—7 rifle brigades—35 fortified areas—2 tank brigades—8	685,600	12,088	30,340	42,428	1,212
N. Caucasus Front (24.01–04.02.43)	—	—	2,970	6,986	9,956	830
Black Sea Fleet (01.01–04.02.43)	—	65,900	216	222	438	13
Total	Divisions—59 Tank and mechanised corps—5 Brigades—53 Fortified areas—5	1,145,300	69,627	84,912	154,539	4,415

Outcome of the operation. In the course of the advance the Germans' Army Group A suffered a major defeat at the hands of the Soviets, who reached the approaches to

Rostov north-east of Krasnodar and the River Kuban line. Although the operation was not entirely successful in that the main enemy forces managed to retreat to the Donbass and avoid utter defeat, the Germans were prevented from occupying the oil-rich lands of the Caucasus. Stavropol territory, the autonomous republics of Chechen-Ingushetia, North Ossetia and Kabardino-Balkaria, part of the Rostov region and Krasnodar territory were all liberated by the Red Army.

The Operation to Break the Siege of Leningrad, Code-Named 'Iskra' ('Spark'), 12–30 January 1943

The stategic offensive to break the seige of Leningrad was carried out by the Leningrad and Volkhov Front battle groups, with support from part of the Baltic Fleet and the long-range air force.

The operation lasted 19 days. The fighting ranged over a front 45km wide. The Soviet troops advanced 60km. The average rate of advance was 3–3.5km a day.

Fighting Strength, Numerical Strength and Losses

Name of force, period involved in operation	Fighting strength and numerical strength of troops at start of operation		Losses during the operation			
	No of formations	Numerical strength	Irrecoverable losses	Sick and wounded	Total	Average daily losses
Leningrad Front (whole period)	rifle divisions—6 rifle brigades—7 tank brigades—3 fortified areas—1	133,300	12,320	28,944	41,264	2,172
Including: 67th Army	rifle divisions—6 rifle brigades—7 tank brigades—3 fortified areas—1	130,780	12,268	28,726	40,994	2,158
13th Air Army (aircrew)	—	2,520	52	218	270	14
Volkhov Front (whole period)	rifle divisions—15 rifle brigades—7 tank brigades—4	169,500	21,620	52,198	73,818	3,885
Including: 2nd Shock Army	rifle divisions—11 rifle brigades—4 tank brigades—4	114,000	19,017	46,301	65,318	3,138
8th Army	rifle divisions—4 rifle brigades—3	52,500	2,593	5,871	8,164	445
14th Air Army (aircrew)	—	3,000	10	26	36	2
Total	Divisions—21 Brigades—21 Fortified areas—1	302,800	33,940	81,142	115,082	6,057

Outcome of the operation. In the course of the offensive the Leningrad and Volkhov Front troops broke through the enemy blockade, creating a corridor 8–11km wide so that overland lines of communication between the city and the country beyond could be re-established. The whole southern shore of Lake Ladoga was cleared of enemy troops. In spite of the fact that the Soviet troops did not press home their attack, the operation to penetrate the blockade was of considerable strategic significance and proved to be the turning point in the battle for Leningrad. The enemy's plans to starve out the city's defenders and its citizens had failed and the initiative in this sector passed to the Red Army.

The Voronezh-Kharkov Strategic Offensive Operation, 13 January–3 March 1943

The operation was conducted by the troops of the Voronezh Front, the Bryansk Front's 13th Army and the South-Western Front's 6th Army. In addition, the headquarters of the 69th and 64th Armies, a tank corps, a cavalry corps, nine divisions and five brigades were brought in during the operation. The Voronezh-Kharkov strategic operation included the Ostrogozhsk-Rossosh, Voronezh-Kastornoye and Kharkov army group offensive operations.

The operation lasted 50 days. The fighting ranged over a front 250–400km wide. The Soviet troops advanced 360–520km, the average rate of advance being 7–10km per day.

Fighting Strength, Numerical Strength and Losses

Name of force, period involved in operation	No of formations	Numerical strength	Irrecoverable losses	Sick and wounded	Total	Average daily losses
	Fighting strength and numerical strength of troops at start of operation		Losses during the operation			
Bryansk Front 13th Army (13.01–03.03.43)	rifle divisions—7 anti-tank rifle divisions—1 tank brigades—2	95,000	13,876	23,547	37,423	748
Voronezh Front (13.01–03.03.43)	rifle divisions—20 anti-tank rifle divisions—1 cavalry divisions—2 rifle brigades—10 tank corps—2 ind. tank brigades—10	347,200	33,331	62,384	95,715	1,914
S.W. Front, 6th Army (13.01–03.03.43)	rifle divisions—5 rifle brigades—1 tank brigades—2	60,200	8,268	12,155	20,423	408
Total	Divisions—36 Tank corps—2 Brigades—25	502,400	55,475	98,086	153,561	3,071

Outcome of the operation. In the course of the advance the enemy's Army Group B was heavily defeated by the Soviet forces. The 2nd Hungarian Army and the 8th Italian Army which were part of Army Group B were almost completely routed. A large area was liberated, including the major industrial and administrative centres of Voronezh, Kursk, Belgorod and Kharkov. By the beginning of March, however, the advancing troops' resources were exhausted, and they were forced to abandon the rest of their mission and go over to the defensive.

The Kharkov Defensive Operation, 4–25 March 1943

The operation was conducted by the left wing of the Voronezh Front and South-Western Front's 6th Army. In addition, the headquarters of the 21st Army, and also six divisions and one tank corps, were brought in during the operation, which lasted 22 days. The fighting ranged over a front 200–240km wide, the Soviet troops retreating 100–150km.

Fighting Strength, Numerical Strength and Losses

Name of force, period involved in operation	Fighting strength and numerical strength of troops at start of operation		Losses during the operation				
	No of formations	Numerical strength	Irrecoverable losses	Sick and wounded	Total	Average daily losses
Voronezh Front (whole period), left wing: 3rd Tank Army, 40th and 69th Armies	rifle divisions— 8 anti-tank rifle divisions—1 cavalry divisions—2 rifle brigades—4 tank corps —1 ind. tank brigades—5	281,800	29,807	28,437	58,244	2,647
S.W. Front's 6th Army (whole period)	rifle divisions—5 cavalry divisions— 3 rifle brigades—1 ind. tank brigades —1	64,100	15,412	12,813	28,225	1,283
Total	Divisions—19 Brigades—11 Tank corps—1	345,900	45,219	41,250	86,469	3,930

Outcome of the operation. Under attack by superior enemy forces, the troops of the Voronezh Front's left wing and South-Western Front's 6th Army were forced to abandon Kharkov and retreat to the Krasnopolye–Berezov–Belgorod line and the River Severski Donets. However, the Germans failed to encircle and destroy the Soviet troops in the Kharkov area or seize the strategic initiative for the German Command.

The Kursk Strategic Defensive Operation, 5–23 July 1943

The operation was conducted by the troops of the Central, Voronezh and Steppe Fronts. In addition, the headquarters of Steppe Front and of the 27th, 47th and 53rd Combined-Arms, the 5th Guards Tank and 5th Air Armies, and also five tank and one mechanised corps, nineteen divisions and one brigade, were brought in during the operation.

It lasted 19 days. The fighting ranged over a front 550km wide. The Soviet troops retreated 12–35km.

Fighting Strength, Numerical Strength and Losses

Name of force, period involved in operation	Fighting strength and numerical strength of troops at start of operation		Losses during the operation				
	No of formations	Numerical strength	Irrecoverable losses	Sick and wounded	Total	Average daily losses
Central Front (05.07–11.07.43)	rifle divisions—41 anti-tank rifle divisions—1 rifle brigades—5 tank corps—4 ind. tank brigades—3 fortified areas—3	738,000	15,336	18,561	33,897	4,842
Voronezh Front (whole period)	rifle divisions—35 mechanised corps—1 tank corps—4 ind. tank brigades—6	534,700	27,542	46,350	73,892	3,889
Steppe Front (09.07–23.07.43)	—	—	27,452	42,606	70,058	4,670
Total	Divisions—77 Mechanised corps—1 Tank corps—8 Brigades—14 Fortified areas—3	1,272,700	70,330	107,517	177,847	9,360

Outcome of the operation. In its scope and intensity, the Kursk defensive operation, which was the first stage in the Battle of Kursk, was one of the biggest battles of World War II. In the course of the fighting the Central and Voronezh Front troops first rendered ineffective, then stopped the advance by, the German Army's battle groups, paving the way for going over to the counter-offensive in the Orel and Belgorod-Kharkov sectors. Hitler's plans to rout the Soviets in the area of the Kursk salient were a total failure.

The Orel Strategic Offensive Operation, Code-Named 'Kutuzov', 12 July–18 August 1943

The operation was conducted by the troops of the Bryansk and Central Fronts and part of the Western Front. In addition, the headquarters of the 11th Combined-

Arms, the 3rd Guards and 4th Tank Armies, and five tank, one mechanised and one cavalry corps, plus eleven divisions, were brought in during the operation.

It lasted 38 days. The fighting ranged over a front 400km wide and the Soviet troops advanced 150km, the average rate of advance being 4–5km per day (rifle formations) and 7–10km per day (tank and mechanised formations).

Fighting Strength, Numerical Strength and Losses

Name of force, period involved in operation	Fighting strength and numerical strength of troops at start of operation		Losses during the operation			
	No of formations	Numerical strength	Irrecover- able losses	Sick and wounded	Total	Average daily losses
Western Front (left wing):	rifle divisions—19 tank corps—2 ind. tank brigades—5	233,300	25,585	76,856	102,441	4,241
11th Guards Army (12.07–30.07.43)	rifle divisions—12 tank corps—2 ind. tank brigades—4	170,500	12,768	38,513	51,281	2,699
50th Army (12.07–18.08.43)	rifle divisions—7 ind. tank brigades—1	62,800	5,395	17,767	23,162	609
11th Army (20.07–18.08.43)	—	—	4,979	15,580	20,559	685
4th Tank Army (20.07–18.08.43)	—	—	2,443	4,996	7,439	248
Bryansk Front (whole period)	rifle divisions—21 rifle brigades—1 tank corps—2 ind. tank brigades—1	409,000	39,173	123,234	162,407	4,274
Central Front (whole period)	rifle divisions—41 anti-tank rifle divisions—1 rifle brigades—3 tank corps—4 ind. tank brigades—4 fortified areas—3	645,300	47,771	117,271	165,042	4,343
Total	Divisions—82 Tank corps—8 Brigades—14 Fortified areas—3	1,287,600	112,529	317,361	429,890	11,313

Outcome of the operation. In the course of the offensive Army Group Centre was heavily defeated and a large area liberated, including Orel, the regional centre. With the elimination of the enemy's Orel bridgehead from which his advance on Kursk had begun, the situation in the central section of the Soviet-German front changed radically, giving ample opportunity for the Soviets to press home the attack in the Bryansk sector and reach the eastern part of Byelorussia.

The Belgorod-Kharkov Strategic Offensive
Operation, Code-Named 'Rumyantsev', 3–23 August 1943

The concluding operation in the Battle of Kursk was conducted by the troops of the Voronezh and Steppe Fronts. In addition, the headquarters of the 4th Guards Army and of the 47th and 57th Armies, a tank and a mechanised corps, 19 divisions and two brigades were brought in during the operation.

It lasted 21 days. The fighting ranged over a front 300–400km wide, the Soviet troops advancing 140km. The average rate of advance was 7km per day (rifle formations) and 10–15km per day (tank and mechanised formations).

Fighting Strength, Numerical Strength and Losses

Name of force, period involved in operation	Fighting strength and numerical strength of troops at start of operation		Losses during the operation				
	No of formations	Numerical strength	Irrecoverable losses	Sick and wounded	Total	Average daily losses
Voronezh Front (whole period)	rifle divisions—28 tank corps—8 mechanised corps—2 ind. tank brigades—2	739,400	48,339	108,954	157,293	7,490
Steppe Front (whole period)	rifle divisions—22 mechanised corps—1 ind. tank brigades—3	404,600	23,272	75,001	98,273	4,680
Total	Divisions—50 Tank and mechanised corps—11 Brigades—5	1,144,000	71,611	183,955	255,566	12,170

Outcome of the operation. In the course of the advance the Voronezh and Steppe Front troops routed the enemy's powerful Belgorod-Kharkov Group, liberating the Kharkov industrial area, Belgorod and Kharkov. This paved the way for the liberation of the left-bank Ukraine.

The Smolensk Strategic Offensive Operation,
Code-Named 'Suvorov', 7 August–2 October 1943

The operation was conducted by the troops of the Kalinin and Western Fronts. In addition, the 2nd Guards Tank Corps, the 3rd Guards Cavalry Corps and two divisions were brought in during the operation. The Smolensk strategic operation included the Spas-Demensk, Yelnya-Dorogobuzh, Dukhovshchina-Demidov and Smolensk-Roslavl army group offensive operations.

The operation lasted 57 days. The fighting ranged over a front 400km wide and the Soviet troops advanced 200–250km. The average rate of advance was 4–5km per day for rifle formations and 6–10km per day for tank and mechanised formations.

Fighting Strength, Numerical Strength and Losses

Name of force, period involved in operation	Fighting strength and numerical strength of troops at start of operation		Losses during the operation				
	No of formations	Numerical strength	Irrecoverable losses	Sick and wounded	Total	Average daily losses
Kalinin Front (whole period)	rifle divisions—26 rifle brigades—10 ind. tank brigades—4 fortified areas—3	428,400	28,106	90,172	118,278	2,075
Western Front (whole period)	rifle divisions—58 cavalry divisions—3 rifle brigades—2 mechanised corps—1 ind. tank brigades—10 fortified areas—2	824,200	79,539	253,649	333,188	5,845
Total	Divisions—87 Corps—1 Brigades—26 Fortified areas—5	1,252,600	107,645	343,821	451,466	7,920

Outcome of the operation. In the course of the offensive the Kalinin and Western Front troops liberated the Smolensk region and part of the Kalinin region with the towns of Yelnya, Dukhovshchina, Roslavl and Smolensk and entered Byelorussia. The rapid advance by the Soviet troops destroyed the Ostwall in the upper reaches of the Dnieper and threatened the northern flank of Army Group Centre. The German Command was forced to transfer additional forces from the Orel-Bryansk sector, which contributed to the success of the Soviet advance at Kursk.

The Donbass Strategic Offensive Operation, 13 August–22 September 1943

The operation was conducted by the troops of the Southern and South-Western Fronts. In addition, the 11th Tank Corps, the 5th Guards Cavalry Corps and four divisions were brought in during the operation.

It lasted 41 days. The fighting ranged over a front 450km wide. The Soviet troops advanced 250–300km and the average rate of advance was 7–8km per day (rifle formations) and 10–15km per day (tank and mechanised formations).

Fighting Strength, Numerical Strength and Losses

Name of force, period involved in operation	Fighting strength and numerical strength of troops at start of operation		Losses during the operation				
	No of formations	Numerical strength	Irrecover- able losses	Sick and wounded	Total	Average daily losses
S.W. Front (whole period)	rifle divisions—41 rifle brigades—1 cavalry divisions—3 tank corps—1 mechanised corps—1 motor rifle brigades—1 ind. tank brigades—4	565,200	40,275	117,074	157,349	3,838
Southern Front (whole period)	rifle divisions—30 cavalry divisions—3 rifle brigades—1 mechanised corps—2 ind. tank brigades—4 fortified areas—3	446,700	25,891	90,282	116,173	2,833
Total	Divisions—77 Tank and mechanised corps—4 Brigades—11 Fortified areas—3	1,011,900	66,166	207,356	273,522	6,671

Outcome of the operation. In the course of the offensive the Southern and South-Western Front troops liberated the Donbass, reached the Zaporozhye area and the River Molochnaya and captured a bridgehead on the right bank of the Dnieper. Thus the country recovered an area of considerable economic importance. The Soviet troops' arrival at the Dnieper and Molochnaya paved the way for a successful advance in the southern parts of the right-bank Ukraine (to the west of the Dnieper) and in Northern Tavria (southern Ukraine to the north of the Crimea).

The Chernigov-Poltava Strategic
Offensive Operation, 26 August–30 September 1943

The operation was conducted by the troops of the Central, Voronezh and Steppe Fronts and was the first stage in the battle for the Dnieper. There was a major re-grouping of forces in these fronts during the operation; in addition, the headquarters of the 37th, 46th and 61st Armies and of the 3rd Guards Tank Army, and also one mechanised and two cavalry corps, fourteen divisions and five brigades, were brought in. At the same time one combined-arms and two tank armies were taken off the fronts' fighting strength. The Chernigov-Poltava strategic operation included the Chernigov-Pripyet, Sumy-Priluki and Poltava army group offensive operations.

The operation lasted 36 days. The fighting ranged over a front 600km wide. The Soviet troops advanced 250–300km. The average rate of advance was 7–8km per day.

Fighting Strength, Numerical Strength and Losses

Name of force, period involved in operation	Fighting strength and numerical strength of troops at start of operation		Losses during the operation				
	No of formations	Numerical strength	Irrecover-able losses	Sick and wounded	Total	Average daily losses
Central Front (whole period)	rifle divisions—35 airborne divisions—3 anti-tank rifle divisions—1 rifle brigades—3 tank corps—3 mechanised corps—1 ind. tank brigades—3	579,600	33,523	107,878	141,401	3,928
Voronezh Front (whole period)	rifle divisions—42 airborne divisions—5 tank corps—7 mechanised corps—2 ind. tank brigades—1	665,500	46,293	131,211	177,504	4,930
Steppe front (whole period)	rifle divisions—30 tank corps—2 mechanised corps—2 ind. tank brigades—5	336,200	23,141	85,906	109,047	3,029
Total	Divisions—116 Corps—17 Brigades—12	1,581,300	102,957	324,995	427,952	11,887

Outcome of the operation. Once the troops of the Central, Voronezh and Steppe Fronts had broken through the enemy's defences, their advance turned to pursuit, in the course of which the Soviet troops reached the Dnieper and captured a bridgehead on its right bank. Sizeable areas of the left-bank Ukraine were liberated, as were a number of major cities, including the regional centres of Sumy, Chernigov and Poltava. The German Command's plans for a long drawn out defence of the left-bank Ukraine were frustrated and the way was paved for the liberation of the right-bank Ukraine.

The Novorossiysk-Taman Strategic Offensive Operation, 10 September–9 October 1943

This was the final operation in the battle for the Caucasus. It was conducted by the troops of the North Caucasus Front supported by the Black Sea Fleet and Azov Flotilla. The Novorossiysk-Taman strategic operation included the Novorossiysk amphibious operation.

It lasted 30 days. The fighting ranged over a front 80km wide. The Soviet troops advanced 150km, the average rate of advance being 5–6km per day.

Fighting Strength, Numerical Strength and Losses

Name of force, period involved in operation	Fighting strength and numerical strength of troops at start of operation		Losses during the operation			
	No of formations	Numerical strength	Irrecoverable losses	Sick and wounded	Total	Average daily losses
N. Caucasus Front (whole period)	rifle divisions—20 rifle brigades—5 tank brigades—2	248,700	13,912	50,323	64,235	2,141
Black Sea Fleet, Azov Flotilla (whole period)	—	68,700	652	623	1,275	43
Total	Divisions—20 Brigades—7	317,400	14,564	50,946	65,510	2,184

Outcome of the operation. The North Caucasus Front and Black Sea Fleet forces defeated Army Group A, liberated Novorossiysk with a combination of land and sea strikes, reached the coast at the Kerch strait and concluded the liberation of the Caucasus. The bridgehead from which the enemy had defended the Crimea was destroyed. The liberation of Novorossiysk and the Taman peninsula gave the Black Sea Fleet a more secure base and paved the way for strikes from the sea and across the Kerch strait against the enemy's Crimean Group.

The Lower Dnieper Strategic
Offensive Operation, 26 September–20 December 1943

The final operation in the battle for the Dnieper was conducted by the troops of the Steppe (2nd Ukrainian), South-Western (3rd Ukrainian) and Southern (4th Ukrainian) Fronts. The Lower Dnieper strategic operation included the Melitopol, Zaporozhye, Pyatikhatki, Dnepropetrovsk and Znamenka army group offensive operations.

The operation lasted 86 days, the fighting ranging over a front 750–800km wide. The Soviet troops advanced 100–300km and the average rate of advance was 2–4km per day (rifle formations) and 5–10km per day (tank and mechanised formations).

Fighting Strength, Numerical Strength and Losses

Name of force, period involved in operation	Fighting strength and numerical strength of troops at start of operation		Losses during the operation			
	No of formations	Numerical strength	Irrecoverable losses	Sick and wounded	Total	Average daily losses
Steppe (2nd Ukrainian) Front (whole period)	rifle divisions—38 airborne divisions—4 mechanised corps—1 ind. tank brigades—5	463,500	77,400	226,217	303,617	3,530

Name of force, period involved in operation	Fighting strength and numerical strength of troops at start of operation		Losses during the operation				
	No of formations	Numerical strength	Irrecoverable losses	Sick and wounded	Total	Average daily losses
S.W. (3rd Ukrainian) Front (whole period)	rifle divisions—29 tank corps—1 mechanised corps—1 motor rifle brigades—1 ind. tank brigades—2	461,600	34,821	132,248	167,069	1,943
Southern (4th Ukrainian) Front (whole period)	rifle divisions—35 cavalry divisions—6 rifle brigades—4 tank corps—3 mechanised corps—2 ind. tank brigades—5 fortified areas—3	581,300	60,980	222,726	283,706	3,299
Total	Divisions—112 Corps—8 Brigades—17 Fortified areas—3	1,506,400	173,201	581,191	754,392	8,772

Outcome of the operation. The troops of the 2nd, 3rd and 4th Ukrainian Fronts liberated the left-bank Ukraine in the lower reaches of the Dnieper, blockaded the enemy's Crimean Group from the land and captured a bridgehead on the west bank of the Dnieper about 400km wide and about 100km deep, which was to play a major part in the liberation of the right-bank Ukraine.

The Kiev Strategic Offensive Operation, 3–13 November 1943
The operation was conducted by the troops of the 1st Ukrainian Front, with the aim of routing the enemy's Kiev Group and liberating Kiev, the capital of the Ukraine.

The operation lasted 11 days. The fighting ranged over a front 320–500km wide. The Soviet troops advanced 150km, the average rate of advance being 12–14km per day.

Fighting Strength, Numerical Strength and Losses

Name of force, period involved in operation	Fighting strength and numerical strength of troops at start of operation		Losses during the operation				
	No of formations	Numerical strength	Irrecoverable losses	Sick and wounded	Total	Average daily losses
1st Ukrainian Front (whole period)	rifle divisions—42 airborne divisions—3 cavalry divisions—3 rifle brigades—2 tank corps—5 mechanised corps—1 ind. tank brigades—4	671,000	6,491	24,078	30,569	2,779

Outcome of the operation. The troops advanced rapidly, liberating Kiev and forming a strategic bridgehead 300km wide and 150km deep on the right bank of the Dnieper which was to play a significant part in the operations to liberate the right-bank Ukraine.

The Dnieper-Carpathian Strategic Offensive Operation (Liberation of the Right-Bank Ukraine), 24 December 1943–17 April 1944

This was one of the largest operations of World War II and was made up of ten inter-connected army group operations. It was conducted by the troops of the 1st, 2nd, 3rd and 4th Ukrainian Fronts. In the final stage, the troops of the 2nd Byelorussian Front also took part.

The headquarters of the 2nd Byelorussian Front, of the 47th, 61st and 70th Armies and of the 2nd, 4th and 6th Tank and 6th Air Armies, and also six tank and two mechanised corps and 33 divisions, were brought in during the advance.

The operation lasted 116 days. The fighting ranged over a front 1,300–1,400km wide and the Soviet troops advanced 250–450km, the average rate of advance being 2–4km per day.

The Dnieper-Carpathian operation included the Zhitomir-Berdichev, Kirovo-grad, Korsun-Shevchenkovsky, Rovno-Lutsk, Nikopol-Krivoy Rog, Proskurov-Chernovtsy, Uman-Botosani, Bereznegovatoye-Snigirevka, Polesskoe and Odessa army group offensive operations.

Fighting Strength, Numerical Strength and Losses

Name of force, period involved in operation	Fighting strength and numerical strength of troops at start of operation		Losses during the operation			
	No of formations	Numerical strength	Irrecover-able losses	Sick and wounded	Total	Average daily losses
1st Ukrainian Front (whole period)	rifle divisions—62 airborne divisions—1 cavalry divisions—3 tank corps—6 mechanised corps—2 ind. tank brigades—5 fortified areas—2	924,300	124,467	331,902	456,369	3,934
2nd Ukrainian Front (whole period)	rifle divisions—52 airborne divisions—7 cavalry divisions—3 tank corps—3 mechanised corps—4 ind. tank brigades—3	594,700	66,059	200,914	266,973	2,301
3rd Ukrainian Front (whole period)	rifle divisions—19 tank corps—1 ind. tank brigades—1	336,900	54,997	214,238	269,235	2,321

Name of force, period involved in operation	Fighting strength and numerical strength of troops at start of operation		Losses during the operation				
	No of formations	Numerical strength	Irrecoverable losses	Sick and wounded	Total	Average daily losses
4th Ukrainian Front (whole period)	rifle divisions—38 cavalry divisions—3 tank corps—1 mechanised corps—2 ind. tank brigades—3 ind. motor rifle brigades—1 fortified areas—3	550,200	21,914	83,905	105,819	912
2nd Byelorussian Front (15.03–05.04.44)	—	—	2,761	8,371	11,132	506
Total	Divisions—188 Corps—19 Brigades—13 Fortified areas—5	2,406,100	270,198	839,330	1,109,528	9,565

Outcome of the operation. The entire southern wing of Nazi Germany's Eastern Front was routed, bringing about a radical change in the situation in other theatres of operations. The German Command was forced to transfer major forces to the right-bank Ukraine from Western Europe (34 divisions and four brigades), which weakened its groupings there. The Soviet troops liberated the vast area of the right-bank Ukraine, moved forward to the approaches to southern Poland and Czechoslovakia and, on 28 March, forced the River Prut and entered Romania. For the first time during the war, the fighting was taken beyond the borders of the USSR.

The Leningrad-Novgorod Strategic
Offensive Operation, 14 January–1 March 1944

The operation was conducted by the troops of the Leningrad and Volkhov Fronts and part of the 2nd Baltic Front. The headquarters of the 3rd Shock and 10th Guards Armies and of the 22nd Army, together with 30 divisions and six brigades, were brought in during the operation. The Leningrad-Novgorod strategic operation included the Krasnoye Selo-Ropsha, Novgorod-Luga, Kingisepp-Gdov and Starorussk-Novorzhev army group offensive operations.

The operation lasted 48 days. The fighting ranged over a front 600km wide and the Soviet troops advanced 220–280km, the average rate of advance being 5–6km per day.

Fighting Strength, Numerical Strength and Losses

Name of force, period involved in operation	Fighting strength and numerical strength of troops at start of operation		Losses during the operation			
	No of formations	Numerical strength	Irrecoverable losses	Sick and wounded	Total	Average daily losses
Leningrad Front, minus 23rd Army (whole period)	rifle divisions—30 rifle brigades—3 fortified areas—3 ind. tank brigades—4	417,600	56,564	170,876	227,440	4,738
Volkhov Front (14.01–15.02.44)	rifle divisions—22 rifle brigades—6 fortified areas—2 ind. tank brigades—4	260,000	12,011	38,289	50,300	1,524
2nd Baltic Front's 1st Shock Army (14.01–10.02.44)	rifle divisions—5 rifle brigades—1	54,900	1,283	3,759	5,042	180
2nd Baltic Front (10.02–01.03.44)	—	—	6,659	23,051	29,710	1,485
Baltic Fleet (whole period)	—	89,600	169	1,292	1,461	30
Total	Divisions—57 Brigades—18 Fortified areas—5	822,100	76,686	237,267	313,953	6,541

Outcome of the operation. In the course of the offensive Army Group North was heavily defeated and the blockade of Leningrad ended. The Soviet troops liberated almost all of the Leningrad region, all of the Novgorod region and most of the Kalinin region and entered Estonia. The Soviet advance in the north-western sector meant that the German Command was unable to transfer Army Group North forces to the south, where the Soviet armed forces were delivering the main strike of the winter campaign.

The Crimean Strategic Offensive, 8 April–12 May 1944

The operation was conducted by the troops of the 4th Ukrainian Front, the Independent Maritime Army, the Black Sea Fleet and the Azov Flotilla.

It lasted 35 days and the fighting ranged over a front 160km wide. The Soviet troops advanced 200–260km, the average rate of advance being 20km per day until they drew near Sevastopol and 3–5km per day as they breached the defences there.

Fighting Strength, Numerical Strength and Losses

Name of force, period involved in operation	Fighting strength and numerical strength of troops at start of operation		Losses during the operation			
	No of formations	Numerical strength	Irrecover- able losses	Sick and wounded	Total	Average daily losses
4th Ukrainian Front (whole period)	rifle divisions—18 tank corps—1 ind. tank brigades—2 fortified areas—2	278,400	13,332	50,498	63,830	1,824
Independent Maritime and 4th Air Army (whole period)	rifle divisions—12 rifle brigades—2 ind. tank brigades—1	143,500	4,196	16,305	20,501	586
Black Sea Fleet, Azov Flotilla (whole period)	—	40,500	226	262	488	14
Total	Divisions—30 Corps—1 Brigades—5 Fortified areas—2	462,400	17,754	67,065	84,819	2,423

Outcome of the operation. The Soviet troops broke through the deep, echeloned enemy defences on the Perekop isthmus, on the Kerch peninsula and in the Sevastopol area and routed the 17th Field Army. The last major enemy bridgehead threatening the rear area of fronts operating in the right-bank Ukraine was eliminated. The Black Sea Fleet regained its main base of Sevastopol, which gave it a much more secure base from which to carry out operations.

The Vyborg-Petrozavodsk Strategic Offensive Operation, 10 June–9 August 1944

The final operation in the battle for Leningrad was conducted by the right wing of the Leningrad Front and the left wing of the Karelian Front, with support from the Baltic Fleet and the Ladoga and Onega Flotillas. No additional forces were brought in during the operation.

It lasted 61 days. The fighting ranged over a front 280km wide. The Soviet troops advanced 110–250km. The average rate of advance was 2–5km per day. The Vyborg-Petrozavodsk strategic operation included the Vyborg and Svir-Petrozavodsk army group offensive operations.

Fighting Strength, Numerical Strength and Losses

Name of force, period involved in operation	Fighting strength and numerical strength of troops at start of operation		Losses during the operation				
	No of formations	Numerical strength	Irrecoverable losses	Sick and wounded	Total	Average daily losses
Karelian Front, left wing (7th and 32nd Armies, 7th Air Army; 21.06–09.08.44)	rifle divisions—16 rifle brigades—3 ind. tank brigades—2 fortified areas—2	202,300	16,924	46,679	63,603	1,272
Leningrad Front, right wing (21st and 23rd Armies, 13th Air Army; 10.06–20.06.44)	rifle divisions—15 fortified areas—2 ind. tank brigades—1	188,800	6,018	24,011	30,029	2,730
Baltic Fleet, Ladoga and Onega Flotillas (whole period)	—	60,400	732	2,011	2,743	45
Total	Divisions—31 Brigades—6 Fortified areas—4	451,500	23,674	72,701	96,375	1,580

Outcome of the operation. The Soviet troops liberated the Karelian-Finnish Autonomous Republic and the northern parts of the Leningrad region, heavily defeating the Finnish Army. The success of this operation made an appreciable difference to the situation in the northern section of the Soviet-German front, made Finland's withdrawal from the war inevitable and paved the way for the liberation of the Soviet Arctic and northern Norway.

The Byelorussian Strategic Offensive Operation, 23 June–29 August 1944

This was one of the major strategic operations of World War II. It was conducted by the troops of the 1st Baltic and the 1st, 2nd and 3rd Byelorussian Fronts, with support from the Dnieper Flotilla. The 1st Polish Army also took part, fighting with the 1st Byelorussian Front. In addition, the headquarters of the 2nd Guards Army and of the 51st Army, and also the 19th Tank Corps and 24 divisions, were brought in during the operation.

The Byelorussian strategic operation may be divided into two stages according to the nature and purpose of the action. Stage one (23 June–4 July) includes the Vitebsk-Orsha, Mogilev, Bobruisk, Polotsk and Minsk army group offensive operations and stage two (5 July–29 August) the Shyaulyai, Vilnius, Kaunas, Bialystok and Lublin-Brest army group offensive operations.

The operation lasted 68 days. The fighting ranged over a front 1,100km wide. The Soviet troops advanced 550–600km, and the average rate of advance was 20–25km per day during stage one and 13–14km per day during stage two.

Fighting Strength, Numerical Strength and Losses

Name of force, period involved in operation	Fighting strength and numerical strength of troops at start of operation		Losses during the operation			
	No of formations	Numerical strength	Irrecoverable losses	Sick and wounded	Total	Average daily losses
1st Baltic Front (whole period)	rifle divisions—24 rifle brigades—1 tank corps—1 ind. tank brigades—4 mechanised brigades—1 fortified areas—1	359,500	41,248	125,053	166,301	2,446
3rd Byelorussian Front (whole period)	rifle divisions—33 cavalry divisions—3 tank corps—3 mechanised corps—1 ind. tank brigades—5 fortified areas—1	579,300	45,117	155,165	200,282	2,945
2nd Byelorussian Front (whole period)	rifle divisions—22 ind. tank brigades—4 fortified areas—1	319,500	26,315	91,421	117,736	1,731
1st Byelorussian Front (whole period)	rifle divisions—77 cavalry divisions—9 rifle brigades—1 tank corps—6 mechanised corps—1 ind. tank brigades—2 self-propelled artillery brigades—2 fortified areas—4	1,071,100	65,779	215,615	281,394	4,138
Dnieper Flotilla (whole period)	—	2,300	48	54	102	2
Total	Divisions—168 Corps—12 Brigades—20 Fortified areas—7	2,331,700	178,507	587,308	765,815	11,262
1st Polish Army	infantry divisions—4 cavalry brigades—1 ind. tank brigades—1	79,900	1,533	3,540	5,073	75

Outcome of the operation. The troops of the advancing fronts routed Army Group Centre, one of the strongest enemy groupings; 17 divisions and three brigades were destroyed and 50 divisions lost over half their strength. Byelorussia and part of Lithuania and Latvia were liberated. The Red Army entered Poland and moved forwards towards the East Prussian border. In the course of the offensive the major water obstacles of the Berezina, Neman and Vistula were forced and important bridgeheads captured on their west banks, with the aim of paving the way for strikes into the heart of Eastern Prussia and central Poland. In order to stabilise the forward edge of the battle area the German Command was forced to transfer 46 divisions and four brigades to Byelorussia from other sectors, taking some of the pressure off the British and American troops in France.

The Lvov-Sandomierz Strategic
Offensive Operation, 13 July–29 August 1944

The operation was conducted by the troops of the 1st Ukrainian Front. It may be divided into two stages from the point of view of the purpose and progress of the operation. In stage one (13–27 July) the troops broke through the enemy's defences, encircled then destroyed the Brodsk Group and routed the Lvov and Rava-Russkaya Groups, liberating Lvov, Rava-Russkaya, Przemysl, Stanislav, etc. In stage two (28 July–29 August) the troops pressed home their attack, forced the Vistula and captured a bridgehead on its west bank in the region of Sandomierz.

The operation lasted 48 days. The fighting ranged over a front 440km wide and the Soviet troops advanced 350km. While the defences were being breached, the average rate of advance was 3–10km per day; during the advance towards the Vistula, the rate was 17–22km (rifle formations) and 50–65km (tank and motorised formations) per day.

Fighting Strength, Numerical Strength and Losses

Name of force, period involved in operation	Fighting strength and numerical strength of troops at start of operation		Losses during the operation				
	No of formations	Numerical strength	Irrecoverable losses	Sick and wounded	Total	Average daily losses
1st Ukrainian Front (whole period)	rifle divisions—72 cavalry divisions—6 airborne divisions—2 tank corps—7 mechanised corps—3 ind. tank brigades—4	1,002,200	65,001	224,295	289,296	6,027

Outcome of the operation. The Soviet troops routed the strategic enemy grouping Army Group North Ukraine and liberated the Ukraine's western regions and south-east Poland. They captured a major bridgehead on the west bank of the Vistula, from which they continued their advance towards Silesia, central Poland and the German border.

The Iasi-Kishinev Strategic Offensive Operation, 20–29 August 1944

The operation was conducted by the troops of the 2nd and 3rd Ukrainian Fronts, with support from the Black Sea Fleet and the Danube Flotilla. In addition, the 4th Guards Cavalry Corps (of three cavalry divisions) and two rifle brigades were brought in during the operation.

It lasted 10 days. The fighting ranged over a front 500km wide. The Soviet troops advanced 300–320km, the average rate of advance being 20–25km per day (rifle formations) and 30–32km per day (tank and mechanised formations).

Fighting Strength, Numerical Strength and Losses

Name of force, period involved in operation	Fighting strength and numerical strength of troops at start of operation		Losses during the operation				
	No of formations	Numerical strength	Irrecoverable losses	Sick and wounded	Total	Average daily losses
2nd Ukrainian Front (whole period)	rifle divisions—46 airborne divisions—7 cavalry divisions—3 tank corps—3 mechanised corps—2 ind. tank brigades—1 self-propelled artillery brigades—1 fortified areas—2	771,200	7,316	32,669	39,985	3,998
3rd Ukrainian Front (whole period)	rifle divisions—34 airborne divisions—1 mechanised corps—1 ind. tank brigades—1 ind. motor rifle brigades—1 fortified areas—1	523,000	5,820	21,126	26,946	2,695
Black Sea Fleet, Danube Flotilla (whole period)	—	20,000	61	138	199	20
Total	Divisions—91 Corps—6 Brigades—4 Fortified areas—3	1,314,200	13,197	53,933	67,130	6,713

Outcome of the operation. The Soviet troops quickly routed Army Group South Ukraine's main forces, destroying 22 German and almost all the Romanian divisions deployed on the Soviet-German front. Moldavia was liberated, and Romania withdrew from the fascist block and declared war on Germany. With the enemy defences breached across a wide front, the way was clear for the Soviet troops to advance rapidly into the Romanian interior and into Hungary and Bulgaria.

The East Carpathian Strategic
Offensive Operation, 8 September–28 October 1944

The operation was conducted by the troops of the 4th Ukrainian Front and the left wing of the 1st Ukrainian Front, with the aim of giving support to the Slovak national uprising. The 1st Czechoslovak Army Corps also took part in the operation. In addition, the 4th Guards and 31st Tank Corps and five divisions were brought in during the operation. The East Carpathian operation included the Carpathian-Duka and Carpathian-Uzhgorod army group operations.

The operation lasted 51 days. The fighting ranged over a front 400km wide. The Soviet troops advanced 50–110km, the average rate of advance being 1–2km per day.

Fighting Strength, Numerical Strength and Losses

Name of force, period involved in operation	Fighting strength and numerical strength of troops at start of operation		Losses during the operation				
	No of formations	Numerical strength	Irrecoverable losses	Sick and wounded	Total	Average daily losses
1st Ukrainian Front (38th Army, 2nd Air Army, 1st Guards Cavalry Corps, 25th Tank Corps; whole period)	rifle divisions—9 cavalry divisions—3 tank corps—1	99,100	13,264	48,750	62,014	1,216
4th Ukrainian Front (whole period)	rifle divisions—20 airborne divisions—1 ind. tank brigades—2	264,000	13,579	50,618	64,197	1,259
Total	Divisions—33 Corps—1 Brigades—2	363,100	26,843	99,368	126,211	2,475
1st Czechoslovak Army Corps (whole period)	infantry brigades—2 airborne brigades—1 ind. tank brigades—1	14,900	1,630	4,069	5,699	112

Outcome of the operation. The Soviet troops defeated the Heinrici Army Group, liberated the Trans-Carpathian part of the Ukraine and, crossing the main Carpathian ridge, entered Czechoslovakia. These actions caused the diversion of major enemy forces and thereby assisted the Slovak national uprising. The Germans lost a significant strategic position covering Czechoslovakia from the east.

The Baltic Strategic Offensive
Operation, 14 September–24 November 1944

The operation was conducted by the troops of the 1st, 2nd and 3rd Baltic Fronts and part of the Leningrad Front, supported by the Baltic Fleet. The Baltic strategic operation included the Riga, Tallin and Memel army group and Moonzund amphibious operations. In addition, the headquarters of the 39th Army, six divisions and one brigade were brought in during the operation.

It lasted 72 days. The fighting ranged over a front 1,000km wide, the Soviet troops advancing 300km at an average rate of 4–5km per day.

Fighting Strength, Numerical Strength and Losses

Name of force, period involved in operation	Fighting strength and numerical strength of troops at start of operation		Losses during the operation			
	No of formations	Numerical strength	Irrecoverable losses	Sick and wounded	Total	Average daily losses
Leningrad Front (2nd Shock Army, 8th Army, 13th Air Army; whole period)	rifle divisions—16 fortified areas—3	195,000	6,219	22,557	28,776	400
3rd Baltic Front (14.09–10.10.44)	rifle divisions—35 tank corps—1 ind. tank brigades—2 fortified areas—2	345,500	11,867	43,621	55,488	2,055
2nd Baltic Front (14.09–20.10.44)	rifle divisions—33 tank corps—1 ind. tank brigades—3 fortified areas—1	339,400	15,735	58,000	73,735	1,993
1st Baltic Front (14.09–20.10.44)	rifle divisions—51 tank corps—4 mechanised corps—1 ind. tank brigades—6	621,000	24,188	79,758	103,946	2,809
3rd Byelorussian Front's 39th Army (01.10–31.10.44)	—	—	3,201	13,154	16,355	528
Baltic Fleet (whole period)	—	45,500	258	1,532	1,790	25
Total	Divisions—135 Corps—7 Brigades—11 Fortified areas—6	1,546,400	61,468	218,622	280,090	3,890

Outcome of the operation. Army Group North was heavily defeated by the Soviet forces, its remaining formations finding themselves trapped by the sea at Courland near Memel, with no land access to Eastern Prussia. Almost all of the Baltic was liberated and the way cleared for an advance into Eastern Prussia.

The Belgrade Strategic Offensive Operation, 28 September–20 October 1944

This was a joint operation by the troops of the 3rd Ukrainian Front and part of the 2nd Ukrainian Front with the Yugoslav People's Liberation Army and the Bulgarian Patriotic Front. The Danube Flotilla also took part in the operation.

It lasted 23 days. The fighting ranged over a front 400–620km wide. The Soviet troops advanced 200km. The average rate of advance was 8–9km per day.

Fighting Strength, Numerical Strength and Losses

Name of force, period involved in operation	Fighting strength and numerical strength of troops at start of operation		Losses during the operation			
	No of formations	Numerical strength	Irrecoverable losses	Sick and wounded	Total	Average daily losses
3rd Ukrainian Front (57th Army, 17th Air Army, 4th Guards Mech. Corps, 236th Rifle Div., 5th Motor Rifle Brigade, 96th Ind. Tank Brigade; whole period)	rifle divisions—10 rifle brigades—3 fortified areas—1 mechanised corps—1 ind. tank brigade—1	200,000	3,242	9,498	12,740	554
2nd Ukrainian Front (46th Army, 5th Air Army; whole period)	rifle divisions—9	93,500	1,100	4,990	6,090	265
Danube Flotilla (whole period)	—	6,500	8	—	8	—
Total	Divisions—19 Corps—1 Brigades—4 Fortified areas—1	300,000	4,350	14,488	18,838	819

Complete casualty figures for the Yugoslav and Bulgarian Armies are not available.

Outcome of the operation. The Soviet troops, coordinating closely with the Yugoslav National Liberation Army, routed Army Group Serbia, much of which was completely destroyed. The eastern and north-eastern parts of Yugoslavia and the capital Belgrade were liberated and the way was cleared for an advance towards Budapest. The enemy troops in the Balkan peninsula were pushed back over 200km and main lines of communications between Belgrade and Salonika were disrupted. The German Command was forced to move out troops in a hurry from the south of the Balkan peninsula across inaccessible mountain areas controlled by Yugoslav partisans.

The Petsamo-Kirkenes Strategic
Offensive Operation, 7–29 October 1944

The operation was conducted by the Karelian Front and the Northern Fleet. No additional forces were brought in.

The operation lasted 23 days. The fighting ranged over a front 80km wide and the Soviet troops advanced 150km, the average rate of advance being 6–7km per day.

Fighting Strength, Numerical Strength and Losses

Name of force, period involved in operation	Fighting strength and numerical strength of troops at start of operation		Losses during the operation				
	No of formations	Numerical strength	Irrecoverable losses	Sick and wounded	Total	Average daily losses
Karelian Front (14th Army, 7th Air Army; whole period)	rifle divisions—8 rifle brigades—5 ind. tank brigades—1 fortified areas—1	113,200	5,298	13,137	18,435	801
Northern Fleet (whole period)	—	20,300	786	2,012	2,798	122
Total	Divisions—8 Brigades—6 Fortified areas—1	133,500	6,084	15,149	21,233	923

Outcome of the operation. The troops of the 14th Army coordinated with the Northern Fleet to defeat the enemy in harsh Arctic conditions. They liberated the occupied part of Murmansk region, the Petsamo (Pechengi) area and northern Norway, including Kirkenes, assisting the Norwegian people to rid their country of the Nazi occupiers. The taking of Petsamo and Kirkenes greatly limited the activities of the German Fleet in the far north and cut off Germany's supply of nickel ore.

The Budapest Strategic Offensive
Operation, 29 October 1944–13 February 1945

The operation was conducted by the troops of the 2nd and 3rd Ukrainian Fronts and the Danube Flotilla. The 1st and 4th Romanian Armies took part in the operation as part of the 2nd Ukrainian Front. In addition, the headquarters of the 3rd Ukrainian Front and of the 4th Guards Army, the 5th Air Army and the 26th and 57th Armies, and also 22 divisions, were brought in during the operation.

It lasted 108 days. The fighting ranged over a front 420km wide. The Soviet troops advanced 250–400km at an average rate of 2.5–4km per day.

Fighting Strength, Numerical Strength and Losses

Name of force, period involved in operation	Fighting strength and numerical strength of troops at start of operation		Losses during the operation				
	No of formations	Numerical strength	Irrecoverable losses	Sick and wounded	Total	Average daily losses
2nd Ukrainian Front (whole period)	rifle divisions—39 airborne divisions—4 cavalry divisions—9 tank corps—3 mechanised corps—4 ind. tank brigades—1 self-propelled artillery brigades—1 fortified areas—2	712,000	35,027	130,156	165,183	1,529
3rd Ukrainian Front (12.12.44–13.02.45)	—	—	44,887	109,900	154,787	2,418
Danube Flotilla	naval infantry brigades—1	7,500	112	—	112	1
Total	Divisions—52 Corps—7 Brigades—3 Fortified areas—2	719,500	80,026	240,056	320,082	2,964

Outcome of the operation. The troops of the 2nd and 3rd Ukrainian Fronts liberated central Hungary, including the capital Budapest. The enemy's 188,000-strong grouping was destroyed. Hungary withdrew from the German block. With the end of the operation a large number of forces were freed up, which meant that conditions were now right for pressing home the attack in Czechoslovakia and Austria.

The Vistula-Oder Strategic Offensive Operation, 12 January–3 February 1945

One of the biggest operations of World War II was conducted by the troops of the 1st Byelorussian and 1st Ukrainian Fronts. The 1st Polish Army took part in the operation, fighting with the 1st Byelorussian Front. No additional forces were brought in.

The operation lasted 23 days. The fighting ranged over a front 500km wide. The Soviet troops advanced 500km. The average rate of advance was 20–22km per day (rifle formations) and 30–35km a day (tank and mechanised formations). The Vistula-Oder strategic operation included the Warsaw-Poznan and Sandomierz-Silesian army group offensive operations.

Fighting Strength, Numerical Strength and Losses

Name of force, period involved in operation	Fighting strength and numerical strength of troops at start of operation		Losses during the operation			
	No of formations	Numerical strength	Irrecoverable losses	Sick and wounded	Total	Average daily losses
1st Byelorussian Front (whole period)	rifle divisions—63 cavalry divisions—6 tank corps—5 mechanised corps—2 ind. tank brigades—4 self-propelled artillery brigades—2 fortified areas—2	1,028,900	17,032	60,310	77,342	3,363
1st Ukrainian Front (whole period)	rifle divisions—65 airborne divisions—1 cavalry divisions—3 tank corps—6 mechanised corps—3 ind. tank brigades—3 self-propelled artillery brigades—3 fortified areas—1	1,083,800	26,219	89,564	115,783	5,034
Total	Divisions—138 Corps—16 Brigades—12 Fortified areas—3	2,112,700	43,251	149,874	193,125	8,397
1st Polish Army (whole period)	infantry divisions—5 cavalry brigades—1 ind. tank brigades—1	90,900	225	841	1,066	46

Outcome of the operation. The Soviet troops liberated large areas of Poland and crossed into Germany, reaching the Oder and capturing a number of bridgeheads on its west bank. In all, 35 German divisions were destroyed and 25 suffered heavy losses. The Soviet troops' successful action paved the way for advances in Pomerania and Silesia and towards Berlin.

The Western Carpathian Strategic Offensive Operation, 12 January–18 February 1945

The operation was conducted by the troops of the 4th Ukrainian Front and the right wing of the 2nd Ukrainian Front. The 1st and 4th Romanian Armies and the 1st Czechoslovak Army Corps also took part in the operation, the two former fighting with the 2nd Ukrainian Front and the latter with the 4th Ukrainian Front. In addition the 5th Guards Mechanised Corps, the headquarters of two light mountain rifle corps (six brigades) and a self-propelled artillery brigade were brought in during the operation.

The operation lasted 38 days. The fighting ranged over a front 440km wide and the Soviet troops advanced 170–230km, the average rate being 4–6km per day.

Fighting Strength, Numerical Strength and Losses

Name of force, period involved in operation	No of formations	Numerical strength	Irrecover-able losses	Sick and wounded	Total	Average daily losses
	Fighting strength and numerical strength of troops at start of operation		Losses during the operation			
4th Ukrainian Front (whole period)	rifle divisions—24 airborne divisions—1 ind. tank brigades—3 fortified areas—1	267,500	12,316	45,836	58,152	1,530
2nd Ukrainian Front (night wing; whole period)	rifle divisions—25 airborne divisions—4 cavalry divisions—6 tank corps—1 mechanised corps—2 ind. tank brigades—1 fortified areas—1	214,700	4,021	16,815	20,836	548
Total	Divisions—60 Corps—3 Brigades—4 Fortified areas—2	482,200	16,337	62,651	78,988	2,078
1st and 4th Romanian Armies	infantry divisions—5 mountain rifle divisions—3 cavalry divisions—2	99,300	2,486	9,488	11,974	315
1st Czechoslovak Army Corps	infantry brigades—2 ind. tank brigades—1	11,500	257	713	970	25

Outcome of the operation. The troops of the 2nd and 4th Ukrainian Fronts liberated most of Slovakia and the southern part of Poland. Crossing the Western Carpathians, they arrived at the upper reaches of the Vistula, which meant that the 1st Ukrainian Front was able to rout the German grouping in Silesia. Conditions were now right for pressing home the attack with the aim of taking the Moravia-Ostrava industrial area. The difficult winter battles of 1945 helped cement relations between Soviet, Romanian and Czechoslovak troops.

The East Prussian Strategic Offensive Operation, 13 January–25 April 1945

The operation was conducted by the troops of the 2nd and 3rd Byelorussian Fronts with support from the Baltic Fleet. In addition the headquarters of the 19th Army and nine divisions were brought in during the operation.

It lasted 103 days. The fighting ranged over a front 550km wide and the Soviet troops advanced 120–200km. The average rate of advance while breaking through the enemy's tactical zone of defence (13–18 January 1945) was 2–6km per day, and thereafter, until the enemy grouping was encircled (19–30 January 1945), 15km per day (rifle formations) and 22–36km per day (tank and mechanised formations). The East Prussian strategic operation included the Insterburg, Mlawo-Elbing, Heilsberg, Königsberg and Zemland army group operations.

Fighting Strength, Numerical Strength and Losses

Name of force, period involved in operation	Fighting strength and numerical strength of troops at start of operation		Losses during the operation			
	No of formations	Numerical strength	Irrecoverable losses	Sick and wounded	Total	Average daily losses
3rd Byelorussian Front (whole period)	rifle divisions—54 tank corps—2 ind. tank brigades—6 fortified areas—1	708,600	89,463	332,300	421,763	4,095
2nd Byelorussian Front (13.01–10.02.45)	rifle divisions—63 cavalry divisions—3 tank corps—5 mechanised corps—1 ind. tank brigades—3 fortified areas—3	881,500	36,396	123,094	159,490	5,500
1st Baltic Front's 43rd Army (13.01–20.01.45)	rifle divisions—13 ind. tank brigades—1	79,000	195	1,265	1,460	183
Baltic Fleet (01.02–25.04.45)	—	—	410	1,655	2,065	25
Total	Divisions—133 Corps—8 Brigades—10 Fortified areas—4	1,669,100	126,464	458,314	584,778	5,677

Outcome of the operation. The Soviet troops took over Eastern Prussia and wiped out the defending enemy forces. In the course of the advance 25 enemy divisions were destroyed and 12 divisions suffered heavy casualties. The German Navy lost its most important naval bases, which meant that supplies to the Germans' Courland Group were badly affected. The elimination of the enemy's East Prussian Group weakened the Wehrmacht's forces considerably and adversely affected their overall strategic position on the Soviet-German front.

The East Pomeranian Strategic Offensive Operation, 10 February–4 April 1945

The operation was conducted by the troops of the 2nd Byelorussian Front and the right wing of the 1st Byelorussian Front. From 1 March 1945 the 1st Polish Army also took part in the operation.

It lasted 54 days. The fighting ranged over a front 460km wide. The Soviet troops advanced 130–150km at an average rate of 2–3km per day.

Fighting Strength, Numerical Strength and Losses

Name of force, period involved in operation	Fighting strength and numerical strength of troops at start of operation		Losses during the operation				
	No of formations	Numerical strength	Irrecoverable losses	Sick and wounded	Total	Average daily losses
2nd Byelorussian Front (whole period)	rifle divisions—45 cavalry divisions—3 tank corps—3 mechanised corps—1 ind. tank brigades—1 fortified areas—1	560,900	40,471	132,918	173,389	3,211
1st Byelorussian Front (3rd Shock, 1st and 2nd Guards Tank and 16th Air Armies, 47th and 61st Armies; 01.03–04.04.45)	rifle divisions—27 cavalry divisions—3 tank corps—4 mechanised corps—2 ind. tank brigades—2 self-propelled artillery brigades—1 fortified areas—1	359,600	12,269	40,034	52,303	1,494
Total	Divisions—78 Corps—10 Brigades—4 Fortified areas—2	920,500	52,740	172,952	225,692	4,179
1st Polish Army (01.03–04.04.45)	infantry divisions—5 cavalry brigades—1 ind. tank brigades—1	75,600	2,575	6,093	8,668	248

Outcome of the operation. The Soviet troops, incorporating the 1st Polish Army, reached the Baltic coast and took Kolberg, Gdynia and Danzig. Trapped by the sea, the enemy capitulated. The defeat of Army Group Vistula eliminated the threat of counterstrike by the enemy against the flank and rear of the 1st Byelorussian Front's main forces, who were preparing for the advance on Berlin. The whole of the Polish seaboard with the major towns and ports on the Baltic coast were returned to Poland.

The Vienna Strategic Offensive Operation, 16 March–15 April 1945

The operation was conducted by the troops of the 3rd Ukrainian Front, part of the 2nd Ukrainian Front and the Danube Flotilla. The 1st Bulgarian Army, which was incorporated into the 3rd Ukrainian Front, also took part in the operation.

It lasted 31 days. The fighting ranged over a front 230km wide. The Soviet troops advanced 150–250km. The average rate of advance was 5–8km per day.

Fighting Strength, Numerical Strength and Losses

Name of force, period involved in operation	Fighting strength and numerical strength of troops at start of operation		Losses during the operation				
	No of formations	Numerical strength	Irrecoverable losses	Sick and wounded	Total	Average daily losses
3rd Ukrainian Front (whole period)	rifle divisions—42 airborne divisions—4 cavalry divisions—3 tank corps—3 mechanised corps—2 mechanised brigades—1 self-propelled artillery brigades—1 fortified areas—1	536,700	32,846	106,969	139,815	4,510
2nd Ukrainian Front (46th Army, 2nd Guards Mechanised Corps, part of 5th Air Army; whole period)	rifle divisions—12 mechanised corps—1	101,500	5,815	22,310	28,125	907
Danube Flotilla (whole period)	naval infantry brigades—1	6,500	—	—	—	—
Total	Divisions—61 Corps—6 Brigades—3 Fortified areas—1	644,700	38,661	129,279	167,940	5,417
1st Bulgarian Army (whole period)	infantry divisions—6	100,900	2,698	7,107	9,805	316

Outcome of the operation. Advancing rapidly, the 3rd Ukraininan Front and the left wing of the 2nd Ukrainian Front routed Army Group South's main forces, liberating the whole of Hungary, the southern part of Czechoslovakia and the eastern part of Austria, including Vienna. The successful advance towards Vienna and the 3rd Ukrainian Front's march into eastern Austria speeded up the liberation of Yugoslavia. Army Group E, which was operating there, found itself isolated and was forced to start a general withdrawal.

The Berlin Strategic Offensive Operation, 16 April–8 May 1945

The operation was conducted by the troops of the 1st and 2nd Byelorussian and 1st Ukrainian Fronts, with the aim of taking Berlin and reaching the Elbe in order to join up with the Allied troops. The Dnieper Flotilla, part of the Baltic Fleet and the 1st and 2nd Polish Armies also took part in the operation. In addition, the 28th and 31st Armies, each with nine rifle divisions, were brought in during the operation.

It lasted 23 days. The fighting ranged over a front 300km wide. The Soviet troops advanced 100–220km. The average rate of advance was 5–10km per day.

Fighting Strength, Numerical Strength and Losses

Name of force, period involved in operation	Fighting strength and numerical strength of troops at start of operation		Losses during the operation				
	No of formations	Numerical strength	Irrecoverable losses	Sick and wounded	Total	Average daily losses
2nd Byelorussian Front (minus 5th Guards Tank Army and 19th Army; whole period)	rifle divisions—33 cavalry divisions—3 tank corps—3 mechanised corps—1 ind. tank brigades—1 self-propelled artillery brigades—1	441,600	13,070	46,040	59,110	2,570
1st Byelorussian Front (whole period)	rifle divisions—72 cavalry divisions—6 tank corps—5 mechanised corps—2 ind. tank brigades—6 fortified areas—2 self-propelled artillery brigades—2	908,500	37,610	141,880	179,490	7,804
1st Ukrainian Front (3rd and 5th Guards, 3rd and 4th Guards Tank and 2nd Air Armies; 13th and 52nd Armies; whole period)	rifle divisions—44 cavalry divisions—3 tank corps—5 mechanised corps—4 ind. tank brigades—2 self-propelled artillery brigades—3	550,900	27,580	86,245	113,825	4,949
Dnieper Flotilla (whole period)	—	5,200	16	11	27	1
Baltic Fleet (ships and air force; 20.04–08.05.45)	—	—	15	8	23	1
Total	Divisions—161 Corps—20 Brigades—15 Fortified areas—2	1,906,200	78,291	274,184	352,475	15,325
1st and 2nd Polish Armies (whole period)	infantry divisions—10 tank corps—1 cavalry brigades—1	155,900	2,825	6,067	8,892	387

Outcome of the operation. The Soviet troops routed the Germans' Berlin Group and stormed Berlin itself. Pressing home their attack, they reached the river Elbe where they joined up with the British and American troops. With the fall of Berlin and the loss of key areas, Germany was no longer capable of organised resistance and soon capitulated. With the end of the Berlin operation the way was cleared for encircling and destroying the final major enemy groupings in Austria and Czechoslovakia.

The Prague Strategic Offensive Operation, 6–11 May 1945

This was the Red Army's final operation in Europe. It was conducted by the troops of the 1st, 2nd and 4th Ukrainian Fronts. The 2nd Polish Army, the 1st and 4th Romanian Armies and the 1st Czechoslovak Army Corps also took part in the operation.

It lasted six days and the fighting ranged over a front 1,200km wide. The Soviet troops advanced 160–200km. The average rate of advance was 20–30km per day (rifle formations) and 50–60km per day (tank and mechanised formations).

Fighting Strength, Numerical Strength and Losses

Name of force, period involved in operation	No of formations	Numerical strength	Irrecoverable losses	Sick and wounded	Total	Average daily losses
	Fighting strength and numerical strength of troops at start of operation		Losses during the operation			
1st Ukrainian Front (whole period)	rifle divisions—71 cavalry divisions—3 tank corps—5 mechanised corps—4 ind. tank brigades—3 self-propelled artillery brigades—3	806,400	6,384	16,999	23,383	3,897
4th Ukrainian Front (whole period)	rifle divisions—34 tank corps—1 rifle brigades—6 ind. tank brigades—2 fortified areas—1	350,900	2,299	9,230	11,529	1,922
2nd Ukrainian Front (whole period)	rifle divisions—37 cavalry divisions—6 tank corps—1 mechanised corps—3 rifle brigades—1 ind. tank brigades—1 self-propelled artillery brigades—2 fortified areas—1	613,400	2,582	11,854	14,436	2,406
Total	Divisions—151 Corps—14 Brigades—18 Fortified areas—2	1,770,700	11,265	38,083	49,348	8,225
2nd Polish Army (whole period)	infantry divisions—5 tank corps—1	69,500	300	587	887	148
1st and 4th Romanian Armies (whole period)	infantry divisions—12 cavalry divisions—3	139,500	320	1,410	1,730	288
1st Czechoslovak Army Corps (whole period)	infantry brigades—4 ind. tank brigades—1	48,400	112	421	533	89

Outcome of the operation. The 1st, 2nd and 4th Ukrainian Fronts advanced rapidly, destroying the 860,000-strong enemy grouping which had continued to offer resistance after the surrender document had been signed. Czechoslovakia and its capital, Prague, were liberated. On 11 May Soviet troops reached the Chemnitz-Karlovy Vari-Plzen line, where they met up with advance units of the US Army.

The Manchurian Strategic Offensive Operation, 9 August–2 September 1945

The operation was conducted by the Trans-Baikal and 1st and 2nd Far Eastern Fronts, the Pacific Fleet and the Amur Flotilla. Units and formations of the Mongolian People's Army also took part in the operation. In addition, the 3rd Guards Mechanised and 126th Light Rifle Corps were brought in during the operation.

It lasted 25 days. The fighting ranged over a front 2,700km wide and the Soviet troops advanced 200–800km. The average rate of advance was 35–40km per day (rifle formations) and 70–90km per day (tank and mechanised formations). The Manchurian strategic operation included the Khingan-Mukden, Harbin-Kirin, Sungari and South Sakhalin army group operations.

Fighting Strength, Numerical Strength and Losses

Name of force, period involved in operation	Fighting strength and numerical strength of troops at start of operation		Losses during the operation			
	No of formations	Numerical strength	Irrecoverable losses	Sick and wounded	Total	Average daily losses
Trans-Baikal Front (whole period)	rifle divisions—27 motor rifle divisions—2 motor rifle brigades—1 tank divisions—2 airborne divisions—1 cavalry divisions—1 tank corps—1 mechanised corps—2 ind. tank brigades—6 self-propelled artillery brigades—2 fortified areas—2	638,300	2,228	6,155	8,383	335
2nd Far Eastern Front (whole period)	rifle divisions—11 rifle brigades—4 ind. tank brigades—9 fortified areas—5	334,700	2,449	3,134	5,583	223
1st Far Eastern Front (whole period)	rifle divisions—31 cavalry divisions—1 mechanised corps—1 ind. tank brigades—11 fortified areas—14	586,500	6,324	14,745	21,069	843

Name of force, period involved in operation	Fighting strength and numerical strength of troops at start of operation		Losses during the operation			
	No of formations	Numerical strength	Irrecoverable losses	Sick and wounded	Total	Average daily losses
Pacific Fleet (whole period)	naval infantry brigades—1	97,500	998	300	1,298	52
Amur Flotilla (whole period)	—	12,500	32	91	123	5
Total	Divisions—76 Corps—4 Brigades—34 Fortified areas—21	1,669,500	12,031	24,425	36,456	1,458
Mongolian People's Revolutionary Army formations (whole period)	cavalry divisions—4 motor rifle brigades—1	16,000	72	125	197	8

Outcome of the operation. The troops of Trans-Baikal and 1st and 2nd Far Eastern Fronts, supported by the Pacific Fleet and Amur Flotilla, quickly routed Japan's strongest grouping, the Kwantung Army, thereby liberating Manchuria, North-Eastern China, the northern part of Korea, southern Sakhalin and the Kurile Islands. The defeat of the Kwantung Army and Japan's loss of its military and economic base in China and Korea meant that Japan no longer had any real forces or means of continuing the war. On 2 September 1945 Japanese government representatives were forced to sign an unconditional surrender document.

LOSSES OF FRONTS AND INDEPENDENT ARMIES

The most important link in the armed forces' structure during the Great Patriotic War was the front (army group). These were strategic formations which were capable of undertaking both strategic and operational tasks. They usually encompassed several armies, mechanised, tank, air force and artillery corps and other formations. The very first months of the war proved that success depended on the efforts of not one but two, three or even four fronts. In the course of the war about 90% of defensive and offensive strategic operations were carried out by groupings of this kind.

At the beginning of the war with Germany five fronts were deployed, by December 1941 there were 10, at the end of 1942 there were 12 and in 1943 there were 13 (see Table 76). These changes occurred partly because the fighting spread over a wider area and partly because it was necessary to break the groupings up into smaller units to make them easier to handle.

Table 76. Operational Fronts and Independent Armies

Year, quarter-year, month

Front, independent army	No of days
FRONTS	
Northern	64
North-Western	882
Western, 3rd Byelorussian	1,418
South-Western (1st formation)	386
Southern (1st formation)	399
Central (1st formation)	32
Reserve (1st formation)	76
Bryansk (1st and 2nd formations)	529
Leningrad	1,353
Karelian	1,172
Kalinin, 1st Baltic; Zemland Group	1,262
Volkhov (1st and 2nd formations)	746
Caucasus, Crimean	140
Trans-Caucasus (2nd formation)	320
North Caucasus (1st and 2nd formations)	408
Voronezh, 1st Ukrainian	1,036
Stalingrad (1st formation), Don	218
South-Eastern, Stalingrad (2nd formation)	147
South-Western (2nd formation), 3rd Ukrainian	928

Year, quarter-year, month

Front, independent army	No of days
Southern (2nd formation), 4th Ukr. (1st and 2nd formation)	795
Reserve (2nd formation). Kursk, Orel, Bryansk (3rd formation)	213
Steppe, 2nd Ukrainian	671
Baltic, 2nd Baltic	539
Central (2nd formation), Byelorussian, 1st Byelorussian	815
2nd Byelorussian (1st and 2nd formations)	423
3rd Baltic	179
Trans-Baikal	25
1st Far Eastern	25
2nd Far Eastern	25
Moscow Defensive Zone	667
INDEPENDENT ARMIES	
51st Independent Army	94
7th Independent Army	883
52nd Independent Army	81
4th Independent Army	80
Maritime and Independent Maritime Armies	862
14th Independent Army	176
37th Independent Army	146

In the course of the war the *Stavka* (GHQ) of the Supreme Commander-in-Chief gradually increased the number of operational army formations. If at the outbreak of war operational fronts included 14 combined-arms armies, by 1 December 1941 there were 49. By November 1942 there were 67 combined-arms, two tank and 11 air armies. By 1 July 1943 there were 69 combined-arms, five tank and 13 air armies.

Depending on how the strategic situation developed, individual fronts were disbanded, new ones were formed, some were reorganised, etc. In July 1942, for example, the South-Western Front was disbanded and its troops incorporated into the Stalingrad Front; the same happened to the Southern Front, which was also disbanded in July 1942 and its troops incorporated into the North Caucasus Front.

In the second half of 1943 the number of fronts began to be reduced, so that by the end of the war there were eight: the Leningrad, the 1st, 2nd and 3rd Byelorussian and the 1st, 2nd, 3rd and 4th Ukrainian. Three independent armies also remained, the 14th, the 37th and the Maritime. This was both because the length of the front line had been reduced and because military leaders now had experience in commanding larger fronts.

The tables which follow give the casualty figures for each front and independent army for the period they existed and for each year of the war,[9] except for air defence and military district fronts and armies and *Stavka* reserve formations and units which did not form part of the army on active service. Casualty figures for these forces are included in tables which summarise army and navy losses by year and quarter-year of the war.

The percentage ratio of losses to numerical strength was determined by comparing the number of losses in the front or fleet concerned with the average monthly listed strength for a specific period of time.

The Trans-Caucasus Front's 1st Formation (August–December 1941), which was not directly involved in combat, is not included in Table 76.

The Karelian Front's losses (see tables) for the period December 1944–April 1945 include non-combat losses for the front's headquarters and troops which on 15 November 1944 were transferred to the Supreme Command HQ Reserve. This five-month period is not included in the 1,172 days of the Karelian Front's existence.

Northern Front Personnel Losses (Total for 64 Days)

	Loss category		Officers	Sergeants	Men	Total
Irrecoverable losses	Killed in action, died during casualty evacuation	No	1,938	3,326	17,070	22,334
		% of losses	19.54	18.20	14.20	15.05
	Missing in action, POWs	No	3,791	7,075	50,671	61,537
		% of losses	38.20	38.71	42.17	41.48
	Non-combat losses	No	137	313	1,138	1,588
		% of losses	1.38	1.71	0.95	1.07
	Total irrecoverable losses	No	5,866	10,714	68,879	85,459
		% of losses	59.12	58.62	57.32	57.60
	% of personnel strength: All losses		9.18	11.28	13.77	12.97
	Average monthly losses		4.37	5.37	6.56	6.18

	Loss category		Officers	Sergeants	Men	Total
Sick and wounded (including those evacuated to hospitals)	Wounded, burns and concussion cases	No	3,826	7,279	49,166	60,271
		% of losses	38.56	39.83	40.92	40.62
	Sick	No	231	284	2,119	2,634
		% of losses	2.32	1.55	1.76	1.78
	Frostbite cases	No				
		% of losses				
	Total sick and wounded	No	4,057	7,563	51,285	62,905
		% of losses	40.88	41.38	42.68	42.40
		% of personnel strength:				
		All losses	6.35	7.96	10.26	9.55
		Average monthly losses	3.02	3.79	4.88	4.55
	Total losses	No	9,923	18,277	120,164	148,364
		% of losses	100	100	100	100
		% of personnel strength:				
		All losses	15.53	19.24	24.03	22.52
		Average monthly losses	7.39	9.16	11.44	10.73

North-Western Front Personnel Losses (Total for 882 Days)

	Loss category		Officers	Sergeants	Men	Total
Irrecoverable losses	Killed in action, died during casualty evacuation	No	19,446	42,772	180,629	242,847
		% of losses	23.21	23.16	20.15	20.85
	Missing in action, POWs	No	10,877	26,066	155,498	192,441
		% of losses	12.98	14.12	17.35	16.53
	Non-combat losses	No	1,422	2,280	16,335	20,037
		% of losses	1.71	1.23	1.83	1.72
	Total irrecoverable losses	No	31,745	71,118	352,462	455,325
		% of losses	37.90	38.51	39.33	39.10
		% of personnel strength:				
		All losses	64	110.78	159.05	135.76
		Average monthly losses	2.21	3.83	5.50	4.70
Sick and wounded (including those evacuated to hospitals)	Wounded, burns and concussion cases	No	45,032	99,542	446,587	591,161
		% of losses	53.76	53.90	49.83	50.75
	Sick	No	6,928	13,824	95,097	115,849
		% of losses	8.27	7.49	10.61	9.95
	Frostbite cases	No	63	188	2,060	2,311
		% of losses	0.07	0.10	0.23	0.20
	Total sick and wounded	No	52,023	113,554	543,744	709,321
		% of losses	62.10	61.49	60.67	60.90
		% of personnel strength:				
		All losses	104.89	176.88	245.37	211.49
		Average monthly losses	3.63	6.12	8.49	7.32
	Total losses	No	83,768	184,672	896,206	1,164,646
		% of losses	100	100	100	100
		% of personnel strength:				
		All losses	168.89	287.66	404.43	347.25
		Average monthly losses	5.84	9.95	13.99	12.02

North-Western Front Personnel Losses, by Year

	Loss category		Losses by year				
			1941	1942	1943	1944	1945
Irrecoverable losses	Killed in action, died during casualty evacuation	No	31,511	133,573	77,763		
		% of losses	11.67	23.89	23.18		
	Missing in action, POWs	No	142,190	41,720	8,531		
		% of losses	52.64	7.47	2.54		
	Non-combat losses	No	8,563	8,970	2,504		
		% of losses	3.17	1.60	0.75		
	Total irrecoverable losses	No	182,264	184,263	88,798		
		% of losses	67.48	32.96	26.47		
		% of personnel strength:					
		All losses	70.17	51.26	25.84		
		Average monthly losses	11.14	4.27	2.44		
Sick and wounded (including those evacuated to hospitals)	Wounded, burns and concussion cases	No	83,816	319,111	188,234		
		% of losses	31.03	57.07	56.11		
	Sick	No	3,741	53,878	58,230		
		% of losses	1.39	9.64	17.36		
	Frostbite cases	No	266	1,856	189		
		% of losses	0.10	0.33	0.06		
	Total sick and wounded	No	87,823	374,845	246,653		
		% of losses	32.52	67.04	73.53		
		% of personnel strength:					
		All losses	33.81	104.28	71.79		
		Average monthly losses	5.37	8.69	6.77		
	Total losses	No	270,087	559,108	335,451		
		% of losses	100	100	100		
		% of personnel strength:					
		All losses	103.99	155.54	97.63		
		Average monthly losses	16.51	12.96	9.21		

Western Front Personnel Losses (Total for 1,037 Days)

	Loss category		Officers	Sergeants	Men	Total
Irrecoverable losses	Killed in action, died during casualty evacuation	No	46,086	104,016	436,234	586,336
		% of losses	18.22	18.72	16.01	16.59
	Missing in action, POWs	No	61,875	130,511	674,218	866,604
		% of losses	24.46	23.48	24.74	24.52
	Non-combat losses	No	3,623	9,421	69,305	82,349
		% of losses	1.43	1.69	2.54	2.33
	Total irrecoverable losses	No	111,584	243,948	1,179,757	1,535,289
		% of losses	44.11	43.89	43.29	43.44
		% of personnel strength:				
		All losses	102.46	163.29	231.64	200.01
		Average monthly losses	3.01	4.80	6.81	5.88

	Loss category		Officers	Sergeants	Men	Total
Sick and wounded (including those evacuated to hospitals)	Wounded, burns and concussion cases	No	122,483	279,888	1,301,150	1,703,521
		% of losses	48.41	50.35	47.74	48.20
	Sick	No	18,637	31,310	238,096	288,043
		% of losses	7.37	5.63	8.73	8.15
	Frostbite cases	No	270	707	6,445	7,422
		% of losses	0.11	0.13	0.24	0.21
	Total sick and wounded	No	141,390	311,905	1,545,691	1,998,986
		% of losses	55.89	56.11	56.71	56.56
		% of personnel strength: All losses	129.83	208.77	303.50	260.42
		Average monthly losses	3.82	6.14	8.93	7.66
	Total losses	No	252,974	555,853	2,725,448	3,534,275
		% of losses	100	100	100	100
		% of personnel strength: All losses	232.29	372.06	535.14	460.43
		Average monthly losses	6.83	10.94	15.74	13.54

Western Front Personnel Losses, by Year

			Losses by year				
	Loss category		1941	1942	1943	1944	1945
Irrecoverable losses	Killed in action, died during casualty evacuation	No	106,997	244,574	195,525	39,240	
		% of losses	8.24	22.46	20.81	18.87	
	Missing in action, POWs	No	798,465	44,966	21,333	1,840	
		% of losses	61.52	4.13	2.27	0.88	
	Non-combat losses	No	50,831	25,095	5,541	882	
		% of losses	3.92	2.31	0.59	0.43	
	Total irrecoverable losses	No	956,293	314,635	222,399	41,962	
		% of losses	73.68	28.90	23.67	20.18	
		% of personnel strength: All losses	190.83	32.89	28.96	7.87	
		Average monthly losses	30.29	2.74	2.41	2.13	
Sick and wounded (including those evacuated to hospitals)	Wounded, burns and concussion cases	No	328,735	665,341	582,977	126,468	
		% of losses	25.33	61.11	62.05	60.81	
	Sick	No	9,069	105,540	133,954	39,480	
		% of losses	0.70	9.69	14.26	18.98	
	Frostbite cases	No	3,857	3,249	245	71	
		% of losses	0.29	0.30	0.02	0.03	
	Total sick and wounded	No	341,661	774,130	717,176	166,019	
		% of losses	26.32	71.10	76.33	79.82	
		% of personnel strength: All losses	68.18	80.92	93.41	31.15	
		Average monthly losses	10.82	6.74	7.79	8.42	
	Total losses	No	1,297,954	1,088,765	939,575	207,981	
		% of losses	100	100	100	100	
		% of personnel strength: All losses	259.01	113.81	122.37	39.02	
		Average monthly losses	41.11	9.48	10.20	10.55	

3rd Byelorussian Front Personnel Losses (Total for 381 Days)

	Loss category		Officers	Sergeants	Men	Total
Irrecoverable losses	Killed in action, died during casualty evacuation	No	15,196	33,642	112,848	161,686
		% of losses	22.61	21.30	18.25	19.17
	Missing in action, POWs	No	826	1,488	6,978	9,292
		% of losses	1.22	0.94	1.13	1.10
	Non-combat losses	No	496	987	3,669	5,152
		% of losses	0.74	0.63	0.59	0.61
	Total irrecoverable losses	No	16,518	36,117	123,495	176,130
		% of losses	24.57	22.87	19.97	20.88
		% of personnel strength:				
		All losses	17.17	24.29	32.10	27.97
		Average monthly losses	1.37	1.94	2.57	2.24
Sick and wounded (including those evacuated to hospitals)	Wounded, burns and concussion cases	No	42,309	104,987	409,189	556,485
		% of losses	62.95	66.48	66.19	65.99
	Sick	No	8,389	16,800	85,586	110,775
		% of losses	12.48	10.64	13.84	13.13
	Frostbite cases	No	1	8	28	37
		% of losses		0.01		
	Total sick and wounded	No	50,699	121,795	494,803	667,297
		% of losses	75.43	77.13	80.03	79.12
		% of personnel strength:				
		All losses	52.70	81.91	128.62	105.99
		Average monthly losses	4.22	6.55	10.29	8.48
	Total losses	No	67,217	157,912	618,298	843,427
		% of losses	100	100	100	100
		% of personnel strength:				
		All losses	69.87	106.20	160.72	133.96
		Average monthly losses	5.59	8.49	12.86	10.72

3rd Byelorussian Front Personnel Losses, by Year

	Loss category		Losses by year				
			1941	1942	1943	1944	1945
Irrecoverable losses	Killed in action, died during casualty evacuation	No				77,733	83,953
		% of losses				18.44	19.91
	Missing in action, POWs	No				5,518	3,774
		% of losses				1.31	0.89
	Non-combat losses	No				3,323	1,829
		% of losses				0.79	0.43
	Total irrecoverable losses	No				86,574	89,556
		% of losses				20.54	21.23
		% of personnel strength:					
		All losses				15.54	12.01
		Average monthly losses				1.87	2.86

			Losses by year				
	Loss category		1941	1942	1943	1944	1945
Sick and wounded (including those evacuated to hospitals)	Wounded, burns and concussion cases	No				258,611	297,874
		% of losses				61.34	70.61
	Sick	No				76,379	34,396
		% of losses				18.12	8.15
	Frostbite cases	No					37
		% of losses					0.01
	Total sick and wounded	No				334,990	332,307
		% of losses				79.46	78.77
		% of personnel strength: All losses				60.13	44.57
		Average monthly losses				7.25	10.61
	Total losses	No				421,564	421,863
		% of losses				100	100
		% of personnel strength: All losses				75.67	56.58
		Average monthly losses				9.12	13.47

South-Western Front (1st Formation) Personnel Losses (Total for 386 Days)

	Loss category		Officers	Sergeants	Men	Total
Irrecoverable losses	Killed in action, died during casualty evacuation	No	10,144	18,580	89,441	118,165
		% of losses	9.98	9.94	8.66	8.94
	Missing in action, POWs	No	65,552	121,847	656,044	843,443
		% of losses	64.49	65.16	63.51	63.82
	Non-combat losses	No	2,227	5,098	48,165	55,490
		% of losses	2.19	2.72	4.66	4.20
	Total irrecoverable losses	No	77,923	145,525	793,650	1,017,098
		% of losses	76.66	77.82	76.83	76.96
		% of personnel strength: All losses	127.12	185.38	237.90	214.85
		Average monthly losses	10.09	14.71	18.88	17.05
Sick and wounded (including those evacuated to hospitals)	Wounded, burns and concussion cases	No	21,536	37,815	211,716	271,067
		% of losses	21.19	20.22	20.50	20.50
	Sick	No	1,747	2,226	16,194	20,167
		% of losses	1.72	1.19	1.57	1.53
	Frostbite cases	No	445	1,440	11,411	13,296
		% of losses	0.43	0.77	1.10	1.01
	Total sick and wounded	No	23,728	41,481	239,321	304,530
		% of losses	23.34	22.18	23.17	23.04
		% of personnel strength: All losses	38.71	52.84	71.74	64.33
		Average monthly losses	3.07	4.19	5.69	5.11
	Total losses	No	101,651	187,006	1,032,971	1,321,628
		% of losses	100	100	100	100
		% of personnel strength: All losses	165.83	238.22	309.64	279.18
		Average monthly losses	13.16	18.90	24.57	22.16

South-Western Front (1st Formation) Personnel Losses, by Year

	Loss category		Losses by year				
			1941	1942	1943	1944	1945
Irrecoverable losses	Killed in action, died during casualty evacuation	No	60,016	58,149			
		% of losses	7.05	12.38			
	Missing in action, POWs	No	607,860	235,583			
		% of losses	71.36	50.14			
	Non-combat losses	No	49,957	5,533			
		% of losses	5.87	1.17			
	Total irrecoverable losses	No	717,833	299,265			
		% of losses	84.28	63.69			
		% of personnel strength:					
		All losses	151.39	63.29			
		Average monthly losses	24.03	10.05			
Sick and wounded (including those evacuated to hospitals)	Wounded, burns and concussion cases	No	128,973	142,094			
		% of losses	15.14	30.24			
	Sick	No	4,069	16,098			
		% of losses	0.48	3.43			
	Frostbite cases	No	888	12,408			
		% of losses	0.10	2.64			
	Total sick and wounded	No	133,930	170,600			
		% of losses	15.72	36.31			
		% of personnel strength:					
		All losses	28.25	36.08			
		Average monthly losses	4.48	5.72			
	Total losses	No	851,763	469,865			
		% of losses	100	100			
		% of personnel strength:					
		All losses	179.64	99.37			
		Average monthly losses	28.51	15.77			

Southern Front (1st Formation) Personnel Losses (Total for 399 Days)

	Loss category		Officers	Sergeants	Men	Total
Irrecoverable losses	Killed in action, died during casualty evacuation	No	9,302	17,159	87,997	114,458
		% of losses	16.91	16.30	13.91	14.44
	Missing in action, POWs	No	20,769	32,030	252,631	305,430
		% of losses	37.73	30.44	39.95	38.53
	Non-combat losses	No	1,092	2,904	24,775	28,771
		% of losses	1.98	2.76	3.92	3.63
	Total irrecoverable losses	No	31,163	52,093	365,403	448,659
		% of losses	56.62	49.50	57.78	56.60
		% of personnel strength:				
		All losses	53.00	66.28	103.02	91.17
		Average monthly losses	4.05	5.07	7.88	6.97

	Loss category		Officers	Sergeants	Men	Total
Sick and wounded (including those evacuated to hospitals)	Wounded, burns and concussion cases	No	20,289	46,379	216,302	282,970
		% of losses	36.86	44.07	34.20	35.70
	Sick	No	2,959	4,471	33,435	40,865
		% of losses	5.38	4.26	5.29	5.15
	Frostbite cases	No	630	2,285	17,280	20,195
		% of losses	1.14	2.17	2.73	2.55
	Total sick and wounded	No	23,878	53,135	267,017	344,030
		% of losses	43.38	50.50	42.22	43.40
		% of personnel strength:				
		All losses	40.61	67.60	75.28	69.91
		Average monthly losses	3.10	5.17	5.76	5.34
	Total losses	No	55,041	105,228	632,420	792,689
		% of losses	100	100	100	100
		% of personnel strength:				
		All losses	93.61	133.88	178.30	161.08
		Average monthly losses	7.15	10.24	13.64	12.31

Southern Front (1st Formation) Personnel Losses, by Year

			Losses by year				
	Loss category		1941	1942	1943	1944	1945
Irrecoverable losses	Killed in action, died during casualty evacuation	No	32,362	82,096			
		% of losses	10.36	17.09			
	Missing in action, POWs	No	188,306	117,124			
		% of losses	60.30	24.38			
	Non-combat losses	No	17,909	10,862			
		% of losses	5.73	2.26			
	Total irrecoverable losses	No	238,577	210,082			
		% of losses	76.39	43.73			
		% of personnel strength:					
		All losses	62.50	36.79			
		Average monthly losses	10.08	5.33			
Sick and wounded (including those evacuated to hospitals)	Wounded, burns and concussion cases	No	66,809	216,161			
		% of losses	21.39	45			
	Sick	No	4,927	35,938			
		% of losses	1.58	7.48			
	Frostbite cases	No	2,004	18,191			
		% of losses	0.64	3.79			
	Total sick and wounded	No	73,740	270,290			
		% of losses	23.61	56.27			
		% of personnel strength:					
		All losses	19.32	47.34			
		Average monthly losses	3.12	6.86			
	Total losses	No	312,317	480,372			
		% of losses	100	100			
		% of personnel strength:					
		All losses	81.82	84.13			
		Average monthly losses	13.20	12.19			

Central Front (1st Formation) Personnel Losses (Total for 32 days)

	Loss category		Officers	Sergeants	Men	Total
Irrecoverable losses	Killed in action, died during casualty evacuation	No	931	1,330	6,938	9,199
		% of losses	8.61	7.06	6.12	6.43
	Missing in action, POWs	No	2,568	4,093	39,163	45,824
		% of losses	23.77	21.75	34.54	32.05
	Non-combat losses	No	4,797	9,741	41,447	55,985
		% of losses	44.39	51.76	36.56	39.15
	Total irrecoverable losses	No	8,296	15,164	87,548	111,008
		% of losses	76.77	80.57	77.22	77.63
		% of personnel strength:				
		All losses	30.06	44.34	44.64	43.04
		Average monthly losses	30.06	44.34	44.64	43.04
Sick and wounded (including those evacuated to hospitals)	Wounded, burns and concussion cases	No	2,442	3,588	25,620	31,650
		% of losses	22.60	19.06	22.60	22.13
	Sick	No	69	68	210	347
		% of losses	0.63	0.37	0.18	0.24
	Frostbite cases	No				
		% of losses				
	Total sick and wounded	No	2,511	3,656	25,830	31,997
		% of losses	23.23	19.43	22.78	22.37
		% of personnel strength:				
		All losses	9.10	10.69	13.17	12.41
		Average monthly losses	9.10	10.69	13.17	12.41
	Total losses	No	10,807	18,820	113,378	143,005
		% of losses	100	100	100	100
		% of personnel strength:				
		All losses	39.16	55.03	57.81	55.45
		Average monthly losses	39.16	55.03	57.81	55.45

Reserve Front (1st Formation) Personnel Losses (Total for 76 Days)

	Loss category		Officers	Sergeants	Men	Total
Irrecoverable losses	Killed in action, died during casualty evacuation	No	2,942	6,246	29,267	38,455
		% of losses	12.84	15.89	11.19	11.88
	Missing in action, POWs	No	10,003	21,384	107,243	138,630
		% of losses	43.67	54.41	41.01	42.82
	Non-combat losses	No	262	750	5,944	6,956
		% of losses	1.14	1.91	2.27	2.15
	Total irrecoverable losses	No	13,207	28,380	142,454	184,041
		% of losses	57.65	72.21	54.47	56.85
		% of personnel strength:				
		All losses	31.98	46.75	40.67	40.69
		Average monthly losses	12.79	18.70	16.27	16.28

	Loss category		Officers	Sergeants	Men	Total
Sick and wounded (including those evacuated to hospitals)	Wounded, burns and concussion cases	No	9,588	10,800	118,063	138,451
		% of losses	41.86	27.48	45.14	42.76
	Sick	No	113	123	1,033	1,269
		% of losses	0.49	0.31	0.39	0.39
	Frostbite cases	No				
		% of losses				
	Total sick and wounded	No	9,701	10,923	119,096	139,720
		% of losses	42.35	27.79	45.53	43.15
		% of personnel strength:				
		All losses	23.49	18	34	30.89
		Average monthly losses	9.40	7.20	13.60	12.36
	Total losses	No	22,908	39,303	261,550	323,761
		% of losses	100	100	100	100
		% of personnel strength:				
		All losses	55.47	64.75	74.67	71.58
		Average monthly losses	22.19	25.90	29.87	28.64

Bryansk Front (1st and 2nd Formations) Personnel Losses (Total for 529 Days)

	Loss category		Officers	Sergeants	Men	Total
Irrecoverable losses	Killed in action, died during casualty evacuation	No	8,399	20,049	73,492	101,940
		% of losses	18.83	20.24	16.58	17.37
	Missing in action, POWs	No	13,109	27,817	149,385	190,311
		% of losses	29.40	28.09	33.71	32.43
	Non-combat losses	No	522	1,720	8,616	10,858
		% of losses	1.17	1.73	1.94	1.85
	Total irrecoverable losses	No	22,030	49,586	231,493	303,109
		% of losses	49.40	50.06	52.23	51.65
		% of personnel strength:				
		All losses	54.81	86.57	109.95	104.04
		Average monthly losses	3.17	5	6.36	6.01
Sick and wounded (including those evacuated to hospitals)	Wounded, burns and concussion cases	No	20,227	45,108	179,132	244,467
		% of losses	45.36	45.55	40.42	41.66
	Sick	No	2,278	4,191	30,984	37,453
		% of losses	5.11	4.23	6.99	6.38
	Frostbite cases	No	56	159	1,603	1,818
		% of losses	0.13	0.16	0.36	0.31
	Total sick and wounded	No	22,561	49,458	211,719	283,738
		% of losses	50.60	49.94	47.77	48.35
		% of personnel strength:				
		All losses	56.14	86.34	100.56	97.39
		Average monthly losses	3.24	4.99	5.81	5.63
	Total losses	No	44,591	99,044	443,212	586,847
		% of losses	100	100	100	100
		% of personnel strength:				
		All losses	110.95	172.91	210.51	201.43
		Average monthly losses	6.41	9.99	12.17	11.64

Bryansk Front (1st and 2nd Formations) Personnel Losses, by Year

	Loss category		Losses by year				
			1941	1942	1943	1944	1945
Irrecoverable losses	Killed in action, died during casualty evacuation	No	14,231	49,689	38,020		
		% of losses	7.17	19.59	28.18		
	Missing in action, POWs	No	138,417	46,706	5,188		
		% of losses	69.79	18.42	3.85		
	Non-combat losses	No	3,044	7,088	726		
		% of losses	1.53	2.80	0.54		
	Total irrecoverable losses	No	155,692	103,483	43,934		
		% of losses	78.49	40.81	32.57		
		% of personnel strength:					
		All losses	86.21	30.50	11.22		
		Average monthly losses	29.73	2.54	4.82		
Sick and wounded (including those evacuated to hospitals)	Wounded, burns and concussion cases	No	41,133	122,890	80,444		
		% of losses	20.74	48.46	59.63		
	Sick	No	998	26,215	10,247		
		% of losses	0.50	10.34	7.60		
	Frostbite cases	No	529	1,004	278		
		% of losses	0.27	0.39	0.20		
	Total sick and wounded	No	42,660	150,109	90,969		
		% of losses	21.51	59.19	67.43		
		% of personnel strength:					
		All losses	23.62	44.24	23.23		
		Average monthly losses	8.15	3.69	9.97		
	Total losses	No	198,352	253,592	134,903		
		% of losses	100	100	100		
		% of personnel strength:					
		All losses	109.83	74.74	34.45		
		Average monthly losses	37.88	6.23	14.79		

Leningrad Front Personnel Losses (Total for 1,353 Days)

	Loss category		Officers	Sergeants	Men	Total
Irrecoverable losses	Killed in action, died during casualty evacuation	No	26,789	64,523	240,747	332,059
		% of losses	21.88	21.11	18.14	18.92
	Missing in action, POWs	No	6,664	14,225	90,253	111,142
		% of losses	5.44	4.66	6.80	6.33
	Non-combat losses	No	1971	3,550	18,803	24,324
		% of losses	1.61	1.16	1.42	1.39
	Total irrecoverable losses	No	35,424	82,298	349,803	467,525
		% of losses	28.93	26.93	26.36	26.64
		% of personnel strength:				
		All losses	45.71	72.64	104.85	89.16
		Average monthly losses	1.03	1.64	2.36	2.01

	Loss category		Officers	Sergeants	Men	Total
Sick and wounded (including those evacuated to hospitals)	Wounded, burns and concussion cases	No	67,822	176,583	705,356	949,761
		% of losses	55.39	57.78	53.16	54.12
	Sick	No	19,101	46,252	267,973	333,326
		% of losses	15.61	15.14	20.20	18.99
	Frostbite cases	No	91	452	3,743	4,286
		% of losses	0.07	0.15	0.28	0.25
	Total sick and wounded	No	87,014	223,287	977,072	1,287,373
		% of losses	71.07	73.07	73.64	73.36
		% of personnel strength: All losses	112.27	197.08	292.89	245.49
		Average monthly losses	2.54	4.44	6.60	5.53
	Total losses	No	122,438	305,585	1,326,875	1,754,898
		% of losses	100	100	100	100
		% of personnel strength: All losses	157.98	269.71	397.74	334.65
		Average monthly losses	3.57	6.08	8.96	7.54

Leningrad Front Personnel Losses, by Year

			Losses by year				
	Loss category		1941	1942	1943	1944	1945
Irrecoverable losses	Killed in action, died during casualty evacuation	No	62,187	62,747	74,473	128,999	3,653
		% of losses	18.87	19.65	19.06	19.37	7.40
	Missing in action, POWs	No	74,280	14,560	9,841	12,231	230
		% of losses	22.54	4.56	2.52	1.84	0.46
	Non-combat losses	No	8,284	6,371	4,431	3,872	1,366
		% of losses	2.52	1.99	1.13	0.58	2.77
	Total irrecoverable losses	No	144,751	83,678	88,745	145,102	5,249
		% of losses	43.93	26.20	22.71	21.79	10.63
		% of personnel strength. All losses	28.09	20.14	17.26	23.70	0.86
		Average monthly losses	6.69	1.68	1.44	1.97	0.21
Sick and wounded (including those evacuated to hospitals)	Wounded, burns and concussion cases	No	165,305	153,661	213,602	406,153	11,040
		% of losses	50.17	48.11	54.66	61	22.37
	Sick	No	17,712	80,184	88,263	114,094	33,073
		% of losses	5.37	25.11	22.58	17.14	67
	Frostbite cases	No	1,762	1,861	184	478	1
		% of losses	0.53	0.58	0.05	0.07	
	Total sick and wounded	No	184,779	235,706	302,049	520,725	44,114
		% of losses	56.07	73.80	77.29	78.21	89.37
		% of personnel strength: All losses	35.85	56.73	58.74	85.06	7.27
		Average monthly losses	8.53	4.73	4.89	7.09	1.73
	Total losses	No	329,530	319,384	390,794	665,827	49,363
		% of losses	100	100	100	100	100
		% of personnel strength: All losses	63.94	76.87	76	108.76	8.13
		Average monthly losses	15.22	6.41	6.33	9.06	1.94

Karelian Front Personnel Losses (Total for 1,172 Days)

	Loss category		Officers	Sergeants	Men	Total
Irrecoverable losses	Killed in action, died during casualty evacuation	No	5,192	15,598	54,745	75,535
		% of losses	21.15	20.87	17.06	17.97
	Missing in action, POWs	No	1,897	3,321	25,327	30,545
		% of losses	7.73	4.44	7.89	7.27
	Non-combat losses	No	460	692	3,203	4,355
		% of losses	1.87	0.93	1	1.04
	Total irrecoverable losses	No	7,549	19,611	83,275	110,435
		% of losses	30.75	26.24	25.95	26.28
		% of personnel strength:				
		All losses	21.21	33.87	46.37	40.44
		Average monthly losses	0.56	0.88	1.20	1.05
Sick and wounded (including those evacuated to hospitals)	Wounded, burns and concussion cases	No	11,466	35,925	132,604	179,995
		% of losses	46.71	48.06	41.31	42.83
	Sick	No	5,462	18,795	102,146	126,403
		% of losses	22.25	25.14	31.82	30.08
	Frostbite cases	No	71	418	2,938	3,427
		% of losses	0.29	0.56	0.92	0.81
	Total sick and wounded	No	16,999	55,138	237,688	309,825
		% of losses	69.25	73.76	74.05	73.72
		% of personnel strength:				
		All losses	47.75	95.23	132.34	113.45
		Average monthly losses	1.24	2.48	3.45	2.95
	Total losses	No	24,548	74,749	320,963	420,260
		% of losses	100	100	100	100
		% of personnel strength:				
		All losses	68.96	129.10	178.71	153.89
		Average monthly losses	1.80	3.36	4.65	4

Karelian Front Personnel Losses, by Year

	Loss category		Losses by year				
			1941	1942	1943	1944	1945
Irrecoverable losses	Killed in action, died during casualty evacuation	No	14,720	22,927	8,111	29,777	
		% of losses	18.92	18.53	14.16	18.65	
	Missing in action, POWs	No	18,685	8,086	456	3,318	
		% of losses	24.02	6.53	0.80	2.08	
	Non-combat losses	No	632	1,491	406	1,705	121
		% of losses	0.81	1.21	0.71	1.07	6.58
	Total irrecoverable losses	No	34,037	32,504	8,973	34,800	121
		% of losses	43.75	26.27	15.67	21.80	6.58
		% of personnel strength:					
		All losses	18.55	12.09	3.58	10.56	
		Average monthly losses	4.64	1	0.30	1	

	Loss category		Losses by year				
			1941	1942	1943	1944	1945
Sick and wounded (including those evacuated to hospitals)	Wounded, burns and concussion cases	No	37,092	53,849	15,181	73,873	
		% of losses	47.68	43.53	26.51	46.27	
	Sick	No	5,292	36,202	32,933	50,258	1,718
		% of losses	6.80	29.27	57.50	31.48	93.42
	Frostbite cases	No	1,374	1,154	185	714	
		% of losses	1.77	0.93	0.32	0.45	
	Total sick and wounded	No	43,758	91,205	48,299	124,845	1,718
		% of losses	56.25	73.73	84.33	78.20	93.42
		% of personnel strength:					
		All losses	23.84	33.92	19.25	37.89	
		Average monthly losses	5.96	2.83	1.60	3.61	
	Total losses	No	77,795	123,709	57,272	159,645	1,839
		% of losses	100	100	100	100	100
		% of personnel strength:					
		All losses	42.39	46.01	22.83	48.45	
		Average monthly losses	10.60	3.83	1.90	4.61	

Kalinin Front, 1st Baltic Front and Zemland Group Personnel Losses (Total for 1,262 Days)

	Loss category		Officers	Sergeants	Men	Total
Irrecoverable losses	Killed in action, died during casualty evacuation	No	38,938	95,286	356,422	490,646
		% of losses	24.15	24.22	22.02	22.58
	Missing in action, POWs	No	6,655	13,755	79,888	100,298
		% of losses	4.12	3.50	4.94	4.62
	Non-combat losses	No	1,544	4,069	24,572	30,185
		% of losses	0.96	1.03	1.52	1.39
	Total irrecoverable losses	No	47,137	113,110	460,882	621,129
		% of losses	29.23	28.75	28.48	28.59
		% of personnel strength:				
		All losses	66.20	107.52	147.01	126.79
		Average monthly losses	1.60	2.60	3.55	3.06
Sick and wounded (including those evacuated to hospitals)	Wounded, burns and concussion cases	No	97,351	244,001	955,129	1,296,481
		% of losses	60.37	62.03	59.02	59.67
	Sick	No	16,662	35,706	195,638	248,006
		% of losses	10.34	9.09	12.09	11.41
	Frostbite cases	No	96	516	6,663	7,275
		% of losses	0.06	0.13	0.41	0.33
	Total sick and wounded	No	114,109	280,223	1,157,430	1,551,762
		% of losses	70.77	71.25	71.52	71.41
		% of personnel strength:				
		All losses	160.27	266.37	369.20	316.75
		Average monthly losses	3.87	6.43	8.92	7.65
	Total losses	No	161,246	393,333	1,618,312	2,172,891
		% of losses	100	100	100	100
		% of personnel strength:				
		All losses	226.47	373.89	516.21	443.54
		Average monthly losses	5.47	9.03	12.47	10.71

Kalinin Front, 1st Baltic Front and Zemland Group Personnel Losses, by Year

	Loss category		Losses by year				
			1941	1942	1943	1944	1945
Irrecoverable losses	Killed in action, died during casualty evacuation	No	23,186	221,726	112,753	115,090	17,891
		% of losses	19.56	25.62	22.67	19.22	19.29
	Missing in action, POWs	No	18,866	55,826	9,492	13,788	2,326
		% of losses	15.92	6.45	1.91	2.30	2.51
	Non-combat losses	No	7,973	13,984	2,488	4,379	1,361
		% of losses	6.73	1.61	0.50	0.73	1.47
	Total irrecoverable losses	No	50,025	291,536	124,733	133,257	21,578
		% of losses	42.21	33.68	25.08	22.25	23.27
		% of personnel strength:					
		All losses	25.55	47.97	26.92	27.12	6.86
		Average monthly losses	10.65	4	2.24	2.26	2.28
Sick and wounded (including those evacuated to hospitals)	Wounded, burns and concussion cases	No	65,491	507,607	301,602	367,995	53,786
		% of losses	55.26	58.66	60.66	61.45	57.99
	Sick	No	1,990	60,534	70,615	97,519	17,348
		% of losses	1.68	6.99	14.20	16.28	18.71
	Frostbite cases	No	1,003	5,818	297	124	33
		% of losses	0.85	0.67	0.06	0.02	0.03
	Total sick and wounded	No	68,484	573,959	372,514	465,638	71,167
		% of losses	57.79	66.32	74.92	77.75	76.73
		% of personnel strength:					
		All losses	34.98	94.44	80.38	94.78	22.64
		Average monthly losses	14.57	7.87	6.70	7.90	7.52
	Total losses	No	118,509	865,495	497,247	598,895	92,745
		% of losses	100	100	100	100	100
		% of personnel strength:					
		All losses	60.53	142.41	107.30	121.90	29.50
		Average monthly losses	25.22	11.87	8.94	10.16	9.80

Volkhov Front (1st and 2nd Formations) Personnel Losses (Total for 746 Days)

	Loss category		Officers	Sergeants	Men	Total
Irrecoverable losses	Killed in action, died during casualty evacuation	No	17,428	36,027	145,254	198,709
		% of losses	21.34	22.49	20.06	20.57
	Missing in action, POWs	No	9,788	14,759	64,776	89,323
		% of losses	11.99	9.21	8.95	9.25
	Non-combat losses	No	770	1,267	8,554	10,591
		% of losses	0.94	0.79	1.18	1.10
	Total irrecoverable losses	No	27,986	52,053	218,584	298,623
		% of losses	34.27	32.49	30.19	30.92
		% of personnel strength:				
		All losses	49.53	75.44	99.31	86.41
		Average monthly losses	2.02	3.08	4.05	3.53

	Loss category		Officers	Sergeants	Men	Total
Sick and wounded (including those evacuated to hospitals)	Wounded, burns and concussion cases	No	45,705	94,936	410,073	550,714
		% of losses	55.97	59.25	56.64	57.02
	Sick	No	7,893	12,919	90,974	111,786
		% of losses	9.66	8.06	12.57	11.57
	Frostbite cases	No	81	315	4,338	4,734
		% of losses	0.10	0.20	0.60	0.49
	Total sick and wounded	No	53,679	108,170	505,385	667,234
		% of losses	65.73	67.51	69.81	69.08
		% of personnel strength:				
		All losses	95.01	156.77	229.62	193.06
		Average monthly losses	3.88	6.40	9.37	7.88
	Total losses	No	81,665	160,223	723,969	965,857
		% of losses	100	100	100	100
		% of personnel strength:				
		All losses	144.54	232.21	328.93	279.47
		Average monthly losses	5.90	9.48	13.42	11.41

Volkhov Front (1st and 2nd Formations) Personnel Losses, by Year

	Loss category		Losses by year				
			1941	1942	1943	1944	1945
Irrecoverable losses	Killed in action, died during casualty evacuation	No	199	117,237	69,794	11,479	
		% of losses	9.72	19.80	21.72	22.82	
	Missing in action, POWs	No		82,337	6,520	466	
		% of losses		13.91	2.03	0.93	
	Non-combat losses	No		8,935	1,590	66	
		% of losses		1.51	0.49	0.13	
	Total irrecoverable losses	No	199	208,509	77,904	12,011	
		% of losses	9.72	35.22	24.24	23.88	
		% of personnel strength:					
		All losses	0.08	60.07	22.35	4.10	
		Average monthly losses	0.16	5.72	1.86	2.73	
Sick and wounded (including those evacuated to hospitals)	Wounded, burns and concussion cases	No	1,307	326,477	189,587	33,343	
		% of losses	63.82	55.14	58.99	66.28	
	Sick	No		53,081	53,766	4,939	
		% of losses		8.96	16.73	9.82	
	Frostbite cases	No	542	4,034	147	11	
		% of losses	26.46	0.68	0.04	0.02	
	Total sick and wounded	No	1,849	383,592	243,500	38,293	
		% of losses	90.28	64.78	75.76	76.12	
		% of personnel strength:					
		All losses	0.76	110.52	69.87	13.07	
		Average monthly losses	1.52	10.53	5.82	8.71	
	Total losses	No	2,048	592,101	321,404	50,304	
		% of losses	100	100	100	100	
		% of personnel strength:					
		All losses	0.84	170.59	92.22	17.17	
		Average monthly losses	1.68	16.25	7.68	11.44	

Caucasus Front Personnel Losses (Total for 29 Days)

	Loss category		Officers	Sergeants	Men	Total
Irrecoverable losses	Killed in action, died during casualty evacuation	No	596	1,358	5,950	7,904
		% of losses	21.14	23.42	16.45	17.65
	Missing in action, POWs	No	1,027	2,073	17,292	20,392
		% of losses	36.43	35.75	47.82	45.53
	Non-combat losses	No	141	305	1,805	2,251
		% of losses	5	5.25	4.99	5.03
	Total irrecoverable losses	No	1,764	3,736	25,047	30,547
		% of losses	62.57	64.42	69.26	68.21
		% of personnel strength: All losses	3.21	4.85	6.63	5.99
		Average monthly losses	3.21	4.85	6.63	5.99
Sick and wounded (including those evacuated to hospitals)	Wounded, burns and concussion cases	No	844	1,637	7,068	9,549
		% of losses	29.94	28.23	19.55	21.33
	Sick	No	85	134	1,538	1,757
		% of losses	3.02	2.31	4.25	3.92
	Frostbite cases	No	126	292	2,511	2,929
		% of losses	4.47	5.04	6.94	6.54
	Total sick and wounded	No	1,055	2,063	11,117	14,235
		% of losses	37.43	35.58	30.74	31.79
		% of personnel strength: All losses	1.92	2.68	2.94	2.79
		Average monthly losses	1.92	2.68	2.94	2.79
	Total losses	No	2,819	5,799	36,164	44,782
		% of losses	100	100	100	100
		% of personnel strength: All losses	5.13	7.53	9.57	8.78
		Average monthly losses	5.13	7.53	9.57	8.78

Crimean Front Personnel Losses (Total for 111 Days)

	Loss category		Officers	Sergeants	Men	Total
Irrecoverable losses	Killed in action, died during casualty evacuation	No	2,722	5,952	22,377	31,051
		% of losses	12.52	13.70	10.51	11.17
	Missing in action, POWs	No	12,446	23,835	125,609	161,890
		% of losses	57.27	54.84	59.02	58.22
	Non-combat losses	No	97	206	1,563	1,866
		% of losses	0.45	0.47	0.73	0.67
	Total irrecoverable losses	No	15,265	29,993	149,549	194,807
		% of losses	70.24	69.01	70.26	70.06
		% of personnel strength: All losses	55.31	70.57	87.40	80.76
		Average monthly losses	15.36	19.60	24.28	22.43

	Loss category		Officers	Sergeants	Men	Total
Sick and wounded (including those evacuated to hospitals)	Wounded, burns and concussion cases	No	6,019	12,925	56,803	75,747
		% of losses	27.69	29.75	26.69	27.24
	Sick	No	445	500	6,026	6,971
		% of losses	2.05	1.15	2.83	2.51
	Frostbite cases	No	5	41	472	518
		% of losses	0.02	0.09	0.22	0.19
	Total sick and wounded	No	6,469	13,466	63,301	83,236
		% of losses	29.76	30.99	29.74	29.94
		% of personnel strength:				
		All losses	23.44	31.69	37.00	34.51
		Average monthly losses	6.51	8.80	10.28	9.59
	Total losses	No	21,734	43,459	212,850	278,043
		% of losses	100	100	100	100
		% of personnel strength:				
		All losses	78.75	102.26	124.40	115.27
		Average monthly losses	21.87	28.40	34.56	32.02

Caucasus Front (2nd Formation) Personnel Losses (Total for 320 Days)

	Loss category		Officers	Sergeants	Men	Total
Irrecoverable losses	Killed in action, died during casualty evacuation	No	7,022	14,213	51,454	72,689
		% of losses	21.82	22.41	18.99	19.83
	Missing in action, POWs	No	5,120	10,419	56,790	72,329
		% of losses	15.90	16.43	20.95	19.73
	Non-combat losses	No	532	1,161	7,447	9,140
		% of losses	1.65	1.83	2.75	2.49
	Total irrecoverable losses	No	12,674	25,793	115,691	154,158
		% of losses	39.37	40.67	42.69	42.05
		% of personnel strength:				
		All losses	9.17	14.28	17.41	15.68
		Average monthly losses	0.87	1.36	1.66	1.49
Sick and wounded (including those evacuated to hospitals)	Wounded, burns and concussion cases	No	16,594	32,288	122,637	171,519
		% of losses	51.55	50.92	45.26	46.79
	Sick	No	2,740	4,610	29,459	36,809
		% of losses	8.51	7.27	10.87	10.04
	Frostbite cases	No	180	721	3,207	4,108
		% of losses	0.56	1.14	1.18	1.12
	Total sick and wounded	No	19,514	37,619	155,303	212,436
		% of losses	60.63	59.33	57.31	57.95
		% of personnel strength:				
		All losses	14.12	20.83	23.37	21.60
		Average monthly losses	1.35	1.98	2.22	2.06
	Total losses	No	32,188	63,412	270,994	366,594
		% of losses	100	100	100	100
		% of personnel strength:				
		All losses	23.29	35.11	40.78	37.28
		Average monthly losses	2.22	3.34	3.88	3.55

Caucasus Front (2nd Formation) Personnel Losses, by Year

	Loss category		Losses by year				
			1941	1942	1943	1944	1945
Irrecoverable losses	Killed in action, died during casualty evacuation	No		61,569	11,120		
		% of losses		19.82	19.89		
	Missing in action, POWs	No		69,540	2,789		
		% of losses		22.38	4.99		
	Non-combat losses	No		8,235	905		
		% of losses		2.65	1.62		
	Total irrecoverable losses	No		139,344	14,814		
		% of losses		44.85	26.50		
		% of personnel strength:					
		All losses		13.17	2.16		
		Average monthly losses		1.73	0.74		
Sick and wounded (including those evacuated to hospitals)	Wounded, burns and concussion cases	No		144,250	27,269		
		% of losses		46.43	48.77		
	Sick	No		25,395	11,414		
		% of losses		8.17	20.42		
	Frostbite cases	No		1,696	2,412		
		% of losses		0.55	4.31		
	Total sick and wounded	No		171,341	41,095		
		% of losses		55.15	73.50		
		% of personnel strength:					
		All losses		16.20	5.99		
		Average monthly losses		2.13	2.07		
	Total losses	No		310,685	55,909		
		% of losses		100	100		
		% of personnel strength:					
		All losses		29.37	8.15		
		Average monthly losses		3.86	2.81		

North Caucasus Front (1st Formation) Personnel Losses (Total for 107 Days)

	Loss category		Officers	Sergeants	Men	Total
Irrecoverable losses	Killed in action, died during casualty evacuation	No	1,543	2,545	10,055	14,143
		% of losses	15.23	13.01	10.54	11.31
	Missing in action, POWs	No	4,640	9,958	54,277	68,875
		% of losses	45.81	50.92	56.89	55.06
	Non-combat losses	No	313	872	5,134	6,319
		% of losses	3.09	4.46	5.38	5.05
	Total irrecoverable losses	No	6,496	13,375	69,466	89,337
		% of losses	64.13	68.39	72.81	71.42
		% of personnel strength:				
		All losses	21.51	31.92	51.15	42.97
		Average monthly losses	6.15	9.12	14.62	12.28

		Loss category		Officers	Sergeants	Men	Total
Sick and wounded (including those evacuated to hospitals)		Wounded, burns and concussion cases	No	3,256	5,257	21,938	30,451
			% of losses	32.15	26.88	23	24.34
		Sick	No	377	925	3,999	5,301
			% of losses	3.72	4.73	4.19	4.24
		Frostbite cases	No				
			% of losses				
		Total sick and wounded	No	3,633	6,182	25,937	35,752
			% of losses	35.87	31.61	27.19	28.58
			% of personnel strength:				
			All losses	12.03	14.76	19.10	17.20
			Average monthly losses	3.44	4.22	5.45	4.91
		Total losses	No	10,129	19,557	95,403	125,089
			% of losses	100	100	100	100
			% of personnel strength:				
			All losses	33.54	46.68	70.25	60.17
			Average monthly losses	9.58	13.34	20.07	17.19

North Caucasus Front (2nd Formation) Personnel Losses (Total for 301 Days)

		Loss category		Officers	Sergeants	Men	Total
Irrecoverable losses		Killed in action, died during casualty evacuation	No	10,545	18,763	70,184	99,492
			% of losses	22.45	21.95	18.62	19.54
		Missing in action, POWs	No	2,018	3,355	18,503	23,876
			% of losses	4.30	3.92	4.91	4.69
		Non-combat losses	No	526	902	4,508	5,936
			% of losses	1.11	1.06	1.20	1.16
		Total irrecoverable losses	No	13,089	23,020	93,195	129,304
			% of losses	27.86	26.93	24.73	25.39
			% of personnel strength:				
			All losses	19.50	27.31	35.11	31.02
			Average monthly losses	1.99	2.79	3.58	3.17
Sick and wounded (including those evacuated to hospitals)		Wounded, burns and concussion cases	No	25,588	50,367	210,549	286,504
			% of losses	54.47	58.93	55.87	56.26
		Sick	No	8,098	11,688	69,970	89,756
			% of losses	17.24	13.67	18.57	17.62
		Frostbite cases	No	198	401	3,126	3,725
			% of losses	0.43	0.47	0.83	0.73
		Total sick and wounded	No	33,884	62,456	283,645	379,985
			% of losses	72.14	73.07	75.27	74.61
			% of personnel strength:				
			All losses	50.50	74.09	106.88	91.17
			Average monthly losses	5.15	7.56	10.91	9.30
		Total losses	No	46,973	85,476	376,840	509,289
			% of losses	100	100	100	100
			% of personnel strength:				
			All losses	70.00	101.40	141.99	122.19
			Average monthly losses	7.14	10.35	14.49	12.47

Voronezh and 1st Ukrainian Front Personnel Losses (Total for 1,036 Days)

	Loss category		Officers	Sergeants	Men	Total
Irrecoverable losses	Killed in action, died during casualty evacuation	No	45,533	111,337	344,528	501,398
		% of losses	22.20	21.41	18.37	19.28
	Missing in action, POWs	No	12,881	33,368	135,876	182,125
		% of losses	6.28	6.42	7.24	7
	Non-combat losses	No	2,334	5,807	25,264	33,405
		% of losses	1.13	1.11	1.35	1.28
	Total irrecoverable losses	No	60,748	150,512	505,668	716,928
		% of losses	29.61	28.94	26.96	27.56
		% of personnel strength:				
		All losses	60.87	94.54	113.05	101.50
		Average monthly losses	1.79	2.78	3.33	2.98
Sick and wounded (including those evacuated to hospitals)	Wounded, burns and concussion cases	No	124,254	330,993	1,177,271	1,632,518
		% of losses	60.57	63.64	62.77	62.77
	Sick	No	20,074	38,465	191,709	250,248
		% of losses	9.79	7.39	10.22	9.62
	Frostbite cases	No	57	140	1,001	1,198
		% of losses	0.03	0.03	0.05	0.05
	Total sick and wounded	No	144,385	369,598	1,369,981	1,883,964
		% of losses	70.39	71.06	73.04	72.44
		% of personnel strength:				
		All losses	144.67	232.16	306.28	266.74
		Average monthly losses	4.26	6.83	9	7.85
	Total losses	No	205,133	520,110	1,875,649	2,600,892
		% of losses	100	100	100	100
		% of personnel strength:				
		All losses	205.54	326.70	419.33	368.24
		Average monthly losses	6.05	9.61	12.33	10.83

Voronezh and 1st Ukrainian Front Personnel Losses, by Year

	Loss category		Losses by year				
			1941	1942	1943	1944	1945
Irrecoverable losses	Killed in action, died during casualty evacuation	No		48,984	169,952	172,828	109,634
		% of losses		19.22	19.73	18.09	20.72
	Missing in action, POWs	No		46,949	77,333	45,909	11,934
		% of losses		18.42	8.98	4.80	2.26
	Non-combat losses	No		7,849	12,896	8,748	3,912
		% of losses		3.08	1.50	0.92	0.74
	Total irrecoverable losses	No		103,782	260,181	227,485	125,480
		% of losses		40.72	30.21	23.81	23.72
		% of personnel strength:					
		All losses		34.17	46.42	24.22	12.80
		Average monthly losses		5.89	3.87	2.02	3.05

	Loss category		Losses by year				
			1941	1942	1943	1944	1945
Sick and wounded (including those evacuated to hospitals)	Wounded, burns and concussion cases	No		138,769	536,285	593,361	364,103
		% of losses		54.44	62.26	62.09	68.81
	Sick	No		12,265	64,153	134,361	39,469
		% of losses		4.81	7.45	14.06	7.46
	Frostbite cases	No		68	668	404	58
		% of losses		0.03	0.08	0.04	0.01
	Total sick and wounded	No		151,102	601,106	728,126	403,630
		% of losses		59.28	69.79	76.19	76.28
		% of personnel strength: All losses		49.76	107.25	77.52	41.17
		Average monthly losses		8.58	8.94	6.46	9.80
	Total losses	No		254,884	861,287	955,611	529,110
		% of losses		100	100	100	100
		% of personnel strength: All losses		83.93	153.67	101.74	53.97
		Average monthly losses		14.47	12.81	8.48	12.85

Stalingrad Front (1st Formation) and Don Front Personnel Losses (Total for 218 Days)

	Loss category		Officers	Sergeants	Men	Total
Irrecoverable losses	Killed in action, died during casualty evacuation	No	11,303	22,526	82,301	116,130
		% of losses	17.09	16.25	14.02	14.66
	Missing in action, POWs	No	25,056	50,382	223,692	299,130
		% of losses	37.90	36.35	38.10	37.77
	Non-combat losses	No	571	2,086	11,126	13,783
		% of losses	0.86	1.50	1.89	1.74
	Total irrecoverable losses	No	36,930	74,994	317,119	429,043
		% of losses	55.85	54.10	54.01	54.17
		% of personnel strength: All losses	56.21	88.64	113.05	99.59
		Average monthly losses	7.92	12.49	15.92	14.03
Sick and wounded (including those evacuated to hospitals)	Wounded, burns and concussion cases	No	27,099	60,352	248,031	335,482
		% of losses	40.98	43.53	42.24	42.36
	Sick	No	2,050	3,188	21,133	26,371
		% of losses	3.10	2.30	3.60	3.33
	Frostbite cases	No	44	94	920	1,058
		% of losses	0.07	0.07	0.15	0.14
	Total sick and wounded	No	29,193	63,634	270,084	362,911
		% of losses	44.15	45.90	45.99	45.83
		% of personnel strength: All losses	44.43	75.22	96.29	84.24
		Average monthly losses	6.26	10.59	13.56	11.86
	Total losses	No	66,123	138,628	587,203	791,954
		% of losses	100	100	100	100
		% of personnel strength: All losses	100.64	163.86	209.34	183.83
		Average monthly losses	14.18	23.08	29.48	25.89

Stalingrad Front (1st Formation) and Don Front Personnel Losses, by Year

	Loss category		Losses by year				
			1941	1942	1943	1944	1945
Irrecoverable losses	Killed in action, died during casualty evacuation	No		92,642	23,488		
		% of losses		13.47	22.59		
	Missing in action, POWs	No		297,726	1,404		
		% of losses		43.27	1.35		
	Non-combat losses	No		12,948	835		
		% of losses		1.88	0.81		
	Total irrecoverable losses	No		403,316	25,727		
		% of losses		58.62	24.75		
		% of personnel strength:					
		All losses		88.60	7.19		
		Average monthly losses		15.82	4.79		
Sick and wounded (including those evacuated to hospitals)	Wounded, burns and concussion cases	No		266,644	68,838		
		% of losses		38.76	66.21		
	Sick	No		17,757	8,614		
		% of losses		2.58	8.29		
	Frostbite cases	No		270	788		
		% of losses		0.04	0.75		
	Total sick and wounded	No		284,671	78,240		
		% of losses		41.38	75.25		
		% of personnel strength:					
		All losses		62.54	21.86		
		Average monthly losses		11.17	14.57		
	Total losses	No		687,987	103,967		
		% of losses		100	100		
		% of personnel strength:					
		All losses		151.14	29.05		
		Average monthly losses		26.99	19.36		

South-Eastern Front and Stalingrad Front (2nd Formation) Personnel Losses (Total for 147 Days)

	Loss category		Officers	Sergeants	Men	Total
Irrecoverable losses	Killed in action, died during casualty evacuation	No	6,194	12,505	47,632	66,331
		% of losses	20.84	19.44	19.16	19.36
	Missing in action, POWs	No	8,931	20,259	75,300	104,490
		% of losses	30.05	31.50	30.30	30.50
	Non-combat losses	No	352	1,009	9,116	10,477
		% of losses	1.18	1.57	3.67	3.06
	Total irrecoverable losses	No	15,477	33,773	132,048	181,298
		% of losses	52.07	52.51	53.13	52.92
		% of personnel strength:				
		All losses	30.77	50.33	62.73	55.29
		Average monthly losses	6.41	10.49	13.07	11.52

	Loss category		Officers	Sergeants	Men	Total
Sick and wounded (including those evacuated to hospitals)	Wounded, burns and concussion cases	No	13,215	29,092	108,436	150,743
		% of losses	44.46	45.22	43.62	44
	Sick	No	1,017	1,406	7,651	10,074
		% of losses	3.43	2.19	3.08	2.94
	Frostbite cases	No	12	50	418	480
		% of losses	0.04	0.08	0.17	0.14
	Total sick and wounded	No	14,244	30,548	116,505	161,297
		% of losses	47.93	47.49	46.87	47.08
		% of personnel strength:				
		All losses	28.32	45.53	55.35	49.19
		Average monthly losses	5.90	9.48	11.53	10.25
	Total losses	No	29,721	64,321	248,553	342,595
		% of losses	100	100	100	100
		% of personnel strength:				
		All losses	59.09	95.86	118.08	104.48
		Average monthly losses	12.31	19.97	24.60	21.77

South-Western Front (2nd Formation) and 3rd Ukrainian Front Personnel Losses (Total for 928 Days)

	Loss category		Officers	Sergeants	Men	Total
Irrecoverable losses	Killed in action, died during casualty evacuation	No	28,615	65,155	217,211	310,981
		% of losses	22.05	21.27	18.38	19.22
	Missing in action, POWs	No	6,851	14,994	61,714	83,559
		% of losses	5.27	4.90	5.22	5.16
	Non-combat losses	No	1,025	2,634	12,177	15,836
		% of losses	0.79	0.86	1.03	0.98
	Total irrecoverable losses	No	36,491	82,783	291,102	410,376
		% of losses	28.11	27.03	24.63	25.36
		% of personnel strength:				
		All losses	50.33	80.30	94.64	84.93
		Average monthly losses	1.66	2.64	3.11	2.79
Sick and wounded (including those evacuated to hospitals)	Wounded, burns and concussion cases	No	76,101	193,069	746,988	1,016,158
		% of losses	58.63	63.04	63.20	62.80
	Sick	No	17,042	29,684	139,645	186,371
		% of losses	13.13	9.69	11.81	11.52
	Frostbite cases	No	167	731	4,198	5,096
		% of losses	0.13	0.24	0.36	0.32
	Total sick and wounded	No	93,310	223,484	890,831	1,207,625
		% of losses	71.89	72.97	75.37	74.64
		% of personnel strength:				
		All losses	128.70	216.76	289.61	249.92
		Average monthly losses	4.23	7.13	9.53	8.22
	Total losses	No	129,801	306,267	1,181,933	1,618,001
		% of losses	100	100	100	100
		% of personnel strength:				
		All losses	179.03	297.06	384.25	334.85
		Average monthly losses	5.89	9.77	12.64	11.01

South-Western Front (2nd Formation) and 3rd Ukrainian ... Losses, by Year

	Loss category		1941	1942	
Irrecoverable losses	Killed in action, died during casualty evacuation	No		32,3..	
		% of losses		11.??	
	Missing in action, POWs	No		6,543	
		% of losses		4.4?	
	Non-combat losses	No		3,790	
		% of losses		0.36	
	Total irrecoverable losses	No		42,5..	
		% of losses			
	% of personnel strength:				
	All losses			38.1?	
	Average monthly losses		5.77	3.18	
Sick and wounded (those evacuated to hospital)	Wounded, battle and contusion cases	No		97,707	431,710
		% of losses		65.91	63.3?
	Sick	No		5,651	58,642
		% of losses		1.0?	8.60
	Frostbite cases	No		2,285	2,227
		% of losses		1.5?	0.3?
	Total sick and wounded	No		105,643	492,3?9
		% of losses		71.26	72.27
	% of personnel strength:				
	All losses			31.49	
	Average monthly losses		14.0?	8.29
	Total losses	No		148,2..	381,549
		% of losses		100	100
	% of personnel strength:				
	All losses			44.19	137.49
	Average monthly losses		20.09	11.46	11.36

Southern Front (2nd Formation) and 4th Ukrainian Front (1st and 2nd Formations) Personnel Losses (Total for 795 days)

	Loss category		Officers	Sergeants	Men	Total
Irrecoverable losses	Killed in action, died during casualty evacuation	No	21,911	46,199	174,791	242,901
		% of losses	21.86	21.04	18.41	19.13
	Missing in action, POWs	No	4,971	10,813	41,045	56,829
		% of losses	4.96	4.92	4.32	4.48
	Non-combat losses	No	994	3,085	13,309	17,388
		% of losses	0.99	1.41	1.40	1.37
	Total irrecoverable losses	No	27,876	60,097	229,145	317,118
		% of losses	27.81	27.37	24.13	24.98
	% of personnel strength:					
	All losses		44.07	68.09	87.24	76.57
	Average monthly losses		1.69	2.61	3.34	2.93

	Loss category		Officers	Sergeants	Men	Total
Sick and wounded (including those evacuated to hospitals)	Wounded, burns and concussion cases	No	60,830	139,711	620,296	820,837
		% of losses	60.69	63.63	65.32	64.66
	Sick	No	11,360	19,329	97,165	127,854
		% of losses	11.33	8.81	10.23	10.07
	Frostbite cases	No	172	421	3,061	3,654
		% of losses	0.17	0.19	0.32	0.29
	Total sick and wounded	No	72,362	159,461	720,522	952,345
		% of losses	72.19	72.63	75.87	75.02
		% of personnel strength:				
		All losses	114.41	180.67	274.33	229.95
		Average monthly losses	4.38	6.92	10.51	8.81
	Total losses	No	100,238	219,558	949,667	1,269,463
		% of losses	100	100	100	100
		% of personnel strength:				
		All losses	158.48	248.76	361.57	306.52
		Average monthly losses	6.07	9.53	13.85	11.74

Southern Front (2nd Formation) and 4th Ukrainian Front (1st and 2nd Formations) Personnel Losses, by Year

			Losses by year				
	Loss category		1941	1942	1943	1944	1945
Irrecoverable losses	Killed in action, died during casualty evacuation	No			150,026	58,209	34,666
		% of losses			19.59	18.11	19.02
	Missing in action, POWs	No			48,583	5,542	2,704
		% of losses			6.34	1.73	1.48
	Non-combat losses	No			13,553	2,626	1,209
		% of losses			1.77	0.82	0.66
	Total irrecoverable losses	No			212,162	66,377	38,579
		% of losses			27.70	20.66	21.16
		% of personnel strength:					
		All losses			43.29	18.02	11.59
		Average monthly losses			3.61	1.82	2.76
Sick and wounded (including those evacuated to hospitals)	Wounded, burns and concussion cases	No			488,227	206,611	125,999
		% of losses			63.75	64.30	69.12
	Sick	No			62,646	47,804	17,404
		% of losses			8.18	14.87	9.55
	Frostbite cases	No			2,784	550	320
		% of losses			0.37	0.17	0.17
	Total sick and wounded	No			553,657	254,965	143,723
		% of losses			72.30	79.34	78.84
		% of personnel strength:					
		All losses			112.98	69.23	43.17
		Average monthly losses			9.41	6.99	10.28
	Total losses	No			765,819	321,342	182,302
		% of losses			100	100	100
		% of personnel strength:					
		All losses			156.27	87.25	54.76
		Average monthly losses			13.02	8.81	13.04

Kursk and Orel Fronts, Reserve Front (2nd Formation) and Bryansk Front (3rd Formation) Personnel Losses (Total for 213 Days)

	Loss category		Officers	Sergeants	Men	Total
Irrecoverable losses	Killed in action, died during casualty evacuation	No	6,685	18,498	48,514	73,697
		% of losses	27.67	25.93	21.78	23.16
	Missing in action, POWs	No	312	1,407	6,473	8,192
		% of losses	1.29	1.97	2.91	2.57
	Non-combat losses	No	91	207	1,010	1,308
		% of losses	0.38	0.29	0.45	0.41
	Total irrecoverable losses	No	7,088	20,112	55,997	83,197
		% of losses	29.34	28.19	25.14	26.14
		% of personnel strength:				
		All losses	11	21.45	20.44	19.25
		Average monthly losses	1.57	3.07	2.92	2.75
Sick and wounded (including those evacuated to hospitals)	Wounded, burns and concussion cases	No	15,969	48,920	149,848	214,737
		% of losses	66.09	68.58	67.26	67.47
	Sick	No	1,104	2,301	16,927	20,332
		% of losses	4.57	3.23	7.60	6.39
	Frostbite cases	No	—	—	—	—
		% of losses	—	—	—	—
	Total sick and wounded	No	17,073	51,221	166,775	235,069
		% of losses	70.66	71.81	74.86	73.86
		% of personnel strength:				
		All losses	26.49	54.63	60.88	54.40
		Average monthly losses	3.78	7.80	8.70	7.77
	Total losses	No	24,161	71,333	222,772	318,266
		% of losses	100	100	100	100
		% of personnel strength:				
		All losses	37.49	76.08	81.32	73.65
		Average monthly losses	5.35	10.87	11.62	10.52

Steppe Front and 2nd Ukrainian Front Personnel Losses (Total for 671 Days)

	Loss category		Officers	Sergeants	Men	Total
Irrecoverable losses	Killed in action, died during casualty evacuation	No	25,321	57,558	207,779	290,658
		% of losses	21.37	20.40	17.63	18.41
	Missing in action, POWs	No	5,141	14,024	51,481	70,646
		% of losses	4.34	4.98	4.37	4.47
	Non-combat losses	No	818	2,069	6,199	9,086
		% of losses	0.69	0.73	0.52	0.57
	Total irrecoverable losses	No	31,280	73,651	265,459	370,390
		% of losses	26.40	26.11	22.52	23.45
		% of personnel strength:				
		All losses	33.71	52.91	64.62	57.62
		Average monthly losses	1.53	2.41	2.94	2.62

	Loss category		Officers	Sergeants	Men	Total
Sick and wounded (including those evacuated to hospitals)	Wounded, burns and concussion cases	No	69,973	178,094	764,871	1,012,938
		% of losses	59.05	63.13	64.90	64.15
	Sick	No	17,199	30,334	148,009	195,542
		% of losses	14.52	10.75	12.56	12.38
	Frostbite cases	No	35	28	230	293
		% of losses	0.03	0.01	0.02	0.02
	Total sick and wounded	No	87,207	208,456	913,110	1,208,773
		% of losses	73.60	73.89	77.48	76.55
		% of personnel strength: All losses	93.97	149.75	222.28	188.05
		Average monthly losses	4.27	6.80	10.10	8.55
	Total losses	No	118,487	282,107	1,178,569	1,579,163
		% of losses	100	100	100	100
		% of personnel strength: All losses	127.68	202.66	286.90	245.67
		Average monthly losses	5.80	9.21	13.04	11.17

Steppe Front and 2nd Ukrainian Front Personnel Losses, by Year

			Losses by year				
	Loss category		1941	1942	1943	1944	1945
Irrecoverable losses	Killed in action, died during casualty evacuation	No			118,995	131,318	40,345
		% of losses			19.54	17.68	17.74
	Missing in action, POWs	No			40,462	23,943	6,241
		% of losses			6.64	3.22	2.75
	Non-combat losses	No			3,642	3,937	1,507
		% of losses			0.60	0.53	0.66
	Total irrecoverable losses	No			163,099	159,198	48,093
		% of losses			26.78	21.43	21.15
		% of personnel strength: All losses			32.25	21.65	8.22
		Average monthly losses			5.56	1.81	1.96
Sick and wounded (including those evacuated to hospitals)	Wounded, burns and concussion cases	No			415,395	456,080	141,463
		% of losses			68.20	61.41	62.21
	Sick	No			30,489	127,256	37,797
		% of losses			5.01	17.13	16.62
	Frostbite cases	No			60	194	39
		% of losses			0.01	0.03	0.02
	Total sick and wounded	No			445,944	583,530	179,299
		% of losses			73.22	78.57	78.85
		% of personnel strength: All losses			88.18	79.35	30.65
		Average monthly losses			15.20	6.61	7.30
	Total losses	No			609,043	742,728	227,392
		% of losses			100	100	100
		% of personnel strength: All losses			120.43	101	38.87
		Average monthly losses			20.76	8.42	9.26

Baltic and 2nd Baltic Front Personnel Losses (Total for 539 Days)

	Loss category		Officers	Sergeants	Men	Total
Irrecoverable losses	Killed in action, died during casualty evacuation	No	15,728	35,707	115,804	167,239
		% of losses	21.54	20.85	18.67	19.35
	Missing in action, POWs	No	1,358	1,668	10,092	13,118
		% of losses	1.86	0.97	1.63	1.52
	Non–combat losses	No	370	967	3,566	4,903
		% of losses	0.51	0.57	0.58	0.57
	Total irrecoverable losses	No	17,456	38,342	129,462	185,260
		% of losses	23.91	22.39	20.88	21.43
		% of personnel strength:				
		All losses	24.45	36.24	47.53	41.21
		Average monthly losses	1.38	2.05	2.69	2.33
Sick and wounded (including those evacuated to hospitals)	Wounded, burns and concussion cases	No	44,810	108,806	379,943	533,559
		% of losses	61.37	63.53	61.27	61.72
	Sick	No	10,732	24,051	110,523	145,306
		% of losses	14.70	14.04	17.82	16.81
	Frostbite cases	No	15	70	218	303
		% of losses	0.02	0.04	0.03	0.04
	Total sick and wounded	No	55,557	132,927	490,684	679,168
		% of losses	76.09	77.61	79.12	78.57
		% of personnel strength:				
		All losses	77.81	125.64	180.13	151.06
		Average monthly losses	4.40	7.10	10.17	8.53
	Total losses	No	73,013	171,269	620,146	864,428
		% of losses	100	100	100	100
		% of personnel strength:				
		All losses	102.26	161.88	227.66	192.27
		Average monthly losses	5.78	9.15	12.86	10.86

Baltic and 2nd Baltic Front Personnel Losses, by Year

	Loss category		Losses by year				
			1941	1942	1943	1944	1945
Irrecoverable losses	Killed in action, died during casualty evacuation	No			22,133	110,710	34,396
		% of losses			20.96	19.52	17.94
	Missing in action, POWs	No			1,631	7,831	3,656
		% of losses			1.55	1.38	1.91
	Non–combat losses	No			553	2,823	1,527
		% of losses			0.52	0.50	0.80
	Total irrecoverable losses	No			24,317	121,364	39,579
		% of losses			23.03	21.40	20.65
		% of personnel strength:					
		All losses			5.69	28.42	7.04
		Average monthly losses			2.11	2.37	2.35

	Loss category		Losses by year				
			1941	1942	1943	1944	1945
Sick and wounded (including those evacuated to hospitals)	Wounded, burns and concussion cases	No			62,428	354,284	116,847
		% of losses			59.12	62.46	60.96
	Sick	No			18,814	91,302	35,190
		% of losses			17.82	16.10	18.36
	Frostbite cases	No			35	208	60
		% of losses			0.03	0.04	0.03
	Total sick and wounded	No			81,277	445,794	152,097
		% of losses			76.97	78.60	79.35
		% of personnel strength: All losses			19.03	104.41	27.03
		Average monthly losses			7.05	8.70	9.01
	Total losses	No			105,594	567,158	191,676
		% of losses			100	100	100
		% of personnel strength: All losses			24.72	132.83	34.07
		Average monthly losses			9.16	11.07	11.36

Central Front (2nd Formation), Byelorussian and 1st Byelorussian Front Personnel Losses (Total for 815 Days)

	Loss category		Officers	Sergeants	Men	Total
Irrecoverable losses	Killed in action, died during casualty evacuation	No	36,866	90,258	283,804	410,928
		% of losses	23.43	22.32	19.88	20.66
	Missing in action, POWs	No	4,141	9,384	39,281	52,806
		% of losses	2.63	2.32	2.76	2.66
	Non-combat losses	No	1,647	3,986	15,024	20,657
		% of losses	1.05	0.99	1.05	1.04
	Total irrecoverable losses	No	42,654	103,628	338,109	484,391
		% of losses	27.11	25.63	23.69	24.36
		% of personnel strength: All losses	37.32	56.60	68.08	61.00
		Average monthly losses	1.40	2.12	2.55	2.28
Sick and wounded (including those evacuated to hospitals)	Wounded, burns and concussion cases	No	94,945	261,030	909,182	1,265,157
		% of losses	60.36	64.56	63.71	63.62
	Sick	No	19,701	39,599	179,344	238,644
		% of losses	12.52	9.79	12.57	11.99
	Frostbite cases	No	15	70	474	559
		% of losses	0.01	0.02	0.03	0.03
	Total sick and wounded	No	114,661	300,699	1,089,000	1,504,360
		% of losses	72.89	74.37	76.31	75.64
		% of personnel strength: All losses	100.32	164.23	219.29	189.47
		Average monthly losses	3.75	6.15	8.21	7.10
	Total losses	No	157,315	404,327	1,427,109	1,988,751
		% of losses	100	100	100	100
		% of personnel strength: All losses	137.64	220.83	287.37	250.47
		Average monthly losses	5.15	8.27	10.76	9.38

Central Front (2nd Formation), Byelorussian and 1st Byelorussian Front Personnel Losses, by Year

	Loss category		Losses by year				
			1941	1942	1943	1944	1945
Irrecoverable losses	Killed in action, died during casualty evacuation	No			173,558	140,636	96,734
		% of losses			22.76	18.71	20.38
	Missing in action, POWs	No			31,114	16,321	5,371
		% of losses			4.08	2.17	1.13
	Non-combat losses	No			7,428	9,087	4,142
		% of losses			0.98	1.21	0.87
	Total irrecoverable losses	No			212,100	166,044	106,247
		% of losses			27.82	22.09	22.38
		% of personnel strength: All losses			34.26	19.45	10.26
		Average monthly losses			3.26	1.62	2.44
Sick and wounded (including those evacuated to hospitals)	Wounded, burns and concussion cases	No			489,514	454,419	321,224
		% of losses			64.19	60.47	67.67
	Sick	No			60,447	130,981	47,216
		% of losses			7.93	17.43	9.95
	Frostbite cases	No			475	59	25
		% of losses			0.06	0.01	
	Total sick and wounded	No			550,436	585,459	368,465
		% of losses			72.18	77.91	77.62
		% of personnel strength: All losses			88.90	68.58	35.59
		Average monthly losses			8.47	5.72	8.47
	Total losses	No			762,536	751,503	474,712
		% of losses			100	100	100
		% of personnel strength: All losses			123.16	88.03	45.85
		Average monthly losses			11.73	7.34	10.91

2nd Byelorussian Front (1st Formation) Personnel Losses (Total for 42 Days, 1944)

	Loss category		Officers	Sergeants	Men	Total
Irrecoverable losses	Killed in action, died during casualty evacuation	No	406	1,119	3,462	4,987
		% of losses	25	24.35	21.58	22.40
	Missing in action, POWs	No	28	108	315	451
		% of losses	1.72	2.35	1.96	2.02
	Non-combat losses	No	6	15	63	84
		% of losses	0.37	0.33	0.39	0.38
	Total irrecoverable losses	No	440	1,242	3,840	5,522
		% of losses	27.09	27.03	23.93	24.80
		% of personnel strength: All losses	1.81	3.43	3.29	3.11
		Average monthly losses	1.39	2.64	2.53	2.40

	Loss category		Officers	Sergeants	Men	Total
Sick and wounded (including those evacuated to hospitals)	Wounded, burns and concussion cases	No	991	3,027	10,404	14,422
		% of losses	61.02	65.88	64.85	64.78
	Sick	No	193	326	1,800	2,319
		% of losses	11.89	7.09	11.22	10.42
	Frostbite cases	No				
		% of losses				
	Total sick and wounded	No	1,184	3,353	12,204	16,741
		% of losses	72.91	72.97	76.07	75.20
		% of personnel strength:				
		All losses	4.87	9.26	10.45	9.44
		Average monthly losses	3.75	7.12	8.04	7.26
	Total losses	No	1,624	4,595	16,044	22,263
		% of losses	100	100	100	100
		% of personnel strength:				
		All losses	6.68	12.69	13.74	12.55
		Average monthly losses	5.14	9.76	10.57	9.66

2nd Byelorussian Front (2nd Formation) Personnel Losses (Total for 381 Days)

	Loss category		Officers	Sergeants	Men	Total
Irrecoverable losses	Killed in action, died during casualty evacuation	No	11,676	26,474	82,950	121,100
		% of losses	23.03	21.30	18.19	19.20
	Missing in action, POWs	No	802	1,294	7,255	9,351
		% of losses	1.57	1.04	1.59	1.48
	Non-combat losses	No	557	1,178	3,911	5,646
		% of losses	1.10	0.95	0.86	0.89
	Total irrecoverable losses	No	13,035	28,946	94,116	136,097
		% of losses	25.70	23.29	20.64	21.57
		% of personnel strength:				
		All losses	16.36	21.84	27.36	24.47
		Average monthly losses	1.31	1.75	2.19	1.96
Sick and wounded (including those evacuated to hospitals)	Wounded, burns and concussion cases	No	30,513	80,392	289,777	400,682
		% of losses	60.17	64.68	63.56	63.51
	Sick	No	7,157	14,948	71,965	94,070
		% of losses	14.12	12.02	15.70	14.91
	Frostbite cases	No	5	15	33	53
		% of losses	0.01	0.01	0.01	0.01
	Total sick and wounded	No	37,675	95,355	361,775	494,805
		% of losses	74.30	76.71	79.36	78.43
		% of personnel strength:				
		All losses	47.27	71.97	105.17	88.96
		Average monthly losses	3.78	5.75	8.41	7.12
	Total losses	No	50,710	124,301	455,891	630,902
		% of losses	100	100	100	100
		% of personnel strength:				
		All losses	63.63	93.81	132.53	113.43
		Average monthly losses	5.09	7.50	10.60	9.08

2nd Byelorussian Front (2nd Formation) Personnel Losses, by Year

	Loss category		Losses by year				
			1941	1942	1943	1944	1945
Irrecoverable losses	Killed in action, died during casualty evacuation	No % of losses				40,138 16.81	80,962 20.65
	Missing in action, POWs	No % of losses				3,430 1.44	5,921 1.51
	Non-combat losses	No % of losses				2,592 1.08	3,054 0.78
	Total irrecoverable losses	No % of losses				46,160 19.33	89,937 22.94
		% of personnel strength: All losses Average monthly losses				10.17 1.23	12.49 2.97
Sick and wounded (including those evacuated to hospitals)	Wounded, burns and concussion cases	No % of losses				136,645 57.23	264,037 67.33
	Sick	No % of losses				55,963 23.44	38,107 9.72
	Frostbite cases	No % of losses				12	41 0.01
	Total sick and wounded	No % of losses				192,620 80.67	302,185 77.06
		% of personnel strength: All losses Average monthly losses				42.44 5.11	41.96 9.99
	Total losses	No % of losses				238,780 100	392,122 100
		% of personnel strength: All losses Average monthly losses				52.61 6.34	54.45 12.96

3rd Baltic Front Personnel Losses (Total for 179 Days)

	Loss category		Officers	Sergeants	Men	Total
Irrecoverable losses	Killed in action, died during casualty evacuation	No % of losses	3,773 22.39	7,814 22.53	28,123 19.33	39,710 20.15
	Missing in action, POWs	No % of losses	225 1.33	308 0.89	2,000 1.38	2,533 1.29
	Non-combat losses	No % of losses	80 0.47	154 0.45	678 0.46	912 0.46
	Total irrecoverable losses	No % of losses	4,078 24.19	8,276 23.87	30,801 21.17	43,155 21.90
		% of personnel strength: All losses Average monthly losses	9.08 1.57	13.22 2.28	17.87 3.08	15.42 2.66

	Loss category		Officers	Sergeants	Men	Total
Sick and wounded (including those evacuated to hospitals)	Wounded, burns and concussion cases	No	10,867	22,961	96,599	130,427
		% of losses	64.47	66.22	66.39	66.20
	Sick	No	1,910	3,439	18,100	23,449
		% of losses	11.34	9.91	12.44	11.90
	Frostbite cases	No				
		% of losses				
	Total sick and wounded	No	12,777	26,400	114,699	153,876
		% of losses	75.81	76.13	78.83	78.10
		% of personnel strength:				
		All losses	28.46	42.17	66.53	54.97
		Average monthly losses	4.90	7.27	11.47	9.48
	Total losses	No	16,855	34,676	145,500	197,031
		% of losses	100	100	100	100
		% of personnel strength:				
		All losses	37.54	55.39	84.40	70.39
		Average monthly losses	6.47	9.55	14.55	12.14

Trans–Baikal Front Personnel Losses (Total for 25 Days)

	Loss category		Officers	Sergeants	Men	Total
Irrecoverable losses	Killed in action, died during casualty evacuation	No	162	566	955	1,683
		% of losses	23.28	25.88	17.37	20.08
	Missing in action, POWs	No	5	8	10	23
		% of losses	0.72	0.37	0.18	0.27
	Non-combat losses	No	74	168	280	522
		% of losses	10.63	7.68	5.09	6.23
	Total irrecoverable losses	No	241	742	1,245	2,228
		% of losses	34.63	33.93	22.64	26.58
		% of personnel strength:				
		All losses	0.30	0.48	0.31	0.35
		Average monthly losses	0.30	0.48	0.31	0.35
Sick and wounded (including those evacuated to hospitals)	Wounded, burns and concussion cases	No	271	983	1,905	3,159
		% of losses	38.93	44.95	34.63	37.68
	Sick	No	184	462	2,350	2,996
		% of losses	26.44	21.12	42.73	35.74
	Frostbite cases	No				
		% of losses				
	Total sick and wounded	No	455	1,445	4,255	6,155
		% of losses	65.37	66.07	77.36	73.42
		% of personnel strength:				
		All losses	0.58	0.94	1.05	0.96
		Average monthly losses	0.58	0.94	1.05	0.96
	Total losses	No	696	2,187	5,500	8,383
		% of losses	100	100	100	100
		% of personnel strength:				
		All losses	0.88	1.42	1.36	1.31
		Average monthly losses	0.88	1.42	1.36	1.31

1st Far Eastern Front Personnel Losses (Total for 25 Days)

	Loss category		Officers	Sergeants	Men	Total
Irrecoverable losses	Killed in action, died during casualty evacuation	No	603	1,657	2,894	5,154
		% of losses	30.27	26.53	22.55	24.46
	Missing in action, POWs	No	39	109	233	381
		% of losses	1.96	1.74	1.82	1.81
	Non-combat losses	No	137	201	451	789
		% of losses	6.88	3.22	3.52	3.75
	Total irrecoverable losses	No	779	1,967	3,578	6,324
		% of losses	39.11	31.49	27.89	30.02
		% of personnel strength:				
		All losses	1.03	1.28	1	1.08
		Average monthly losses	1.03	1.28	1	1.08
Sick and wounded (including those evacuated to hospitals)	Wounded, burns and concussion cases	No	1,097	3,824	8,037	12,958
		% of losses	55.07	61.22	62.63	61.50
	Sick	No	116	455	1,216	1,787
		% of losses	5.82	7.29	9.48	8.48
	Frostbite cases	No				
		% of losses				
	Total sick and wounded	No	1,213	4,279	9,253	14,745
		% of losses	60.89	68.51	72.11	69.98
		% of personnel strength:				
		All losses	1.60	2.78	2.59	2.51
		Average monthly losses	1.60	2.78	2.59	2.51
	Total losses	No	1,992	6,246	12,831	21,069
		% of losses	100	100	100	100
		% of personnel strength:				
		All losses	2.63	4.06	3.59	3.59
		Average monthly losses	2.63	4.06	3.59	3.59

2nd Far Eastern Front Personnel Losses (Total for 25 Days)

	Loss category		Officers	Sergeants	Men	Total
Irrecoverable losses	Killed in action, died during casualty evacuation	No	224	564	1,220	2,008
		% of losses	40.0	28.91	39.71	35.97
	Missing in action, POWs	No	3	67	342	412
		% of losses	0.53	3.43	11.13	7.38
	Non-combat losses	No	1	9	19	29
		% of losses	0.18	0.46	0.62	0.52
	Total irrecoverable losses	No	228	640	1,581	2,449
		% of losses	40.71	32.80	51.46	43.87
		% of personnel strength:				
		All losses	0.51	0.75	0.78	0.73
		Average monthly losses	0.51	0.75	0.78	0.73

	Loss category		Officers	Sergeants	Men	Total
Sick and wounded (including those evacuated to hospitals)	Wounded, burns and concussion cases	No	330	1,308	1,474	3,112
		% of losses	58.93	67.04	47.98	55.74
	Sick	No	2	3	17	22
		% of losses	0.36	0.16	0.56	0.39
	Frostbite cases	No				
		% of losses				
	Total sick and wounded	No	332	1,311	1,491	3,134
		% of losses	59.29	67.20	48.54	56.13
		% of personnel strength:				
		All losses	0.73	1.53	0.73	0.93
		Average monthly losses	0.73	1.53	0.73	0.93
	Total losses	No	560	1,951	3,072	5,583
		% of losses	100	100	100	100
		% of personnel strength:				
		All losses	1.24	2.28	1.51	1.66
		Average monthly losses	1.24	2.28	1.51	1.66

Moscow Defensive Zone Personnel Losses (Total for 667 Days)

	Loss category		Officers	Sergeants	Men	Total
Irrecoverable losses	Killed in action, died during casualty evacuation	No	94	132	668	894
		% of losses	18.95	11.11	9.28	10.06
	Missing in action, POWs	No	17	55	668	740
		% of losses	3.43	4.63	9.28	8.33
	Non-combat losses	No	60	288	1,104	1,452
		% of losses	12.10	24.24	15.33	16.35
	Total irrecoverable losses	No	171	475	2,440	3,086
		% of losses	34.48	39.98	33.89	34.74
		% of personnel strength:				
		All losses	1.54	2.45	3.95	3.35
		Average monthly losses	0.07	0.11	0.18	0.15
Sick and wounded (including those evacuated to hospitals)	Wounded, burns and concussion cases	No	157	214	896	1,267
		% of losses	31.65	18.02	12.45	14.26
	Sick	No	168	498	3,858	4,524
		% of losses	33.87	41.92	53.59	50.93
	Frostbite cases	No		1	5	6
		% of losses		0.08	0.07	0.07
	Total sick and wounded	No	325	713	4,759	5,797
		% of losses	65.52	60.02	66.11	65.26
		% of personnel strength:				
		All losses	2.93	3.67	7.71	6.29
		Average monthly losses	0.13	0.17	0.35	0.29
	Total losses	No	496	1,188	7,199	8,883
		% of losses	100	100	100	100
		% of personnel strength:				
		All losses	4.47	6.12	11.66	9.64
		Average monthly losses	0.20	0.28	0.53	0.44

Moscow Defensive Zone Personnel Losses, by Year

	Loss category		Losses by year				
			1941	1942	1943	1944	1945
Irrecoverable losses	Killed in action, died during casualty evacuation	No	477	376	41		
		% of losses	28.16	13.09	0.95		
	Missing in action, POWs	No	739		1		
		% of losses	43.62		0.02		
	Non-combat losses	No	9	790	653		
		% of losses	0.53	27.49	15.13		
	Total irrecoverable losses	No	1,225	1,166	695		
		% of losses	72.31	40.58	16.10		
		% of personnel strength:					
		All losses	0.79	0.98	1.27		
		Average monthly losses	0.79	0.08	0.14		
Sick and wounded (including those evacuated to hospitals)	Wounded, burns and concussion cases	No	452	751	64		
		% of losses	26.68	26.14	1.48		
	Sick	No	15	956	3,553		
		% of losses	0.89	33.28	82.33		
	Frostbite cases	No	2		4		
		% of losses	0.12		0.09		
	Total sick and wounded	No	469	1,707	3,621		
		% of losses	27.69	59.42	83.90		
		% of personnel strength:					
		All losses	0.30	1.44	6.64		
		Average monthly losses	0.30	0.12	0.74		
	Total losses	No	1,694	2,873	4,316		
		% of losses	100	100	100		
		% of personnel strength:					
		All losses	1.09	2.42	7.91		
		Average monthly losses	1.09	0.20	0.88		

51st Independent Army Personnel Losses (Total for 94 Days)

	Loss category		Officers	Sergeants	Men	Total
Irrecoverable losses	Killed in action, died during casualty evacuation	No	542	1,304	7,634	9,480
		% of losses	13.79	17.49	13.47	13.93
	Missing in action, POWs	No	1,852	3,063	27,258	32,173
		% of losses	47.11	41.09	48.10	47.28
	Non-combat losses	No	395	1,023	9,132	10,550
		% of losses	10.05	13.72	16.12	15.50
	Total irrecoverable losses	No	2,789	5,390	44,024	52,203
		% of losses	70.95	72.30	77.69	76.71
		% of personnel strength:				
		All losses	34.43	42.11	51.43	49.02
		Average monthly losses	11.11	13.58	16.59	15.81

	Loss category		Officers	Sergeants	Men	Total
Sick and wounded (including those evacuated to hospitals)	Wounded, burns and concussion cases	No	1,030	1,907	11,451	14,388
		% of losses	26.20	25.58	20.20	21.14
	Sick	No	111	158	1,194	1,463
		% of losses	2.82	2.12	2.11	2.15
	Frostbite cases	No	1			1
		% of losses	0.03			
	Total sick and wounded	No	1,142	2,065	12,645	15,852
		% of losses	29.05	27.70	22.31	23.29
		% of personnel strength:				
		All losses	14.10	16.13	14.77	14.88
		Average monthly losses	4.55	5.20	4.76	4.80
	Total losses	No	3,931	7,455	56,669	68,055
		% of losses	100	100	100	100
		% of personnel strength:				
		All losses	48.53	58.24	66.20	63.90
		Average monthly losses	15.66	18.78	21.35	20.61

7th Independent Army Personnel Losses (Total for 883 Days)

	Loss category		Officers	Sergeants	Men	Total
Irrecoverable losses	Killed in action, died during casualty evacuation	No	1,036	2,785	11,971	15,792
		% of losses	23.37	23.28	18.60	19.55
	Missing in action, POWs	No	235	761	6,014	7,010
		% of losses	5.30	6.36	9.34	8.68
	Non-combat losses	No	79	191	1,265	1,535
		% of losses	1.78	1.60	1.97	1.90
	Total irrecoverable losses	No	1,350	3,737	19,250	24,337
		% of losses	30.45	31.24	29.91	30.13
		% of personnel strength:				
		All losses	12.74	20.42	31.77	27.19
		Average monthly losses	0.44	0.71	1.10	0.94
Sick and wounded (including those evacuated to hospitals)	Wounded, burns and concussion cases	No	2,169	5,681	27,455	35,305
		% of losses	48.92	47.50	42.65	43.72
	Sick	No	907	2,522	17,250	20,679
		% of losses	20.45	21.08	26.80	25.60
	Frostbite cases	No	8	22	411	441
		% of losses	0.18	0.18	0.64	0.55
	Total sick and wounded	No	3,084	8,225	45,116	56,425
		% of losses	69.55	68.76	70.09	69.87
		% of personnel strength:				
		All losses	29.09	44.95	74.45	63.05
		Average monthly losses	1	1.55	2.57	2.18
	Total losses	No	4,434	11,962	64,366	80,762
		% of losses	100	100	100	100
		% of personnel strength:				
		All losses	41.83	65.37	106.22	90.24
		Average monthly losses	1.44	2.26	3.67	3.12

7th Independent Army Personnel Losses, by Year

	Loss category		Losses by year				
			1941	1942	1943	1944	1945
Irrecoverable losses	Killed in action, died during casualty evacuation	No	4,637	9,304	1,781	70	
		% of losses	18.35	22.18	14.04	8.28	
	Missing in action, POWs	No	5,609	1,289	110	2	
		% of losses	22.19	3.07	0.87	0.24	
	Non-combat losses	No	346	908	268	13	
		% of losses	1.37	2.16	2.11	1.54	
	Total irrecoverable losses	No	10,592	11,501	2,159	85	
		% of losses	41.91	27.41	17.02	10.06	
		% of personnel strength:					
		All losses	14.16	11.77	2.49	0.10	
		Average monthly losses	4.42	0.98	0.21	0.05	
Sick and wounded (including those evacuated to hospitals)	Wounded, burns and concussion cases	No	13,112	19,023	3,072	98	
		% of losses	51.88	45.34	24.21	11.60	
	Sick	No	1,245	11,343	7,429	662	
		% of losses	4.93	27.04	58.56	78.34	
	Frostbite cases	No	325	89	27		
		% of losses	1.28	0.21	0.21		
	Total sick and wounded	No	14,682	30,455	10,528	760	
		% of losses	58.09	72.59	82.98	89.94	
		% of personnel strength:					
		All losses	19.62	31.16	12.15	0.90	
		Average monthly losses	6.13	2.60	1.01	0.50	
	Total losses	No	25,274	41,956	12,687	845	
		% of losses	100	100	100	100	
		% of personnel strength:					
		All losses	33.78	42.93	14.64	1	
		Average monthly losses	10.55	3.58	1.22	0.55	

52nd Independent Army Personnel Losses (Total for 81 Days)

	Loss category		Officers	Sergeants	Men	Total
Irrecoverable losses	Killed in action, died during casualty evacuation	No	225	521	2,811	3,557
		% of losses	19.72	20.60	15.51	16.32
	Missing in action, POWs	No	293	989	8,356	9,638
		% of losses	25.68	39.11	46.10	44.22
	Non-combat losses	No	23	166	375	564
		% of losses	2.01	6.56	2.07	2.59
	Total irrecoverable losses	No	541	1,676	11,542	13,759
		% of losses	47.41	66.27	63.68	63.13
		% of personnel strength:				
		All losses	10.02	22.35	29.22	26.26
		Average monthly losses	3.85	8.59	11.24	10.10

	Loss category		Officers	Sergeants	Men	Total
Sick and wounded (including those evacuated to hospitals)	Wounded, burns and concussion cases	No	540	818	6,077	7,435
		% of losses	47.33	32.35	33.53	34.12
	Sick	No	55	23	411	489
		% of losses	4.82	0.91	2.27	2.24
	Frostbite cases	No	5	12	94	111
		% of losses	0.44	0.47	0.52	0.51
	Total sick and wounded	No	600	853	6,582	8,035
		% of losses	52.59	33.73	36.32	36.87
		% of personnel strength:				
		All losses	11.11	11.37	16.66	15.33
		Average monthly losses	4.27	4.37	6.41	5.90
	Total losses	No	1,141	2,529	18,124	21,794
		% of losses	100	100	100	100
		% of personnel strength:				
		All losses	21.13	33.72	45.88	41.59
		Average monthly losses	8.12	12.96	17.65	16

4th Independent Army Personnel Losses (Total for 80 Days)

	Loss category		Officers	Sergeants	Men	Total
Irrecoverable losses	Killed in action, died during casualty evacuation	No	692	1,578	8,676	10,946
		% of losses	26.45	27.56	24.25	24.81
	Missing in action, POWs	No	205	510	4,675	5,390
		% of losses	7.84	8.91	13.06	12.21
	Non combat losses	No	102	220	1,085	1,407
		% of losses	3.90	3.84	3.03	3.19
	Total irrecoverable losses	No	999	2,308	14,436	17,743
		% of losses	38.19	40.31	40.34	40.21
		% of personnel strength:				
		All losses	16.11	26.53	33.19	30.38
		Average monthly losses	6.20	10.20	12.76	11.68
Sick and wounded (including those evacuated to hospitals)	Wounded, burns and concussion cases	No	1,503	3,215	19,750	24,468
		% of losses	57.45	56.16	55.18	55.44
	Sick	No	100	137	880	1,117
		% of losses	3.82	2.39	2.46	2.53
	Frostbite cases	No	14	65	724	803
		% of losses	0.54	1.14	2.02	1.82
	Total sick and wounded	No	1,617	3,417	21,354	26,388
		% of losses	61.81	59.69	59.66	59.79
		% of personnel strength:				
		All losses	26.08	39.28	49.09	45.19
		Average monthly losses	10.03	15.11	18.88	17.38
	Total losses	No	2,616	5,725	35,790	44,131
		% of losses	100	100	100	100
		% of personnel strength:				
		All losses	42.19	65.81	82.28	75.57
		Average monthly losses	16.23	25.31	31.64	29.06

Independent Maritime Army (1st Formation) Personnel Losses (Total for 303 Days)[1]

	Loss category		Officers	Sergeants	Men	Total
Irrecoverable losses	Killed in action, died during casualty evacuation	No	968	1,828	9,224	12,020
		% of losses	7.60	8.98	7.12	7.39
	Missing in action, POWs	No	8,192	12,099	63,930	84,221
		% of losses	64.32	59.42	49.36	51.79
	Non-combat losses	No	126	271	8,130	8,527
		% of losses	0.99	1.33	6.28	5.25
	Total irrecoverable losses	No	9,286	14,198	81,284	104,768
		% of losses	72.91	69.73	62.76	64.43
		% of personnel strength:				
		All losses	122.18	127.91	147.25	141.77
		Average monthly losses	12.22	12.79	14.72	14.18
Sick and wounded (including those evacuated to hospitals)	Wounded, burns and concussion cases	No	3,192	5,706	44,322	53,220
		% of losses	25.05	28.03	34.22	32.73
	Sick	No	253	444	3,490	4,187
		% of losses	1.99	2.18	2.70	2.57
	Frostbite cases	No	6	12	419	437
		% of losses	0.05	0.06	0.32	0.27
	Total sick and wounded	No	3,451	6,162	48,231	57,844
		% of losses	27.09	30.27	37.24	35.57
		% of personnel strength:				
		All losses	45.41	55.51	87.38	78.27
		Average monthly losses	4.54	5.55	8.74	7.83
	Total losses	No	12,737	20,360	129,515	162,612
		% of losses	100	100	100	100
		% of personnel strength:				
		All losses	167.59	183.42	234.63	220.04
		Average monthly losses	16.76	18.34	23.46	22.01

1. Losses for the period 15 July–1 September 1941 are included with Southern Front's Losses.

Independent Maritime Army (1st Formation) Personnel Losses, by Year

			Losses by year				
	Loss category		1941	1942	1943	1944	1945
Irrecoverable losses	Killed in action, died during casualty evacuation	No	6,881	5,139			
		% of losses	9.87	5.53			
	Missing in action, POWs	No	21,350	62,871			
		% of losses	30.64	67.67			
	Non-combat losses	No	7,419	1,108			
		% of losses	10.64	1.19			
	Total irrecoverable losses	No	35,650	69,118			
		% of losses	51.15	74.39			
		% of personnel strength:					
		All losses	54.68	86.74			
		Average monthly losses	13.67	14.46			

	Loss category		Losses by year				
			1941	1942	1943	1944	1945
Sick and wounded (including those evacuated to hospitals)	Wounded, burns and concussion cases	No	32,977	20,243			
		% of losses	47.31	21.79			
	Sick	No	986	3,201			
		% of losses	1.41	3.45			
	Frostbite cases	No	89	348			
		% of losses	0.13	0.37			
	Total sick and wounded	No	34,052	23,792			
		% of losses	48.85	25.61			
		% of personnel strength:					
		All losses	52.22	29.86			
		Average monthly losses	13.05	4.97			
	Total losses	No	69,702	92,910			
		% of losses	100	100			
		% of personnel strength:					
		All losses	106.90	116.60			
		Average monthly losses	26.72	19.43			

Independent Maritime Army (2nd Formation) Personnel Losses (Total for 504 Days)

	Loss category		Officers	Sergeants	Men	Total
Irrecoverable losses	Killed in action, died during casualty evacuation	No	1,327	2,579	7,741	11,647
		% of losses	19.21	17.07	16.08	16.60
	Missing in action, POWs	No	220	332	1,111	1,663
		% of losses	3.19	2.20	2.31	2.37
	Non-combat losses	No	91	178	515	784
		% of losses	1.32	1.17	1.07	1.12
	Total irrecoverable losses	No	1,638	3,089	9,367	14,094
		% of losses	23.72	20.44	19.46	20.09
		% of personnel strength:				
		All losses	11.78	14.37	16.55	15.32
		Average monthly losses	0.71	0.87	1	0.93
Sick and wounded (including those evacuated to hospitals)	Wounded, burns and concussion cases	No	2,883	7,385	22,093	32,361
		% of losses	41.74	48.87	45.89	46.12
	Sick	No	2,369	4,572	16,507	23,448
		% of losses	34.30	30.25	34.29	33.42
	Frostbite cases	No	17	66	177	260
		% of losses	0.24	0.44	0.36	0.37
	Total sick and wounded	No	5,269	12,023	38,777	56,069
		% of losses	76.28	79.56	80.54	79.91
		% of personnel strength:				
		All losses	37.91	55.92	68.51	60.94
		Average monthly losses	2.30	3.39	4.15	3.69
	Total losses	No	6,907	15,112	48,144	70,163
		% of losses	100	100	100	100
		% of personnel strength:				
		All losses	49.69	70.29	85.06	76.26
		Average monthly losses	3.01	4.26	5.15	4.62

Independent Maritime Army (2nd Formation) Personnel Losses, by Year

	Loss category		Losses by year				
			1941	1942	1943	1944	1945
Irrecoverable losses	Killed in action, died during casualty evacuation	No			2,762	8,881	4
		% of losses			19.84	15.97	0.61
	Missing in action, POWs	No			1,302	361	
		% of losses			9.35	0.65	
	Non-combat losses	No			130	638	16
		% of losses			0.94	1.15	2.43
	Total irrecoverable losses	No			4,194	9,880	20
		% of losses			30.13	17.77	3.04
		% of personnel strength:					
		All losses			2	8.88	0.07
		Average monthly losses			1.43	0.81	0.02
Sick and wounded (including those evacuated to hospitals)	Wounded, burns and concussion cases	No			6,075	26,282	4
		% of losses			43.64	47.28	0.61
	Sick	No			3,651	19,164	633
		% of losses			26.23	34.48	96.35
	Frostbite cases	No				260	
		% of losses				0.47	
	Total sick and wounded	No			9,726	45,706	637
		% of losses			69.87	82.23	96.96
		% of personnel strength:					
		All losses			4.64	41.11	2.11
		Average monthly losses			3.31	3.77	0.50
	Total losses	No			13,920	55,586	657
		% of losses			100	100	100
		% of personnel strength:					
		All losses			6.64	49.99	2.18
		Average monthly losses			4.74	4.58	0.52

37th Independent Army Personnel Losses (Total for 146 Days)

	Loss category		Officers	Sergeants	Men	Total
Irrecoverable losses	Killed in action, died during casualty evacuation	No				
		% of losses				
	Missing in action, POWs	No				
		% of losses				
	Non-combat losses	No	39	89	298	426
		% of losses	9.47	8.68	9.06	9.02
	Total irrecoverable losses	No	39	89	298	426
		% of losses	9.47	8.68	9.06	9.02
		% of personnel strength:				
		All losses	0.37	0.41	0.51	0.47
		Average monthly losses	0.07	0.08	0.10	0.09

	Loss category		Officers	Sergeants	Men	Total
Sick and wounded (including those evacuated to hospitals)	Wounded, burns and concussion cases	No			2	2
		% of losses			0.06	0.04
	Sick	No	373	936	2,988	4,297
		% of losses	90.53	91.32	90.88	90.94
	Frostbite cases	No				
		% of losses				
	Total sick and wounded	No	373	936	2,990	4,299
		% of losses	90.53	91.32	90.94	90.98
		% of personnel strength:				
		All losses	3.52	4.36	5.14	4.76
		Average monthly losses	0.73	0.91	1.07	0.99
	Total losses	No	412	1,025	3,288	4,725
		% of losses	100	100	100	100
		% of personnel strength:				
		All losses	3.89	4.77	5.65	5.23
		Average monthly losses	0.80	0.99	1.17	1.08

14th Independent Army Personnel Losses (Total for 176 Days)

	Loss category		Officers	Sergeants	Men	Total
Irrecoverable losses	Killed in action, died during casualty evacuation	No	15	39	107	161
		% of losses	3.23	2.05	1.70	1.86
	Missing in action, POWs	No	6		2	8
		% of losses	1.29		0.03	0.09
	Non-combat losses	No	38	59	146	243
		% of losses	8.17	3.10	2.31	2.80
	Total irrecoverable losses	No	59	98	255	412
		% of losses	12.69	5.15	4.04	4.75
		% of personnel strength:				
		All losses	0.60	0.54	0.55	0.55
		Average monthly losses	0.10	0.09	0.10	0.10
Sick and wounded (including those evacuated to hospitals)	Wounded, burns and concussion cases	No	21	91	254	366
		% of losses	4.52	4.78	4.03	4.22
	Sick	No	384	1,711	5,789	7,884
		% of losses	82.58	89.96	91.82	90.91
	Frostbite cases	No	1	2	7	10
		% of losses	0.21	0.11	0.11	0.12
	Total sick and wounded	No	406	1,804	6,050	8,260
		% of losses	87.31	94.85	95.96	95.25
		% of personnel strength:				
		All losses	4.14	9.97	13.01	11.11
		Average monthly losses	0.73	1.75	2.28	1.85
	Total losses	No	465	1,902	6,305	8,672
		% of losses	100	100	100	100
		% of personnel strength:				
		All losses	4.74	10.51	13.56	11.66
		Average monthly losses	0.83	1.84	2.38	1.95

LOSSES OF FLEETS AND FLOTILLAS

From the beginning of the war the navy included the Northern, Baltic, Black Sea and Pacific Fleets, the Caspian Flotilla and a number of lake and river flotillas which were formed and disbanded as required. During the war the navy conducted active military operations to destroy enemy naval forces and transports, supported Red Army maritime groupings during defensive and offensive operations, defended naval bases and major ports, carried out amphibious landings and protected sea, lake and river transportation of military and non-military supplies.

The Northern and Baltic Fleets were involved in combat operations for 1,418 days, the Black Sea Fleet for 1,183 days. The Baltic and Black Sea Fleets conducted lengthy operations together with the ground forces to defend coastal towns and evacuate their inhabitants. The Northern Fleet severed enemy lines of communication, gave protection to Allied convoys and carried out amphibious landings. The Pacific Fleet trained crews for the operational fleets, sent surface ships and submarines to support the Northern Fleet and organised naval squadrons for the front. The Pacific Fleet helped defeat the Japanese, carrying out amphibious landings in the ports of northern Korea, on the Kurile Islands and in south Sakhalin. The Amur Flotilla contributed to the success of the Soviets' Manchurian offensive operation.

On the rivers and lakes combat operations were carried out by the Azov, Dnieper, Danube, Pinsk, Ladoga, Onega, Volga and Chudskoe (Peipus) Flotillas and a detachment of ships on Lake Ilmen. Table 77 shows for how long the various fleets and flotillas were involved in the fighting. Battle casualties for some of the flotillas are included with those of the fleets of which they were part.

Table 77. Fleets and Flotillas and the Period for which They were Part of the Fighting Army

Flotilla or Fleet	Period when part of fighting army	No of days	Comments
	Fleets		
Baltic	22.06.1941–09.05.1945	1,418	
Northern	22.06.1941–09.05.1945	1,418	
Pacific	09.08.1945–02.09.1945	25	
Black Sea	22.06.1941–16.09.1944	1,183	
	Flotillas		
Azov	22.07.1941–14.10.1942 31.05.1943–20.04.1944	776	Losses included with those of Black Sea Fleet
Amur	09.08.1945–02.09.1945	25	
White Sea	15.08.1941–09.05.1945	1,364	Losses included with those of Northern Fleet
Volga	25.07.1942–02.02.1943	193	
Dnieper	14.09.1943–09.05.1945	604	
Danube (1st and 2nd formations)	22.06.1941–20.11.1941 20.04.1944–09.05.1945	537	
Caspian	08.08.1942–02.02.1943	179	
Ladoga	25.06.1941–02.10.1944	1,197	Losses included with those of Baltic Fleet
Onega	07.08.1941–28.11.1941 13.12.1942–10.07.1944	690	
Pina	22.06.1941–28.09.1941	99	
Chudskoe (Lake Peipus)	03.07.1941–19.10.1941	109	Losses included with those of Baltic Fleet
Naval units under central command	1941–1942		

Table 78. Average Monthly Listed Strength and Personnel Losses of Operational Fleets and Independent Flotillas (Excluding the Pacific Fleet and Amur Flotilla), 22 June 1941–9 May 1945

Period		Average monthly listed strength	Irrecoverable losses				Sick and wounded				All losses			
			No	% of losses	% All losses	Average monthly losses	No	% of losses	% All losses	Average monthly losses	No	% of losses	% All losses	Average monthly losses
1941	3rd quarter	260,200	25,071	70.28	9.64	2.92	10,602	29.72	4.07	1.23	35,673	100	13.71	4.15
	4th quarter	280,600	34,732	75.65	12.38	4.12	11,178	24.35	3.98	1.33	45,910	100	16.36	5.45
	Total for year	274,360	59,803	73.30	21.80	3.46	21,780	26.70	7.94	1.26	81,583	100	29.74	4.72
1942	1st quarter	251,400	20,049	73.71	7.97	2.66	7,150	26.29	2.84	0.95	27,199	100	10.81	3.61
	2nd quarter	283,000	7,426	62.70	2.62	0.87	4,417	37.30	1.56	0.52	11,843	100	4.18	1.39
	3rd quarter	282,000	42,498	90.01	15.07	5.02	4,715	9.99	1.67	0.56	47,213	100	16.74	5.58
	4th quarter	274,900	3,924	42.82	1.43	0.48	5,241	57.18	1.90	0.64	9,165	100	3.33	1.12
	Total for year	284,700	73,897	77.44	25.96	2.16	21,523	22.56	7.56	0.63	95,420	100	33.52	2.79
1943	1st quarter	253,800	2,652	42.82	1.04	0.35	3,541	57.18	1.40	0.47	6,193	100	2.44	0.82
	2nd quarter	255,460	2,995	42.90	1.17	0.39	3,987	57.10	1.56	0.52	6,982	100	2.73	0.91
	3rd quarter	226,800	2,469	42.12	1.09	0.36	3,393	57.88	1.50	0.50	5,862	100	2.59	0.86
	4th quarter	242,250	2,653	31.42	1.10	0.37	5,791	68.58	2.39	0.80	8,444	100	3.49	1.17
	Total for year	257,460	10,769	39.19	4.18	0.35	16,712	60.81	6.49	0.54	27,481	100	10.67	0.89
1944	1st quarter	248,770	2,038	22.06	0.82	0.27	7,200	77.94	2.89	0.96	9,238	100	3.71	1.23
	2nd quarter	262,300	2,653	29.12	1.01	0.34	6,459	70.88	2.46	0.82	9,112	100	3.47	1.16
	3rd quarter	268,750	2,029	37.88	0.75	0.25	3,327	62.12	1.24	0.41	5,356	100	1.99	0.66
	4th quarter	295,800	1,876	35.26	0.63	0.21	3,445	64.74	1.16	0.39	5,321	100	1.79	0.60
	Total for year	273,200	8,596	29.61	3.15	0.26	20,431	70.39	7.48	0.62	29,027	100	10.63	0.88
1945	1st quarter	307,900	386	9.75	0.13	0.04	3,575	90.25	1.16	0.39	3,961	100	1.29	0.43
	2nd quarter	312,700	290	25.39	0.09	0.07	852	74.61	0.27	0.21	1,142	100	0.36	0.28
	Total for year	311,000	676	13.25	0.22	0.05	4,427	86.75	1.42	0.33	5,103	100	1.64	0.38
Total during war		270,000	153,741	64.43	56.94	1.22	84,873	35.57	31.43	0.68	238,614	100	88.37	1.90

Notes

1. Losses for 22–30 June 1941 are included in the third quarter of 1941; losses for 1 April–9 May 1945 are included in the second quarter of 1945.

2. Sick and wounded who later died in hospital are included under 'sick and wounded'.

210

Baltic Fleet Personnel Losses (Total for 1,418 Days)

	Loss category		Officers	Petty officers, sergeants	Men	Total
Irrecoverable losses	Killed in action, died during casualty evacuation	No	3,001	4,038	12,797	19,836
		% of losses	30.38	27.35	19.11	21.66
	Missing in action, POWs	No	3,528	4,920	24,261	32,709
		% of losses	35.72	33.32	36.24	35.71
	Non-combat losses	No	323	624	2,398	3,345
		% of losses	3.27	4.22	3.58	3.65
	Total irrecoverable losses	No	6,852	9,582	39,456	55,890
		% of losses	69.37	64.89	58.93	61.02
		% of personnel strength:				
		All losses	48.15	42.16	64.94	57.20
		Average monthly losses	1.03	0.91	1.4	1.23
Sick and wounded (including those evacuated to hospitals)	Wounded, concussion and burns cases	No	2,038	2,530	20,941	25,509
		% of losses	20.64	17.14	31.28	27.85
	Sick	No	987	2,654	6,552	10,193
		% of losses	9.99	17.97	9.79	11.13
	Frostbite cases	No				
		% of losses				
	Total sick and wounded	No	3,025	5,184	27,493	35,702
		% of losses	30.63	35.11	41.07	38.98
		% of personnel strength:				
		All losses	21.26	22.80	45.25	36.53
		Average monthly losses	0.46	0.49	0.97	0.79
	Total losses	No	9,877	14,766	66,949	91,592
		% of losses	100	100	100	100
		% of personnel strength:				
		All losses	69.41	64.96	110.19	93.73
		Average monthly losses	1.49	1.4	2.37	2.02

Northern Fleet Personnel Losses (Total for 1,418 Days)

	Loss category		Officers	Petty officers, sergeants	Men	Total
Irrecoverable losses	Killed in action, died during casualty evacuation	No	1,291	1,727	4,836	7,854
		% of losses	35.26	26.43	18.61	21.71
	Missing in action, POWs	No	383	299	1,061	1,743
		% of losses	10.46	4.58	4.08	4.81
	Non-combat losses	No	141	224	943	1,308
		% of losses	3.86	3.43	3.63	3.62
	Total irrecoverable losses	No	1,815	2,250	6,840	10,905
		% of losses	49.58	34.44	26.32	30.14
		% of personnel strength:				
		All losses	18.39	14.08	13.53	14.27
		Average monthly losses	0.4	0.30	0.29	0.31

	Loss category		Officers	Petty officers, sergeants	Men	Total
Sick and wounded (including those evacuated to hospitals)	Wounded, concussion and burns cases	No	635	1,589	6,754	8,978
		% of losses	17.34	24.32	25.99	24.81
	Sick	No	1,211	2,695	12,393	16,299
		% of losses	33.08	41.24	47.69	45.05
	Frostbite cases	No				
		% of losses				
	Total sick and wounded	No	1,846	4,284	19,147	25,277
		% of losses	50.42	65.56	73.68	69.86
		% of personnel strength:				
		All losses	18.70	26.81	37.87	33.08
		Average monthly losses	0.40	0.58	0.81	0.71
	Total losses	No	3,661	6,534	25,987	36,182
		% of losses	100	100	100	100
		% of personnel strength:				
		All losses	37.09	40.89	51.40	47.35
		Average monthly losses	0.8	0.88	1.10	1.02

Pacific Fleet Personnel Losses (Total for 25 Days)

	Loss category		Officers	Petty officers, sergeants	Men	Total
Irrecoverable losses	Killed in action, died during casualty evacuation	No	195	201	507	903
		% of losses	83.33	73.90	64.02	69.57
	Missing in action, POWs	No	23	12	60	95
		% of losses	9.83	4.41	7.57	7.32
	Non-combat losses	No				
		% of losses				
	Total irrecoverable losses	No	218	213	567	998
		% of losses	93.16	78.31	71.59	76.89
		% of personnel strength:				
		All losses	1.16	0.59	0.52	0.61
		Average monthly losses	1.16	0.59	0.52	0.61
Sick and wounded (including those evacuated to hospitals)	Wounded, concussion and burns cases	No	16	58	212	286
		% of losses	6.84	21.32	26.77	22.03
	Sick	No		1	13	14
		% of losses		0.37	1.64	1.08
	Frostbite cases	No				
		% of losses				
	Total sick and wounded	No	16	59	225	300[1]
		% of losses	6.84	21.69	28.41	23.11
		% of personnel strength:				
		All losses	0.08	0.16	0.20	0.18
		Average monthly losses	0.08	0.16	0.20	0.18

Loss category		Officers	Petty officers, sergeants	Men	Total
Total losses	No	234	272	792	1,298
	% of losses	100	100	100	100
	% of personnel strength:				
	All losses	1.24	0.75	0.72	0.79
	Average monthly losses	1.24	0.75	0.72	0.79

1. According to reports from the fleet. According to information from medical treatment centres, 4,076 men were admitted to hospitals for treatment from Pacific Fleet ships, units and sub-units: 3,299 sick and 777 wounded.

Black Sea Fleet Personnel Losses (Total for 1,183 Days)

	Loss category		Officers	Petty officers, sergeants	Men	Total
Irrecoverable losses	Killed in action, died during casualty evacuation	No	3,017	3,649	10,276	16,942
		% of losses	30.19	21.93	13.10	16.12
	Missing in action, POWs	No	4,669	7,886	46,824	59,379
		% of losses	46.71	47.41	59.69	56.51
	Non-combat losses	No	458	1,061	4,554	6,073
		% of losses	4.58	6.38	5.80	5.78
	Total irrecoverable losses	No	8,144	12,596	61,654	82,394
		% of losses	81.48	75.72	78.59	78.41
		% of personnel strength:				
		All losses	66.81	64.13	106.63	91.91
		Average monthly losses	1.72	1.65	2.75	2.37
Sick and wounded (including those evacuated to hospitals)	Wounded, concussion and burns cases	No	1,587	3,302	14,147	19,036
		% of losses	15.88	19.85	18.03	18.12
	Sick	No	264	738	2,651	3,653
		% of losses	2.64	4.43	3.38	3.47
	Frostbite cases	No				
		% of losses				
	Total sick and wounded	No	1,851	4,040	16,798	22,689
		% of losses	18.52	24.28	21.41	21.59
		% of personnel strength:				
		All losses	15.18	20.57	29.05	25.30
		Average monthly losses	0.39	0.53	0.75	0.65
	Total losses	No	9,995	16,636	78,452	105,083
		% of losses	100	100	100	100
		% of personnel strength:				
		All losses	81.99	84.70	135.68	117.21
		Average monthly losses	2.11	2.18	3.50	3.02

213

Amur Flotilla Personnel Losses (Total for 25 Days)

	Loss category		Officers	Petty officers, sergeants	Men	Total
Irrecoverable losses	Killed in action, died during casualty evacuation	No	4	6	22	32
		% of losses	57.14	17.14	27.16	26.02
	Missing in action, POWs	No				
		% of losses				
	Non-combat losses	No				
		% of losses				
	Total irrecoverable losses	No	4	6	22	32
		% of losses	57.14	17.14	27.16	26.02
		% of personnel strength:				
		All losses	0.24	0.19	0.29	0.26
		Average monthly losses	0.24	0.19	0.29	0.26
Sick and wounded (including those evacuated to hospitals)	Wounded, concussion and burns cases	No	3	16	28	47
		% of losses	42.86	45.72	34.57	38.21
	Sick	No		13	31	44
		% of losses		37.14	38.27	35.77
	Frostbite cases	No				
		% of losses				
	Total sick and wounded	No	3	29	59	91
		% of losses	42.86	82.86	72.84	73.98
		% of personnel strength:				
		All losses	0.18	0.91	0.77	0.72
		Average monthly losses	0.18	0.91	0.77	0.72
	Total losses	No	7	35	81	123
		% of losses	100	100	100	100
		% of personnel strength:				
		All losses	0.41	1.10	1.06	0.98
		Average monthly losses	0.41	1.10	1.06	0.98

Volga Flotilla Personnel Losses (Total for 193 Days)

	Loss category		Officers	Petty officers, sergeants	Men	Total
Irrecoverable losses	Killed in action, died during casualty evacuation	No	43	65	164	272
		% of losses	31.16	29.41	27.70	28.60
	Missing in action, POWs	No	19	17	116	152
		% of losses	13.77	7.69	19.60	15.98
	Non-combat losses	No	21	60	117	198
		% of losses	15.21	27.15	19.76	20.82
	Total irrecoverable losses	No	83	142	397	622
		% of losses	60.14	64.25	67.06	65.40
		% of personnel strength:				
		All losses	6.29	8.02	8.58	8.06
		Average monthly losses	1	1.27	1.36	1.28

	Loss category		Officers	Petty officers, sergeants	Men	Total
Sick and wounded (including those evacuated to hospitals)	Wounded, concussion and burns cases	No	54	77	193	324
		% of losses	39.14	34.85	32.60	34.08
	Sick	No	1	2	2	5
		% of losses	0.72	0.90	0.34	0.52
	Frostbite cases	No				
		% of losses				
	Total sick and wounded	No	55	79	195	329
		% of losses	39.86	35.75	32.94	34.60
		% of personnel strength:				
		All losses	4.16	4 46	4.21	4.26
		Average monthly losses	0.66	0.71	0.67	0.68
	Total losses	No	138	221	592	951
		% of losses	100	100	100	100
		% of personnel strength:				
		All losses	10.45	12.48	12.79	12.32
		Average monthly losses	1 66	1 98	2.03	1.96

Dnieper Flotilla Personnel Losses (Total for 604 Days)

	Loss category		Officers	Petty officers, sergeants	Men	Total
Irrecoverable losses	Killed in action, died during casualty evacuation	No	35	57	186	278
		% of losses	79.55	53.27	57.59	58.65
	Missing in action, POWs	No	3	6	17	26
		% of losses	6.81	5.61	5.26	5.49
	Non-combat losses	No	2	17	38	57
		% of losses	4.55	15.89	11.76	12.02
	Total irrecoverable losses	No	40	80	241	361
		% of losses	90.91	74.77	74.61	76.16
		% of personnel strength:				
		All losses	5.41	6.40	6.97	6.63
		Average monthly losses	0.27	0.32	0.35	0.33
Sick and wounded (including those evacuated to hospitals)	Wounded, concussion and burns cases	No	4	27	82	113
		% of losses	9.09	25.23	25.39	23.84
	Sick	No				
		% of losses				
	Frostbite cases	No				
		% of losses				
	Total sick and wounded	No	4	27	82	113
		% of losses	9.09	25.23	25.39	23.84
		% of personnel strength:				
		All losses	0.54	2.16	2.37	2.07
		Average monthly losses	0.03	0.11	0.12	0.10
	Total losses	No	44	107	323	474
		% of losses	100	100	100	100
		% of personnel strength:				
		All losses	5.95	8.56	9.34	8.70
		Average monthly losses	0.30	0.43	0.47	0.43

Danube Flotilla Personnel Losses (Total for 537 Days)

	Loss category[1]		Officers	Petty officers, sergeants	Men	Total
Irrecoverable losses	Killed in action, died during casualty evacuation	No	34	41	99	174
		% of losses	97.14	83.67	86.09	87.44
	Missing in action, POWs	No	1	8	16	25
		% of losses	2.86	16.33	13.91	12.56
	Non-combat losses	No				
		% of losses				
	Total irrecoverable losses	No	35	49	115	199
		% of losses	100	100	100	100
		% of personnel strength: All losses	3	2.58	2.26	2.44
		Average monthly losses	0.17	0.15	0.13	0.14

1. As there are no figures for sick and wounded for the Danube, Caspian or Onega Flotillas, the section has been omitted in this and the following two tables.

Caspian Flotilla Personnel Losses (Total for 179 Days)

	Loss category		Officers	Petty officers, sergeants	Men	Total
Irrecoverable losses	Killed in action, died during casualty evacuation	No	18	15	61	94
		% of losses	58.06	27.27	27.23	30.32
	Missing in action, POWs	No				
		% of losses				
	Non-combat losses	No	13	40	163	216
		% of losses	41.94	72.73	72.77	69.68
	Total irrecoverable losses	No	31	55	224	310
		% of losses	100	100	100	100
		% of personnel strength: All losses	2.42	1.92	3.80	3.09
		Average monthly losses	0.41	0.32	0.64	0.53

Onega Flotilla Personnel Losses (Total for 690 Days)

	Loss category		Officers	Petty officers, sergeants	Men	Total
Irrecoverable losses	Killed in action, died during casualty evacuation	No	8	13	51	72
		% of losses	88.89	56.52	80.95	75.79
	Missing in action, POWs	No	1	1	3	5
		% of losses	11.11	4.35	4.76	5.26
	Non-combat losses	No			9	9	18
		% of losses		39.13	14.29	18.95

Loss category		Officers	Petty officers, sergeants	Men	Total
Total irrecoverable losses	No	9	23	63	95
	% of losses	100	100	100	100
	% of personnel strength:				
	All losses	5.63	7.93	9.84	8.72
	Average monthly losses	0.25	0.35	0.44	0.39

Pinsk Flotilla Personnel Losses (Total for 99 Days)

	Loss category		Officers	Petty officers, sergeants	Men	Total
Irrecoverable losses	Killed in action, died during casualty evacuation	No	33	12	37	82
		% of losses	11.79	11.65	11.42	11.60
	Missing in action, POWs	No	221	44	165	430
		% of losses	78.93	42.72	50.93	60.82
	Non-combat losses	No	2			2
		% of losses	0.71			0.28
	Total irrecoverable losses	No	256	56	202	514
		% of losses	91.43	54.37	62.35	72.70
		% of personnel strength:				
		All losses	80	11.20	13.29	21.97
		Average monthly losses	25	3.50	4.15	6.86
Sick and wounded (including those evacuated to hospitals)	Wounded, concussion and burns cases	No	24	47	122	193
		% of losses	8.57	45.63	37.65	27.30
	Sick	No				
		% of losses				
	Frostbite cases	No				
		% of losses				
	Total sick and wounded	No	24	47	122	193
		% of losses	8.57	45.63	37.65	27.30
		% of personnel strength:				
		All losses	7.50	9.40	8.03	8.25
		Average monthly losses	2.34	2.94	2.51	2.58
	Total losses	No	280	103	324	707
		% of losses	100	100	100	100
		% of personnel strength:				
		All losses	87.50	20.60	21.32	30.22
		Average monthly losses	27.34	6.44	6.66	9.44

217

Naval Units under Central Control: Personnel Losses (Total for 1941–42)

	Loss category		Officers	Petty officers, sergeants	Men	Total
Irrecoverable losses	Killed in action, died during casualty evacuation	No	400	102	658	1,160
		% of losses	62.99	24.40	33.43	38.40
	Missing in action, POWs	No	162	65	474	701
		% of losses	25.51	15.55	24.09	23.20
	Non-combat losses	No	36	142	412	590
		% of losses	5.67	33.97	20.94	19.53
	Total irrecoverable losses	No	598	309	1,544	2,451
		% of losses	94.17	73.92	78.46	81.13
		% of personnel strength: All losses Average monthly losses				
Sick and wounded (including those evacuated to hospitals)	Wounded, concussion and burns cases	No	37	109	424	570
		% of losses	5.83	26.08	21.54	18.87
	Sick	No				
		% of losses				
	Frostbite cases	No				
		% of losses				
	Total sick and wounded	No	37	109	424	570
		% of losses	5.83	26.08	21.54	18.87
		% of personnel strength: All losses Average monthly losses				
	Total losses	No	635	418	1,968	3,021
		% of losses	100	100	100	100
		% of personnel strength: All losses Average monthly losses				

LOSSES IN THE ARMS OF SERVICE

At the time of the Great Patriotic War the fighting army encompassed various arms of service. The rifle troops (infantry), who made up the main part of the ground forces, were the most numerous. Together with the armoured and mechanised troops, the artillery, etc., they carried out the most important tasks and bore the brunt of the fighting in both offensive and defensive operations. Consequently they suffered particularly heavy casualties. Table 79, which gives total casualty numbers by arm of service for 28 months of the war (1943–45), confirms this.

Table 79. Red Army Losses by Arm of Service, 1943–45

Arm of service	Irrecoverable losses											Sick and wounded (including those evacuated to hospitals)										Total losses		
	Killed in action, died during casualty evacuation		Non-combat losses (died as result of sickness or accident)		Missing in action POWs		Total			Wounded, concussion and burns cases		Sick, frostbite cases		Total										
	No	% of losses	No	% of losses	No	% of losses	No	% of losses	% of numerical strength	No	% of losses	No	% of losses	No	% of losses	% of numerical strength			No	% of losses	% of numerical strength
Rifle troops	2,850,139	85.95	303,329	68.48	439,313	78.29	3,392,781	84.23	126.93	9,263,165	88.84	1,946,637	80.98	11,209,802	87.37	419.39	14,602,583	86.62	546.32
Fortified areas	11,866	0.36	1,142	0.76	1,845	0.33	14,853	0.37	18.27	27,741	0.27	16,938	0.70	44,679	0.35	54.97	59,532	0.35	73.24
Cavalry	54,546	1.64	2,828	1.87	19,773	3.52	77,147	1.92	61.94	131,223	1.26	20,483	0.85	151,706	1.18	121.81	228,853	1.36	183.75
Armoured and mechanised troops	241,236	7.27	8,071	5.35	61,180	10.90	310,487	7.71	71.95	637,857	6.12	73,175	3.04	711,032	5.54	164.78	1,021,519	6.06	236.73
GHQ Reserve artillery	76,365	2.30	6,424	4.25	14,123	2.52	96,912	2.41	17.15	194,421	1.86	82,113	3.42	276,534	2.16	48.93	373,446	2.22	66.08
Rocket units	4,118	0.12	392	0.26	1,117	0.20	5,627	0.14	5.88	9,134	0.09	5,416	0.23	14,550	0.11	15.21	20,177	0.12	21.09
GHQ Reserve air defence units	9,213	0.28	7,750	5.14	1,290	0.23	18,253	0.45	10.89	20,406	0.20	42,780	1.78	63,186	0.49	37.71	81,439	0.48	48.59
Flame-thrower units	2,219	0.07	331	0.22	666	0.12	3,216	0.08	26.12	5,479	0.05	2,785	0.12	8,264	0.06	67.12	11,480	0.07	93.24
Signals units	3,159	0.10	1,380	0.91	619	0.11	5,158	0.13	3.35	6,744	0.06	15,902	0.66	22,646	0.18	14.70	27,804	0.16	18.05
Engineers	30,222	0.91	5,296	3.52	6,415	1.14	41,933	1.04	21.91	72,811	0.71	45,830	1.91	119,641	0.93	62.51	161,574	0.96	84.41
Road units	2,072	0.06	2,923	1.94	322	0.06	5,317	0.13	3.55	4,454	0.04	38,853	1.62	43,307	0.34	28.90	48,624	0.29	32.44
MT units	398	0.01	576	0.38	51	0.01	1,025	0.03	1.07	714	0.01	6,988	0.29	7,702	0.06	8.01	8,727	0.05	9.08
Other units and departments	21,063	0.64	6,008	3.98	3,483	0.62	30,554	0.75	2.32	45,314	0.44	87,423	3.64	133,737	1.04	10.14	164,291	0.97	12.46
Air force	9,456	0.29	4,438	2.94	10,941	1.95	24,835	0.63	6.30	5,632	0.05	18,526	0.76	24,158	0.19	6.12	48,993	0.29	12.42
Total, 01.01.1943–09.05.1945	3,316,072	100	150,888	100	561,138	100	4,028,098	100		10,427,095	100	2,403,849	100	12,830,944	100		16,859,042	100	

Notes

1. As there is insufficient information on losses by arm of service for 1941–42, the table only gives a summary of the figures for 1 January 1943–9 May 1945.

2. Casualty figures for airborne troops are included with rifle troops; figures for artillery units which formed part of rifle and tank divisions/brigades are included with these arms of service as appropriate.

3. Figures for air defence units are included with 'other units and departments'; this also includes figures for other units which do not come under the arms of service listed, including reserve, training and logistic units and military training establishments.

4. The column '% of numerical strength' indicates the proportion of total losses in relation to average monthly numerical strength for the arm of service concerned between 1 January 1943 and 9 May 1945.

In this period alone total losses for the arms of service were 16,859,000: 4,028,000 irrecoverable losses and 12,831,000 sick and wounded. Of these, 86.6% were rifle troops, 6% armoured troops, 2.2% GHQ Reserve artillery, 0.29% air force, etc.

Comparing the total number of casualties in each arm of service during this period with the average monthly listed strength, it may be concluded that over 28 months the percentage who became casualties was as follows: rifle troops 546.3% of average monthly strength; armoured troops 236.7%; cavalry 183.7%; flame-thrower units 93.2%; engineers 84.4%; artillery 66% etc.

If the losses for 1941–42 were added to these figures then the proportion would be significantly higher, especially for the rifle troops.

OFFICER CASUALTIES (IRRECOVERABLE LOSSES)

The figures for officer casualties during the Great Patriotic War are based on information and statistics from the Chief Personnel Directorate of the USSR Ministry of Defence, which were compiled in 1963 by a group of authors under the supervision of Army General A. P. Byeloborodov.

As officers are the backbone of the army and it is they who organise and lead operations against the enemy, in all wars there have been an appreciable number of officer casualties. In World War I, for example, Tsarist Russia's army lost over 72,000 officers alone, or 14.6% of officer strength. The breakdown of casualties by rank is as follows: 208 generals; 3,368 staff officers; 30,330 senior officers; 37,392 junior officers; 1,076 military doctors; and 485 clerical staff.

All Red Army and Navy officers bore a heavy responsibility in the bitter struggle against the Nazi invaders. Over a million[10] were killed, died of wounds, were missing in action or were taken prisoner during the Great Patriotic War, which was 35% of the total number of officers serving in the armed forces during the war.

By rank, this figure breaks down as follows: 421 generals and admirals; 2,502 colonels; 4,887 lieutenant-colonels; 19,404 majors; 71,738 captains; 168,229 senior lieutenants; 353,040 lieutenants; 279,967 junior lieutenants; and 122,905 acting officers not holding officer rank.

The Red Army and Navy lost 14 times more officers in the Great Patriotic War than the Tsarist Army lost in World War I. Irrecoverable losses were as follows: killed, died of wounds or disease—631,008 (61.68%); missing in action, POWs—392,085% (38.32%). According to figures from repatriation organisations, by 1 January 1950 over 126,000 officer POWs had been repatriated.

Irrecoverable losses by section, Service and arm of service are shown in Tables 80 and 81.

These figures show that 90% of officer casualties during the war were command personnel and political staff. Although officers in other sections made up only a small proportion of casualties compared with command personnel and political staff, there

Table 80. Irrecoverable Losses by Section

Section	Killed or died	Missing in action, POWs	Total	% of total losses
Command personnel	536,364	284,571	820,935	80.3
Political staff	57,608	42,126	99,734	9.7
Technical staff	14,033	21,803	35,836	3.5
Administrative staff	8,746	22,914	31,660	3.1
Medical personnel	11,971	15,431	27,402	2.7
Veterinary personnel	1,642	3,798	5,440	0.5
Legal staff	644	1,442	2,086	0.2
Total	631,008	392,085	1,023,093	100

were still a large number of them. By way of comparison, in World War I support staff (doctors and clerical staff) made up only 2.1% of the total number of officers killed. With more sophisticated military hardware, the involvement of the air force and high troop manoeuvrability, however, it was of course not only units and formations fighting on the battlefield which came under attack and suffered heavy casualties, but also units and establishments in the rear.

Table 81. Irrecoverable Losses by Service and Arm of Service

Service, arm of service (service)	Killed or died	Missing in action, POWs	Total	% of total casualties
Army	607,217	366,043	973,260	95.13
No of command personnel losses:				
Infantry	389,467	180,327	569,794	58.54
Artillery	56,610	37,576	94,186	9.68
Armoured and mechanised troops	35,166	11,939	47,105	4.84
Engineers	10,260	8,047	18,307	1.88
Signallers	11,172	13,167	24,339	2.50
Cavalry	6,757	5,836	12,593	1.29
Other arms of service and services	4,401	6,385	10,786	1.11
Air force	18,420	20,684	39,104	3.82
No of command personnel losses	17,170	18,753	35,923	91.87
Navy	5,371	5,358	10,729	1.05
No of command personnel losses	3,413	3,431	6,844	63.79
Total	631,008	392,085	1,023,093	

As can be seen from Table 81, the heaviest losses (95.13% of total officer casualties) were in the ground forces. A further 3.82% were in the air force and 1.05% in the navy.

According to figures from the Chief Personnel Directorate, the greatest number of irrecoverable losses among army and naval officers were in the first years of the war, over 50% of all such losses during the war occurring in 1941–42.

In 1942, 161,857 officers were killed on active service in the army and navy and 124,488 were missing in action. About 125,000 of these were platoon leaders, about 16,000 were commanders of companies, batteries or squadrons and about 5,500 were battalion commanders. It was the rifle units which suffered the heaviest casualties: 50% of the total number of officers killed or missing in action were infantry commanders. Senior officer casualties were also high. Suffice it to say that in 1942 11 corps commanders, 76 division commanders and 16 brigade commanders were killed.

In the air force it was the air crews that suffered the heaviest losses. In 1942 6,178 pilots were killed, which was about 24% of combat crews in the operational air force.

In the navy the heaviest casualties were in the infantry, which took part in the defence of Sevastopol and Novorossiysk and in combat operations in other maritime sectors.

As well as the large number of irrecoverable losses, a large number of officers also fell sick or were wounded. About 300,000 were sent to hospital in the course of the year.

Thus in 1942 total officer casualties were over 550,000.

In 1943 in the army and navy 173,584 were killed and 43,423 missing in action, a total of 217,007 officers. In addition, over 400,000 officers were discharged from active combat on medical grounds.

As in previous years, the heaviest losses were in the ground forces, where there were over 200,000 officers killed or missing in action.

The fierce fighting for control of the air, especially during the Soviet advance on Stalingrad, during the Battle of Kursk and during the air battles over the Kuban in April and May 1943, meant that there were exceptionally heavy air force casualties, which were heavier in 1943 than in any other year of the war. There were 8,255 casualties, or 39.2% of active combat crews.

In the navy, almost 2,000 commanders became casualties.

In 1944 there was a noticeable reduction in the number of officers killed in battle, as the army became better equipped and gained in fighting skill, and also as commanders improved their organisational skills. Even then, however, casualty numbers remained high. In the course of the year 169,553 army and naval officers were killed and 36,704 were missing. The total officer casualties, including sick and wounded, came to over 500,000.

In 1945 over 80,000 army and naval officers were killed or missing.

Table 82 gives combat losses among command personnel in the army, navy and air force, by rank.

Table 82. Combat Losses among Command Personnel in the Army, Navy and Air Force, by Rank

Position	Killed or died	Missing in action	Total
Army			
Commanders of Fronts	5	—	5
Chiefs of staff of Fronts	3	—	3
Army commanders	19	—	19
Army chiefs of staff	9	2	11
Corps commanders	42	6	48
Corps chiefs of staff	12	—	12

Position	Killed or died	Missing in action	Total
Division (brigade) commanders	400	163	563
Division (brigade) chiefs of staff	345	221	566
Division chief military administrative officers	160	153	313
Regiment commanders	2,545	1,114	3,659
Regiment chiefs of staff	1,372	775	2,147
Battalion commanders	14,547	6,366	20,913
Company (battery, squadron) commanders	90,210	34,554	124,764
Platoon leaders	296,744	137,766	434,510
Air Force			
Air corps, division and regiment commanders and deputy commanders	464	294	758
Air squadron commanders and deputy commanders	1,946	2,110	4,056
Detachment and flight commanders	2,792	2,587	5,379
Aircraft commanders, pilots	7,855	10,609	18,464
Staff officers responsible for radio-gunners' training	154	181	335
Air regiment and air division navigators	51	118	169
Air squadron navigators, chief political officers	258	320	578
Flight navigators	729	878	1,607
Airborne rifle service and air squadron senior signals officers	44	74	118
Reconnaissance pilots and bombadier-gunners	1,715	2,659	4,374
Air corps division and regt. chiefs of staff and deputy COS.	58	17	75
Air corps, division and regt. chief operations officers and chief military information officers	60	17	77
Air corps, division and regt. senior signals officers and chiefs CW service	73	57	130
Adjutants	32	14	46
Navy			
Squadron and brigade commanders	2	—	2
Ships' commanders 1st rank and deputy commanders	2	—	2
Ships' commanders 2nd and 3rd rank and submarine commanders	364	49	413
Ships' commanders 4th class	283	59	342
Commanders of detachments and squadrons of ships	98	14	112
Commanders of divisions of ships	45	8	53
Surface ship navigators	111	29	140
Submarine navigators	124	9	133
Ships' gunners	112	30	142
Surface ship mine specialists	65	18	83
Submarine mine specialists	107	9	116
Naval signallers	57	28	85
Submarine mechanics	117	4	121
Surface ship mechanics	172	39	211
Officers i/c radio-technical service	8	6	14
Naval staff officers	20	3	23
Naval infantry staff officers	27	37	64
Naval infantry brigade commanders	3	—	3
Battalion commanders	30	29	59
Coast defence battery commanders and deputy commanders	45	78	123
Naval infantry platoon commanders	569	1,292	1,861
Naval infantry company commanders and deputy commanders	150	233	383

These figures show that the majority of officers killed or missing in action were command personnel with the field army (operational fleet), corps, division and regiment commanders, unit and formation chiefs of staff, platoon leaders and company commanders (the two last suffering the heaviest casualties).

True to their military and patriotic duty and to their oath of allegiance, officers inspired their men on the battlefield by their personal example and led them into the attack. Together with their men they won victories, and together with them they died. The military leaders who laid down their lives for the liberation of their country from the Nazis will always be remembered by its people: commanders of fronts Army Generals I. D. Chernyakhovski, N. F. Vatutin, I. R. Apanasenko and D. G. Pavlov and Colonel-General M. P. Kirponos; chiefs of staff of fronts Lieutenant-General P. I. Bodin and Major-Generals G. D. Stelmakh and V. I. Tupikov; army commanders Lieutenant-Generals S. D. Akimov, P. P. Korzun, A. M. Gorodnyanski, M. G. Yefremov, A. I. Zygin, V. Ya. Kachalov, I. F. Nikolaev, K. P. Podlas, P. S. Pshennikov, A. K. Smirnov, P. M. Filatov, F. M. Kharitonov and V. A. Khomenko and Major-Generals A. I. Lizyukov, M. P. Petrov and K. I. Rakutin; members of military councils of fronts Divisional Commissars D. A. Lestev and Ye. P. Rykov; members of military councils of armies Major-Generals B. O. Galstyan, I. A. Gavrilov and I. V. Vasiliev, Divisional Commissar I. P. Sheklanov, etc.

In all during the war 421 generals and admirals were killed, missing in action or died of disease or from other causes: 344 major-generals, seven rear-admirals, 59 lieutenant-generals, two vice-admirals, four colonel-generals (Kirponos, I. G. Zakharkin, K. N. Leselidze and V. I. Pestov), four army generals (Apanasenko, Vatulin, Chernyakhovski and Pavlov) and a Marshal of the Soviet Union (B. M. Shaposhnikov).

Under the leadership of their officers, the Soviet troops fought heroically during the Great Patriotic War, driving the aggressors from their homeland and, together with the Allies, liberating the peoples of Europe.

THE PRICE OF VICTORY

For almost eighteen months the firestorm of war swept eastwards, burning villages and destroying towns in its path. Its first victims were those in uniform who were defending the country. Amid heavy fighting and at the cost of many casualties, Soviet troops crushed the Nazi divisions which were racing towards the rich resources of the Ukraine, Byelorussia, the Baltic republics, central Russia and the Caucasus. With increasing combat experience and powerful support from the rear, the Red Army won more and more battles, striking ever harder at the enemy. They fought to turn the tide westwards, to liberate the peoples of these regions from the Nazi invasion.

It was the battle of Moscow between September 1941 and January 1942 that put paid to Hitler's plans for a blitzkrieg against the USSR. The enemy was thrown back a long way from the walls of the capital and the myth that the German Army was invincible was dispelled. In spite of temporary setbacks for the Soviets, the Nazi invaders came up against unprecedented resistance put up by the Red Army and the tremendous force of spirit with which they defended their country. Both those who fought at the front and those who laboured day and night in the rear believed in the rightness of their cause and that ultimately victory would be theirs.

Both in pronouncements by the leaders of the Soviet state and in the many international documents they signed, the joint tasks were posed of defeating Nazism, liberating Europe and Asia from fascism and assisting their peoples to restore national independence.

People in the occupied countries closely followed events in the Soviet Union. They saw the Red Army as their liberators and therefore wished them success, at the same time redoubling their resistance to the Nazi troops. Once the Soviet Union entered the war, the socio-political character of World War II changed. Gradually, anti-Hitler alliances of peoples in the countries fighting Germany were formed. The leaders of Britain and the United States placed a high value on the USSR's role in the overall fight against fascism. In a personal message to Stalin in July 1941 Winston Churchill stated: 'All of us here are very pleased that the Russian armies are putting up such strong and courageous resistance to the totally unprovoked and merciless Nazi invasion. The bravery and determination of the Soviet soldiers and people are widely admired ...'[11] In spring 1942, when Soviet troops were engaged in heavy fighting across a broad front, a telegram expressing approval arrived from across the ocean. In the name of the American people, President Roosevelt wrote: 'The determination of your armies and people to defeat Hitler is an inspiration to the free nations of the world.'[12] Similar messages reached Moscow from different parts of the globe. Many countries recognised that the Red Army was fighting and incurring heavy casualties not just for Russia, but to save the freedom-loving nations of the world. It may therefore be said that the Soviet troops began their liberators' mission not when they crossed the USSR's western border and entered Romania, Poland, Czechoslovakia and Hungary, but with the first frontier battles of 1941, and that it continued for the entire 1,418 days of the Great Patriotic War. The Red Army only achieved final victory after many ordeals and sacrifices.

In spring 1944 the actual liberation of Europe from Nazi occupation began. The first country to be liberated was Romania, Soviet troops forcing the natural border of the River Prut on the night of 28 March 1944.

They inflicted a crushing defeat on the enemy at Iasi and Kishinev, paving the way for an armed uprising in Romania and Romania's withdrawal from the fascist block. The 2nd Ukrainian Front fought with Romanian units which went over to the side of the people and by the end of October had completely liberated Romania. Soviet casualties in the Iasi-Kishinev operation were 13,197 killed or missing in action and 53,933 wounded or sick, a total of 67,130 men and officers.

In September 1944 the Bulgarians welcomed the liberating army with flowers and the traditional greeting of bread and salt. Power was transferred to the Patriotic Front, and Bulgaria declared war on Germany.

The liberation of Hungary was achieved only after heavy fighting. The Debrecen offensive operation lasted from 6 to 28 October 1944. Then began the Budapest operation, as a result of which the 188,000-strong enemy grouping was encircled by the 2nd Ukrainian Front, advancing on Budapest from the east and north-east, and the 3rd Ukrainian Front, attacking from the south. After the Balaton defensive operation the Soviets joined forces with the Bulgarian and Yugoslav armies to liberate Hungary on 4 April.

Driving the Nazis out of Poland was achieved with great difficulty and cost many lives. The liberation of the country began in the second half of 1944 during the Byelorussian operation, which lasted from 23 June to 29 August. Its aim was to rout Army Group Centre and completely liberate Byelorussia. The Soviets were opposed by 63 divisions and three brigades numbering 1.2 million men, which were blocking the route to Warsaw.

After heavy fighting Army Group Centre was defeated and its main forces encircled and routed. In stage two of the operation, from 5 July to 29 August, the rout of the encircled enemy troops was completed and heavy losses were inflicted on formations which had been newly formed or transferred from other sectors.

The Soviet troops now entered Poland. Here, too, they met with stubborn resistance from the enemy, who was supported by a powerful system of defences. As a result of the Vistula-Oder operation, the Red Army, together with the Polish Army, liberated the western and southern parts of Poland and entered Nazi Germany. Twenty-five enemy divisions were routed and 35 were completely destroyed.

There were a large number of Soviet casualties—43,251 killed or missing in action and 149,874 sick or wounded, a total of 193,125 men.

Soviet troops also helped Czechoslovakia and the Yugoslav Army to liberate their countries from Nazi occupation. In Austria, Norway and Denmark, too, the heroism of the Soviet soldier is remembered.

In order to hasten the end of World War II and help China, Korea and the other Asian countries to rid themselves of Japanese domination, the Soviet Union fulfilled its commitment to the Allies by entering the war with Japan. The people of China, Indonesia, Korea and the other countries were overjoyed at the move. In the United States, too, a wave of enthusiasm spread across the country.

The Manchurian strategic offensive operation (9 August–2 September 1945) was conducted by the Trans-Baikal and the 1st and 2nd Far Eastern Fronts, the Pacific Fleet and the Red Banner Amur Flotilla. The People's Revolutionary Army of the Mongolian People's Republic also took part in the operation. The million-strong Kwantung Army was subjected to simultaneous air, sea and land strikes.

In the first six days the advancing troops in all sectors broke the Japanese resistance, forced the Amur and Ussuri rivers, crossed the Lesser Khingan and Greater Khingan ranges, many other mountain ranges and the desert steppes of Inner Mongolia and reached the central part of Manchuria. The Kwantung Army was split and its lines of withdrawal were cut off. The Pacific Fleet put ashore assault landing forces in the ports of northern Korea. Airborne assault forces were landed at Harbin, Kirin, Dalyan, Chang-chun, Shen-yang and other towns.

The Chinese and Koreans gave the Soviet liberators a rapturous welcome. The Red Army's successful attack left the way open for further actions by the Chinese People's Liberation Army.

Also at this time the South Sakhalin offensive operation and the Kurile amphibious operation were taking place (11–25 August and 18 August–1 September respectively). The outcome of these operations was that the occupied southern part of Sakhalin island and the Kurile Islands, which had long been a cause of Japan's anti-Soviet policies, were liberated.

An area of over 1.3 million square kilometres, with a population of over 40 million, was liberated. This paved the way for the rise of national liberation struggles in many countries of East and South-East Asia.

The liberation of the West and East in 1944–45 involved a number of major operations by the Soviet armed forces, including the Byelorussian, Iasi-Kishinev, Lvov-Sandomierz, Budapest, Vienna, Belgrade, Vistula-Oder, Berlin, Prague and Manchurian operations, in which 11 fronts, four fleets, 50 combined-arms, six tank and 13 air armies and three flotillas took part. For over a year about 7 million Soviet soldiers fought bitterly, fully or partially liberating 13 European and Asian countries with a total population of over 147 million.[13]

The final defeat of Nazi Germany and of Japan's militarist regime, and the liberation of Europe and Asia, cost the Soviet armed forces great hardship and many sacrifices. Casualty figures are given in Table 83.

Table 83. Casualty Figures for the Soviet Armed Forces

Country[1]	Irrecoverable losses		Sick and wounded		Total losses	
	Total	Killed, died of wounds or disease	Total	Wounded, concussion and frostbite cases	No	%
Poland	600,212	541,029	1,416,032	1,145,329	2,016,244	51.83
Czechoslovakia	139,918	122,392	411,514	346,044	551,432	14.18
Hungary	140,004	112,625	344,296	290,136	484,300	12.45
Germany	101,961	92,316	262,861	241,522	364,822	9.38
Romania	68,993	59,499	217,349	150,311	286,342	7.36
Austria	26,006	23,128	68,179	60,143	94,185	2.42
Yugoslavia	7,995	6,307	21,589	14,617	29,584	0.76
Norway	3,436	2,887	14,726	4,750	18,162	0.47
Bulgaria	977	154	11,773	514	12,750	0.33
China	9,272	6,729	20,630	15,885	29,902	0.77
N. Korea	691	528	1,272	1,154	1,963	0.05
Total	1,099,465	967,594[2]	2,790,221	2,270,405	3,889,686	100

1. Soviet personnel losses are based on post-war borders.
2. Includes 10,825 who died of disease.

As the table shows, about a million Soviet soldiers lie buried in the countries they helped liberate in Europe and Asia.

The Soviet people paid a high price for the liberation of Europe and Asia from German fascism and Japanese militarism. In all, including sick and wounded, there were about four million Soviet casualties during this period. Table 84 gives a breakdown of these casualties by rank.

Table 84. Breakdown of Soviet Casualties, by Rank

	Loss category	Officers	Sergeants	Men	Total
Irrecoverable losses	Killed in action, died of wounds	86,203	205,848	664,718	956,769
	Missing in action, POWs	6,467	17,725	70,392	94,584
	Non-combat losses (died in accident, of disease etc.)	4,228	9,688	34,196	48,112
	Total irrecoverable losses	96,898	233,261	769,306	1,099,465
Sick and wounded (incl. those evacuated to hospitals)	Wounded, concussion and burns cases etc.	174,539	459,340	1,636,526	2,270,405
	Sick	43,696	91,399	383,420	518,515
	Frostbite cases	73	201	1,027	1,301
	Total sick and wounded	218,308	550,940	2,020,973	2,790,221
	Total losses	315,206	784,201	2,790,279	3,889,686

The Soviet people and army regarded the defence of their own country and the defeat of the Nazis there and the liberation of the other occupied countries as inextricably linked, and the Soviet armed forces played their part in this with honour.

Their troops showed exceptional military skill and moral qualities during the war. They fought bravely and risked their lives to preserve ancient cities and centres of world culture. They treated humanely the people of the aggressor country which had caused so much bloodshed, caring for rescued women, children and old people. They helped build a new life on the ruins of despotism. They shared their food with the German population, providing food for 3.5 million people in Berlin alone.

In the post-war years much was done in the liberated countries to preserve the memory of the Soviet soldiers who had brought liberation from fascism. Unfortunately, however, recent events have shown that in some of these countries there are people with short memories. The increasingly frequent attempts to consign to oblivion the heroism of the Soviet troops and any relics connected with their role in the war, and also the vandalism of monuments to the liberators and their graves outside Russia, are regarded here with dismay and disbelief.

LOSSES OF OTHER FORMATIONS

As well as the army and navy, an active part was played in the struggle against Nazi occupation by the people's militia, the partisans and the underground resistance. However, there is only information on casualty figures for people's militia units and formations which were part of operational fronts and armies. Because the military archives do not contain the necessary documents on other formations, it has not been possible to calculate their losses.

It should be borne in mind that people's militia formations were put together under the supervision of local Party and soviet organisations. They included volunteers who were not among the first who were liable for call-up. People's militia divisions and regiments played a significant role in the defence of Moscow, Leningrad, Smolensk, Tula, Stalingrad and other cities. They suffered many casualties, not a few because they were insufficiently armed and had little combat training.

Over 4 million people in all volunteered for the people's militia, and from those who were selected for training the formations, units and sub-units of the militia were formed. Not everywhere was it possible to complete the formation process, however. Only about 2 million people actually joined the fighting troops via the people's militia. Volunteer formations were given additional arms and reinforcements so they were staffed like regular units and incorporated into the Red Army. In all, 40 people's militia divisions were brought into the fighting army, 26 of these for the whole duration of the war.

In territory which was temporarily under enemy occupation, partisans and underground resistance fighters were active. A sizeable proportion of those fighting in the enemy's rear area had broken out of encirclement or captivity.

By the end of 1941 there were over 2,000 partisan detachments (more than 90,000 men) in occupied territory. Altogether in the enemy's rear area there were over 6,000 partisan detachments, numbering more than a million men, over 10,000 of whom were Red Army officers who had escaped from encirclement or captivity.

Overall strategic control of the partisan struggle was exercised by the Supreme Command Headquarters. On 30 May 1942 the Central Headquarters of the Partisan Movement was set up. It existed until 13 January 1944, when control of the partisan detachments was transferred to Central Committees of the union republics and to regional Party committees. In working on this book, the authors studied short reports on the partisan struggle by several regional committees and reports by the Central Headquarters of the Partisan Movement. Although these were not enough to give a full picture of partisan losses, they did provide one source of information to help determine partisan numbers and losses during the war.

One report from the Orel region, for example, shows that by 1 July 1942 there were 9,693 partisans fighting the occupying forces in the region. By 15 April 1943 this number had increased to 14,142. Between 2 May and 6 July 1943 the Germans carried out punitive raids against the Orel partisans, as a result of which 841 partisans were killed, 128 were drowned, 697 were wounded, 30 were taken prisoner and 2,450 were missing in action (the majority of these later, one by one, joined up with Soviet troops).

According to incomplete figures received from the Chernigov, Stalino (Donetsk), Kirovograd, Nikolaev, Poltava, Odessa, Dnepropetrovsk and Orel regions, Krasnodar territory, the Kalmyk Autonomous Republic and the Karelian-Finnish Union Republic, 6,528 partisans were killed, wounded, missing in action or taken prisoner.

It is known that over 127,000 were awarded 'Great Patriotic War Partisan' 1st and 2nd class medals, and over 184,000 were awarded orders and medals of the USSR.

This book does not cover losses in the merchant navy and river transport, whose workers played an active part in the war. Many crews took part in amphibious operations and transported supplies to the front under constant enemy attack from air and sea.

A heavy burden also fell on rail and road transport workers and special formations. These kept up a steady supply of replacements for the front, evacuated equipment from factories and the wounded to hospitals and repaired damaged track or roads. Trains and road convoys were frequently bombed by the German air force, and in these circumstances casualties were inevitable.

It is said that war is not a matter for women, but when the country was under threat from the Nazis women fought alongside men. At the front they served as pilots, doctors, medical assistants, anti-aircraft gunners, snipers, signallers, laundresses, weather forecasters, etc. A total of 490,235 women were called up, and many of these did not return from the war.

While this book was being prepared for publication, a major study was under way in the republics, territories and regions of the USSR to discover the names of all who perished during the Great Patriotic War, including members of the people's militia, the partisans and the resistance, road, sea, river and rail transport workers, health workers and communications workers who served in special formations under different departments. The aim is to name all those who, like the soldiers who served at the front, gave their lives to save their country. Their names will be published in Books of Remembrance which are currently under preparation.

On the basis of this record of the names of all who were killed or missing in action during the war it will be possible to establish more exactly the total number of Soviet losses.

The figures once again show that it was the Soviet Union and its armed forces which bore the brunt of the fighting against the Germans and Japanese in World War II.

The cost of victory was high, but it was a price that had to be paid for the country's freedom and independence, to save many nations from enslavement, to crush fascism and militarism and bring about a lasting peace.

PRISONERS OF WAR AND MEN MISSING IN ACTION

The problem of determining the exact number of casualties in the Great Patriotic War is particularly difficult in the case of prisoners of war and men missing in action.

The sudden attack by Nazi Germany caught troops unawares in western frontier military districts, which at the beginning of the war were reorganised into fronts. The rapid deployment of superior enemy forces in the main sectors, the highly unfavourable conditions in which the Soviet troops had to operate in the first days of the war and the breakdown in communications and command structures all led to large gaps in their defences and to not only individual units and formations but entire armies being encircled and cut off from their fronts' main forces. At the same time the rapid advance by enemy tanks, which reached the flanks and rear of the defending troops, continuous air strikes and acts of sabotage by different enemy groups often led to confusion among command personnel as well as the rank and file. By no means all were able to withstand such an ordeal, or the exceptional physical and emotional strain. As a result, with all possibilities of further resistance exhausted and lacking any support, large groups of retreating troops were taken prisoner. Some were wounded, some were psychologically broken and some were worn to the limit by cold, hunger and other privations.

Consequently, in the early months of the war a large number of prisoners of war taken by the Germans swelled the numbers missing in action, but loss of communication to and from army, front and General HQ meant that it was not possible to submit regular reports on either the outcome of operations or casualty numbers.

In any war there have always been prisoners taken and men missing. This is inevitable in armed conflict. For example, in the 40 months of war from 1914 to 1917 there were 3,638,271 missing in action and prisoners of war in the Russian Army, while 1,961,333 enemy prisoners were taken on Russian territory during the same period.[14]

The intensity of the fighting in the Great Patriotic War and the fact that it involved large numbers of people and a large amount of military hardware explains but does not justify the high casualty numbers.

Of course, there were different reasons why soldiers were taken prisoner. As a rule it happened after they had been wounded, were physically exhausted or out of ammunition. They all knew that to give oneself up voluntarily through cowardice or lack of spirit has always been considered a military offence. However, for most Soviet soldiers the word 'voluntarily' does not apply. Almost all who were captured by the Nazis felt it as a severe psychological blow to be torn from the ranks of the Soviet Army and taken prisoner. Many preferred death to the dreadful disgrace.

Unfortunately, for many years both during and after the war discussion of this subject was banned on the orders of Stalin and his entourage, yet the matter was one which concerned millions of Soviet men and officers who had fallen into the hands of the Nazis. Therefore, before embarking on a calculation of the losses, let us first dwell on the tragic fate of those who were taken prisoner by the Germans.

Nazi Germany's aim was the total destruction of the Soviet Union. This was reflected in the particularly brutal way that Soviet prisoners of war were treated by the Nazis. The 'Barbarossa' plan and other documents stipulated that they were to be eliminated *en masse*.

Some Western historians have tried to whitewash the Nazis' crimes and have painted a false picture of the conditions in which Soviet prisoners of war were held. What was in fact mass extermination is referred to as 'entirely proper' treatment. This is patently untrue. Soviet people died in their thousands as a result of this 'proper treatment': they died of cold and disease, and they were tortured or shot. The many prison camps become their graveyards, and the Nuremberg Trial documents on the major war criminals are evidence of this. In particular, it was noted that the Hitler government and the High Command of the German Army had drawn up special instructions before they attacked the USSR that Soviet prisoners of war, both men and officers, were to be exterminated.

Research into the preparations for the 'Barbarossa' campaign shows that the Wehrmacht Command and Nazi leadership gave only superficial attention to the question of conditions for POWs. All their calculations were based on a quick victory, which outcome they did not doubt. As for the High Command of the German Ground Forces, they gave unconditional support to the political leadership's directive to the effect that expenditure on the upkeep of POWs must be kept to a minimum. This had another quite different purpose—that of improving supplies to the German population by mercilessly exploiting resources in the occupied parts of the USSR.

Soviet prisoners of war were treated barbarically and the conditions they were subjected to were very different from those in which prisoners from other countries were kept. The despotism, violence and inhumanity with which they were treated led to their dying in their thousands.

It may be stated with full justification that the treatment of Soviet POWs was the result of the general policy of destroying the peoples of the Soviet Union. This manifested itself first and foremost in the agreement in principle of the German military leadership to the unchecked extermination of Soviet POWs by special SS commands (detachments) in camps situated in areas of fighting. Troops were issued with the so-called 'instructions re commissars' and several other orders to the effect that all Party and soviet workers, and also Jews and 'Soviet intellectuals', were to be exterminated—in other words anyone who might pose a threat to 'Greater Germany'. The Nazi leadership's justification for their treatment of POWs was that the USSR had not ratified the Geneva Convention on Prisoners of War.

Only after the blitzkrieg strategy had failed and the need arose for additional labour to work in German military production did the treatment of POWs change somewhat. Attempts were now made to keep some POWs alive. The measures taken did not signify any fundamental change in their treatment, however, and mortality rates in POW camps remained high.

There are hardly any German documents containing information on the number of Soviet POWs prior to 1942. This is because in 1941 the number of reports received from the Eastern Front was insufficient and on close examination those that were submitted often proved to be improbable. Orders that accurate information on Soviet POWs was to be submitted were issued by the Ground Forces High Command only on 1 January 1942, by which time considerably fewer Soviet prisoners were being taken.

It must be borne in mind that responsibility for all matters concerning POWs in Nazi Germany (camp conditions, how prisoners were to be kept, what use was to be made of them) was divided between the Wehrmacht High Command (Oberkommando der Wehrmacht—OKW) and the Army High Command (Oberkommando des Heeres—OKH). On the territory of the Reich and annexed countries and regions, responsibility for these matters lay with the POW Section of the Wehrmacht High Command (Abt. Kriegsgefangene im OKW/AWA). In the occupied regions of the Soviet Union that responsibility lay with the military-administrative section of the Chief of Army Rear Areas (Befehlshaber des Rück-wärtigen Heeresgebeite—Befh. R. H. Geb.) (Quartermaster-General Branch).

Right from the start of the war within the so-called zone of competence of the Wehrmacht High Command (OKW), proper attention was not paid to the accurate recording of statistics relating to POW numbers. The directive from the POW Department of 16 June 1941 did not make it compulsory to provide such information. On 2 July this was changed, but only as far as POWs on the territory of the Reich were concerned.

By the end of July 1941 a large number of POWs had accumulated at assembly points and transit camps situated within the ground forces' zone of responsibility, while there were neither the means nor the resources for holding them. As a result, an order was issued by the quartermaster-general (No 11/4590 of 25 July 1941) to the effect that Soviet POWs of certain nationalities were to be freed (Volga Germans, Balts, Ukrainians and later Byelorussians). This order was subsequently suspended, in OKW directive No 3900 of 13 November 1941. In all, 318,770 prisoners were freed during this period, of whom 292,702 were within the OKH zone and 26,068 within the OKW zone. Those freed included 277,761 Ukrainians. In 1942-44 mainly those who entered volunteer guard and other formations or the police were freed. By 1 May 1944 a total of 823,230 POWs had been released, 535,523 within the OKH zone and 287,707 within the OKW zone.[15]

On 30 September 1941 camp commandants in the East were issued with instructions to start card-indexes for registering POWs so as to introduce some order into the record-keeping process. However, it was emphasised that the directive was to be implemented only after the campaign on the Eastern Front was at an end, and also that only information on prisoners who 'after selection', to be carried out by the Einsatzkommandos (Sonderkommandos), 'would finally stay in the camps or in appropriate work' should be passed on to the Central Information Department.

It followed that information on POWs who were killed during redeployment and filtration was not to be included in Central Information Department documents. It is therefore likely that there is no statistical information at all on Soviet POWs in Reichskommissariats Ostland (the Baltic) and Ukraine, where there were large numbers of prisoners of war in autumn 1941.

The report by the OKW's POW Department to the International Committee of the Red Cross only concerned those camps which were under OKW control. Information on Soviet POWs only started to appear from February 1942, that is, after the decision had been taken to use them as labour in German military production (see Table 85).

Table 85. Reports on the Number of Soviet POWs in Camps of the High Command of the German Armed Forces (OKW) and Used as Workers in German Industry in 1942–45.[1]

As of (date):	Number of POWs		Total
	In OKW camps	At work in German military industry (concentration camps)	
1 February 1942	1,020,531	147,736	1,168,267
1 March 1942	976,458	153,674	1,130,132
1 April 1942	643,237	166,881	810,118
1 June 1942	734,544	242,146	976,690
1 September 1942	1,675,626	375,451	2,051,077
1 October 1942	1,118,011	455,054	1,573,065
1 November 1942	766,314	487,535	1,253,849
1 January 1943	1,045,609	No figures available	—
1 February 1943	1,038,512	493,761	1,532,373
1 July 1943	647,545	505,975	1,153,520
1 August 1943[2]	807,603	496,106	1,303,709
1 December 1943	766,314	564,692	1,331,006
1 March 1944	861,052	594,279	1,455,331
1 May 1944	877,980	618,528	1,496,508
1 June 1944	875,733	618,528	1,494,261
1 August 1944	889,309	631,559	1,520,868
1 September 1944	905,864	765,444	1,671,308
1 October 1944	911,990	No figures available	—
1 November 1944	929,100	No figures available	—
1 January 1945	930,287	750,000	1,680,287
25 April 1945	—	—	800,000

1. Based on German records in the German federal and military archives and in the Central Archive of the Ministry of Defence of the Russian Federation (f. 500, op. 12450, d. 86), and also on material from works of military history published in the German Federal Republic.
2. Between February 1942 and August 1943 these reports did not include POWs held in reception and transit camps or at centres which came within the zone of responsibility of the OKH. From autumn 1943 these were placed under the control of the OKW.

On 7 July 1943 there was a meeting at Hitler's main HQ on the use of labour in the mining industry. Directive No 02358/43 of 8 July 1943, signed by Himmler, stated: 'On 7 July the Führer ordered that in order to extend the programme of iron and steel production, the production of coal must be increased, and to achieve this the work force must be augmented by prisoners of war ...

'Prisoners who are men aged 16–55 and who were captured during the struggle against gangs in areas of fighting, in the army's rear, in eastern commissariats, in govenor-generalships and in the Balkans are considered prisoners of war. This also applies to men in newly conquered regions of the East. They are to be sent to prisoner-of-war camps and from there to work in Germany ...'[16]

It should be borne in mind that in POW camps there were large numbers of ordinary Soviet citizens who were not servicemen but were taken prisoner by the Germans in contravention of the Hague and Geneva Conventions. This was confirmed by the former head of the Danzig Military District POW Department, Kurt Österreich, for example, in evidence given on 28 December 1945. He wrote that in the camps under his command in the Ukraine about 20,000 Soviet citizens were being held along with servicemen in separate barracks. They had been taken as hostages in a number of areas where partisans were active.[17] Even more hostages were held in POW camps in Byelorussia and the Baltic states.

A close examination of German documentary sources is therefore needed in order to establish the correct number of Soviet servicemen who were taken prisoner. This would bring us closer to the truth. In the meantime the figures quoted in many publications both in the Soviet Union and elsewhere give figures which are contradictory and at times clearly exaggerated.

In overseas publications (mainly German), the number of Soviet POWs is put at between 5,200,000 and 5,750,000, most of these relating to the initial phase of the war (June 1941–November 1942). In the absence of reliable documentary evidence it is to be assumed that these figures are based on information submitted by the HQs of Army Groups North, Centre and South during the period of offensive operations in 1941. Reports from the German High Command stated that 300,000 prisoners were taken in encirclements at Bialystok, Grodno and Minsk, 103,000 at Uman, 450,000 at Vitebsk, Orsha, Mogilev and Gomel, 180,000 at Smolensk, 665,000 in the Kiev area, 100,000 at Chernigov, 100,000 in the Mariupol area and 663,000 at Bryansk and Vyazma. A total of 2,561,000 prisoners were taken in 1941.

These figures are impressive but not entirely accurate, as the Nazi leadership included all Party and soviet workers, and also all men, irrespective of age, who had left with retreating troops and who then became caught in encirclements. Sometimes the number of prisoners taken exceeds the numerical strength of the army or front involved in the operation. For example the German Command reported that 665,000 Soviet men and officers were taken prisoner east of Kiev, while the entire strength of the South-Western Front at the start of the Kiev defensive operation was 627,000, of whom 150,000 escaped encirclement. Similarly, in the German Command's report that 100,000 prisoners of war had been taken at Sevastopol, the Nazis must have counted the entire population of the town, whom it had not been possible to evacuate.

On the same subject, it is appropriate to quote here the English historian D. Fuller, who stated that it was not possible to believe German communiqués on their victories as the figures they gave were often astronomically high.[18]

What information from Soviet sources is there, then, on the number of Soviet servicemen taken prisoner by the Germans during the war? The main official source is the casualty reports submitted by fronts, armies, formations and individual units. These have been analysed at the Main Staff and amended and added to using information on unlisted casualties.

By comparing and analysing all the sources it has been established that 4,559,000 Soviet servicemen were missing in action or taken prisoner during the war. Further research revealed that a significant number of these were POWs. That there is no clear dividing line between these two categories is explained by the fact that with the situation at the front changing rapidly, it was extremely difficult even to establish whether prisoners had been taken, let alone how many had been taken. Therefore, many who were missing from their units after a battle were listed as missing in action. The contemptuous attitude to being taken prisoner which prevailed in the army at the time was also a factor which often led commanders and leaders to understate the number, even when it was obvious that men had been taken prisoner, and to put them down in their reports as missing.

On the basis of the documents available the total number of Soviet servicemen who were taken prisoner or missing in action (4,559,000) can be calculated as follows.

It is known for certain that 1,836,000 servicemen returned from prison camps after the end of the war and that 939,700 servicemen who had been missing or taken prisoner were redrafted as occupied territory was liberated.[19] According to German sources, 673,000 died in captivity. Of the remaining 1,110,300, Soviet sources indicate that over half also died in captivity. Thus a total of 4,059,000 Soviet servicemen were prisoners of war and about 500,000 were killed on the battlefield, although according to reports from the front they were listed as missing in action.

These figures do not and indeed cannot correspond with those published outside the Soviet Union. The discrepancy is mainly explained by the fact that German figures include not only servicemen but also personnel from special formations coming under various civilian departments (railways, sea-going and river fleets, defence construction, civil aviation, communications, healthcare, etc.), reports from which were not submitted to army and fleet HQs. For example, USSR Council of People's Commissars, NKVD and People's Commissariat for Defence Construction Directorate personnel included only a small percentage of servicemen (command personnel), while the main body of workers, which was quite sizeable, consisted of ordinary workers and employees. They worked on the construction of defensive lines, fortified areas, roads and aerodromes. Many were caught in encirclements and taken prisoner. Among them was General D. M. Karbyshev, who had been sent to check the progress of the construction of fortified areas. Partisans, resistance fighters, members of incomplete people's militia formations, the local air defence, fighter battalions and the militia (police) were not servicemen either. However, citizens in all the above categories who were on territory taken by the Nazis were counted by the German Command as prisoners of war and sent to POW camps.

Moreover, in the first weeks of the war, when general mobilisation was under way, a large number of citizens who had been called up by military commissariats in Byelorussia, the Ukraine and the Baltic republics were captured by the enemy along the line of march before they had been taken on strength. They were taken prisoner but were not on any army or front records. According to a report from the General Staff Mobilisation Directorate compiled in June 1942, the number of persons liable for military service who were taken prisoner by the enemy was over 500,000.[20] If one takes into account a further 5% of citizens in western republics and regions of the country who for various reasons had been exempted from military service and who also found themselves on occupied territory, and some of whom were taken prisoner, the total number captured who had been called up or were liable for military service was about a million.

Sick and wounded who were in hospitals undergoing treatment when they were taken prisoner were also counted as POWs. They had previously been listed in reports from the field under 'sick and wounded'.

Consequently, information published outside the USSR on POW numbers cannot be taken as a basis on which to calculate the exact number of Soviet servicemen taken prisoner by the Germans.

At the end of the war, when Soviet troops entered Nazi Germany, a USSR Council of People's Commissars Repatriation Directorate was set up. It was headed by Colonel-General F. I. Golikov. The files of this directorate contain statistical information for 3 October 1945 on the 1,368,849 Soviet servicemen who returned from prison camps. Some of the figures are given below.

By Length of Time Spent in Captivity

Held prisoner since (year):	Officers	Sergeants	Men	Total
1941	52,025	76,359	544,321	672,705
1942	48,796	52,046	348,110	448,952
1943	13,083	18,350	128,082	159,515
1944	5,876	9,449	54,705	70,030
1945	1,344	1,665	14,638	17,647

By Nationality

Russians	—657,339	or	48.02%;
Ukrainians	—386,568	or	28.24%;
Byelorussians	—103,053	or	7.53%;
Uzbeks	— 28,228	or	2.06%;
Kazakhs	— 23,143	or	1.69%;
Georgians	— 23,816	or	1.74%;
Azerbaijanis	— 20,850	or	1.52%;
Lithuanians	— 2,749	or	0.20%;
Moldavians	— 4,739	or	0.35%;
Latvians	— 3,286	or	0.24%;
Kirghiz	— 4,014	or	0.29%;
Tajiks	— 3,948	or	0.29%;
Armenians	— 20,067	or	1.47%;
Turkmens	— 3,511	or	0.26%;
Estonians	2,484	or	0.18%;
Bashkirs	— 4,248	or	0.31%;
Kalmyks	— 3,772	or	0.28%;
Karelians	— 1,989	or	0.14%;
Tatars	— 30,698	or	2.24%;
Jews	— 4,457	or	0.32%;
Others	— 35,890	or	2.63%.
Total listed	1,368,849		

Allowing a small margin for error, these figures can be taken as reflecting the total number of Soviet POWs (4,059,000).

Unfortunately it is not possible to be precise about the fate of those who did not return to the Soviet Union. The difficult job of research is continuing, the results of which may bring us nearer to the truth.

ARMS AND EQUIPMENT: PRODUCTION AND LOSSES

The fighting efficiency, strike capability and manoeuvrability of troops and the range and effectiveness of the operations they are able to carry out, as well as being dependent on personnel numbers and thorough training, also depend on troops being properly equipped. The wars fought in the early part of the twentieth century by large armies showed that strategic goals could only be achieved by well-equipped forces armed with a diversity of weapons and equipment.

During World War I new weapons were already appearing, such as tanks, aircraft, improved artillery systems and small arms. This gave the English military theorist, Fuller, cause to suggest that the outcome of a war was 99% dependent on weapons, while other factors such as strategy, leadership, bravery, discipline, organisation of supplies, etc. accounted for only 1%.

This over-emphasis of the role of equipment in war may be found in a number of works by other military theorists. For example, the Italian General Douhet believed that daily strikes against 50 industrial centres by 500 bombers would weaken any front and cause the enemy to capitulate. The German General Guderian preferred large-scale tank strikes which, in his opinion, would be able to overwhelm any defences. At the beginning of the twentieth century the American Admiral Mahan put forward the idea that sea power should be a decisive factor in war.

In the Soviet Union in the 1920s and 1930s the military commanders V. Triandafillov, M. Tukhachevski and others developed and put into practice the theory of battle in depth and of operations using large-scale groupings of tank troops, aircraft and airborne assault forces. Military doctrines were formulated, the armed forces built up and orders placed for the mass production of arms and equipment, all on the basis of these theories. The theories and doctrines contained a paradox, however: the better-equipped armies were, the less able they were to conduct a blitzkrieg with little bloodshed on the battlefield when confronted by equally strong, well-organised enemy opposition.

The process of equipping armies with the new kinds of arms and equipment which had appeared during World War I carried on apace into the 1930s. Wishing to exact revenge for their defeat in World War I and gain world supremacy, Nazi Germany went ahead with active preparations for a new war. The Germans were to rely on an army which would have tank and motorised divisions, a strong air force and an infantry equipped with modern small arms and powerful artillery.

The Soviet Union also prepared to defend itself. During this period the defence industry produced the following:

(a) Tanks: T-26, BT-7M, T-50 and KV;

(b) Artillery systems: 45mm ATG,[21] 76mm G, 122mm H, 122mm G, 152mm GH, 152mm H, 152mm G, 203mm H, 210mm G, 280mm mortar, 305mm H, 25mm AAG, 37mm AAG, 76mm AAG, 85mm AAG, 50mm M, 82mm M and 120mm M; and

(c) Aircraft: TB-3, Pe-8 (TB-7), Yer-2, DB-3F (Il-4), R-Zet, MBR-2, Yak-2 (BB-22), Yak-4, Su-2, SB, Ar-2, R-10, Kor-2, Il-2, I-15bis, I-153, I-16, Yak-1, LaGG-3, MiG-3, Po-2, etc.

Technical specifications for the arms and fighting equipment produced in the USSR on the eve of the 1941–45 war are given in Tables 86–88.

Table 86. Technical Specifications of the Main Types of Tanks Produced in the USSR just before the War[1]

Specifications	T-26	BT-7	T-50	T-34	KV
Year of production	1937	1939	1941	1940	1939
Laden weight, t	10.5	14.6	14	30.9	47.5
Max. speed, kph	30	62	52	55	35
Range, km	200	600	340	300	250
Engine power, hp	97	400	85	500	600
Height, m	2.33	2.70	1.90	2.40	2.71
Width, m	2.46	2.23	2.35	3	3.32
Armour thickness:					
front, mm	15	20	37	45	75
sides, mm	15	13	37	45	75
Gun calibre, mm	45	45	45	76.2	76.2
Gun range, km	4.8	4.8	4.8	12	12
Muzzle velocity, m/sec	760	760	760	662	662
Shells per tank	165	188	150	100	114
No of machine guns	3	3	2	2	4

1. The specifications given in Tables 86, 87 and 88 are based on figures from the Chief and Central Directorates of the USSR Ministry of Defence.

Table 87. Technical Specifications of Artillery Pieces and Mortars Produced in the USSR just before the War

Weapon	Weight in firing position, kg	Range, km[1]	Weight of shell, kg	Muzzle velocity, m/sec	Rate of fire, rounds/min
45mm ATG, 1937 model	560	4.6	1.4	760	20
76mm regt G, 1927 model	780	8.5	6.2	387	10–12
76mm div G, 1939 model	1,480	13.3	6.2	680	15–20
122mm H, 1938 model	2,500	11.8	21.7	515	5–6
122mm G, 1931/37 model	7,120	19.7	25	800	5–6
152mm H, 1938 model	4,150	12.3	40	508	3–4
152mm GH, 1937 model	7,128	17.2	43.5	655	3–4
152mm G, 1935 model	17,200	27	49	880	0.5–1
203mm H, 1931 model	17,500	18	100	607	0.5–1
210mm G, 1939 model	44,000	28.6	133	800	0.5
280mm M, 1939 model[2]	17,600	14.1	286	356	0.5
305mm H, 1939 model[2]	45,700	10.4	465	410	0.5
25mm AAG, 1940 model	1,060	2.4/2	0.28	910	250

Weapon	Weight in firing position, kg	Range, km[1]	Weight of shell, kg	Muzzle velocity, m/sec	Rate of fire, rounds/min
37mm AAG, 1939 model	2,100	4/	0.77	880	180
76mm AAG, 1938 model	4,300	14/9.5	6.6	813	20
85mm AAG, 1939 model	4,300	15.5/10.5	9.2	800	15–20
50mm M, 1938 model	10	3	0.9		30
82mm M, 1937 model	61	3.1	3.4		25
120mm M, 1938 model	280	5.7	16	272	12–15

1. Two figures are given for AA guns, the first denoting the ground range, the second denoting the ceiling.
2. Production was halted shortly before the Great Patriotic War.

Table 88. Technical Specifications of Aircraft Manufactured in the USSR just before the War

Aircraft	Came into service (year)	Engine power, hp	Range, km	Max. speed, kph	Ceiling, m	Weapons[1]	Bomb load, kg
Fighters							
I-15bis	1935	1×730	770	367	9,000	4×7.62	150
I-16	1934	1×900	625	462	9,700	4×7.62	100
I-153	1938	1×900	690	427	10,000	4×7.62	200
Yak-1	1941	1×1,050	700	572	9,600	1×20 2×7.62	—
LaGG-3	1941	1×1,050	556	549	9,600	1×20 1×12.7 2×7.62	200
MiG-3	1940	1×1,200	1,000	620	12,000	1×12.7 2×7.62	200
Ground-attack aircraft							
Il-2	1941	1×1,600	510	412	5,500	2×20 2×7.62 8 rocket missiles	600
Bombers							
TB-3	1934	4×850	4,000	288	7,740	8×7.62	4,000
DB-3f	1937	2×1,000	2,700	440	10,000	3×7.62	2,500
SB	1935	2×1,050	1,000	445	9,000	4×7.62	1,500
Pe-2	1941	2×1,260	1,100	540	8,800	4×7.62	1,000
Special purpose aircraft							
R-5 (recon.)	1931	1×650	600	230	6,150	3×7.62	400

1. Number of guns and machine guns and their calibres, in mm.

Table 89. Arms and Equipment of the Armed Forces of the USSR and Germany (including Germany's Allies) on 22 June 1941 (Thousands)

Equipment	USSR		Ratio of Soviet to German equipment (field armies)	Germany	
	Fighting troops	IMDs[1] and Supreme High Command Reserve		On Soviet-German front[2]	In reserve and in other theatres of war[3]
Tanks, all types	14.2[4] (3.8)[5]	8.4	3.3 : 1 (1 : 1.1)[5]	4.3	2.4
Guns and mortars, all calibres[6]	48.9 / 32.9	63.9 / 43.6	1 : 1 / 1 : 1.4	47.2	43.1
Combat aircraft, all types	9.2	10.8	1.5 : 1	5.9	7.8

1. IMDs: interior military districts.
2. Of these, the armies of Germany's allies (Finland, Hungary and Romania) had 262 tanks, 5,200 guns and mortars and 978 combat aircraft.
3. Includes 800 tanks, 24,100 guns and mortars and 3,700 combat aircraft in Italy, Finland, Hungary and Romania. In addition, Nazi Germany and the armies of its allies had a large amount of captured equipment from France, Belgium, Poland and other countries.
4. Of this number 29% were in need of major overhaul and 44% in need of medium repair; only 3,800 tanks were fully operational.
5. The figures in brackets show the number of serviceable Soviet tanks and the ratio of these to German tanks.
6. The lower figures show the number of Soviet guns and mortars excluding 50mm mortars; figures for the German army exclude 50mm mortars.

The outbreak of war meant that there were new and higher demands for arms and equipment on both sides. There was a pressing need to increase the fire-power and improve the armour plating of tanks and for anti-tank weapons to be developed. The mobility and fire-power of artillery pieces also needed to be improved, as did the quality of combat aircraft, especially fighter planes to be used for the purpose of winning supremacy in the air, without which successful actions by the ground forces would be impossible.

Immediate pre-war policy on weapons and equipment was well and truly put to the test by the war. At the start of the war the Red Army was obviously short of anti-aircraft and anti-tank weapons. As a consequence, its troops were left defenceless in the face of enemy air and tank strikes. In these conditions Soviet soldiers armed only with rifles and machine guns bore the brunt of the fighting. They put up brave resistance, showing courage, determination and quick-wittedness, often sacrificing their lives for the sake of victory. In critical situations Soviet pilots flew their planes straight into targets and infantrymen threw themselves under tanks with grenade clusters or bottles of flammable liquid, covered pillbox embrasures with their chests and fired rifles at enemy planes. But even the heroism and courage of the troops were not enough to compensate for inadequate arms and equipment. Tanks, aircraft and guns were needed which would enable them to fight back against a strong enemy.

Table 90. Specifications of the Main Models of Tanks and Self-Propelled (SP) Guns Produced in the USSR during the War

Specifications	T-60	T-70	T-34-85	KV-85	IS-2	IS-3	Su-76	Su-85	Su-100	ISU-122	ISU-152
Year of production	1941	1942	1944	1943	1944	1945	1943	1943	1944	1944	1943
Laden weight, t	6.4	10	32	45	46	46.5	10.5	29.6	31.6	45.5	46
Max. speed, kph	42	45	55	42	37	40	45	55	50	35	35
Range, km	450	250	300	225	140	190	250	300	310	220	220
Engine power, hp	70	2×70	500	600	520	520	2×70	2×70	500	520	600
Height, m	1.73	2.04	2.70	3.24	2.73	2.45	2.10	2.10	2.24	2.48	2.48
Width, m	2.30	2.42	3	3.32	3.07	3.15	2.71	2.71	3	3.07	3.07
Armour thickness,											
front, mm	35	45	45	75	120	120	35	45	110	90	90
sides, mm	15	15	45	75	90	90	15	45	45	90	90
Gun calibre, mm	20	45	85	85	122	122	76	85	100	122	152
Gun range, km	2	6	13.6	13.6	13.5	13.5	12.1	13.6	25.4	14.3	6.2
Muzzle velocity, m/sec	815	760	792	792	781	781	680	792	895	781	655
Shells per tank	780	90	56		28	28	60	48	34	30	20
No of machine guns			2	3	4	2					

Of the armoured vehicles produced in the USSR, the T-34 tank was of high quality. It proved itself throughout the war, but even it needed greater fire-power. Soviet engineers and industry had to work intensively on the design and production of new fighter and bomber models and on improvements to ground attack aircraft.

Artillery pieces of almost all calibres and types were also improved and updated. Particular attention was paid to the production and development of rocket artillery (the 'katyusha'), which won international renown.

During the Great Patriotic War in the USSR the following were brought into service:

(a) Tanks: T-60, T-70, T-34/85, KV-85, IS-2 and IS-3;

(b) Self-propelled (SP) guns: Su-76, Su-85, Su-100, Su-122 (ISU-122) and Su-152 (ISU-152);

(c) Artillery systems: 45mm ATG, 57mm ATG, 76mm G (ZIS-3), 76mm G (ob-25), 100mm G (BS-3), 152mm H (D-1) and 160mm M;

(d) Combat aircraft: Tu-2, Il-10, Yak-3, Yak-7, Yak-9, La-5, La-7, Li-2.

Production of pre-war arms and equipment continued but with improvements to the main features.

The technical specifications of tanks, guns, mortars and combat aircraft produced during the war are given in Tables 90–92. A comparison of the specifications of arms and equipment produced before and during the war will show what improvements were made.

Table 91. Specifications of Artillery Pieces Produced in the USSR during the War

Weapon	Weight in firing position, kg	Range, km	Weight of shell, kg	Muzzle velocity, m/sec	Rate of fire, rounds/min
45mm ATG (M-42), 1942 model	570	4.4	1.4	870	30
57mm ATG (ZIS-2), 1943 model	1,150	8.4	3.14	990	15
76mm G (ZIS-3), 1942 model	1,180	13.2	6.2	680	20–25
76mm G (ob-25), 1943 model	600	4.2	6.2	262	10–12
100mm G (BS-3), 1944 model	3,650	20	15.6	900	7
152mm H (D-1), 1943 model	3,600	12.4	40	508	4
160mm M, 1943 model	1,080	5	40		3

Table 92. Specifications of the Main Types of Aircraft Produced in the USSR during the War

Aircraft	Came into service (year)	Engine power, hp	Range, km	Max. speed, kph	Ceiling, m	Weapons, bomb load, kg
Yak-3	1944	1,310	480	645	10,800	1×20 2×12.7
Yak-7	1942	1,260	820	580	10,000	1×20 2×12.7
Yak-9	1943	1,260	1,330	584	10,000	1×20 1×12.7
La-5	1942	1,500	490	650	11,200	2×20 200
La-7	1944	1,850	500	680	11,200	2×20 200
Il-10	1944	2,000	600	600	6,000	2×23 2×7.62 4 rocket missiles 400–600
Tu-2	1942	2×1,550	2,000	550	9,500	3×12.7 1,000–3,000

Figures showing output of the main types of arms and equipment produced in the USSR during the war are given in Table 93.

Table 93. Output of the Main Types of Arms and Equipment in the USSR

Arms, equipment	1941	1942	1943	1944	1945, January–April	Total
Small arms, all types, millions[1]	1.76	5.91	5.92	4.86	1.38	19.83
Tanks and SP guns, all types, 1000s	4.7	24.5	24.1	29	16	98.3
Guns and mortars, all types and calibres, 1000s[2]	53.6	287	126	47.3	11.3	525.2
Aircraft, all types, 1000s	11.5	25.4	34.9	40.2	10.1	122.1
No of combat aircraft, 1000s	8.2	21.7	29.9	33.2	8.2	101.2
Combatant ships, main classes, actual no	35	15	14	4	2	70

1. Excludes pistols and revolvers.
2. Excludes production of tank guns, SP guns and guns for aircraft and ships.

Table 93 shows that on the outbreak of war Soviet industry rapidly increased its output of medium and heavy tanks, SP guns, anti-tank artillery and fighter and ground attack aircraft. This meant that the turning point in the war and ultimate victory were now achievable.

Increasing output of arms and equipment during the war meant that the requirements of the fighting troops could be adequately met, combat effectiveness could be rapidly re-established and losses during operations replaced.

Table 94. Quantities of the Main Categories of Arms and Equipment in the Red Army, by Year[1]

		Tanks and SP guns, 1000s	Guns and mortars,[2] 1000s	Combat aircraft, 1000s
As of 22.06.1941	Total	22.6	76.5	20
	In the theatre of operations	14.2	32.9	9.2
As of 01.01.1942	Total	7.7	48.6	12
	In the theatre of operations	2.2	30	5.4
As of 01.01.1943	Total	20.6	161.6	21.9
	In the theatre of operations	8.1	91.4	12.3
As of 01.01.1944	Total	24.4	244.4	32.5
	In the theatre of operations	5.8	101.4	13.4
As of 01.01.1945	Total	35.4	244.4	43.3
	In the theatre of operations	8.3	114.6	21.5
As of 09.05.1945	Total	35.2	239.6	47.3
	In the theatre of operations	8.1	94.4	22.3

1. Includes unserviceable arms and equipment.
2. Excludes 50mm mortars

Table 94 shows that by the end of 1941 the number of tanks operated by the fighting troops had fallen by almost 6.5 times since the start of the war, and the number of combat aircraft by 1.7 times. This was mainly because of high material losses, but also because of reduced supplies from factories. In autumn 1941 defence industry factories in the Ukraine, Byelorussia and parts of Russia were evacuated to the east of the country and to Central Asia. It was not until autumn 1942 that there was a significant increase in supplies of arms and equipment to the front. Furthermore, the field army had far less substantial quantities of these than did the armed forces as a whole: at the beginning of the war a large quantity of arms was held by formations and forces in interior military districts and the Supreme Command HQ Reserve, and also by forces in the Far East, Central Asia and the Trans-Caucasus.

During the war a large amount of equipment was supplied to newly deployed forces and to formations and units withdrawn from the front so that they could be restored to fighting efficiency, and also to military schools and training and reserve formations and units.

Towards the end of the war an increasing amount of arms and equipment was under repair or had been dispatched to the forces in the Far East. At any one time during the war 8–10% of the army's arms and equipment was in transit to or from the front, either to be repaired or during regrouping.

Table 95 gives an overall picture of changes in quantities of arms and equipment in the Red Army.

Table 95. Detailed Summary of Availability, Supplies and Losses of Arms and Equipment during the Great Patriotic War, 1941–45, by Year

I. Small-arms

Arms, equipment (1000s or millions)	No available, 22.06.41	1941 (22.06–31.12)				1942					1943				
		Received	Total stock	Losses	% of total stock lost	No available, 01.01.42	Received	Total stock	Losses	% of total stock lost	No available, 01.01.43	Received	Total stock	Losses	% of total stock lost
1	2	3	4	5	6	7	8	9	10	11	12	13	14	15	16
Revolvers and pistols, millions	1.24	0.13	1.37	0.44	32.1	0.93	0.17	1.10	0.39	35.5	0.71	0.37	1.08	0.08	7.4
Rifles and carbines, millions	7.74	1.57	9.31	5.55	59.6	3.76	4.04	7.80	2.18	27.9	5.62	3.85	9.47	1.26	13.3
Sub-machine guns, millions	0.10	0.10	0.20	0.10	50	0.10	1.56	1.66	0.55	33.1	1.11	2.06	3.17	0.53	16.7
Light machine guns, 1000s	170.4	45.3	215.7	134.7	62.4	81	172.8	253.8	76.7	30.2	177.1	250.2	427.3	82.8	19.4
Medium machine guns, 1000s	76.3	8.4	84.7	54.7	64.6	30	58	88	24.5	27.8	63.5	90.5	154	21	13.6
Heavy machine guns, 1000s	2.2	1.4	3.6	1.4	38.9	2.2	7.4	9.6	4.9	51	4.7	14.4	19.1	0.9	4.7
Anti-tank rocket launchers, 1000s	—	17.7	17.7	8.8	49.7	8.9	249	257.9	86.9	33.7	171	164.5	335.5	46.6	13.9
Total, millions	9.33	1.87	11.20	6.29	56.2	4.91	6.26	11.17	3.31	29.6	7.86	6.20	14.06	2.02	14.4

Arms, equipment (1000s or millions)	1944						1945 (01.01–10.05)					During war as a whole			
	No available, 01.01.44	Re-ceived	Total stock	Losses	% of total stock lost	No available, 01.01.45	Re-ceived	Total stock	Losses	% of total stock lost	No available, 09.05.45	Re-ceived	Total stock	Losses	% of total stock lost
1	17	18	19	20	21	22	23	24	25	26	27	28	29	30	31
Revolvers and pistols, millions	1	0.57	1.57	0.15	9.6	1.42	0.21	1.63	0.06	3.7	1.57	1.45	2.69	1.12	41.6
Rifles and carbines, millions	7.61	2.06	9.67	1.61	16.6	8.06	0.24	8.30	0.67	8.1	7.63	11.16	18.90	11.27	59.6
Sub-machine guns, millions	2.64	1.78	4.42	0.84	19	3.58	0.03	3.61	0.26	7.2	3.35	5.53	5.63	2.28	40.5
Light machine guns, 1000s	344.5	179.7	524.2	106.1	20.2	418.1	14.5	432.6	27.2	6.3	405.4	662.5	832.9	427.5	51.3
Medium machine guns, 1000s	133	89.9	222.9	38.2	17.1	184.7	10.8	195.5	12.9	6.6	182.6	257.6	333.9	151.3	45.3
Heavy machine guns, 1000s	18.2	14.8	33	1.9	5.8	31.1	7.3	38.4	0.9	2.3	37.5	45.3	47.5	10	21
Anti-tank rocket launchers, 1000s	288.9	37.7	326.6	56.5	17.3	271.9	0.8	272.7	15.2	5.6	257.5	471.5	471.5	214	45.4
Total, millions	12.04	4.73	16.77	2.81	16.8	14.06	0.69	14.75	1.04	7	13.71	19.85	29.18	15.47	53

II. Artillery

Arms, equipment (1000s)	1941 (22.06–31.12)					1942					1943				
	No available, 22.06.41	Re-ceived	Total stock	Losses	% of total stock lost	No available, 01.01.42	Re-ceived	Total stock	Losses	% of total stock lost	No available, 01.01.43	Re-ceived	Total stock	Losses	% of total stock lost
1	2	3	4	5	6	7	8	9	10	11	12	13	14	15	16
Anti-aircraft guns, 1000s	8.6	3.4	12	4.1	34.2	7.9	6.8	14.7	1.6	10.9	13.1	12.2	25.3	0.8	3.2
Breakdown:															
25mm AAG	—	0.3	0.3	0.1	33.3	0.2	0.2	0.4	—	—	0.4	1.5	1.9	0.1	5.3
37 and 40mm AAG	1.4	1.4	2.8	1.2	42.8	1.6	3.8	5.4	0.6	11.1	4.8	6.9	11.7	0.4	3.4
76, 85 and 90mm AAG	7.2	1.7	8.9	2.8	31.5	6.1	2.8	8.9	0.9	10.1	8	3.8	11.8	0.3	2.5
Anti-tank guns, 1000s	14.9	2.5	17.4	12.1	69.5	5.3	20.5	25.8	11.5	44.6	14.3	23.4	37.7	5.5	14.6
Breakdown:															
45mm G	14.9	2.1	17	12	70.6	5	20.5	25.5	11.3	44.3	14.2	21.5	35.7	5.2	14.6
57mm G	—	0.4	0.4	0.1	25	0.3	—	0.3	0.2	66.7	0.1	1.9	2	0.3	15

Arms, equipment (1000s)	1944					1945 (01.01–10.05)						During war as a whole			
	No available, 01.01.44	Re-ceived	Total stock	Losses	% of total stock lost	No available, 01.01.45	Re-ceived	Total stock	Losses	% of total stock lost	No available, 09.05.45	Re-ceived	Total stock	Losses	% of total stock lost
1	17	18	19	20	21	22	23	24	25	26	27	28	29	30	31
Anti-aircraft guns, 1000s	24.6	13.4	38	1	2.6	37	2.6	39.6	0.6	1.5	39	38.4	47	8	17
Breakdown:															
25mm AAG	1.8	2.4	4.2	0.3	7.1	3.9	0.5	4.4	0.1	2.3	4.3	4.9	4.9	0.6	12.2
37 and 40mm AAG	11.3	9	20.3	0.5	2.5	19.8	1.5	21.3	0.4	1.9	20.9	22.6	24	3.1	12.9
76, 85 and 90mm AAG	11.5	2	13.5	0.2	1.5	13.3	0.6	13.9	0.1	0.7	13.8	10.9	18.1	4.3	23.8
Anti-tank guns, 1000s	32.2	6.4	38.6	9.3	24.1	29.3	1.4	30.7	4	13	26.7	54.2	69.1	42.4	61.4
Breakdown:															
45mm G	30.5	4.1	34.6	8.2	23.7	26.4	0.6	27	3.5	13	23.5	48.8	63.7	40.2	63.1
57mm G	1.7	2.3	4	1.1	27.5	2.9	0.8	3.7	0.5	13.5	3.2	5.4	5.4	2.2	40.7

II. Artillery (continued)

Arms, equipment (1000s)	1941 (22.06–31.12)					1942					1943				
	No available, 22.06.41	Received	Total stock	Losses	% of total stock lost	No available, 01.01.42	Received	Total stock	Losses	% of total stock lost	No available, 01.01.43	Received	Total stock	Losses	% of total stock lost
1	2	3	4	5	6	7	8	9	10	11	12	13	14	15	16
Field guns, 1000s	33.2	10.1	43.3	24.4	56.3	18.9	30.1	49	12.3	25.1	36.7	22.1	58.8	5.7	9.7
Breakdown:															
76mm G	15.3	6.5	21.8	12.3	56.4	9.5	23.6	33.1	10.1	30.5	23	16.6	39.6	5	12.6
100 and 107mm G	0.9	0.1	1	0.4	40	0.6	—	0.6	0.1	16.7	0.5	—	0.5	—	—
122mm H	8.1	1.9	10	6	60	4	4.5	8.5	1.5	17.6	7	3.8	10.8	0.6	5.6
122mm G	1.3	0.3	1.6	0.9	56.2	0.7	0.3	1	—	—	1	0.5	1.5	—	—
152mm H	3.8	0.3	4.1	2.6	63.4	1.5	—	1.5	0.2	13.3	1.3	0.1	1.4	—	—
152mm GH, G	2.8	0.9	3.7	2.1	56.8	1.6	1.7	3.3	0.4	12.1	2.9	1.1	4	0.1	2.5
203mm and above	1	0.1	1.1	0.1	9.1	1	—	1	—	—	1	—	1	—	—
Mortars, 1000s	56.1	42.4	98.5	60.5	61.4	38	230.3	268.3	82.2	30.6	186.1	67.9	254	26.7	10.5
Breakdown:															
50mm	36.3	23.2	59.5	38	63.9	21.5	104.4	125.9	37.3	29.6	88.6	17.5	106.1	13.3	12.5
82mm	14.5	16.6	31.1	18.5	59.5	12.6	100.5	113.1	34.8	30.8	78.3	33.6	111.9	10.3	9.2
107 and 120mm	5.3	2.6	7.9	4	50.6	3.9	25.4	29.3	10.1	34.5	19.2	16.8	36	3.1	8.6
160mm	—	—	—	—	—	—	—	—	—	—	—	—	—	—	—
Guns and mortars, 1000s	112.8	58.4	171.2	101.1	59	70.1	287.7	357.8	107.6	30.1	250.2	125.6	375.8	38.6	10.3
Rocket artillery, 1000s	—	1	1	—	—	1	3.3	4.3	0.7	16.3	3.6	3.3	6.9	2.1	30.4
Breakdown:															
BM-8	—	0.4	0.4	—	—	0.4	0.9	1.3	0.3	23.1	1	0.4	1.4	0.5	35.7
BM-13	—	0.6	0.6	—	—	0.6	2.4	3	0.4	13.3	2.6	2.9	5.5	1.6	29.1
BM-31-12	—	—	—	—	—	—	—	—	—	—	—	—	—	—	—

Arms, equipment (1000s)	1944						1945 (01.01 – .05)					During war as a whole			
	No available, 01.01.44	Received	Total stock	Losses	% of total stock lost	No available, 01.01.45	Received	Total stock	Losses	% of total stock lost	No available, 09.05.45	Received	Total stock	Losses	% of total stock lost
1	17	18	19	20	21	22	23	24	25	26	27	28	29	30	31
Field guns, 1000s	53.1	21.5	74.6	12.3	16.5	62.3	5.8	68.1	6.8	10	51.3	89.6	122.8	61.5	50.1
Breakdown:															
76mm G	34.6	17.3	51.9	10.8	20.8	41.1	4.8	45.9	5.8	12.6	40.1	68.8	84.1	44	52.3
100 and 107mm G	0.5	0.3	0.8	—	—	0.8	0.3	1.1	0.1	9.1	1	0.7	1.6	0.6	37.5
122mm H	10.2	3.1	13.3	1.2	9.0	12.1	0.3	12.4	0.7	5.6	11.7	13.6	21.7	10	46.1
122mm G	1.5	0.2	1.7	0.1	5.9	1.6	0.1	1.7	—	—	1.7	1.4	2.7	1	37
152mm H	1.4	0.3	1.7	0.1	5.9	1.5	0.1	1.7	0.1	5.9	1.6	0.8	4.6	3	65.2
152mm GH, G	3.9	0.3	4.2	0.1	2.4	4.1	0.2	4.3	0.1	2.3	4.2	4.2	7	2.8	40
203mm and above	1	—	1	—	—	1	—	1	—	—	1	0.1	1.1	0.1	9.7
Mortars, 1000s	227.3	2	229.3	29.2	12.7	200.1	1.4	201.5	7	3.5	194.5	344	400.1	205.6	51.4
Breakdown:															
50mm	92.8	—	92.8	8.5	9.2	84.3	—	84.3	2.4	2.8	81.9	145.1	181.4	99.5	54.9
82mm	101.6	0.6	102.2	14.6	14.3	87.2	1	88.3	3.7	4.2	84.6	152.3	166.8	82.2	49.3
107 and 120mm	32.9	1.4	34.3	5.8	16.9	28.5	0.4	28.9	0.9	3.1	28	46.6	51.9	23.9	46
160mm	—	0.6		—	—	0.6	0.8	1.4	—	—	1.4	1.4	1.4	—	—
Guns and mortars, 1000s	337.2	43.3	380.5	51.8	13.6	328.7	11.2	339.9	18.4	5.4	321.5	526.2	639	317.5	49.7
Rocket artillery, 1000s	4.8	2.6	7.4	1.5	20.3	5.9	0.8	6.7	0.6	8.9	6.1	11	11	4.9	44.5
Breakdown:															
BM-8	0.9	0.5	1.4	0.5	35.7	0.9	0.2	1.1	0.1	9.1	1	2.4	2.4	1.4	58.3
BM-13	3.9	0.9	4.8	1	20.8	3.8	—	2.8	0.4	10.5	3.4	6.8	6.8	3.4	50
BM-31-12	—	1.2	1.2	—	—	1.2	0.6	1.8	0.1	5.6	1.7	1.8	1.8	0.1	5.6

III. Armoured vehicles

Arms, equipment (1000s)	1941 (22.06–31.12)						1942					1943			
	No available, 22.06.41	Received	Total stock	Losses	% of total stock lost	No available, 01.01.42	Received	Total stock	Losses	% of total stock lost	No available, 01.01.43	Received	Total stock	Losses	% of total stock lost
1	2	3	4	5	6	7	8	9	10	11	12	13	14	15	16
Tanks, 1000s	22.6	5.6	28.2	20.5	72.7	7.7	27.9	35.6	15	42.1	20.6	22.9	43.5	22.4	51.5
Breakdown:															
Heavy	0.5	1	1.5	0.9	60	0.6	2.6	3.2	1.2	37.5	2	0.9	2.9	1.3	44.8
Medium	0.9	2.2	3.1	2.3	74.2	0.8	13.4	14.2	6.6	46.5	7.6	16.3	23.9	14.7	61.5
Light	21.2	2.4	23.6	17.3	73.3	6.3	11.9	18.2	7.2	39.6	11	5.7	16.7	6.4	38.3
SP guns, 1000s	—	—	—	—	—	—	0.1	0.1	0.1	100	—	4.4	4.4	1.1	25
Breakdown:															
Heavy	—	—	—	—	—	—	0.03	0.03	0.03	100	—	1.3	1.3	0.5	38.5
Medium	—	—	—	—	—	—	—	—	—	—	—	0.8	0.8	0.1	12.5
Light	—	—	—	—	—	—	0.03	0.03	0.03	100	—	2.3	2.3	0.5	21.7
Tanks and SP guns, 1000s	22.6	5.6	28.2	20.5	72.7	7.7	28	35.7	15.1	42.3	20.6	27.3	47.9	23.5	49.1
Armoured cars, tractors, other armoured vehicles	13.1	10.8	23.9	3	12.5	20.9	10.2	31.1	9	28.9	22.1	10.6	32.7	12.5	38.2

1	1944					1945 (01.01–10.05)						During war as a whole			
Arms, equipment (1000s)	No available, 01.01.44	Received	Total stock	Losses	% of total stock lost	No available, 01.01.45	Received	Total stock	Losses	% of total stock lost	No available, 09.05.45	Received	Total stock	Losses	% of total stock lost
	17	18	19	20	21	22	23	24	25	26	27	28	29	30	31
Tanks, 1000s	21.1	21.2	42.3	16.9	40	25.4	8.5	33.9	8.7	25.7	25.2	86.1	108.7	83.5	76.8
Breakdown:															
Heavy	1.6	4	5.6	0.9	16.1	4.7	1.5	6.2	0.9	14.5	5.3	10	10.5	5.2	49.5
Medium	9.2	17	26.2	13.8	52.7	12.4	6.1	18.5	7.5	40.5	11	55	55.9	44.9	80.3
Light	10.3	0.2	10.5	2.2	21.9	8.3	0.9	9.2	0.3	3.3	8.9	21.1	42.3	33.4	79.1
SP guns, 1000s	3.3	13.6	16.9	6.8	40.2	10.1	5	15.1	5.0	33.1	10.1	23.1	23.1	13	56.3
Breakdown:															
Heavy	0.8	2.5	3.3	0.9	27.3	2.4	1.2	3.6	0.9	25	2.7	5	5	2.3	46
Medium	0.7	2.4	3.1	1	32.3	2.1	0.8	2.9	1	34.5	1.9	4	4	2.1	52.5
Light	1.8	8.6	10.4	4.9	47.1	5.5	3	8.5	3.1	36.5	5.4	14	14	8.6	61.4
Tanks and SP guns, 1000s	24.4	34.7	59.1	23.7	40.1	35.4	13.5	48.9	13.7	28	35.2	109.1	131.7	96.5	73.3
Armoured cars, tractors, other armoured vehicles	20.2	17	37.2	12.5	33.6	24.7	10.6	35.3	0.6	1.7	34.6	59.1	72.2	37.6	52.1

IV. Aircraft

Arms, equipment (1000s)	1941 (22.06–31.12)					1942					1943				
	No available, 22.06.41	Re-ceived	Total stock	Losses	% of total stock lost	No available, 01.01.42	Re-ceived	Total stock	Losses	% of total stock lost	No available, 01.01.43	Re-ceived	Total stock	Losses	% of total stock lost
1	2	3	4	5	6	7	8	9	10	11	12	13	14	15	16
Bombers, 1000s	8.4	2.5	10.9	7.2 / 4.6	42.2	3.7	4.1	7.8	2.5 / 1.6	20.5	5.3	5.1	10.4	3.6 / 1.7	16.3
Ground-attack aircraft, 1000s	0.1	1.4	1.5	1.1 / 0.6	40	0.4	7.2	7.6	2.6 / 1.8	23.7	5	11	16	7.2 / 3.9	24.4
Fighters, 1000s	11.5	6	17.5	9.6 / 5.1	29.1	7.9	10.7	18.6	7 / 4.4	23.7	11.6	17	28.6	11.7 / 5.6	19.6
Total combat aircraft, 1000s	20	9.9	29.9	17.9 / 10.3	34.4	12	22	34	12.1 / 7.8	22.9	21.9	33.1	55	22.5 / 11.2	20.4
Training, transport and other aircraft, 1000s	12.1	1.1	13.2	3.3 / 0.3	2.3	9.9	5.7	15.6	2.6 / 1.3	8.3	13	5.1	18.1	4.2 / 0.5	2.8
Total aircraft, 1000s	32.1	11	43.1	21.2 / 10.6	24.6	21.9	27.7	49.6	14.7 / 9.1	18.3	34.9	38.2	73.1	26.7 / 11.7	16

Arms, equipment (1000s)	1944						1945 (01.01–10.05)					During war as a whole			
	No available, 01.01.44	Re-ceived	Total stock	Losses	% of total stock lost	No available, 01.01.45	Re-ceived	Total stock	Losses	% of total stock lost	No available, 09.05.45	Re-ceived	Total stock	Losses	% of total stock lost
1	17	18	19	20	21	22	23	24	25	26	27	28	29	30	31
Bombers, 1000s	6.8	5.3	12.1	3.2 / 1.5	12.4	8.9	2.2	11.1	1.4 / 0.6	5.4	9.7	19.2	27.6	17.9 / 10	36.2
Ground-attack aircraft, 1000s	8.8	10.3	19.1	8.9 / 4.1	21.5	10.2	3.7	13.9	3.8 / 2	14.4	10.1	33.6	33.7	23.6 / 12.4	36.8
Fighters, 1000s	16.9	20	36.9	12.7 / 4.1	11.1	24.2	9.1	33.3	5.8 / 1.5	4.5	27.5	62.8	74.3	46.8 / 20.7	27.9
Total combat aircraft, 1000s	32.5	35.6	68.1	24.8 / 9.7	14.2	43.3	15	58.3	11 / 4.1	7	47.3	115.6	135.6	88.3 / 43.1	31.8
Training, transport and other aircraft, 1000s	13.9	7.5	21.4	5.7 / 0.7	3.3	15.7	3.5	19.2	2.3 / 0.2	1	16.9	22.9	35	18.1 / 3	8.6
Total aircraft, 1000s	46.4	43.1	89.5	30.5 / 10.4	11.6	59.9	18.5	77.5	13.3 / 4.3	5.5	64.2	138.5	170.6	106.4 / 46.1	27

V. Ships (actual no)

Arms, equipment	1941 (22.06–31.12)					1942					1943				
	No available, 22.06.41	Received	Total stock	Losses	% of total stock lost	No available, 01.01.42	Received	Total stock	Losses	% of total stock lost	No available, 01.01.43	Received	Total stock	Losses	% of total stock lost
1	2	3	4	5	6	7	8	9	10	11	12	13	14	15	16
Surface ships (excl. cutters)	235	264	499	121	24.2	378	62	440	46	10.4	394	—	394	22	5.6
Military cutters	466	682	1,148	168	14.6	980	548	1,528	159	10.4	1,369	311	1,680	210	12.5
Submarines	212	20	232	36	15.5	196	13	209	37	17.7	172	14	186	19	10.2
Total	913	966	1,879	325	17.3	1,554	623	2,177	242	11.1	1,935	325	2,260	251	11.1

Arms, equipment	1944					1945 (01.01–10.05)						During war as a whole			
	No available, 01.01.44	Received	Total stock	Losses	% of total stock lost	No available, 01.01.45	Received	Total stock	Losses	% of total stock lost	No available, 09.05.45	Received	Total stock	Losses	% of total stock lost
1	17	18	19	20	21	22	23	24	25	26	27	28	29	30	31
Surface ships (excl. cutters)	372	8	380	21	5.5	359	54	413	2	0.5	411	388	623	212	34
Military cutters	1,470	568	2,038	141	6.9	1,897	40	1,937	22	1.1	1,915	2,149	2,615	700	26.8
Submarines	167	3	170	9	5.3	161	1	162	1	0.6	161	51	263	102	38.8
Total	2,009	579	2,588	171	6.6	2,417	95	2,512	25	1	2,487	2,588	3,501	1,014	29

VI. Motor vehicles, 1000s

Arms, equipment	1941 (22.06–31.12)					1942					1943				
	No available, 22.06.41	Re-ceived	Total stock	Losses	% of total stock lost	No available, 01.01.42	Re-ceived	Total stock	Losses	% of total stock lost	No available, 01.01.43	Re-ceived	Total stock	Losses	% of total stock lost
1	2	3	4	5	6	7	8	9	10	11	12	13	14	15	16
Motor vehicles, all types	272.6	204.9	477.5	159	33.3	318.5	152.9	470.7	66.2	14.1	404.5	158.5	563	67	11.9

Arms, equipment	1944					1945 (01.01–10.05)					During war as a whole				
	No available, 01.01.44	Re-ceived	Total stock	Losses	% of total stock lost	No available, 01.01.45	Re-ceived	Total stock	Losses	% of total stock lost	No available, 09.05.45	Re-ceived	Total stock	Losses	% of total stock lost
1	17	18	19	20	21	22	23	24	25	26	27	28	29	30	31
Motor vehicles, all types	496	157.9	653.9	32.6	5	621.3	70.9	692.2	27	3.9	665.2	744.4	1,017	351.8	34.6

VII. Radio sets, 1000s

Arms, equipment	1941 (22.06–31.12)					1942					1943				
	No available, 22.06.41	Received	Total stock	Losses	% of total stock lost	No available, 01.01.42	Received	Total stock	Losses	% of total stock lost	No available, 01.01.43	Received	Total stock	Losses	% of total stock lost
1	2	3	4	5	6	7	8	9	10	11	12	13	14	15	16
Radio sets, all types	37.4	5.6	43	23.7	55.1	19.3	27.5	46.8	7	15	39.8	49.5	89.3	17.7	19.8

Arms, equipment	1944					1945 (01.01–10.05)					During war as a whole				
	No available, 01.01.44	Received	Total stock	Losses	% of total stock lost	No available, 01.01.45	Received	Total stock	Losses	% of total stock lost	No available, 09.05.45	Received	Total stock	Losses	% of total stock lost
1	17	18	19	20	21	22	23	24	25	26	27	28	29	30	31
Radio sets, all types	71.6	48.7	120.3	13.3	11.1	107	20.1	127.1	13.4	10.5	113.7	151.4	188.8	75.1	39.8

Notes

1. These figures were compiled after a close examination of archive material from the Great Patriotic War period.

2. The columns showing the number of items available include arms and equipment which were under repair, worn out or with a limited service life (fighting vehicles with limited range or engine life, guns with worn barrels, etc.).

3. The columns showing the number of items received include arms and fighting equipment received from factories, under Lend–Lease or after repair (complete overhaul). They do not include about 43,000 small arms, 17,100 guns and mortars, 1,300 tanks and 1,600 aircraft supplied by the Soviet Union during the war to Bulgarian, Polish, Romanian and Yugoslav formations and units.

4. The 'losses' columns show both combat and non-combat losses combined, as the proportion of non-combat losses was insignificant, except in the case of the air force. Two figures are given for air force losses, the upper figure representing total losses, the lower figure losses in combat.

5. The columns showing the percentage of total stock lost show the percentage of losses in relation to total stock (number available at start of war, plus number received), by year and for the war as a whole.

6. Under Lend–Lease and other schemes, 151,700 small arms, 9,400 guns and mortars, 11,900 tanks and self-propelled guns, over 5,000 armoured personnel carriers, 18,300 aircraft and 520 ships and other vessels were received from the United States, Britain and Canada. These figures only include arms and equipment actually received by the army and navy. They do not include losses during transportation, unserviceable items or weapons and equipment handed over to other departments.

Table 96 shows that, in terms of percentages, the heaviest losses were of tanks and SP guns: 427% of those available on 22 June 1941 and over 73% of total stock were lost.

Table 96. Irrecoverable Material Losses during the Great Patriotic War: Main Categories of Arms and Combat Equipment

Arms, equipment	Number			% lost	
	Available 22.06.41	Total stock[1]	Losses	of no available on 22.06.41	of total stock
Small arms, all types, millions	9.33	29.18	15.47	166	53
Tanks and SP guns, 1000s	22.6	131.7	96.5	427	73.3
Guns and mortars,[2] all calibres, 1000s	112.8	639	317.5	281	49.7
Combat aircraft, all types, 1000s	20	135 6	88.3[3] 43.1	442 216	65.1 31.8

1. Total stock comprises the amount of weapons and equipment as of 22 June 1941, plus those supplied to the armed forces during the war.
2. In this and the following tables the figure for total guns and mortars lost includes 50mm mortars, which made up between 29 and 30% in 1941-42 and 3% in 1945 of the field army's weapons in this category.
3. Combat aircraft: the upper figure represents total losses, the lower figure losses in combat. In the case of other types of arms and equipment, these are not differentiated, as non-combat losses were insignificant.

A high percentage of combat aircraft were lost in relation to the number available on 22 June 1941: 442% (total losses) or 216% (combat losses). Losses as a percentage of total stock were also high: 65.1% (total losses) or 31.8% (combat losses). In the air force over a half of losses were non-combat losses. This was mainly because of inadequate pilot training and reduced training time, especially the time allowed for mastering new equipment, but also because of lack of discipline during flight training among aircrews and officers in charge of flying. Design and manufacturing faults in aircraft also contributed to the number of non-combat losses.

Table 97. Irrecoverable Material Losses during the War: Main Categories of Arms and Equipment, by Year

Arms, equipment	Total losses during war	1941		1942		1943		1944		1945	
		No	%	No	%	No	%	No	%	No	%
Small arms, all types, millions	15.47	6.29	40.7	3.31	21.4	2.02	13	2.81	18.2	1.04	6.7
Tanks and SP guns, 1000s	96.5	20.5	21.2	15.1	15.6	23.5	24.4	23.7	24.6	13.7	14.2
Guns and mortars, 1000s	317.5	101.1	31.8	107.6	33.9	38.6	12.2	51.8	16.3	18.4	5.8
Combat aircraft, 1000s	88.3 43.1	17.9 10.3	20.3 23.9	12.1 7.8	13.7 18.1	22.5 11.2	25.5 26	24.8 9.7	28.1 22.5	11 4.1	12.4 9.5

As the table shows, the heaviest losses incurred by the Soviet forces were of small arms, when they were retreating in 1941 and 1942 (over 60% of small arms losses occurred during this time). Large numbers of tanks and SP guns were lost in 1941, 1943 and 1944. In the first year of the war it was mostly obsolete tanks which were lost. In 1943–44 enemy anti-tank weapons caused an increase in losses, especially as German defensive lines were breached. The greatest number of guns and mortars were lost in 1941–42 (65.7% of losses). During withdrawals guns and mortars were abandoned even when they were hardly damaged, sometimes because tractors were unserviceable or not available. These proved to be irrecoverable losses for the Soviet Union. The highest number of combat aircraft lost was in 1943–44 (48.5% of combat losses). This was when the fight for air supremacy was at its height. Intense air battles over the Kuban and Kursk, and also strategic operations conducted with support from air force groupings, all meant heavy losses.

Figures for the main categories of arms and equipment lost, by strategic operation and phase of the war, are given in Table 98.

Table 98. Material Losses, by Strategic Operation and Phase of the War

Name of operation, dates, duration (no of days)	Losses							
	Small arms, 1000s		Tanks, SP guns, actual no		Guns and mortars, actual no		Combat aircraft, actual no	
	During operation	Average daily losses	During operation	Average daily losses	During operation	Average daily losses	During operation	Average daily losses
Phase I (22.06.1941–18.11.1942)								
Baltic defensive operation, 22.06–09.07.1941 (18)	341	18.9	2,523	140	3,561	198	990	55
Byelorussian defensive operation, 22.06–09.07.1941 (18)	521.2	28.9	4,799	267	9,427	524	1,777	99
Defensive operation in W. Ukraine, 22.06–06.07.1941 (15)	169.8	11.3	4,381	292	5,806	387	1,218	81
Defensive operation in Arctic and Karelia, 29.06–10.10.1941 (104)	40.2	0.4	546	5	540	5	64	1
Kiev defensive operation, 07.07–26.09.1941 (82)	1,764.9	21.5	411	5	28,419	347	343	4
Leningrad defensive operation, 10.07–30.09.1941 (83)	733.3	8.8	1,492	18	9,885	119	1,702	20–21
Battle of Smolensk, 10.07–10.09.1941 (63)	233.4	3.7	1,348	21	9,290	147	903	14
Donbass–Rostov defensive operation, 29.09–16.11.1941 (49)	369	7.5	101	2	3,646	74	240	5

| Name of operation, dates, duration (no of days) | Losses | | | | | | | |
| | Small arms, 1000s | | Tanks, SP guns, actual no | | Guns and mortars, actual no | | Combat aircraft, actual no | |
	During operation	Average daily losses	During operation	Average daily losses	During operation	Average daily losses	During operation	Average daily losses
Moscow defensive operation, 30.09–05.12.1941 (67)	250.8	3.7	2,785	42	3,832	57	293	4
Tikhuin offensive operation, 10.11–30.12.1941 (51)	31.1	0.6	70	1–2	2,293	45	82	1–2
Rostov offensive operation, 17.11–02.12.1941 (16)	66.8	4.2	42	2–3	1,017	64	42	2–3
Moscow offensive operation, 05.12.1941–07.01.1942 (34)	1,093.8	32.2	429	13	13,350	393	140	4
Kerch-Feodosia amphibious operation, 25.12.1941–02.01.1942 (9)	11.2	1.2	35	4	133	15	39	4–5
Rzhev-Vyazma offensive operation, 08.01–20.04.1942 (103)	305.5	3	957	9	7,296	71	550	5
Voronezh-Voroshilovgrad defensive operation, 28.06–24.07.1942 (27)	488.0	18.1	2,436	90	13,716	508	783	29
Stalingrad defensive operation, 17.07–18.11.1942 (125)	412.6	3.3	1,426	11–12	12,137	97	2,063	16–17
N. Caucasus defensive operation, 25.07–31.12.1942 (160)	139.2	0.9	990	6	5,049	31–32	644	4
Total during strategic operations of Phase I of the war (1,024)[1]	6,972.4	6.81	24,771	24	129,397	126	11,873	11–12
Phase II (19.11.1942–31.12.1943)								
Stalingrad offensive operation, 19.11.1942–02.02.1943 (76)	112.2	1.5	2,915	38	3,591	47	706	9
N. Caucasus offensive operation, 01.01–04.02.1943 (35)	36.7	1	220	6	895	26	236	6–7
Operation to break the siege of Leningrad, 12.01–30.01.1943 (19)	17.4	0.9	41	2	417	22	41	2
Voronezh-Kharkov defensive operation, 13.01–03.03.1943 (50)	81.5	1.6	1,023	20	2,106	42	307	6

Name of operation, dates, duration (no of days)	Small arms, 1000s		Tanks, SP guns, actual no		Guns and mortars, actual no		Combat aircraft, actual no	
	During operation	Average daily losses	During operation	Average daily losses	During operation	Average daily losses	During operation	Average daily losses
Kharkov defensive operation, 04.03–25.03.1943 (22)	116.5	5.3	322	15	3,185	145	110	5
Kursk defensive operation, 05.07–23.07.1943 (19)	70.8	3.7	1,614	85	3,929	207	459	24
Orel offensive operation, 12.07–18.08.1943 (38)	60.5	1.6	2,586	68	892	23	1,014	27
Belgorod-Kharkov offensive operation, 03.08–23.08.1943 (21)	21.7	1	1,864	89	423	20	153	7
Smolensk offensive operation, 07.08–02.10.1943 (57)	33.7	0.6	863	15	234	4	303	5
Donbass offensive operation, 13.08–22.09.1943 (41)	37.9	0.9	886	22	814	20	327	8
Chernigov-Poltava offensive operation, 26.08–30.09.1943 (36)	48	1.3	1,140	32	916	25	269	7
Novorossiysk-Taman offensive operation, 10.09–09.10.1943 (30)	4.5	0.2	111	4	70	2	240	8
Lower Dnieper offensive operation, 26.09–20.12.1943 (86)	179.9	2.1	2,639	31	3,125	36	430	5
Kiev offensive operation, 03.11–13.11.1943 (11)	8.6	0.8	271	25	104	9	125	11
Total during strategic operations of Phase II of the war (541)	829.9	1.5	16,495	30	20,701	38	4,720	8–9

Phase III (January 1944–May 1945)

Name of operation, dates, duration (no of days)	Small arms, 1000s		Tanks, SP guns, actual no		Guns and mortars, actual no		Combat aircraft, actual no	
Liberation of right-bank Ukraine, 24.12.1943–17.04.1944 (116)	362.6	3.1	4,666	40	7,532	65	676	6
Leningrad-Novgorod offensive operation, 14.01–01.03.1944 (48)	77.1	1.6	462	10	1,832	38	260	5
Crimean offensive operation, 08.04–12.05.1944 (35)	29.7	0.8	171	5	521	15	179	5
Vyborg-Petrozavodsk offensive operation, 10.06–09.08.1944 (61)	24.1	0.4	294	5	489	8	311	5

Name of operation, dates, duration (no of days)	Losses							
	Small arms, 1000s		Tanks, SP guns, actual no		Guns and mortars, actual no		Combat aircraft, actual no	
	During operation	Average daily losses	During operation	Average daily losses	During operation	Average daily losses	During operation	Average daily losses
Byelorussian offensive operation, 23.06–29.08.1944 (68)	183.5	2.7	2,957	43	2,447	36	822	12
Lvov-Sandomierz offensive operation, 13.07–29.08.1944 (48)	79	1.6	1,269	26	1,832	38	289	6
Iasi-Kishinev offensive operation, 20.08–29.08.1944 (10)	6.2	0.6	75	7–8	108	10–11	111	11
E. Carpathian offensive operation, 08.09–28.10.1944 (51)	47.9	0.9	478	9	962	19	192	4
Baltic offensive operation, 14.09–24.11.1944 (71)	172.7	2.4	522	7	2,593	37	779	11
Belgrade offensive operation, 28.09–20.10.1944 (23)	16.6	0.7	53	2	184	8	66	3
Petsamo-Kirkenes offensive operation, 07.10 29.10.1944 (23)	2.9	0.1	21	1	40	2	62	3
Budapest offensive operation, 29.10.1944–13.02.1945 (108)	135.1	1.3	1,766	16	4,127	38	293	2–3
Vistula-Oder offensive operation, 12.01–03.02.1945 (23)	25.3	1.1	1,267	55	374	16	343	15
W. Carpathian offensive operation, 12.01–18.02.1945 (38)	21.5	0.6	359	9	753	20	94	2
E. Prussian offensive operation, 13.01–25.04.1945 (103)	119.4	1.2	3,525	34	1,644	16	1,450	14
E. Pomeranian offensive operation, 10.02–04.04.1945 (54)	89.4	1.7	1,027	19	1,005	19	1,073	20
Vienna offensive operation, 16.03–15.04.1945 (31)	29.6	0.9	603	19	764	25	614	20
Berlin offensive operation, 16.04–08.05.1945 (23)	215.9	9.4	1,997	87	2,108	92	917	40
Prague offensive operation, 06.05–11.05.1945 (6)	59.8	10	373	62	1,006	168	80	13
Total during strategic operations of Phase III of the war (940)	1,698.3	1.8	21,885	23	30,321	32	8,611	9

Name of operation, dates, duration (no of days)	Losses							
	Small arms, 1000s		Tanks, SP guns, actual no		Guns and mortars, actual no		Combat aircraft, actual no	
	During operation	Average daily losses	During operation	Average daily losses	During operation	Average daily losses	During operation	Average daily losses
Campaign in Far East (August 1945)								
Manchurian offensive operation, 09.08–02.09.1945 (25)	11	0.4	78	3	232	9	62	2
Total during strategic operations of the Great Patriotic War (2,530)	9,511.6	3.75	63,229	25	180,651	71	25,266	10

1. The figure in brackets at the end of each phase of the war shows the total number of days for which strategic operations continued during that phase.

Losses during strategic operations accounted for 61.48% of small-arms losses, 65.52% of tank and SP gun losses, 56.89% of gun and mortar losses and 58.6% of combat aircraft losses during the war. On average 11,000 small arms, 68 tanks, 224 guns and mortars and 30 aircraft were lost each day. In such as the Baltic, Byelorussian, Kiev and Voronezh-Voroshilovgrad defensive operations, 20–30,000 small arms, 90–290 tanks, 200–520 guns and mortars and 30–100 combat aircraft were lost daily. Losses were also high during the Battle of Kursk and the Berlin offensive, with 70–90 tanks, 90–210 guns and mortars and 25–40 aircraft lost each day.

The number of small arms lost declined steadily after 1941. The percentage of light tanks lost also declined, but this was because fewer were being produced. In battles and operations it was heavy and medium tanks which played the major role, and increasing numbers of these were lost, especially in 1943. This was the year the Nazi command attempted to exact revenge for Stalingrad, again relying on more sophisticated marks of tank and assault gun as they had done at the start of the war. There were major battles fought with large numbers of tank troops on both sides in the Donbass, at Kharkov and at Kursk.

In 1944 there were a number of major strategic offensive operations from the Barents to the Black Sea, the aim of which was to drive the enemy from Soviet territory and liberate the countries of eastern and south-eastern Europe from Nazi occupation. In these operations the artillery played a major part both in preparations for attacks and by giving support to rifle and tank troops in the heart of the enemy's defences. In these circumstances increased numbers of all kinds of artillery weapons were lost, except for mortars. The number of mortars lost decreased as fewer were used in offensive operations, especially 50mm mortars, which ceased to be used by infantry divisions and brigades at the end of 1944.

In 1942 air force losses stabilised and remained at approximately the same level. During the Great Patriotic War 351,800 motor vehicles were lost (34.6% of stock),

75,100 radio sets of all types (40% of stock), about 10,000 items of engineer equipment (ferries, towing launches, graders, scrapers, compressor units, battery-charging trucks and mobile power units, water lifts, workshop trucks, etc.), over 24 million items of anti-CW equipment, over 31,000 special bulk decontamination vehicles, CW detection kits and anti-CW units, and several thousand items of logistic equipment.

During the war 1,014 ships of various classes went down. Of these, 314 were 1st, 2nd or 3rd class surface ships and submarines (a list of these is given in Table 99, together with the date and location where they sank), 139 motor torpedo boats, 128 submarine-chasers, 77 armoured launches, 168 minesweepers and 188 patrol (escort) and other boats.

Table 99. List of Soviet Navy Ships Lost during the Great Patriotic War, 1941–45

No	Date	Name of vessel	Fleet, flotilla	Where lost	Additional information
		Cruisers			
1	18.09.41	Petropavlovsk	Baltic Fleet	Leningrad	Raised
2	12.11.41	Chervóna Ukraina	Black Sea Fleet	Sevastopol	
		Flotilla leaders			
1	26.06.41	Moscow	Black Sea Fleet	S.E. of Constanţa	
2	23.09.41	Minsk	Baltic Fleet	Kronstadt	Raised
3	02.07.42	Tashkent	Black Sea Fleet	Novorossiysk	
4	06.10.43	Kharkov	Black Sea Fleet	Middle of Black Sea	
		Destroyers			
1	23.06.41	Gnevnyi	Baltic Fleet	Entrance to Gulf of Finland	
2	23.06.41	Lenin	Baltic Fleet	Liepāja	
3	01.07.41	Bystryi	Black Sea Fleet	Sevastopol	
4	19.07.41	Serdityi	Baltic Fleet	Moonzundski proliv	
5	20.07.41	Stremitelnyi	Northern Fleet	Yekaterinskaya gavan	
6	27.07.41	Smelyi	Baltic Fleet	Gulf of Riga	
7	08.08.41	Karl Marx	Baltic Fleet	Loksa bay	
8	18.08.41	Statnyi	Baltic Fleet	Moonzundski proliv	
9	24.08.41	Engels	Baltic Fleet	Off mys Yuminda	
10	28.08.41	Yakov Sverdlov	Baltic Fleet	Off Mokhni island	
11	28.08.41	Skoryi	Baltic Fleet	Off mys Yuminda	
12	28.08.41	Kalinin	Baltic Fleet	Off mys Yuminda	
13	28.08.41	Volodarski	Baltic Fleet	Off mys Yuminda	
14	28.08.41	Artem	Baltic Fleet	Off mys Yuminda	
15	21.09.41	Steregushchi	Baltic Fleet	Kronstadt	Raised
16	21.09.41	Frunze	Black Sea Fleet	Off Tendrovskaya kosa	
17	05.11.41	Smetlivyi	Baltic Fleet	Off Naissaar island	
18	14.11.41	Surovyi	Baltic Fleet	Off Keri island	
19	14.11.41	Gordyi	Baltic Fleet	Off Naissaar island	
20	06.03.42	Smyshlenyi	Black Sea Fleet	Off mys Zheleznyi Rog	
21	03.04.42	Shaumyan	Black Sea Fleet	Gelendzhik area	
22	14.05.42	Dzerzhinski	Black Sea Fleet	Sevastopol area	
23	08.06.42	Sovershennyi	Black Sea Fleet	Sevastopol	

No	Date	Name of vessel	Fleet, flotilla	Where lost	Additional information
24	10.06.42	Svobodnyi	Black Sea Fleet	Sevastopol	
25	26.06.42	Bezuprechnyi	Black Sea Fleet	Yalta area	
26	02.07.42	Bditelnyi	Black Sea Fleet	Novorussiysk	
27	20.11.42	Sokrushitelnyi	Northern Fleet	Middle of Barents Sea	
28	06.10.43	Besposhchadnyi	Black Sea Fleet	Middle of Black Sea	
29	06.10.43	Sposobnyi	Black Sea Fleet	Middle of Black Sea	
30	16.01.45	Deyatelnyi	Northern Fleet	Off Bolshoi Olenic island	

Submarines

No	Date	Name of vessel	Fleet, flotilla	Where lost	Additional information
1	23.06.41	M-78	Baltic Fleet	Ventspils area	
2	23.06.41	S-1	Baltic Fleet	Liepāja	
3	23.06.41	Ronis	Baltic Fleet	Liepāja	
4	23.06.41	Spidola	Baltic Fleet	Liepāja	
5	23.06.41	M-71	Baltic Fleet	Liepāja	
6	23.06.41	M-80	Baltic Fleet	Liepāja	
7	24.06.41	S-3	Baltic Fleet	Near Uzhava lighthouse	
8	26.06.41	M-83	Baltic Fleet	Liepāja	
9	28.06.41	S-10	Baltic Fleet	Danzig bay	
10	28.06.41	M-99	Baltic Fleet	Off Hiiumaa island	
11	01.07.41	M-81	Baltic Fleet	Off Vormsi island	
12	06.07.41	Shch-206	Black Sea Fleet	Off Shabler cape	
13	21.07.41	M-94	Baltic Fleet	Near Ristna lighthouses	
14	02.08.41	S-11	Baltic Fleet	Soela Väin channel	
15	08.41	M-49	Pacific Fleet	Vladivostok area	
16	08.41	M-63	Pacific Fleet	Vladivostok area	
17	28.08.41	S-5	Baltic Fleet	Gulf of Finland	
18	28.08.41	Shch-301	Baltic Fleet	Off mys Yuminda	
19	08.41	S-6	Baltic Fleet	Karlskrona area	
20	08.41	M-103	Baltic Fleet	Gulf of Finland	
21	09.41	P-1	Baltic Fleet	Gulf of Finland	
22	09.41	Shch-319	Baltic Fleet	Gulf of Finland	
23	23.09.41	M-74	Baltic Fleet	Kronstadt	Raised
24	10.41	S-8	Baltic Fleet	Gulf of Finland	
25	10.41	Shch-322	Baltic Fleet	Gulf of Finland	
26	10.41	M-58	Black Sea Fleet	Off Constanţa	
27	10–11.41	M-59	Black Sea Fleet	Sulina area	
28	10–11.41	M-34	Black Sea Fleet	Constanţa area	
29	11.41	S-34	Black Sea Fleet	Off Emine cape	
30	11.41	Shch-211	Black Sea Fleet	Varna area	
31	14.11.41	L-2	Baltic Fleet	Off Keri island	
32	14.11.41	M-98	Baltic Fleet	Off Naissaar island	
33	11.41	Kalev	Baltic Fleet	Off Naissaar island	
34	11.41	L-1	Baltic Fleet	Leningrad	
35	11.41	Shch-324	Baltic Fleet	Gulf of Finland	
36	11–12.41	Shch-204	Black Sea Fleet	Varna area	
37	10.01.42	M-175	Northern Fleet	Varangerfjord	
38	03.42	Shch-210	Black Sea Fleet	Off Shabler cape	
39	08.04.42	Shch-421	Northern Fleet	Off Nordkapp cape	
40	04.42	Shch-401	Northern Fleet	Off Fulei island	
41	12.05.42	K-23	Northern Fleet	Off Nordkinn cape	
42	13.06.42	Shch-405	Baltic Fleet	Off Seskar island	

No	Date	Name of vessel	Fleet, flotilla	Where lost	Additional information
43	15.06.42	M-95	Baltic Fleet	Off Gogland island	
44	20.06.42	Shch-214	Black Sea Fleet	Off mys Aitodor	
45	06.42	D-3	Northern Fleet	Tanafjord	
46	26.06.42	S-32	Black Sea Fleet	Off mys Aitodor	
47	26.06.42	D-6	Black Sea Fleet	Sevastopol	
48	26.06.42	A-1	Black Sea Fleet	Sevastopol	
49	04.07.42	M-176	Northern Fleet	Varangerfjord	
50	18.07.42	Shch-138	Pacific Fleet	Nikolaevsk-na-Amure	
51	07.42	Shch-317	Baltic Fleet	Gulf of Finland	
52	08.42	M-173	Northern Fleet	Vardö area	
53	08.42	M-33	Black Sea Fleet	Odessa area	
54	08–09.42	Shch-208	Black Sea Fleet	Constanţa area	
55	08–09.42	K-2	Northern Fleet	Tanafjord	
56	09.42	M-97	Baltic Fleet	Off Gogland island	
57	09.42	M-60	Black Sea Fleet	Odessa area	
58	01.10.42	M-118	Black Sea Fleet	Off mys Burnas	
59	10.42	Shch-320	Baltic Fleet	Gulf of Finland	
60	10.42	Shch-302	Baltic Fleet	Gulf of Finland	
61	11.10.42	L-16	Pacific Fleet	Pacific Ocean, off U.S. coast	
62	14.10.42	Shch-213	Black Sea Fleet	Constanţa area	
63	10.42	Shch-311	Baltic Fleet	Gulf of Finland	
64	10.42	Shch-308	Baltic Fleet	Gulf of Finland	
65	21.10.42	S-7	Baltic Fleet	Gulf of Bothnia	
66	29.10.42	Shch-304	Baltic Fleet	Gulf of Finland	
67	05.11.42	Shch-305	Baltic Fleet	Gulf of Bothnia	
68	11.42	Shch-306	Baltic Fleet	Gulf of Finland	
69	11.42	M-121	Northern Fleet	Varangerfjord	
70	12.42	L-24	Black Sea Fleet	Off Shabler cape	
71	12.42	M-31	Black Sea Fleet	Zhebriany bay	
72	12.42	Shch-212	Black Sea Fleet	Off Sinop cape	
73	12.42	M-72	Baltic Fleet	Leningrad	Raised
74	02.43	K-22	Northern Fleet	Off coast of Norway	
75	10.04.43	K-3	Northern Fleet	Off coast of Norway	
76	01.05.43	Shch-323	Baltic Fleet	Kronstadt area	Raised
77	14.05.43	M-122	Northern Fleet	Off mys Tsyp-Navolok	
78	22.05.43	Shch-408	Baltic Fleet	Off Vaindlo island	
79	01.06.43	Shch-406	Baltic Fleet	Gulf of Finland	
80	05.07.43	M-106	Northern Fleet	Varangerfjorden	
81	07.43	Shch-422	Northern Fleet	Off coast of Norway	
82	01.08.43	S-12	Baltic Fleet	Gulf of Finland	
83	13.08.43	S-9	Baltic Fleet	Off Bolshoi Tyuters island	
84	08–09.43	Shch-203	Black Sea Fleet	Sevastopol area	
85	09.43	K-1	Northern Fleet	Off Novaya Zemlya	
86	22.09.43	M-51	Black Sea Fleet	Ochamchire area	
87	10.43	M-172	Northern Fleet	Varangerfjord	
88	10.43	Shch-403	Northern Fleet	Tanafjord	
89	10.43	M-174	Northern Fleet	Varangerfjord	
90	28.10.43	A-3	Black Sea Fleet	Kalamitski zaliv	
91	12.43	D-4	Black Sea Fleet	Kalamitski zaliv	
92	12.43	S-55	Northern Fleet	Off coast of Norway	

No	Date	Name of vessel	Fleet, flotilla	Where lost	Additional information
93	04.01.44	M–36	Black Sea Fleet	Kobuleti area	
94	17.01.44	L–23	Black Sea Fleet	Karkinitski zaliv	
95	02.44	M–108	Northern Fleet	Kongsfjord	
96	02–03.44	Shch–216	Black Sea Fleet	Off mys Tarkhankut	
97	03.44	S–54	Northern Fleet	Off coast of Norway	
98	04.44	L–6	Black Sea Fleet	Sevastopol area	
99	27.07.44	V–1	Northern Fleet	Off coast of England	
100	09.44	M–96	Baltic Fleet	Narvski zaliv	
101	21.09.44	Shch–402	Northern Fleet	Gamvik area	
102	06.01.45	S–4	Baltic Fleet	Danzig bay	

Monitors

No	Date	Name of vessel	Fleet, flotilla	Where lost	Additional information
1	16.07.41	Vinnitsa	Pina Flotilla	River Berezina	
2	12.08.41	Zhemchuzhin	Pina Flotilla	River Dnieper	
3	31.08.41	Bobruisk	Pina Flotilla	River Dnieper	
4	01.09.41	Zhitomir	Pina Flotilla	River Dnieper	
5	15.09.41	Smolensk	Pina Flotilla	River Desna	
6	18.09.41	Martynov	Danube Flotilla	River Dnieper	
7	18.09.41	Levachev	Pina Flotilla	Kiev area	
8	18.09.41	Flyaghin	Pina Flotilla	Kiev area	
9	18.09.41	Rostovtsev	Pina Flotilla	Kiev area	
10	18.09.41	Vitebsk	Pina Flotilla	Kiev area	
11	19.09.41	Udarnyi	Danube Flotilla	Off Kinburnskaya kosa	

Patrol (escort) vessels

No	Date	Name of vessel	Fleet, flotilla	Where lost	Additional information
1	13.07.41	Passat	Northern Fleet	Off Kharlov island	
2	19.07.41	Shtil	Northern Fleet	Guba Ura	
3	10.08.41	Tuman	Northern Fleet	Kildinski ples	
4	11.08.41	Zhemchug	Northern Fleet	Entrance to White Sea	
5	26.08.41	Reka	Pina Flotilla	River Dnieper	
6	26.08.41	Parizhskaya kommuna	Pina Flotilla	River Dnieper	
7	28.08.41	Sneg	Baltic Fleet	Off mys Yuminda	
8	28.08.41	Tsiklon	Baltic Fleet	Off mys Yuminda	
9	28.08.41	Rulevoi	Pina Flotilla	River Dnieper	
10	28.08.41	Vodopiyanov	Pina Flotilla	River Dnieper	
11	31.08.41	Tekhnik	Pina Flotilla	River Dnieper	
12	31.08.41	Bolshevik	Pina Flotilla	River Dnieper	
13	09.09.41	Pushkin	Pina Flotilla	River Desna	
14	09.41	Karl Marx	Pina Flotilla	River Dnieper	
15	09.41	Engels	Pina Flotilla	River Dnieper	
16	18.09.41	Voroshilov	Pina Flotilla	River Dnieper	
17	22.09.41	Vikhr	Baltic Fleet	Kronstadt	Raised
18	26.09.41	Shchors	Baltic Fleet	Off Lavensaari island	Raised
19	10.41	SKR–11 (RT–66)	Northern Fleet	Near Tersko-Orlovski lighthouse	
20	03.12.41	Virsaitis	Baltic Fleet	Gulf of Finland	
21	01.42	SKR–24 (Iceberg)	Northern Fleet	Off Lumbouski island	
22	08.03.42	Mgla (RT–38)	Northern Fleet	Off mys Tsyp-Navolok	
23	12.05.42	Brilliant	Northern Fleet	Iokanga	Raised
24	17.05.42	SKR–21 (RT–73)	Northern Fleet	Iokanga	
25	15.07.42	LK–2	Baltic Fleet	Gulf of Finland	

No	Date	Name of vessel	Fleet, flotilla	Where lost	Additional information
26	20.08.42	Voikov	Azov Flotilla	Kerchenski proliv	
27	24.08.42	Shturman	Azov Flotilla	Temryuk	
28	24.08.42	Burya	Baltic Fleet	Gulf of Finland	
29	01.09.42	Purga	Ladoga Flotilla	Lake Ladoga	Raised
30	11.10.42	Musson (RT-54)	Northern Fleet	Proliv Matochkin Shar	
31	05.11.42	SKR-23 (RT-57)	Northern Fleet	Iokanga area	
32	08.12.42	Smerch	Northern Fleet	Rosta	Raised
33	12.05.43	SKR-31 (RT-43)	Northern Fleet	Off mys Tsyp-Navolok	
34	03.08.43	Priliv (RT-5)	Northern Fleet	Kildinski ples	
35	17.10.43	SKR-14 (RT-86)	Northern Fleet	Yeniseyski zaliv	
36	23.09.44	Brilliant	Northern Fleet	Middle of Kara Sea	

Gunboats

No	Date	Name of vessel	Fleet, flotilla	Where lost	Additional information
1	23.07.41	Narova	Chudskoe (Peipus) Flotilla	Lake Chudskoe	
2	11.08.41	Peredovoi	Pina Flotilla	River Dnieper	
3	11.08.41	Issa	Chudskoe (Peipus) Flotilla	Lake Chudskoe	
4	13.08.41	Embakh	Chudskoe (Peipus) Flotilla	Lake Chudskoe	
5	25.08.41	Vernyi	Pina Flotilla	River Dnieper	
6	26.08.41	Dimitrov	Pina Flotilla	River Dnieper	
7	27.08.41	Kreml	Pina Flotilla	River Dnieper	
8	28.08.41	I-8	Baltic Fleet	Off mys Yuminda	
9	31.08.41	Trudovoi	Pina Flotilla	River Dnieper	
10	15.09.41	Kaganovich	Pina Flotilla	River Dnieper	
11	18.09.41	Smolnyi	Pina Flotilla	River Dnieper	
12	21.09.41	Krasnaya Armeniya	Black Sea Fleet	Off Tendrovskaya kosa	
13	27.09.41	Pioneer	Baltic Fleet	Leningrad	Raised
14	06.10.41	Olekma	Ladoga Flotilla	Lake Ladoga	Raised
15	19.10.41	Krenkel	Azov Flotilla	Taganrog	
16	11.05.42	Rion	Azov Flotilla	Kerchenski proliv	
17	02.07.42	No 4	Azov Flotilla	Temryuk	
18	28.07.42	Serafimovich	Azov Flotilla	River Don	
19	31.07.42	KL-13 (Izhoryets-18)	Onega Flotilla	Lake Onega	
20	10.08.42	Dnestr	Azov Flotilla	Temryuk	
21	21.08.42	Ural	Azov Flotilla	Temryukski zaliv	
22	21.08.42	Burlak	Azov Flotilla	Temryukski zaliv	
23	22.08.42	No 1 (IP-22)	Azov Flotilla	River Kuban	
24	24.08.42	Don	Azov Flotilla	Temryuk	
25	24.08.42	Bug	Azov Flotilla	Temryuk	
26	02.09.42	Rostov-Don	Azov Flotilla	Tamanski zaliv	
27	02.09.42	Oktyabr	Azov Flotilla	Tamanski zaliv	
28	16.11.42	Krasnoye Znamya	Baltic Fleet	Off Lavensaari island	Raised
29	27.02.43	Krasnaya Gruziya	Black Sea Fleet	Myskhako area	
30	17.05.43	Krasnyi Daghestan	Volga Flotilla	River Volga	
31	26.05.43	Krasnogvardeyets	Volga Flotilla	River Volga	
32	01.06.43	KL-12 (Kalyaev)	Onega Flotilla	Lake Onega	
33	22.06.43	Kama	Baltic Fleet	Off Lavensaari island	Raised
34	10.11.44	Amgun	Baltic Fleet	Off Aegna island	Raised

No	Date	Name of vessel	Fleet, flotilla	Where lost	Additional information
		Minelayers			
1	11.08.41	Surop	Baltic Fleet	Kuivastu area	
2	28.08.41	Mina	Pina Flotilla	River Dnieper	
3	21.09.41	Kolkhoznik	Danube Flotilla	Off Kinburnskaya kosa	
4	11.02.42	Doob	Black Sea Fleet	Sevastopol area	
5	23.03.42	Ostrovski	Black Sea Fleet	Tuapse	
6	10.10.42	Comintern	Black Sea Fleet	Mouth of River Khopi	
7	05.03.43	Zarya	Black Sea Fleet	Myskhako area	
		Minesweepers			
1	24.06.41	T-208 (Shkiv)	Baltic Fleet	Glotova bank	
2	01.07.41	T-299 (Imanta)	Baltic Fleet	Off Saaremaa island	
3	06.07.41	T-216	Baltic Fleet	Near Takhkun lighthouse	
4	07.07.41	No 39 (Petrozavodsk)	Baltic Fleet	Kronstadt area	Raised
5	09.07.41	T-890 (Nalim)	Northern Fleet	Guba Zapadnaya Litsa	
6	29.07.41	No 51 (Zmei)	Baltic Fleet	Soela Väin channel	
7	30.07.41	T-201 (Zaryad)	Baltic Fleet	Near Ristna lighthouse	
8	31.07.41	No 46 (Izhoryets-25)	Baltic Fleet	Tallinn	
9	03.08.41	T-212 (Shtag)	Baltic Fleet	Soela Väin channel	
10	11.08.41	T-213 (Krambol)	Baltic Fleet	Off mys Yuminda	
11	13.08.41	No 41 (Lenvodput-12)	Baltic Fleet	Gulf of Finland	
12	15.08.41	T-202 (Bui)	Baltic Fleet	Off mys Yuminda	
13	18.08.41	No 80 (Izhoryets-21)	Baltic Fleet	Moonzundski proliv	
14	18.08.41	T-503 (Baikal)	Black Sea Fleet	Ochakov area	
15	19.08.41	T-487 (Ochakovski Canal)	Black Sea Fleet	Kherson area	
16	24.08.41	T-214 (Bughel)	Baltic Fleet	Off Keri island	
17	24.08.41	T-209 (Knecht)	Baltic Fleet	Off Keri island	
18	25.08.41	T-898 (RT-411)	Northern Fleet	Entrance to White Sea	
19	28.08.41	No 71 (Crab)	Baltic Fleet	Off mys Yuminda	
20	28.08.41	No 42 (Lenvodput-13)	Baltic Fleet	Off mys Yuminda	
21	06.09.41	T-493 (Hadjibei)	Black Sea Fleet	Odessa	
22	12.09.41	T-402 (Minrep)	Black Sea Fleet	Off Feodosia	
23	16.09.41	No 81 (Izhoryets-22)	Baltic Fleet	Middle of Baltic Sea	
24	17.09.41	No 122 (Som)	Ladoga Flotilla	Lake Ladoga	
25	19.09.41	No 53 (Izhoryets-39)	Baltic Fleet	Leningrad	Raised
26	20.09.41	No 33 (Molotov)	Baltic Fleet	Leningrad	Raised
27	22.09.41	No 41 (S. Kirov)	Baltic Fleet	Gulf of Finland	
28	23.09.41	No 31 (Ozernyi)	Baltic Fleet	Kronstadt	
29	30.09.41	No 64 (Izhoryets-71)	Baltic Fleet	Gulf of Finland	Raised
30	09.41	No 82 (Izhoryets-23)	Baltic Fleet	Interned in Sweden	
31	09.41	No 87 (Izhoryets-34)	Baltic Fleet	Interned in Sweden	
32	09.41	No 89 (Izhoryets-83)	Baltic Fleet	Interned in Sweden	
33	09.41	No 85 (Izhoryets-29)	Baltic Fleet	Middle of Baltic Sea	
34	25.10.41	T-203 (Patron)	Baltic Fleet	Off Keri island	
35	27.10.41	T-507 (Delegat)	Black Sea Fleet	Kerch	
36	29.10.41	No 36 (Moskva)	Baltic Fleet	Off Lavensaari island	Raised
37	01.11.41	No 43 (Izhoryets-65)	Baltic Fleet	Off Lavensaari island	
38	02.11.41	T-504 (Rabotnik)	Black Sea Fleet	Off mys Aitodor	
39	02.11.41	T-498 (Yegurcha)	Black Sea Fleet	Novorossiysk	

No	Date	Name of vessel	Fleet, flotilla	Where lost	Additional information
40	03.11.41	No 177 (Beluga)	Baltic Fleet	Leningrad	Raised
41	07.11.41	No 178 (Ulyanov)	Baltic Fleet	Neva inlet	Raised
42	07.11.41	T-484 (Khenkin)	Black Sea Fleet	Off mys Sarych	
43	14.11.41	T-206 (Verp)	Baltic Fleet	Off Keri island	
44	15.11.41	T-889 (RT-3)	Northern Fleet	Off Ostrye Ludki islands	
45	22.11.41	No 35 (Menzhinski)	Baltic Fleet	Gulf of Finland	
46	25.11.41	No 56 (Klyuz)	Baltic Fleet	Gulf of Finland	
47	30.11.41	No 67 (Izhoryets-53)	Baltic Fleet	Gulf of Finland	Raised
48	30.11.41	No 171 (Norek)	Ladoga Flotilla	Lake Ladoga	
49	28.12.41	T-485 (Kakhovka)	Black Sea Fleet	Off Kerch peninsula	
50	05.01.42	T-405 (Vzryvatel)	Black Sea Fleet	Yeupatoria area	
51	02.03.42	T-491 (Kiziltash)	Black Sea Fleet	Kerch	
52	29.04.42	T-494 (Sary-Kamysh)	Azov Flotilla	Yasenski zaliv area	
53	13.06.42	T-413	Black Sea Fleet	Sevastopol area	
54	03.08.42	No 39 (Petrozavodsk)	Baltic Fleet	Demansteinskaya bank	
55	24.08.42	T-204 (Fougasse)	Baltic Fleet	Gulf of Finland	
56	02.10.42	No 57 (Udarnik)	Baltic Fleet	Off Seskar island	
57	20.11.42	No 48 (Izhoryets-33)	Baltic Fleet	Kronstadt	Raised
58	24.11.42	T 105	Northern Fleet	Off Danilov island	
59	27.02.43	T-403 (Gruz)	Black Sea Fleet	Myskhako area	
60	04.03.43	T-514 (Ost)	Black Sea Fleet	Myskhako area	
61	26.03.43	T-511 (Chervonyi kozak)	Black Sea Fleet	Tsemesskaya bay	
62	10.04.43	No 126 (Izhoryets-66)	Ladoga Flotilla	Mouth of River Volkhov	Raised
63	15.06.43	T-411 (Zashchitnik)	Black Sea Fleet	Sukhumi area	
64	25.07.43	T-904 (RT-94)	Northern Fleet	By proliv Yugorski Shar	
65	30.07.43	T-911 (RT-76)	Northern Fleet	Off Novaya Zemliya	
66	29.08.43	Djalita	Black Sea Fleet	Sukhumi area	
67	01.10.43	T-896 (RT-308)	Northern Fleet	Off Mikhailov peninsula	
68	23.12.43	Raduga	Baltic Fleet	Off Seskar island	
69	09.05.44	T-886 (RT-15)	Northern Fleet	Kolski zaliv	
70	21.06.44	No 47 (Izhoryets-26)	Baltic Fleet	Bierkezund	
71	21.06.44	No 53 (Izhoryets-39)	Baltic Fleet	Bierkezund	
72	02.07.44	T-210 (Gak)	Baltic Fleet	Vyborgski zaliv	Raised
73	02.08.44	T-37 (Tyulyen)	Baltic Fleet	Narvski zaliv	
74	03.08.44	No 127 (Izhoryets-32)	Ladoga Flotilla	Lake Ladoga	
75	12.08.44	T 118	Northern Fleet	Middle of Kara Sea	
76	13.08.44	T-114	Northern Fleet	Middle of Kara Sea	
77	26.08.44	T-45 (Antikainen)	Baltic Fleet	Off Nerva island	
78	02.09.44	T-410 (Vzryv)	Black Sea Fleet	Constanta area	
79	08.09.44	T-353	Baltic Fleet	Narvski zaliv	
80	19.09.44	No 49 (Izhoryets-31)	Baltic Fleet	Vigrund bank	
81	24.09.44	T-120	Northern Fleet	Middle of Kara Sea	
82	23.10.44	T-379	Baltic Fleet	Tallinn	
83	22.11.44	T-109	Northern Fleet	Off Kolguyev island	
84	28.11.44	T-387	Baltic Fleet	Tallinn area	
85	05.12.44	T-82 (Izhoryets-82)	Baltic Fleet	Ust-Dvinsk	
86	05.12.44	T-377	Baltic Fleet	Gulf of Riga	
87	29.12.44	T-883 (RT-45)	Northern Fleet	Off mys Svyatoi Nos	
88	11.01.45	T-76 (Corall)	Baltic Fleet	Off Aegna island	

Soviet material losses were enormous, and it is natural to want to know how they compare with enemy losses. However, it is beyond the scope of this work to calculate the losses incurred by Nazi Germany and its allies while fighting the USSR. It can only be said that everything they produced before and during the war was lost irretrievably and that the figures were high: 42,700 tanks and assault guns, 379,400 guns and mortars and 75,700 combat aircraft were lost. It was the end of the Nazi army.

By the end of the war the Red Army had considerably more arms and equipment than at the start of the war. By 9 May 1945 it had 35,200 tanks and SP guns (1.6 times more than on 22 June 1941), 321,500 guns and mortars (2.9 times more) and 47,300 combat aircraft (2.4 times more than at the start of the war). The Soviet armed forces had also gained a great deal of experience in conducting operations and fighting battles and were fully ready for action. Part of their forces in the Far East rapidly routed the Japanese Kwantung Army and took many prisoners.

After the war the striking power of both army and navy increased considerably. The Soviet armed forces acquired nuclear weapons and various kinds of missiles, while several generations of tanks, artillery systems, combat aircraft and ships were replaced. Nowadays, the weapons and equipment which brought victory against the Nazis and Japanese are just museum pieces: the famous 34s, Ilyushins, katyushas, 45s, 76mm guns, 122mm howitzers, submarines and motor torpedo boats, together with those workhorses of the road to the front, the three-ton truck and one-and-a-half tonner ... For millions of people these remain symbols of the Soviet Army's feat of arms in routing and driving out the Nazi aggressor and liberating other nations from fascism.

ENEMY CASUALTIES

A close examination of Soviet and German documents from the World War II period and of many overseas publications on military history has shown that it is extremely difficult to establish reliable, accurate figures for the number of casualties incurred by Nazi Germany and its allies during World War II.

Casualty reports submitted by German HQs were more or less objective until about January 1945. In the last stage of the war, however, when the Germans were suffering major defeats, the OKW stopped producing accurate information and gave only approximate figures. Generally this meant that figures were calculated on the basis of information pertaining to the preceding months. The systematic recording of casualty numbers was also disrupted at this stage, and reports were contradictory and imprecise. This was particularly true of statistics from logistic and servicing units, subunits and departments and also police and other paramilitary formations made up of foreign nationals (Serbs, Croats, Czechs, Slovaks, Poles, French, Belgians, Dutch, etc.).

The figures for Nazi Germany's war losses do not include losses incurred by Germany's allies (Finland, Hungary, Romania and Bulgaria) or by several Slovak divisions, a Spanish division, a French and a Croat infantry regiment, a Belgian infantry battalion and a number of other foreign units which fought with the Germans against the Soviets. Nor did the reports include casualties from Volkssturm subdivisions or from military formations made up of Germany's so-called 'volunteer helpers' from the Soviet Union (Balts, Muslims, Ukrainians, the Russian Liberation Army, etc.). By mid-July 1944 the personnel strength of such formations, including police and auxiliary formations, was over 800,000. During the war more than 150,000 former Soviet citizens served in the SS alone.

It should be explained what is meant by 'total personnel losses of the German armed forces'. In German documents these figures included only servicemen. Casualties from various paramilitary services supporting the armed forces were included with civilian losses.

'Irrecoverable losses' includes deaths in battle, deaths from wounds and disease in treatment centres or at home in incidents connected with the use of weapons, missing in action, and non-combat losses (died in accident, executed, etc.). Wehrmacht documents do not include the category of prisoner of war, POWs being listed as 'missing in action'.

'Sick and wounded' includes wounded, concussed, sick, frostbite and burns cases, but only those who were undergoing hospital treatment or had been evacuated to the rear.

During World War II there were three independent channels in the German armed forces for the submitting of casualty reports. The first channel was for gathering reports from HQs, the aim being to give superior commands an idea of the number of casualties and of reinforcements needed. The second channel was via the medical service and its purpose was that hospitals' workloads could thus be assessed, and to ascertain whether hospitals needed to be relocated or their capacity increased. The third channel was to provide personal details of armed services' casualties. Reports via all three channels were submitted, depending on their purpose, to the relevant headquarters (of the army, navy or air force) so that the necessary decisions could be taken.

The task of analysing and summarising findings from casualty reports at the General Staff of the Armed Forces High Command (OKW) was assigned to a central bureau (department) which recorded armed forces personnel losses, to which all information on the matter was submitted. The monthly summaries of German armed forces casualties drawn up by this bureau are the most comprehensive and are fairly accurate. In the final stage of the war, however, because of the general confusion on the German-Soviet front, the accuracy of these summaries fell sharply. This is confirmed by looking at the central bureau's final summary of 14 March 1945, which gives the same number of German casualties as for 31 January 1945.

Table 100 reproduces the casualty figures from the summaries for 31 December 1944 and 31 January 1945 so that their accuracy may be assessed.

Table 100. Casualty Figures from the Summaries for 31 December 1944 and 31 January 1945

Loss category	Army & SS troops		Air force		Navy		Total	
	01.09.39–31.12.44	01.09.39–31.01.45	01.09.39–31.12.44	01.09.39–31.01.45	01.09.39–31.12.44	01.09.39–31.01.45	01.09.39–31.12.44	01.09.39–31.01.45
Irrecoverable losses	3,359,979	3,425,877	303,464	319,138	160,285	159,088	3,823,728	3,904,103
Breakdown:								
Killed in action, died of wounds or from other causes	1,750,281	1,779,561	155,014	163,006	60,029	58,832	1,965,324	2,001,399
Missing in action, POWs	1,609,698	1,646,316	148,450	156,132	100,256	100,256	1,858,404	1,902,704
Wounded	5,026,404	4,188,037	192,594	216,579	21,002	25,259	5,240,000	4,429,875
Total	8,386,383	7,613,914	496,058	535,717	181,287	184,347	9,063,728	8,333,978

From these figures it would appear that the number of navy personnel killed or who had died by 31 December 1944 was greater than the number killed by the end of January 1945. In the ground forces and SS there is a similar discrepancy in the number of wounded, with apparently 838,400 fewer wounded in January 1945 than in December 1944. The January figure for total losses in the German armed forces as a whole is 729,750 lower than the December figure.

The main failing of these figures, however, is that they do not include losses during the last months of the war in Europe, i.e. when the situation at the front was going against Nazi Germany and in the space of four months the German armed forces suffered their heaviest casualties. Because of the lack of statistical data in the archives on casualties for 1945, the number was estimated by the Wehrmacht's casualty records department after the war and is only approximate.

According to the German Command's calculations, casualties for the period 1 January–30 April 1945 were as shown in Table 101.

Table 101. German Casualties, 1 January–30 April 1945

Loss category	Army and SS troops	Air force	Navy	Total
Irrecoverable losses	1,250,000	17,000	10,000	1,277,000
Breakdown:				
Killed	250,000	10,000	5,000	265,000
Missing in action, POWs	1,000,000	7,000	5,000	1,012,000
Wounded	750,000	30,000	15,000	795,000
Total	2,000,000	47,000	25,000	2,072,000

The accuracy of their calculations is doubtful, however. First, they do not include losses in combat operations between 1 and 11 May; secondly, the calculations were based on average monthly losses over a three-month period in 1944, which could not possibly be the same as 1945 losses; and thirdly, they contradict figures from the headquarters of the German Armed Forces High Command published in B. Müller-Hillebrand's work (Moscow, Voenizdat Publishers, 1976), where on page 328 it states that there were about 1,900,000 killed and missing, not 1,277,000 as indicated in Table 101.

Let us now examine another document from the Wehrmacht's casualty records department which was written after hostilities had ceased. A radio-telegram to the OKW quartermaster-general dated 22 May 1945 contains the following information:

'In answer to the radio-telegram from the OKW quartermaster-general, No 82/266 of 18 May 1945, I hereby inform you:

1. (a) Killed in action, including 500,000 deaths from wounds: 2.03 million. In addition, died as a result of accidents or disease: 200,000.

    (b) Wounded: 5.24 million

    (c) Missing in action: 2.4 million
    Total losses: 9.73 million.[22]

2. Since 2 May 45, about 70,000 wounded have been held by the Russians and about 135,000 by the Americans and British.

3. Total number of wounded at present in the Reich: about 700,000 ...

Wehrmacht casualty records department, 22 May 1945.'[23]

On the basis of this report, the German armed forces' irrecoverable losses amounted to 4,630,000. This figure does not, however, correspond with figures from other sources. Thus, according to the OKH Organisational Department memorandum of 10 May 1945, the ground forces and SS alone (excluding the navy and air force) lost 4,617,000 men between 1 September 1939 and 1 May 1945 (2,007,000 killed and 2,610,000 missing in action or POWs).[24]

For comparison, the different totals are given in Table 102.

Table 102. German Armed Forces' Irrecoverable Losses

Period, source	Casualties, 1000s				
	Irrecoverable losses				
	Killed, died of wounds	Missing in action, POWs	Total	Wounded	Overall total
01.09.1939–31.12.1944 (according to casualty records)	1,965.3	1,858.5	3,823.8	5,240	9,063.8
01.01–30.04.1945 (according to calculations)	265	1,012	1,277	795	2,072
Total for war	2,230.3	2,870.5	5,100.8	6,035	11,135.8
According to report from OKW casualty records department dated 22 May 1945	2,230	2,400	4,630	5,240	9,870

As can be seen from the table, there is a discrepancy of 1,265,800 in the total figures, the biggest discrepancies being in the number of missing in action and wounded.

According to material from the German Information Service (the supplement to the law of the Federal Republic of Germany 'On the preservation of places of burial'), the total number of German soldiers buried in the Soviet Union and other East European countries alone is 3,226,000, of whom the names of 2,395,000 have been established. Figures for the number of Wehrmacht servicemen buried in Western countries (Germany, France, Italy, Greece, Norway, etc.) and in North Africa are not included in this document.

As for those missing in action and POWs, it is known that 1,939,000 German servicemen returned home after the war from the USSR alone, and that 450,600 died while in captivity (356,700 in NKVD camps, the remaining 93,900 while in transit or at transit centres).

The figures in Wehrmacht documents relating to Germany's war losses are therefore contradictory and unreliable.

It is safe to assume that the number of missing and POWs was significantly higher (by about 1,200,000), particularly taking into account the number that died on the battlefield or were taken prisoner when Germany capitulated. An analysis of German personnel losses during World War II confirms this.

There is also information on German prisoner of war numbers in the Soviet archives. According to statistics submitted by fronts, fleets and independent armies and collated at the General Staff, the number of prisoners of war taken by the Soviets in the war with Germany was 3,777,300[25] (see Table 103). Of these, over 600,000 prisoners of various nationalities were freed at the front without being sent to camps in the rear, and at the same time documents were not drawn up for a further 183,619.[26]

Table 103. Prisoners of War Taken by the Soviets in the War with Germany

Period	Personnel				
	Generals	Officers	NCOs	Men	Total
22 June–31 December 1941	—	303	947	9,352	10,602
1 January–30 June 1942	1	161	762	5,759	6,683
1 July–31 December 1942	2	1,173	3,848	167,120	172,143
1 January–30 June 1943	27	2,336	11,865	350,653	364,881
1 July–31 December 1943	—	866	4,469	72,407	77,742
1 January–30 June 1944	12	2,974	15,313	238,116	256,415
1 July–31 December 1944	51	8,160	44,373	895,946	948,530
1 January–30 April 1945	20	10,014	59,870	1,235,440	1,305,344
1–8 May 1945	66	10,424	40,930	583,530	634,950
Total	179	36,411	182,377	3,558,323	3,777,290

Note. Of the total number of prisoners of war (3,777,290), 2,389,560 were Germans, 156,682 were Austrians, 513,767 Hungarians, 201,800 Romanians, 48,957 Italians and 2,377 Finns. The remaining 464,147 were French, Slovaks, Czechs, Belgians, Spaniards, etc. who had previously served in the Wehrmacht or worked in service installations or logistical services.

An analysis of various archive documents and Soviet and overseas publications giving war losses for World War II shows that total German armed forces casualties came to 13,448,000, which was 75.1% of the number mobilised during the war, or 46% of the entire male population of Germany in 1939 including Austria. Their irrecoverable losses on the German-Soviet Front came to 6,923,700.

Germany's allies (Hungary, Italy, Romania and Finland) lost 1,725,800 fighting the Soviet Union (see Table 104).

After 9 May 1945 1,284,000 enemy servicemen surrendered their weapons to Soviet troops.

In fighting the Soviet Union in Europe, Germany and her allies therefore suffered many casualties. In addition their armed forces were routed and they were forced to capitulate. Their irrecoverable losses alone came to 8,649,500.

In Japan's Kwantung Army, too, 83,700 were killed and a further 640,100 taken prisoner while fighting the Soviet Union in the Far East in August and September 1945. Of these, 609,400 were Japanese, 16,100 Chinese, 10,300 Koreans, 3,600 Mongolians and 700 Manchurians or other nationalities.

Table 104. Hungarian, Italian, Romanian and Finnish Losses against the Soviet Union

Country, formation, loss category	No of casualties, 1000s
German Armed Forces	
Wehmacht and SS	6,231.7
Breakdown: Killed, died of wounds or disease	2,869.3
Missing in action	972.8
POWS	2,389.6[1]
Austrians, Sudeten Germans, natives of Alsace, Lorraine and Luxembourg serving in Wehrmacht	462
Breakdown: Killed, died of wounds or disease, missing in action	280
POWs	182
Foreign Wehrmacht formations (Spanish division, Slovak divisions, French, Belgian, Flemish and other formations)	15
Volunteer Wehrmacht formations and SS troops (Vlasovites, Balts, Muslims, etc.)	215
Total	6,923.7
Armed Forces of Germany's Allies	
Hungary	863.7
Breakdown: Killed, died of wounds, missing in action	350
POWs	513.7[2]
Italy	93.9
Breakdown: Killed, died of wounds, missing in action	45
POWs	48.9
Romania	681.8
Breakdown: Killed, died of wounds, missing in action	480
POWs	201.8[3]
Finland	86.4
Breakdown: Killed, died of wounds, missing in action	84
POWs	2.4
Total	1,725.8
Total losses in fascist bloc armies	8,649.5

1. Of these, 450,600 died while in captivity.
2. Of these, 54,700 died while in captivity.
3. Of these, 40,000 died while in captivity.

Although the warring countries recovered some of their losses in prisoner of war exchanges, nonetheless Nazi aggression cost Germany and its allies dear. Their irrecoverable personnel losses on the Soviet-German front were only 30% fewer than corresponding Soviet losses (German losses were 8.6 million, Soviet losses 11.4 million). Thus the ratio of German to Soviet irrecoverable losses was 1:1.3. The excessive number of Soviet losses is mainly due to events during phase one of the Great Patriotic War, with the sudden attack by Nazi Germany and miscalculations by the Soviet military and political leadership before and at the start of the war.

NOTES

1. See *Velikaya Otechestvennaya voina 1941–45* (*The Great Patriotic War: an Encyclopedia*), Moscow, 1985, p. 11.

2. From a military-operational point of view, 'irrecoverable losses' means not only deaths in action or from wounds but also missing in action and prisoners of war.

3. Including 767,750 reservists who were on courses of instruction in the forces when the war started.

4. According to the census, in 1940 the population of the USSR was 194.1 million; 33.9 million manual and white-collar workers and 29 million collective farmers were employed in different sectors of the economy.

5. The table gives average monthly listed strength and losses only for operational fronts and independent armies (i.e. it excludes the navy, military districts, Supreme Command HQ reserve troops and air defence fronts and armies). Average monthly listed strength and losses of operative fleets and independent flotillas are given elsewhere.

6. Average monthly strength for August–December 1941.

7. Losses for June–December 1941.

8. In the tables, which give fighting strength, numerical strength and casualties, the fighting strength figures are for the period before the ground forces were combined. The number of corps only includes tank and mechanised corps formed in May 1942. The tables have been based on the reports from the fronts, which were the fullest and most reliable. In cases where operations lasted less than a month, ten day reports from the fronts were used. Using the monthly or ten-day reports, however, it was not always possible to calculate exactly full casualty numbers throughout the whole operation. In cases where a front took part in an operation for more than five days, as a rule the front's losses for the ten-day period were added to the total figure; or, if it took part in the operation for less than five days, the front's losses for the ten-day period were not added. For example, the Kursk defensive operation began on 5 July 1943. There are casualty figures for the ten days from 1 July. In this case the figures for ten, not five, days have been added to the total number.

9. Deaths in hospital from wounds and disease are included under 'sick and wounded'.

10. Includes about 123,000 acting officers who did not hold officer rank.

11. Correspondence to and from the Chairman of the USSR Council of Ministers, the President of the United States and the Prime Minister of Great Britain during the Great Patriotic War, 1941–45, Moscow, 1976, vol. 1, p. 17.

12. Ibid., vol. 2, p. 17.

13. See *Velikaya Otechestvennaya voina 1941–45* (*The Great Patriotic War*), p. 519.

14. See *Rossiya v mirovoi voine 1914–1918 (v tsifrakh)* (*Russia during the World War (in figures)*), Moscow, 1925, pp. 30, 41.

15. German Federal Archive, RH-23/5-155; RH-53-23/65; R-41/168; H-3/729.

16. TsGAOR (Central State Archive of the October Revolution), f. 7021, op. 148, d. 258, l. 420–1.

17. See *Voenno-istoricheski zhurnal* (*Journal of Military History*), 1991, No 3, p. 40.

18. See Fuller, D., *The Second World War 1939–45*, Moscow, 1956, p. 164.

19. TsAMO, f. 19-A, op. 1914, d. 7, l. 87–96; f. 8-A. op. 1261, d. 2, l. 50, 77.

20. TsAMO, f. 15-A, op. 113, d. 1, l. 116–26, 228–38.

21. Abbreviations: G—gun; ATG—anti-tank gun; H—howitzer; GH—gun-howitzer; AAG—anti-aircraft gun; M—mortar.

22. A mistake has been made in the total figure, which is 140,000 short.

23. Military archive, WF No 01/1913, l. 655.

24. Military archive, WF No 01/1761, l. 123, 124.
25. TsAMO, f. 13-A, op. 3028, d. 10, l. 1–15.
26. TsGA (Central State Archive), f. 1p, op. 32-b, d. 2, l. 8–9.

Chapter Four

The Soviet Armed Forces' Losses while Giving Military Assistance to Other Countries and in Border Conflicts

THE WAR IN KOREA, 1950–53

After the formation of two Korean states in 1948 and the departure from the peninsula first of the Soviet and then the American forces, a military conflict flared up between North and South Korea.

The war began on 25 June 1950. As well as South Korean and American troops, forces from 15 different countries were involved, fighting under the UN flag. These were mostly members of NATO or other blocs (Australia, Belgium, Great Britain, Greece, Turkey, France, etc.).

The government of the Soviet Union regarded the war in Korea as a national liberation struggle by the Korean people, and sent a large quantity of arms, equipment and various material resources to North Korea to help defend the country in its hour of need. Chinese volunteers fought in the war on the North Korean side.

The Soviet government also sent several air force divisions[1] to south-eastern China to help repel air attacks by the US Air Force over Chinese and North Korean territory, and Soviet military advisers were sent to Korea, where they were seconded to formations and HQs in the Korean People's Army.

After three years of fighting by Korean People's Army troops and Chinese volunteers, and with growing demands by the world community to end the war, a ceasefire agreement was signed in 1953.

During the Korean war the Soviet Air Force formations which were involved in repelling USAF air attacks lost a total of 335 planes and 120 pilots.[2] Total Soviet casualties came to 299, 146 officers and 153 sergeants or privates.

LOCAL WARS AND MILITARY CONFLICTS IN ASIA, THE NEAR EAST AND AFRICA

After World War II, national liberation struggles in various parts of the world led to new, developing countries coming into existence which had been freed from colonialism and dependence. Over half the newly created states in Asia, Africa and Latin America won their sovereignty and independence by force of arms. In a number

281

of former colonies popular armies were formed which fought against the restoration of colonial regimes.

The Soviet Union gave all-round support to these newly liberated nations, and from the 1960s many friendly developing countries were helped to set up or build up their own armed forces.

Soviet military units and sub-units, military advisers and specialists were sent to these countries under the terms of inter-governmental agreements, in order to assist their military commands on various aspects of military organisation. They were also supplied with Soviet arms and equipment and given technical help in setting up various military facilities.

In a number of countries where local wars were in progress or military conflicts arose, it was not unusual for Soviet servicemen to be involved in fighting. Casualty figures are given in Table 105.

Table 105. Casualty Figures for Soviet Personnel in Local Wars and Military Conflicts

				Losses			
				Combat losses		Non-combat losses	
Country	Periods of fighting	Personnel sent	Killed or died, total	Total	No of officers	Total	No of officers
Algeria	1962–64 and subsequent years	Military advisers and specialists	25	21	20	4	4
United Arab Republic (Egypt)	18 October 1962– 1 April 1963, 1 October 1969– 16 July 1972, 5 October 1973– 1 April 1974	Specialists	15	5	5	10	10
		Military units	6	6	6	—	—
		Total	21	11	11	10	10
Yemen Republic	18 October 1962– 1 April 1963	Military advisers and specialists	1	1	1	—	—
Vietnam	July 1965– December 1974	Military advisers and specialists	16	13	12	3	3
Syria	5–13 June 1967, March–July 1970, September–November 1972, 6–24 October 1973	Military advisers and specialists	35	30	28	5	5
Angola	November 1975– November 1979	Military advisers and specialists	7	3	2	4	3
Mozambique	1967, 1969, November 1975–November 1979	Military advisers and specialists	6	5	5	1	1
Ethiopia	9 December 1977– May 1990	Military advisers and specialists	34	14[1]	11	20	16

1. Includes seven missing in action, five officers and two men.
Note. Servicemen who died as a result of illness or in an incident unconnected with the conflict are not included in the table.

EVENTS IN HUNGARY, 1956

In 1956 in Hungary there was an armed uprising by forces opposed to socialism. Its organisers took advantange of crude blunders by the leadership of the Hungarian Workers' Party who were responsible for major deviations from economic policy and had committed serious infringements of the law. A certain element of the country's youth and of other sectors of the population were drawn into the conflict.

In this complex situation, on 4 November 1956 a workers' and peasants' revolutionary government was formed by a group of activists in the Hungarian Workers' Party and a temporary Central Committee of the Hungarian Socialist Workers' Party set up. The new government turned to the USSR for help.

Acting under the terms of the Warsaw Pact, Soviet Army units helped put down the armed uprising by anti-government forces.

Soviet casualties during operations in Hungary are shown in Table 106.[3]

Table 106. Soviet Casualties During Operations in Hungary, 1956

Loss category	Officers	Sergeants and men	Total
Irrecoverable losses			
Killed, died of wounds	85	584	669
Missing in action	2	49	51
Total	87	633	720
Sick and wounded			
Wounded, injured	138	1,402	1,540
Total losses	225	2,035	2,260

THE SENDING OF TROOPS INTO CZECHOSLOVAKIA, 1968

On 21 August 1968 troops from five Warsaw Pact countries (the USSR, Bulgaria, Hungary, the GDR and Poland) were sent into Czechoslovakia. At the time it was stated that their aim was to help the Czechoslovak people defend socialism against right-wing revisionist and anti-socialist forces backed by the imperialist West.

The troops did not engage in fighting as they entered the country. Between 21 August and 20 October 1968, while the troops in Czechoslovakia were being deployed, as a result of hostile actions by individual Czechoslovak citizens 11 Soviet servicemen were killed, including one officer, and 87, of whom 19 were officers, were wounded or injured. In addition, 85 were killed in accidents, other incidents or as a result of careless handling of weapons and equipment or died of illness.

In 1989 the decision to send troops into Czechoslovakia was reassessed. It now became evident that what had been termed 'internationalist assistance' essentially put a stop to the process of democratisation in Czechoslovakia. For this reason, on 5 December 1989 a Soviet government announcement and a joint announcement by the leaderships of Bulgaria, Hungary, the GDR, Poland and the USSR were published, acknowledging that the sending of troops into Czechoslovakia had been an illegal act of interference in the internal affairs of a sovereign state, which had disrupted the process of democratic renewal in Czechoslovakia and had long-term negative consequences.

BORDER CONFLICTS IN
THE FAR EAST AND KAZAKHSTAN, 1969

In the 1960s, as the so-called Cultural Revolution began in China, a marked anti-Soviet tendency came to prevail in both internal and foreign policy. The Chinese leadership at that time started trying unilaterally to move the location of the Soviet-Chinese border in a number of places. Groups of civilians and servicemen began systematically to breach the frontier and enter Soviet territory, each time being turned back by border guards without recourse to weapons.

Far more aggressive and dangerous were armed attacks in the area of Damanski island on the Ussuri river and near Lake Zhalanashkol in Kazakhstan.

On 2 March 1969, having secretly concentrated about 300 armed soldiers along the border, the Chinese breached the frontier by seizing the Soviet island of Damanski, 300km south of Khabarovsk. When Soviet border guards reached the place where the frontier had been breached they came under concentrated fire. Decisive action by sub-units of border troops was sufficient to drive the aggressors from Soviet territory.

By 15 March the Chinese Command had concentrated almost a full regiment of infantry reinforced by artillery and tanks in the area and now made another attempt to seize the island. Joint action by Soviet border guards and sub-units from Far Eastern Military District prevented this second act of provocation from succeeding.

Casualties in the fighting at Damanski island between 2 and 21 March 1969 are shown in Table 107.

Table 107. Casualties in the Fighting at Damanski Island, 2 and 21 March 1969

Loss category	Border troops Total	No of officers	Far Eastern MD personnel Total	No of officers	Total	No of officers
Killed, died of wounds	49	4	9	—	58	4
Wounded, concussed	61	7	33	2	94	9
Total	110	11	42	2	152	13

On 13 August 1969 Soviet border guards put down a further act of armed aggression by the Chinese, this time in Kazakhstan.

In the fighting at Lake Zhalanashkol two Soviet border guards were killed and five wounded.

MILITARY ASSISTANCE TO THE GOVERNMENT OF AFGHANISTAN, 25 DECEMBER 1979–15 FEBRUARY 1989

In December 1978 a friendship and cooperation treaty was signed between the USSR and the Democratic Republic of Afghanistan. Clause 4 of this treaty stated that 'The High Contracting Parties, acting in the traditions of friendship and neighbourliness and of the UN Charter, shall hold joint consultations and shall with the agreement of both Parties take the necessary measures to ensure the security, independence and territorial integrity of both Parties.' It was in the light of this clause in the treaty that the Afghan leadership made their request for Soviet troops to be sent to Afghanistan in 1979 to assist in the fight against the anti-government opposition and to help defend the country against outside interference.

In December 1979 the decision was taken to send troops into Afghanistan, it being intended that the various units and formations would be stationed in garrisons and take on the guarding of important targets.

Sending in and deploying the Soviet troop contingent took from 25 December 1979 until mid-January 1980. It consisted of the headquarters of the 40th Army together with supporting and servicing units, four divisions, five independent brigades, four independent regiments, four combat aircraft regiments, three helicopter regiments, one pipeline brigade, a logistic support brigade and several other units and services.

Apart from Soviet Army units and formations in Afghanistan, there were independent sub-units of border troops, and also KGB and MVD personnel.

The Soviet troops in Afghanistan guarded roads, many joint Afghan-Soviet industrial facilities (gasfields, electric power stations, the nitrogen fertiliser plant at Mazar-i-Sharif, etc.). They also guarded aerodromes in major cities and kept them functioning. They gave support to the ruling authorities in 21 provincial centres and escorted convoys carrying military and non-military cargoes both for their own and Afghan use. Together with Afghan units and sub-units they carried out various actions against armed opposition groups and tried to stop convoys bringing in weapons and ammunition from Pakistan and Iran.

At the request of the Afghan leadership, Soviet servicemen also undertook other missions.

Sending troops into Afghanistan did not lead to a reduction in armed resistance by the opposition; on the contrary, from spring 1980 it began to increase.

In answer to countless attacks on Soviet garrisons and transport convoys by opposition detachments, the political leadership in the USSR took a decision that the Soviet forces would begin carrying out joint operations together with Afghan sub-units to search out and defeat the most aggressive enemy groups. However, this merely served to aggravate the situation. The number of refugees fleeing to Pakistan and Iran began to grow, as did the flow of trained and well-armed opposition detachments from these countries to Afghanistan. Thus it was that the Soviet troops sent into

Afghanistan found themselves drawn into an internal conflict on the side of the government.

The Soviet military presence and military activity in Afghanistan may be divided into four stages.

Stage one: December 1979–February 1980. Troops sent into Afghanistan and stationed in garrisons. Defence of places where troops stationed and various other locations organised.

Stage two: March 1980–April 1985. Commencing of active operations, including large-scale actions jointly with Afghan troops. Assistance with reorganisation and building up of Afghan armed forces.

Stage three: May 1985–December 1986. Changeover from active operations to mainly support for actions by Afghan troops from the Soviet Air Force and artillery and sniper sub-units. Deployment of motor rifle, airborne and tank sub-units, mainly in reserve capacity and to bolster morale among Afghan troops. Special sub-units continue trying to stop supplies of arms and ammunition from abroad. Assistance with development of Afghan armed forces. Six Soviet regiments withdrawn and sent home.

Stage four: January 1987–February 1989. Soviet troops participate in implementing the Afghan leadership's policy of national reconciliation. Continued support for combat activity by Afghan troops. Preparations for Soviet troop withdrawal from Afghanistan; complete withdrawal.

Personnel Strength and Losses

Officers serving in the limited contingent of Soviet troops in Afghanistan spent up to two years there, sergeants and men up to 18 months. Between 25 December 1979 and 15 February 1989 a total of 620,000 soldiers served with the forces stationed in Afghanistan, 525,000 in the army, 90,000 with border troop and other KGB sub-units and 5,000 in independent formations of MVD internal service troops and militia. A further 21,000 personnel were with the Soviet troop contingent over the same period doing various white collar or manual jobs.

The annual listed strength of the Soviet Army force was 80,000–104,000 servicemen and 5,000–7,000 white collar or manual workers.

The total irrecoverable personnel losses (killed, died of wounds or disease, and died in accidents or other incidents) of the Soviet armed forces, frontier and internal security troops came to 14,453. Soviet Army formations, units and HQ elements lost 13,833 men, KGB sub-units lost 572, MVD formations lost 28 and other ministries and departments, such as Goskino and Gosteleradio (the Soviet state cinema and broadcasting companies), the Ministry of Construction, etc., lost 20 men.

Also during this period 417 servicemen were missing in action or taken prisoner; 119 of these were later freed, of whom 97 returned to the USSR and 22 went to other countries. A breakdown of casualties by category is given in Table 108.

Table 108. Breakdown of Soviet Casualties in Afghanistan, by Category

Loss categories		Total	Breakdown:			
			Soviet Army	KGB	MVD	Other ministries and departments
Killed in action	No	9,511	8,984	499	28	
	% of losses	65.81	64.95	87.24	100	
Died of wounds	No	2,386	2,337	49		
	% of losses	16.51	16.89	8.57		
Total combat losses	No	11,897	11,321	548	28	
	% of losses	82.32	81.84	95.80	100	
Killed in accident or other incident, committed suicide, etc	No	1,739	1,708	11		20
	% of losses	12.03	12.35	1.92		100
Died as result of disease	No	817	804	13		
	% of losses	5.65	5.81	2.27		
Total non-combat losses	No	2,556	2,512	24		20
	% of losses	17.68	18.16	4.20		100
Total irrecoverable losses	No	14,453	13,833	572	28	20
	% of losses	100	100	100	100	100
Average monthly irrecoverable losses	No	131	126	5	—	—
	% of losses	0.91	0.91	0.87	—	—
Killed and died, breakdown by rank:						
Generals	No	4	4			
	% of losses	0.03	0.03			
Officers	No	2,129	1,975	129	25	
	% of losses	14.73	14.28	22.55	89.29	
Warrant officers	No	632	616	16		
	% of losses	4.37	4.45	2.80		
Sergeants and men	No	11,549	11,120	427	2	
	% of losses	79.91	80.39	74.65	7.14	
Manual and white collar workers	No	139	118	—	1	20
	% of losses	0.96	0.85	—	3.57	100

Note. Those killed include 190 military advisers, 145 of whom were officers.

There were 469,685 sick and wounded, of whom 53,753, or 11.44%, were wounded, were injured or sustained concussion and 415,932 (88.56%) fell sick.

Table 109 gives a breakdown by outcome of treatment for the different categories of sick and wounded.

A high proportion of casualties were those who fell ill (89%). This was because of local climatic and sanitary conditions, which were such that acute infections spread rapidly among the troops. During the 110 months the Soviet troops were in Afghanistan, in spite of measures taken by the medical service, 415,932 men fell sick. There were 115,308 cases of infectious hepatitis, 31,080 of typhoid fever and 140,665 of other infectious diseases.

Table 109. Outcome of Treatment for the Different Categories of Sick and Wounded in Afghanistan

Loss category, outcome of treatment	No	%
Wounded, concussed, injured	53,753	100
Breakdown:		
Returned to duty	44,056	81.96
Invalided out	7,311	13.60
Died*	2,386	4.44
Sick	415,932	100
Breakdown:		
Returned to duty	411,015	98.82
Invalided out	4,343	1.04
Died*	574	0.14
Total sick and wounded	469,685	100
Breakdown:		
Returned to duty	455,071	96.89
Invalided out	11,654	2.48
Died*	2,960	0.63
Sick and wounded: average monthly figures	4,269	0.91
Wounded, concussed, injured and sick, breakdown by rank:		
Officers and warrant officers	10,287	2.19
Sergeants and men	447,493	95.28
Manual and white collar workers	11,905	2.53

* Included with irrecoverable losses.

Of the 11,654 who were discharged from the army after being wounded, maimed or contracting serious diseases, 92%, or 10,751 men, were left disabled; 672 were Category I disabled, 4,216 Category II and 5,863 Category III.

A breakdown of the casualty figures just for the Soviet Army (irrecoverable losses 13,833; sick and wounded 466,425) shows that losses were greatest in stage two of the war (March 1980–April 1985), 49% of all casualties occurring in these 62 months. In all, the number of losses by phase of the war is shown in Table 110.

Material losses were as follows: aircraft 118; helicopters 333; tanks 147; IFVs, AAVs and APCs 1,314; guns and mortars 433; radio sets and command staff vehicles 1,138; engineer plant 510; trucks with sides, and petrol tankers 11,369.

On 15 February 1989 the Soviet troops returned home. They had suffered heavy casualties, however, and those losses will not be forgotten. All those who served with dignity and honour have earned the respect of their fellow countrymen.

Since the truth about the war at last became known in the USSR, it has been acknowledged that, although it did not contravene international law, sending troops into Afghanistan was a mistake.

Table 110. Losses by Phase of War

Stage of conflict in Afghanistan; duration		Irrecoverable losses		Sick and wounded		Total	
		No	%	No	%	No	%
Stage I (December 1979–February 1980) 2 months	All losses	243	1.76	5,306	1.14	5,549	1.15
	Average monthly	121	0.88	2,653	0.57	2,774	0.58
Stage II (March 1980–April 1985) 62 months	All losses	8,945	64.66	226,649	48.59	235,594	49.06
	Average monthly	144	1.04	3,656	0.78	3,800	0.79
Stage III (May 1985–December 1986) 20 months	All losses	2,700	19.52	114,861	24.63	117,561	24.48
	Average monthly	135	0.98	5,743	1.23	5,878	1.22
Stage IV (January 1987–February 1989) 26 months	All losses	1,945	14.06	119,609	25.64	121,554	25.31
	Average monthly	75	0.54	4,600	0.99	4,676	0.97
Total over 110 months	All losses	13,833	100	466,425	100	480,258	100
	Average monthly	126	0.91	4,240	0.91	4,366	0.91

TOTAL CASUALTY FIGURES FOR THE SOVIET ARMED FORCES IN WARS, MILITARY ACTIONS AND CONFLICTS

The sending of troops into Afghanistan and military assistance to the Afghan government is the final episode in the history of the Soviet armed forces. It concludes our analysis of army and navy casualties in various wars, actions and conflicts.

What, then, were the total Soviet personnel losses in large and small wars and among Soviet troops stationed abroad? The answer to this question is given in Table 111.

Table 111. Total Personnel Losses in the Soviet Armed Forces in Wars, Military Actions and Armed Conflicts, 1918–89

War, combat operation or military conflict	Irrecoverable losses (killed in action, died of wounds, disease, in accident etc., missing in action, failed to return from captivity)	Sick and wounded (wounded, concussion and frostbite cases, sick)
Civil war (1918–22)	939,755	6,791,783
Fight against *Basmachi* (1923–31)	626	867
Sino-Soviet military conflict (1929)	187	665
Military assistance to Spanish republic (1936–39) and China (1937–39)	353	Figures unavailable
Repulse of Japanese aggressors near Lake Khasan (1938)	989	3,279
Combat operations near r. Khalkhin Gol (1939)	8,931	15,952
Campaign in W. Ukraine and W. Byelorussia (1939)	1,139	2,383
War with Finland (1939–40)	126,875	264,908[1]
Great Patriotic War (1941–45)	8,668,400	22,326,905[1]
War in Korea (1950–53)	299	Figures unavailable
Military assistance to countries in Asia, Africa and Near East (1962–79)	145[2]	Figures unavailable
Events in Hungary (1956)	720	1,540
Troops sent into Czechoslovakia (1968)	96[3]	87
Border conflicts in Far East and Kazakhstan (1969)	60	99
Military assistance to government of Afghanistan (1979–89)	14,751[4]	469,685
Total	9,763,326	29,878,153

1. According to medical treatment centre records.
2. Represents irrecoverable losses among Soviet servicemen only during periods when military operations were being conducted in the countries where they were stationed.
3. Of these, 85 were non-combat losses.
4. Represents irrecoverable personnel losses of Red Army, MVD and KGB formations and units and other departments, including 298 missing in action.

NOTES

1. See *Istoriya vneshnei politiki SSSR, 1945–75* (*History of Soviet Foreign Policy*), Moscow, 1976, vol. 2, p. 165.
2. TsAMO, f. 16-A, op. 3139, d. 188, l. 2; op. 175512, d. 1, l. 1–45.
3. TsAMO, f. 16-A, op. 3139, d. 193, l. 10, 12, 48, 65, 69–73.